Problems in Prose

Problems in Prose

REVISED EDITION

by

PAUL HAINES

HARPER & BROTHERS PUBLISHERS

NEW YORK   LONDON

Contents

v

vi CONTENTS

Preface

THAT FRESHMEN MAY BE TAUGHT TO READ AND WRITE through the careful study of good prose no longer needs to be demonstrated.

In most of these essays, the thought moves inductively, from observation to explanation and inference, a procedure exemplary for freshmen. Intentionally, the topics are often remote in time and space; usually the student may find similar data within the range of his own observation to think and write about.

The comments and questions are designed to make him see how the writer went about organizing and presenting his material. Each exercise may be the basis of a unified lesson in rhetoric. The earlier passages are analyzed with reference to elementary rhetorical principles and devices, and the first term's work may consist largely of the study and practice of given forms; in the second term the student should be able to evolve forms to suit what he has to say. The later passages exhibit more complex problems of organization and a subtler mastery of expression.

The student's first preparation of any passage should regularly involve reading it with a dictionary. Fairly strict standards of literal comprehension should be set promptly. Those parts of the exercise that the instructor wishes to use may be prepared merely for recitation or for a brief snap quiz; until the student learns to formulate exact answers, however, he should be required to hand in some answers in writing. Technical concepts and the terminology needed for their convenient discussion are explained in sufficient detail to enable the student to answer the questions; the instructor will amplify or revise this commentary. If the exercise is to culminate in a theme assignment, then the rhetoric lesson should include some discussion of the nature of the author's materials and of how the student might treat similar materials in his own essay.

In the preparation and revision of this book, I have been helped by the good counsel of Mr. Warren Bower, Professor Oscar Cargill, Mr. Howard Dunbar, Mr. Paul A. McGhee, Mr. Edward Parker, and Mr. John Terry, of the English Department, and of Dr. J. Alexander Kerns, of the Classics Department, of Washington Square College.

I am grateful to the following teachers for their shared skill and their kindliness: Professor Frank Gees Black, of the University of Oregon; Professor Sharon Brown, of Brown University; Professor Phillips D. Carleton, of the University of Vermont; Professor Cyrus L. Day, of the University of Delaware; Professor Henry A. Doak, of the University of North Dakota; Professor Phil S. Grant, of the University of California; Professor Robert A. Jelliffe, of Oberlin College; Professor Elizabeth Wheeler Manwaring, of Wellesley College; Professor George L. Nesbitt, of Hamilton College; Professor William S. Sale, of Cornell University; Professor Ernest S. Shepard, of George Washington University; Professors Martin S. Shockley and Charles C. Walcutt, of the University of Oklahoma; Professor William Tate, of the University of Georgia; and Professor Don M. Wolfe, of New York University.

June, 1944

PAUL HAINES

Problems in Prose

STEAMBOAT DAYS[1]

MARK TWAIN

•

1. WHEN I WAS A BOY, THERE WAS BUT ONE PERMANENT ambition among my comrades in our village on the west bank of the Mississippi River. That was, to be a steamboatman. We had transient ambitions of other sorts, but they were only transient. When a circus came and went, it left 5 us all burning to become clowns; the first Negro minstrel show that ever came to our section left us all suffering to try that kind of life; now and then we had a hope that, if we lived and were good, God would permit us to be pirates. These ambitions faded out, each in its turn; but the 10 ambition to be a steamboatman always remained.

2. Once a day a cheap, gaudy packet arrived upward from St. Louis, and another downward from Keokuk. Before these events, the day was glorious with expectancy; after them, the day was a dead and empty thing. Not only 15 the boys, but the whole village, felt this. After all these years I can picture that old time to myself now, just as it was then: the white town drowsing in the sunshine of a summer's morning; the streets empty, or pretty nearly so; one or two clerks sitting in front of the Water Street stores, 20 with their splint-bottomed chairs tilted back against the walls, chins on breasts, hats slouched over their faces, asleep—with shingle-shavings enough around to show what broke them down; a sow and a litter of pigs loafing along the sidewalk, doing a good business in watermelon rinds 25 and seeds; two or three lonely little freight piles scattered about the levee; a pile of skids on the slope of the stone-paved wharf, and the fragrant town drunkard asleep in

[1] From *Life on the Mississippi,* by Mark Twain; reprinted by permission of Harper & Brothers, Publishers.

the shadow of them; two or three wood flats at the head
of the wharf, but nobody to listen to the peaceful lapping
of the wavelets against them; the great Mississippi, the
majestic, the magnificent Mississippi, rolling its mile-wide
tide along, shining in the sun; the dense forest away on
the other side; the point above the town, and the point
below, bounding the river-glimpse and turning it into a
sort of sea, and withal a very still and brilliant and lonely
one. Presently a film of dark smoke appears above one of
those remote points; instantly a Negro drayman, famous
for his quick eye and prodigious voice, lifts up the cry,
"S-t-e-a-m-boat a-comin'!" and the scene changes! The town
drunkard stirs, the clerks wake up, a furious clatter of
drays follows, every house and store pours out a human contribution, and all in a twinkling the dead town is alive and
moving. Drays, carts, men, boys, all go hurrying from
many quarters to a common center, the wharf. Assembled
there, the people fasten their eyes upon the coming boat as
upon a wonder they are seeing for the first time. And the
boat *is* rather a handsome sight, too. She is long and sharp
and trim and pretty; she has two tall, fancy-topped chimneys, with a gilded device of some sort swung between
them; a fanciful pilot-house, all glass and gingerbread,
perched on top of the texas deck behind them; the paddle-
boxes are gorgeous with a picture or with gilded rays
above the boat's name; the boiler-deck, the hurricane-deck,
and the texas deck are fenced and ornamented with clean
white railings; there is a flag gallantly flying from the jack-
staff; the furnace doors are open and the fires glaring
bravely; the upper decks are black with passengers; the
captain stands by the big bell, calm, imposing, the envy
of all; great volumes of blackest smoke are rolling and
tumbling out of the chimneys—a husbanded grandeur created with a bit of pitch-pine just before arriving at a town;
the crew are grouped on the forecastle; the broad stage is
run far out over the port bow, and an envied deck-hand
stands picturesquely on the end of it with a coil of rope in
his hand; the pent steam is screaming through the gauge-

cocks; the captain lifts his hand, a bell rings, the wheels stop; then they turn back, churning the water to foam, and the steamer is at rest. Then such a scramble as there is to get aboard, and to get ashore, and to take in freight and to discharge freight, all at one and the same time; and such a yelling and cursing as the mates facilitate it all with! Ten minutes later the steamer is under way again, with no flag on the jack-staff and no black smoke issuing from the chimneys. After ten more minutes the town is dead again, and the town drunkard asleep by the skids once more.

3.   My father was a justice of the peace, and I supposed he possessed the power of life and death over all men, and could hang anybody that offended him. This was distinc-tion enough for me as a general thing; but the desire to be a steamboatman kept intruding, nevertheless. I first wanted to be a cabin-boy, so that I could come out with a white apron on and shake a table-cloth over the side, where all my old comrades could see me; later I thought I would rather be the deck-hand who stood on the end of the stage-plank with the coil of rope in his hand, because he was particularly conspicuous. But these were only day-dreams— they were too heavenly to be contemplated as real possi-bilities. By and by one of our boys went away. He was not heard of for a long time. At last he turned up as apprentice engineer or striker on a steamboat. This thing shook the bottom out of all my Sunday-school teachings. That boy had been notoriously worldly, and I just the reverse; yet he was exalted to this eminence, and I left in obscurity and misery. There was nothing generous about this fellow in his greatness. He would always manage to have a rusty bolt to scrub while his boat tarried at our town, and he would sit on the inside guard and scrub it, where we all could see him and envy him and loathe him. And when-ever his boat was laid up he would come home and swell around the town in his blackest and greasiest clothes, so that nobody could help remembering that he was a steam-boatman; and he used all sorts of steamboat technicalities

105 in his talk, as if he were so used to them that he forgot
common people could not understand them. He would
speak of the "labbord" side of a horse in an easy, natural
way that would make one wish he was dead. And he was
always talking about "St. Looy" like an old citizen; he
110 would refer casually to occasions when he was "coming
down Fourth Street," or when he was "passing by the
Planter's House," or when there was a fire and he took a
turn on the brakes of "the old Big Missouri"; and then he
would go on and lie about how many towns the size of
115 ours were burned down there that day. Two or three of the
boys had been to St. Louis once and had a vague general
knowledge of its wonders, but the day of their glory was
over now. They lapsed into a humble silence, and learned
to disappear when the ruthless cub-engineer approached.
120 This fellow had money, too, and hair-oil. Also an ignorant
silver watch and a showy brass watch-chain. He wore a
leather belt and used no suspenders. If ever a youth was
cordially admired and hated by his comrades, this one was.
No girl could withstand his charms. He cut out every
125 boy in the village. When his boat blew up at last, it diffused
a tranquil contentment among us such as we had not known
for months. But when he came home the next week, alive,
renowned, and appeared in church all battered up and
bandaged, a shining hero, stared at and wondered over by
130 everybody, it seemed to us that the partiality of Providence
for an undeserving reptile had reached a point where it was
open to criticism.

※ ※ ※

1. In Par. 1, Mark Twain has illustrated the abstract term
"transient ambitions" by giving three examples. Mark them
off in the text.

2. After the preliminary statement (ll. 12-16), Par. 2 falls
into three main sections: before the arrival, the arrival, the de-
parture. Mark these off in the text.

3. The materials for the first section may be itemized: white
town, empty streets, lazy clerks. . . . Continue the list; there
are about ten items in all.

4. Mark Twain could have remembered other images from his childhood in Hannibal, Missouri; he used these because they fitted in one way or another with his design in the paragraph. Why did he choose a sunny day? Why did he include the sow and her litter? The drunkard? The freight piles on the levee? The lapping of the wavelets?

You have made just such an outline of this portion of Par. 2 as the author used. Perhaps Mark Twain jotted this list on the margin of his mind; while you are still learning to write, you had better make notes in black and white, on a piece of scratch paper or the back of an old letter. Your outline need not be formal or elaborate, so long as it enables you to plan in advance what you intend to say. For memory is not always logical or literary, and the order in which the writer's materials occur to him may not be the most effective order in which to present them to his reader. It is relatively easy to rearrange the items while they are still in the form of brief phrases.

5. Why are the river scenes put at the end of this section rather than at the beginning? Why do the points follow the forest rather than precede it? Why are the pigs before the town drunkard rather than after?

6. There are several standard principles for the arrangement of materials within a paragraph. One of these is *time order;* this simple and natural principle governs, for instance, the arrangement of the three sections of Par. 2. Your answers to Question 5 show what principle behind the arrangement of materials in lines 18-38?

7. Why, in the outline for this section, should "white town" have been placed at the top of the list? Why should not the pigs precede the nearly empty streets?

The two procedures which you have traced, gathering the materials and arranging them in an intelligible order, are the groundwork for the writing of an effective paragraph. Substance and plan may be conveniently worked out in a list of short phrases which allows the writer to see what he is doing and to revise his plan without wasting time or literary effort. To postpone this preliminary work of the imagination by trying to invent the paragraph as one goes along is to attack the three problems at once instead of singly. The beginner is then likely to fumble all three, to end with skimpy materials clumsily arranged and feebly phrased. Once the outline is reliable, the writer may give his whole attention to his presentation of the material. Working from his notes, he fills in more details— and some of his best touches may occur to him as he writes. This amplification gives the paragraph its texture and its charm.

8. Compare your outline with the text. Which item do you think most effectively written up? Compare the handling of the clerks with that of the river (ll. 31-37); in each, what details and what phrasings create the tone? Compare the handling of the clerks with that of the drunkard.

9. In the description of the steamboat (ll. 48-69), most of the details have been chosen to convey the sense of splendor; are there any which do not? How is it indicated that the splendor was theatrical and conscious?

10. What order do you find in the presentation of these details?

11. In Par. 3, the boy's yearning for the distinction of a steamboatman's life is evoked by three persons; account for the order in which these three persons appear.

12. Consider the following changes of wording:

Transient (l. 4) to *transitory* or *passing*. Permissible, because the words have the same meaning in this context.

Packet (l. 12) to *boat*. *Packet* is better because more precise; a packet is a small boat carrying mail, cargo, and passengers on a schedule.

Burning (l. 6) to *wanting*. Although the general idea is the same, the metaphor is more vivid and so preferable. (Other metaphors would be *keen* and *eager,* though most readers no longer feel the idea of sharpness implicit in *eager.*)

Obscurity (l. 94) to *difficulty*. "Obscurity" means darkness or lack of prominence. "Difficulty" is sometimes a synonym—a dark saying is hard to understand—but not here.

Casually (l. 109) to *dangerously*. "Casually," although related to "casualty," does not contain the idea of danger. A casual event happens by chance, or seems to; a casualty is a mishap, an ill result of chance, especially a loss in battle.

Conspicuous (l. 87) to *distinctive*. No. What is conspicuous calls attention to itself; what is distinctive distinguishes something else. The deckhand's rope was distinctive, in the boy's eyes; the deckhand was conspicuous.

Comment on the following proposed changes, applying the same principles of criticism. You may need a dictionary. Some of the changes may be sound. *Permit* (l. 9) to *allow; empty* (l. 15) to *uninteresting; drayman* (l. 38) to *workman; husbanded* (l. 61) to *masculine; issuing* (l. 74) to *emitting; lapsed* (l. 117) to *passed; withstand* (l. 123) to *resist; shining* (l. 128) to *great.*

13. Why is "old" in line 84 especially delightful?

14. Write a paragraph describing a place and its characteristic activity: the anatomy laboratory, Main Street on Saturday night, the county workhouse, the bunk room of a logging camp, behind the scenes at the theatre, etc. Pick a place you are familiar with, and for your instructor's sake try to avoid the banal subjects which the rest of the class will be writing about. Above all, refrain from the beauties of nature: the realities of tree structure and starlight can hardly be got into words, and you will not, of course, wish to display your own delicate nature-moods to an audience which, not being in love with you, may find them tiresome. Write about some part of the peopled world that we all inhabit and enjoy. Begin by jotting down a list of striking or significant details; then rearrange them before you start to write.

HOMES IN MIDDLETOWN[1]

ROBERT AND HELEN LYND

•

1. THE POORER WORKING MAN, COMING HOME AFTER HIS
nine and a half hours on the job, walks up the frequently
unpaved street, turns in at a bare yard littered with a rusty
velocipede or worn-out automobile tires, opens a sagging
5 door, and enters the living room of his home. From this
room the whole house is visible—the kitchen with table and
floor swarming with flies and often strewn with bread
crusts, orange skins, torn papers, and lumps of coal and
wood; the bedrooms with soiled, heavy quilts falling off the
10 beds. The worn green shades hanging down at a tipsy
angle admit only a flecked half-light upon the ornate calendars or enlarged colored portraits of the children in heavy
gilt frames tilted out at a precarious angle just below the
ceiling. The whole interior is musty with stale odors of
15 food, clothing, and tobacco. On the brown varnished shelf
of the sideboard the wooden-backed family hair brush,
with the baby bottle, a worn purse, and yesterday's newspaper, may be half stuffed out of sight behind a bright blue
glass cake dish. Rust spots the base-burner. A baby in wet,
20 dirty clothes crawls about the bare floor among the odd
pieces of furniture.

2. The working man with more money leeway may go
home through a tidy front yard; whether his home is of
the two-floor variety, a bungalow, or a cottage, there are
25 often geraniums in the front windows, neat with their tan,
tasseled shades and coarse lace curtains. A name-plate of
silvered glass adorns the door. The small living room is

[1] From *Middletown*, by Robert S. and Helen Merrell Lynd; reprinted
by permission of Harcourt, Brace & Company, Inc., Publishers.

light, with a rather hard brightness, from the blue- and pink-flowered rug, bought on installment, to the artificial flowers, elaborately embroidered pillows, and many-colored center pieces. The furniture is probably straight-lined mission of dark or golden oak or, if the family is more prosperous, overstuffed. The sewing machine stands in the living room or dining room, and the ironing board with its neat piles of clothes stretches across one corner of the kitchen. Knickknacks of all sorts are about—easeled portraits on piano or phonograph, a paper knife brought by some traveled relative from Yellowstone Park, pictures that the small daughter has drawn in school, or if the family is of a religious bent, colored mottoes: What will you be doing when Jesus comes? or Prepare to meet thy God. There may even be a standing lamp with a bright silk shade, another recent installment purchase and a mark of prestige. Some magazines may be lying about, but rarely any books.

3. To some more prosperous members of the business group their homes are a source of pride as they walk up a neatly paved, tree-bordered street to homes which are "the last word in the up-to-date small house." The house may be shingled or stuccoed, in a trim terraced yard. Everything from the bittersweet in the flower-holder by the front door to the modern mahogany smoking table by the overstuffed davenport bespeaks correctness. The long living room opens by a double doorway into the dining room. Colors in rugs, chair coverings, curtains, and the elaborate silk shades of the standing lamps match. There are three or four pictures—colored photographs or Maxfield Parrish prints— hung precisely at the level of the eyes, a pair of candlesticks on the sectional bookcase, and a few bowls and trays; the kitchen cabinet has every convenience. Here one sees the complete small house. "It's so hard to know what to give our relatives for Christmas any more," said one woman; "they have their homes and their knickknacks and their pictures just as we have. It's hard to find anything new that they haven't got. We've stopped giving to

our friends except just cards, but we have to give to the family."

※ ※ ※

These paragraphs are taken from the description of the dwellings in which "Middletown's most sacred institution, the family, works out its destiny. Within the privacy of these shabby or pretentious houses, marriage, birth, child-rearing, death, and the personal immensities of family life go forward." The content of these paragraphs is factual, demanding no resources of vocabulary other than words enough to name things.

1. Compare the following sentence with the text, lines 1–5:
   The poorer working man, coming home after an exhausting day's work, enters his pathetic imitation of a "garden," in reality a few square yards of dirt littered with trash and other discarded articles, opens the door, and enters the living room of his home.
Which is more pictorial? What words make it so?

2. Compare the following sentence with the text, lines 5–10:
   From this room the whole house is visible—the kitchen practically "overflowing" with a conglomeration of various assorted and unsavory refuse; the bedrooms in slovenly disarray.
Which leaves more to the reader's imagination? Which exerts more control over the reader's imagination? Which procedure is more effective?

3. Compare the following sentences with lines 24-26:
   The geraniums in the front windows and their tan, tasseled shades and coarse lace curtains reveal an attempt on the part of the housewife to achieve a certain neatness and refinement in these living quarters.
   Here the housewife has tried to achieve a certain neatness and refinement.
Which of the three explains the situation? Which presents it concretely? Which does both? In the text, what one word implies the explanation?

4. What one word in the next sentence—"A name-plate . . ." (ll. 26-27)—has a similar explanatory function?

5. "Bespeaks correctness" (l. 53) is a comment on the psy-

chology of the inhabitants; of which facts given in the text is
the phrase an explanation?

6. Can you find any similar explanatory comment in Par. 1?
In Par. 2? In Par. 3?

7. Suppose this sentence inserted in line 5:

An atmosphere of poverty seems to predominate everywhere—

and this at the end of the paragraph:

One cannot contemplate such desolate hovels as these without receiving a strong impression of the lack of mere physical well-being which prevails.

In these sentences, just which words or phrases are explanatory? How is the paragraph improved by the addition?

8. In view of what you have learned from Questions 3-7,
formulate a rule for the use of the explanatory and the illustrative in effective description. (Which should make up the bulk
of the paragraph? Which, if either, may be omitted?)

9. Did every working man in Middletown have a wet baby
at home?—and a blue glass cake dish? If these images were
omitted, or if they were qualified by "perhaps" or "in many
cases," no one would be deceived. Is it permissible to lie for
the sake of vividness?

10. Suppose the following phrase inserted after "phonograph" in line 37: "a snapshot of the wife and two children, in
bathing suits, of an eldest son who is now selling insurance
in Chicago." Why is the phrase objectionable? Because it may
not be true? Because the details are irrelevant? Because the
children are in bathing suits? Because it is too long?

11. Why have the authors noted the position in a room
of some pieces of furniture and not of others? Would the rule
implied for the reporting of furniture apply to the description
of a particular room as well as to the description of a type of
room?

In an account of lively action, the writer may use lively
verbs; in a static description he must often be content with
the colorless verb "to be." This distresses the beginner, especially if he sees little and has little to say and therefore thinks
of style as a literary yeast cake. He commonly resorts to laborious variations of "to be": A rusty velocipede *may be seen* in

the otherwise barren yard—*If one should enter* this house, *one could smell* the musty odors of food—Spots of rust *are plainly visible* on the base-burner. "To be" does not impede a reader; these equally empty evasions make him feel that his time is being wasted.

12. Can the predication "is visible" be justified in line 6?

13. One is not, however, restricted to "is" and "are" even in static descriptions: e.g., "shades *admit* light." Check the sentences in which the verb is not "to be," and in each underline the subject, the verb or verbs, and the object if any.

14. Compare the following passages:
   A. Scattered about the walls of the bedroom may be found pictures of the children of the family. Sometimes these portraits are former photographs which have been colored and enlarged. The frames are of gilt and very ponderous. These likenesses, which are usually high on the walls, are suspended in most cases so that they tilt way out. A visitor would also notice illustrations from old calendars on the walls, colored in a wide variety of bright and garish colors. The sleeping quarters are usually kept dark, however, by means of the "holy" (?) curtain shades at the windows.
   B. The worn green shades hanging at a tipsy angle admit only a flecked half-light upon the ornate calendars or enlarged colored portraits of the children in heavy gilt frames tilted out at a precarious angle just below the ceiling.
   a) In A, what are the elaborate variations of "to be"?
   b) "About the walls," twice repeated in A, does not appear in B; what other qualifiers in A may mere common sense dispense with?
   c) Would the fifth sentence in A be better if it read "garish hues," thus avoiding the repetition of "color"?
   d) Underline, in A, "picture" and every variation of it; do the same in B.
   e) Where do the "former photographs . . . enlarged" of A appear in B? Underline the phrase in B; what is its syntax?
   f) Trace the further significant details of A in the same way, underlining the equivalent phrase in B and giving its syntax.

15. Comment on the following changes of wording; some may be sound. *Strewn* (l. 7) to *scattered; heavy* (l. 12) to *mas-*

sive; odors (l. 14) to *aromas; odd* (l. 20) to *curious; bent* (l. 40) to *twist; woman* (l. 63) to *lady.*

16. One thing conducive to a homely familiarity with the language is the habit of recognizing common elements in words of slightly different form. Thus *frequently* is related to *frequency* and to the verb *to frequent.* Not all similarly spelled or sounded syllables have the same origin; while *homely* is an adjective made from *home* (the word was applied to domestic, intimate things, then to persons unfitted for worldly society, and finally to the plain-featured), there is no etymological connection between *home* and *homicide.* In *velocipede* we recognize the roots of *velocity* (*velox,* swift) and of *pedal* (*pes, pedis,* foot); this element appears also in *expedite,* to get one's foot loose, and in *pedestal,* a foot place. But *peddler* is not a cognate of this group, even though peddlers wander on foot to sell their wares.

a) What other cognates of *pedal* can you think of? Check your answers by a dictionary.

b) Give at least one cognate of each of the following words: table, shade, family, picture, school, elaborate, candle, cabinet.

17. Write descriptions of two places of the same class but of different kinds—two students' rooms, two hotel lobbies, a home in which there are children and one in which there are not, streets in two sections of town, etc. Avoid excessive explanations and let the comparisons be implied rather than explicit. You ought to base the essay on fresh observations made with notebook and pencil in hand.

THE GOLD TOOTH[1]

FONTENELLE

•

1. LET US BE SURE OF OUR FACTS BEFORE WE RACK OUR WITS to explain them. This cautious procedure may seem tedious to most people, who assume the truth of an alleged fact in their eagerness to understand its meaning. In the long run, however, it may spare us the absurdity of having accounted for what is not so.

2. Such a misfortune drolly befell several German philosophers about a century ago. In 1593 it was widely rumored that in Silesia a child of seven, having cast its baby teeth, had cut a gold tooth, a molar. By 1595 Horstius, a professor of medicine at the University of Helmstad, had published a full account of this tooth, pointing out that it partook both of the natural and of the supernatural and explaining that God had decreed it to the gums of this baby in order that the Christians languishing under Turkish persecution might be reassured of His power. We may imagine how the news of this miracle consoled the despondent Christians and dismayed their infidel oppressors. In the same year Rullandus contributed another history of the Silesian tooth to the store of human learning, and two years later Ingolsteterus, an equally competent scholar, disputed the opinions of Rullandus, who promptly defended his views in a reply no less eloquent than profound. The whole literature of the tooth was reviewed and summarized by another savant, named Libavius, who concluded with his independent interpretation of it. In these magnificent works every resource of philosophy and rhetoric had been brought to bear upon the tooth, excepting only its verification. When a goldsmith examined it, he found that one of

[1] From *Histoire des oracles*, by Bernard Le Bovier, sieur de Fontenelle.

the child's natural teeth had been covered with gold leaf, 30
very adroitly. The pedants first made books; then they
consulted the goldsmith.

3. The blunder is congenial, easy to make on any subject. Human ignorance is revealed less in the number of
existing things which man cannot account for than in the 35
nonexistent things for which he finds a satisfying explanation. For in his perplexity he wants a logic to discover the
truth; his facile speculations show him encumbered with
another kind of logic, which readily adapts itself to error.
Renowned physicists have ingeniously explained why cav- 40
erns are warm in winter and cold in summer; greater
scientists have since determined that they are not so. Historical discussions are even more open to this kind of error.
We confidently rest our arguments upon the narratives of
historians, who may have been prejudiced, credulous, mis- 45
informed, or careless. An eyewitness impartial in his observation and scrupulous in his reporting is the only reliable authority.

❊ ❊ ❊

1. What is the logical relation between Pars. 1 and 2?
There is also a *rhetorical* relation between them: a purpose
in the way the materials are presented to the reader's mind.
Suppose Par. 1 placed after Par. 2, perhaps on the theory that
the story might better be allowed to speak for itself. Then the
reader, unprepared, would not at first be sure whether the
story was intended to expose the liars of Silesia, to deride the
credulity of scholars, or to lament the futility of miracles. In
general, in *expository* narrative—a story which is to be understood rather than to be imaginatively experienced—the reader
should be given some hint of the point of the story *before* it is
told.

2. What sentence or phrase in Par. 2 reiterates the point?

3. When the story has been told, the point may be stated
again; what sentence in Par. 3 does this?

4. The subsequent explanation, however, may carry the
argument further; so the reader may feel that he is progressing.
What sentences in Par. 3 extend the argument?

5. The absurdity of the pedants in the apologue is emphasized by ironic phrasings. For instance, "By 1595" (l. 8) seems to praise Horstius for his promptness. Find several other examples of irony in the paragraph.

6. In the best irony, the words are to be understood in their literal sense. To say of a miser that he is charitable would be crude; a more skillful ironist would say that he never encourages the poor to suppose that money can buy happiness. Does Fontenelle's irony meet this test?

7. In the second sentence of Par. 2, "widely," "of seven," and "a molar" might have been omitted; how do these words add to the effect of the paragraph?

8. In this passage Fontenelle has undertaken to correct a fault which his readers presumably made themselves. How does he manage to deliver his lecture, offering the cap to whomever it may fit, without giving offense?

9. If "useful" were written for "reliable" in the last sentence, would the statement be true? Explain.

10. College students of history and the sciences surely break the rule laid down by Fontenelle; how are they to be justified?

11. *Console* is related to *solace,* as may be guessed if the prefix *con-* is detached. (Not, however, to *solitude, solicitous,* or *insolent,* as may be determined by consulting another kind of goldsmith.) What words do you know that are related to *infidel, eloquent, conclude, prejudice, credulous?*

12. Why did Fontenelle, in Par. 2, describe the university men as "napping" rather than as "reluctant to profit by their studies"? Because a metaphor is always more vivid? Or because a shorter phrase is always better than a longer one?

13. Write an instructive account of an experience from which you learned something—other than what goes in textbooks.

THE COUNTRY DOCTOR[1]

JOHN BACH McMASTER

•

1. NOT LESS IMPORTANT THAN THE SCHOOLMASTER, IN THE opinion of his townsmen, was the doctor. With the exception of the minister and the judge, he was the most important personage in the district. His professional education would now be thought insufficient to admit him to practice; 5 for there were then but two medical schools in the country, nor were they, by reason of the expense and dangers of travelling, by any means well attended. In general, the medical education of a doctor was such as he could pick up while serving an apprenticeship to some noted practitioner 10 in Boston or New York, during which he combined the duties of a student with many of the menial offices of a servant. He ground the powders, mixed the pills, rode with the doctor on his rounds, held the basin when the patient was bled, helped to adjust plasters and sew wounds, and 15 ran with vials of medicine from one end of the town to the other. In the moments snatched from duties such as these he swept out the office, cleaned the bottles and jars, wired skeletons, tended the night bell, and, when a feast was given, stood in the hall to announce the guests. 20

2. It was a white day with such a young man when he enjoyed the rare good fortune of dissecting a half-putrid arm or examining a human heart and lungs. So great, indeed, was the difficulty of procuring anatomical subjects that even at the medical school which had just been started 25 at Harvard College, a single body was made to do duty for a whole year's course of lectures. It was only by filching

[1] From *A History of the People of the United States,* by John Bach McMaster; reprinted by permission of D. Appleton-Century Company, Inc.

from graveyards or begging the dead bodies of criminals from the governor that subjects could be obtained.

30   3. His apprenticeship ended, the half-educated lad returned to his native town to assume the practice and to follow in the footsteps of his father. There as years went by he grew in popularity and wealth. His genial face, his engaging manners, his hearty laugh, the twinkle with 35 which he inquired of the blacksmith when the next boy was expected, the sincerity with which he asked after the health of the carpenter's daughter, the interest he took in the family of the poorest laborer, the good nature with which he stopped to chat with the farm hands about the prospect 40 of the corn crop and the turnip crop, made him the favorite of the county for miles around. When he rode out he knew the names and personal history of the occupants of every house he passed. The farmers' lads pulled off their hats, and the girls dropped courtesies to him. Sunshine and rain, 45 daylight and darkness, were alike to him. He would ride ten miles on the darkest night, over the worst of roads, in a pelting storm, to administer a dose of calomel to an old woman or to attend a child in a fit. He was present at every birth; he attended every burial; he sat with the minister at 50 every deathbed, and put his name with the lawyer's to every will.

4. Only a few of the simplest drugs were then to be found stowed away on the shelves of the village store, among heaps of shoes, balls of twine, packages of seed, 55 and flitches of bacon. The physician was therefore compelled to combine the duties both of the doctor and the apothecary. He pounded his own drugs, made his own tinctures, prepared his own infusions, and put up his own prescriptions. His saddlebag was the only drugstore within 60 forty miles, and there, beside his horn balances and his china mortar, were medicines now gone quite out of fashion or at most but rarely used. Homeopathy, with its tasteless mixtures and diminutive doses, was unknown, and more medicine was then taken every year by the well 65 than is now taken in the same space of time by the sick.

Each spring the blood must be purified, the bowels must be purged, the kidneys must be excited, the bile must be moved, and large doses of senna and manna and loathsome concoctions of rhubarb and molasses were taken daily. In a thousand ways the practice of medicine has changed since that day. Remedies now in the medicine box of every farmer were then utterly unknown. Water was denied the patient tormented with fever, and in its stead he was given small quantities of clam-juice. Mercurial compounds were taken till the lips turned blue and the gums fell away from the teeth. The damsel who fainted was bled profusely. Cupping and leeching were freely prescribed. The alkaloid quinia was unknown till 1820. The only cure for malarial diseases was powdered cinchona bark, but the amount required to restore the patient was so great and the supply so small that the remedy was all but useless. Vaccination was not made known by Jenner till 1798. Inoculation was still held by many to be attended by divine punishment. Smallpox was almost as prevalent as pneumonia now is. The discovery of anaesthesia by the inhalation of ether or chloroform was not given to the world by Morton till 1846. Not one of the many remedies which assuage pain, which destroy disease, which hold in check the most loathsome maladies and the most violent epidemics, was in use. Every few years during the dog days the yellow fever raged with more violence in the northern cities than it has ever done in this generation in the cities of the far South. Whole streets were depopulated. Every night the dead-cart shot its scores of corpses into the pits of the potter's field. Better surgery is now generously given to every laborer injured by the fall of a scaffold than could then have been purchased at any price.

※ ※ ※

McMaster's problem, in this selection from his survey of American life after the Revolution, was to describe the experience, not of any one doctor, but of doctors in general and still to make the account vivid and human. The prose is by no means distinguished or brilliant; it is the journeywork of a highly competent craftsman. Its virtues are technical; they have become standard in our magazine articles and are such as a skillful freshman may, within his course of study, make his own.

1. Outline the passage by giving a title to each paragraph.

2. Pars. 2 and 4 both deal with the history of medicine; why should not both follow Par. 3? (Assume that proper transitions would be made between the rearranged topics.) Why should not both precede Par. 3?

3. What phrase summarizes the sentence "He ground . . . other" (ll. 13-17)? The sentence "In the moments . . . guests" (ll. 17-20)?

4. Compare the following sentences with the text, lines 13-17:

> He ground the powders when necessary, or, if pills had to be mixed, that task also fell to him. When the doctor rode on his rounds, he was accompanied by the apprentice, whose duty it was to help bleed a patient by holding the basin. Sometimes he adjusted a plaster or was even allowed to sew wounds. Usually at the end of the day his feet were weary from running from one end of the town to the other, carrying vials of medicine to patients.

The reader grasps McMaster's version more readily, not only because it is shorter but also because the material has been reduced to a simple logical pattern. The logical symmetry makes the rhetorical compactness possible.

A common term, the apprentice, appears in each sentence of the alternative version; underline the words in which he appears (he, him, whose, etc.) and give the syntax of each.

Since all these sentences report actions performed by the apprentice, he may logically appear as the grammatical subject of each statement: he ground the powders; he mixed the pills; he rode, etc. Then—just as the mathematician may factor out $(ax + ay + az)$ to read $a(x + y + z)$—the writer may make one subject govern a series of verbs, as in the text. In grammatical terms, the $x, y,$ and z are said to be parallel. One verb may have several parallel objects: cleaned (bottles + jars). Or a noun may be modified by several adjectives; a preposition may have several objects; a verb may take several infinitive complements: He returned (to assume . . . + to follow . . .).

...ie logical simplification is not always obvious. It re-
...that the writer keep his mind on what he is writing
...bout and not merely on the phrases in which he happens to
have thought of his material. Compare the following sentences
with the text, lines 23-29:

> Sometimes the townsmen were enraged to discover that
> graves had been robbed by students in quest of anatomical
> subjects. The difficulty of procuring such subjects is further
> revealed by the fact that at the medical school which had just
> been started at Harvard College, a single body was made to
> do duty for a whole year's course of lectures. One solution
> of the difficulty was to beg from the governor the bodies of
> executed criminals.

Underline in this version the statements of those ideas which
are presented as parallels in the text.

The brace is a convenient device for testing the grammatical
soundness of parallel structures:

$$
he \begin{cases} ground \dots \\ mixed \dots \\ helped\ to \\ and \\ ran \dots \end{cases} \begin{cases} adjust \\ and \\ sew \end{cases}
$$

The parallels must all be the same part of speech, and they
must all have the same syntax, i.e., they must all have the
same relation to the common factor, the word which stands at
the point of the brace. Here four verbs have a common subject. Had the fourth term been written "and errands are
run . . ." or "and running with vials . . . ," it would not
have been grammatically parallel. The beginner should use the
brace diagram to test the accuracy of his own phrasings.

6. Make a diagram of this sort for each of the parallel
structures in constructions in Pars. 3 and 4. There are seventeen.

7. Are we to assume, from lines 36-37, that the country
doctor snubbed the tinsmith?—From line 40, that he was indifferent to the prospects of the potato crop?—From line 46,
that a patient who lived twelve miles away had to wait until
morning? Explain.

McMaster's prose is imaginative. Par. 2 would have been
logically complete without its first sentence, but it would not

have made the reader understand so plainly what the
meant to the young man; McMaster translated "scarcity
specimens" into terms of human experience. Lines 34-40 might
have been written: "the cordiality with which he discussed
the topics of the day with even the humblest laborer"; McMaster
brought us closer to the reality. It was not, in line 76, "persons"
who fainted but "the damsel"; the single word brings the
sentence to life and helps enliven a paragraph which, in the
nature of its materials, might have been colorless. The purpose
of imaginative writing is to convince and reassure the reader
that the discussion relates to the actual world—that the med
student, for instance, was not merely a word on the page but an
eager youngster with a scalpel in his fingers, bending over the
table and what was on it. Exposition must often generalize,
analyze, schematize, reduce the world to an intelligible pattern.
If the thinker is not to lose himself in his verbal pattern, he
must keep his feet on the ground, referring constantly in his
own imagination to the world as it was before he applied his
words to it. As a writer, he must keep his reader likewise in
touch with the practical world. To this end the skillful ex-
positor will deliberately insert imaginative strokes—phrases or
sentences—throughout his paragraph. Witness the procedure in
the following passage, by another historian of Macaulay's great
school, on the comfort and elegance of domestic architecture
under the elder Stuarts:

> Military barbarism in castle and moat-house was already
> a thing of the past. . . . These mansions were of every
> variety of size and style; there were modest halls and manors
> . . . and lofty rural palaces of red brick and carved stone,
> decorating wooded parks and retired valleys. The increased
> profits from land newly enclosed went chiefly to the pocket
> of the landlord; and at this period he was more ready to em-
> ploy money in raising a great Jacobean mansion than in
> further improving his estate. In these halcyon days of pride in
> new prosperity, when the final success of the Tudor rule
> seemed to have secured the island from all chance of again
> becoming the scene of military operations, houses were built
> for peace that were yet to taste of war; mullions and gables
> rose from which the sentinel would soon look forth; garden
> walks were laid out across which the iron shot would tear;
> and carved oak adorned the staircase, on whose broad land-

5. T⸱the pikes of the last defenders would go down before the
q⸱⸱res ⸱r and the tramp of the rush that ends the day.[2]
a⸱ Imaginative writing is a routine part of expository technic,
and it is by no means the most difficult. It does not require that
the writer be fanciful or visionary, prone to sentimental revery.
It does require that he be able to put himself into the situation
he is writing about.

8. Underline the imaginative phrases or sentences in Par. 4.

9. Why is McMaster's inventory of the village store (ll. 54-
55) better than the following: "among flitches of bacon, cases
of tea, barrels of molasses, and tubs of salt fish"?

10. What words do you know that are related to *announce,
obtain, prescription*?

11. Explain the relation, if any, between the words in each
of the following groups: *popular* and *depopulate; malaria* and
hilarious; calomel, callisthenics, callous, and *callow; menial,
mansion,* and *menagerie; mercury* and *market.*

12. Write an essay describing a profession or occupation,
other than medicine: the truck-driver, the hairdresser, the
tourist guide, the sideshow barker, the bartender, the organ-
grinder, the department store Santa Claus, the bridge player,
the social worker, etc. Do not present the adventures of a particular individual; if you use your own experiences as a door-
step peddler or a lifeguard, generalize them so that they illustrate the experiences of most persons so employed. You will
have to set some sort of limit to your topic, of time or place or
rank; thus you might describe the *country* barber, the preacher
in a wealthy parish, the movie pianist *in the days before the
talkies.* You need not copy the outline of this passage; your topic
may not call for a paragraph on apprenticeship, or it may require some description of social setting.

Make check marks in the margin to call your instructor's
attention to skillful parallel constructions; use little stars in the
margin to mark the imaginative strokes of which you are
especially proud.

[2] From *England Under the Stuarts,* by George Macaulay Trevelyan; reprinted by permission of G. P. Putnam's Sons and of Methuen and Co.

PLAY[1]

STUART CHASE

●

1. BEFORE THE DAYS OF THE BICYCLE, PLAY IN A NEW ENG-
land town has been thus described by Mr. Benton MacKaye.
I can still remember happy vestiges of it in my own boy-
hood in Massachusetts.

5   There was the swimming-hole in the mill-stream—and the
flooding of the meadow for skating around the evening bonfire.
There was the "after haying" picnic on the river intervale, and
the coasting parties by February moonlight. There was baseball
and shinny; rainy day pout fishing and tracking rabbits. There
10 was the mud scow on the spring meadow—and there was
fishing through the ice. There was the illustrated lecture, on
the stars or on the Norman Conquest. There was *Evangeline*
read aloud on a long solstice evening; there was "drop the
handkerchief" on the Common. There was the strawberry
15 festival on the green; the corn husking on the barn floor. There
was the Grand Masquerade in the January thaw—and quadrilles
and reels and slides. The church bells rang out on the night
before the Fourth (with the parade of the Antiques and Hor-
ribles to come), as the sleigh bells did on the night before
20 Christmas.[2]

With variations due to local customs, this picture might
hold for all of America, outside of the big cities, in 1875.

2. On a summer Sunday in America today [1929], people also play. Some forty millions of them are being carried
25 by a machine at thirty miles an hour, past Goodrich Tire
signs and Travelers' Rests; and anon creeping in single
line at one mile an hour to the escarpments of bridges, fer-

---

[1] From *Men and Machines,* by Stuart Chase. By permission of The
Macmillan Company, publishers.
[2] From *The New Exploration,* by Benton MacKaye; by permission of
Harcourt, Brace & Co.

ries, tunnels, and bottle-neck highways, in a steamy sweat of
oil and dust. Millions are eating the inevitable steak or
chicken dinner at the inevitable blowsy road house, while 30
the gin gurgles into the Canada Dry, the radio drowns the
engulfing of the canned tomato soup, and Jim and Ethel
essay the Black Bottom. Ten millions are seated in the dark
watching a personable young woman alternately mislay
and recover her virtue for six thick rolls of celluloid. For 35
some hours of the day, practically the entire population of
the Republic disappears under something in the nature of
60,000 tons of wood pulp, to the accompaniment of a noisy
if not positively sanguinary struggle between the younger
generation as to which has prior right to Mutt and Jeff.   40

3. Along the Atlantic, the Pacific, the Gulf of Mexico,
and the Great Lakes, stretch 10,000 miles of fine hard
beaches, deserted save for the seagull, the sandpiper, and the
crab. From point to point between the lonely stretches, to
a total linear measurement of perhaps fifty miles, more 45
millions congregate, each with his bottle of pop, his banana,
and his cheese sandwich. Running and leaping is not seemly
in such mass formations, but phonographs, embellished
with a little sand, are always welcome.

4. When the pop bottle and the banana peel have been 50
duly deposited to add their quota to the littoral, there is
more play to be had immediately to the rear. Here rise
fantastic towers of white plaster, which, as twilight gathers,
glow and sparkle with innumerable lights. Here tram loads
of shrieking shop girls rush down frightful declivities; here 55
may be viewed the fattest, the tallest, the shortest, the
most convoluted of the species. Here one meets oneself with
a resounding thwack in mirror mazes, is deftly bereft of
equilibrium by spinning, heaving floors; loses hat and
modesty by jets of compressed air. Here a five-dollar bill 60
melts like the snows of April.

5. Fifty thousand are roaring as the Home Run King
lifts a horsehide pellet over a board fence; hot, disquieted
matrons are reading confession magazines in stuffy par-
lors; far into the reeking night in a haze of smoke, thin 65

men sit in shirt sleeves bowed over pieces of cardboard
and round, brightly colored discs; while throughout the day
five hundred thousand ampler men alternately strike and
curse at a small white ball, magnetically attracted to pits
70 of sand or to pools of water.

6. All that remains of Mr. MacKaye's tradition is the
small fraction of the population who, with knapsacks on
their backs and maps in their hip pockets, are to be found
here and there clambering over hills and mountains or
75 striding back-country roads, too rough for any vehicles
save the surviving buggies and an occasional reluctant Ford.

❊ ❊ ❊

1. Par. 1 is of the simplest pattern: it contains two elements,
a series of details and a unifying term—a bundle of sticks tied
with a cord. Without the sticks, the cord hangs limp and useless; without the cord, the sticks fall helter-skelter. Distinguish
these two elements in Par. 1, underlining the phrase which
summarizes and defines the substance of the paragraph.

2. The last sentence of Par. 1 does not merely repeat an
idea but carries it a little further. What is the added thought?
Mr. Chase's argument would have been as complete if he had
inserted his last sentence at line 4, before the quoted passage,
but then the paragraph would not have had quite the same
effect on the reader; what is the rhetorical virtue of his arrangement?

3. Show that logically and rhetorically Pars. 2-6 might have
been printed as a single paragraph.

Later in the essay from which this passage is excerpted,
Mr. Chase offers a number of propositions about play in the
1920's: that it was conditioned by machinery, that it was
largely passive rather than active, that it did not involve and
express the whole personality, as did older forms of play, that
it did not restore the psychological balance lost in machine
work, and that the shortening of working hours might have
no value for people who have lost the faculty of playing. In
this preliminary section, however, he develops no theses; here
his aim is to make an imaginative survey of the whole field:

play in the machine age. To this end, the illustrative materials had to be widely diversified, panoramic. An account of the various amusements of shop girls, no matter how entertaining in itself, would not have had sufficient range. Nor would a list of spectator sports have covered enough ground.

4. Just how much ground is covered in Pars. 2-6? There are children (ll. 38-40) as well as adults, highways (ll. 24-29) as well as beaches (Par. 3). Continue the inventory.

The materials for Pars. 2-6 were presumably gathered and arranged in the form of curt notes: cars, roadhouse meal, gin, jazz, funnies. . . . The writer's next problem was to find a compact and vivid way of phrasing each item. The roughly worded ideas of the outline have been worked over into a series of telling little pictures, a page of candid camera shots.

"Many weary hours are spent driving along the highways, getting caught in a traffic jam before the return" would have indicated a kind of popular amusement; the phrasing of the text presents the idea more graphically, as an incident seen and sensed. The method is plain enough. Fix the situation in a simple, blunt statement: Millions go driving. Add qualifying details: through ugly countryside, slow at bottlenecks, breathing impure air. Sharpen the wording; a simple rule is to prefer the phrase of narrower meaning: "past billboards" or, more precisely, "Goodrich Tire signs," "one mile an hour," "bridges, ferries, tunnels," "oil and dust." This is an analysis of the process; a practiced writer does all these things not in stages but at one stroke. The procedure may be followed mechanically; it takes skill and insight, at every stage, to produce a good result.

5. Select the five sentences (or parts of compound sentences) in Pars. 2-5 which you think most successful. In each of these, decide which words or phrases are most effective and comment on them.

6. In Pars. 2-6, point out three elaborate or felicitous instances of parallel structure; make a brace diagram for each of these.

7. Demonstrate that the illustrative materials quoted in Par. 1 have—or have not—sufficient variety to fulfill their purpose.

8. On what principle does Mr. MacKaye seem to have arranged these items? Suggest one or two other possible plans for arranging such materials.

9. Mr. MacKaye presumably had not room for much imaginative amplification of the items in his list. Where is its chief weakness, in nouns, verbs, or modifiers?

10. Had there been room, the first item might have been written so: At the swimming hole in the mill stream, naked boys splashed and shouted, jumping from the rickety diving board or the rope swing, or basking on the bank under the July sun. Take any two other items in lines 5-20 and amplify them.

11. Explain the derivations of *dollar, gin, knapsack, magnet, phonograph, twilight.*

12. Write a "panoramic" sketch. Possible topics: Rush week; Before the Homecoming Game; How the war has affected our town; What happens to a household when the electric power goes off; Why movie ushers chew gum; The life of a metropolitan taxi driver; The work of the ——— Settlement House; Quacks. Broader topics: The automobile in American life; How the masses suffer under capitalism; How the New Deal has undermined national morale. The method is always useful in demonstrating that modern society is terrible or that modern society is up to finer things. Whatever your subject, be sure that your illustrative materials are as varied as possible within the limits of the subject.

SUPERSTITIONS[1]

JOSEPH ADDISON

•

1. GOING YESTERDAY TO DINE WITH AN OLD ACQUAINTANCE, I had the misfortune to find his whole family very much dejected. Upon asking him the occasion of it, he told me that his wife had dreamt a very strange dream the night before, which they were afraid portended some misfortune 5 to themselves or to their children. At her coming into the room I observed a settled melancholy in her countenance, which I should have been troubled for, had I not heard from whence it proceeded. We had no sooner sat down than, after having looked upon me a little while, "My dear," 10 says she, turning to her husband, "you may now see the stranger that was in the candle last night." Soon after this, as they began to talk of family affairs, a little boy at the lower end of the table told her that he was to go into join-hand on Thursday. "Thursday?" says she; "No, child, if it 15 please God, you shall not begin upon Childermas day; tell your writing-master that Friday will be soon enough." I was reflecting with myself on the oddness of her fancy and wondering that anybody would establish it as a rule to lose a day in every week. In the midst of these my musings she 20 desired me to reach her a little salt upon the point of my knife, which I did in such a trepidation and hurry of obedi-ence that I let it drop by the way; at which she immediately startled and said it fell towards her. Upon this I looked very blank and, observing the concern of the whole table, 25 began to consider myself, with some confusion, as a person that had brought a disaster upon the family. The lady, how-ever, recovering herself after a little space, said to her hus-band with a sigh, "My dear, misfortunes never come

[1] From *The Spectator*, No. 7, by Joseph Addison.

30 single." My friend, I found, acted but an under part at his
table and, being a man of more good nature than understanding, thinks himself obliged to fall in with all the
passions and humors of his yoke-fellow. "Do not you remember, child," says she, "that the pigeon-house fell the
35 very afternoon that our careless wench spilt the salt upon
the table?" "Yes," says he, "my dear, and the next post
brought us an account of the battle of Almanza." The reader
may guess at the figure I made, after having done all this
mischief. I dispatched my dinner as soon as I could; when,
40 to my utter confusion, the lady seeing me quitting my
knife and fork and laying them across one another upon my
plate, desired me that I would humor her so far as to take
them out of that figure and place them side by side. What
the absurdity was which I had committed I did not know,
45 but I suppose there was some traditionary superstition in it;
and therefore, in obedience to the lady of the house, I disposed of my knife and fork in two parallel lines, which is
the figure I shall always lay them in for the future, though
I do not know any reason for it. It is not difficult for a
50 man to see that a person has conceived an aversion to him.
For my own part, I quickly found, by the lady's looks,
that she regarded me as a very odd kind of fellow, with
an unfortunate aspect, for which reason I took my leave
immediately after dinner and withdrew to my own lodg-
55 ings.

2. Upon my return home, I fell into a profound contemplation on the evils that attend these superstitious follies
of mankind, how they subject us to imaginary afflictions
and additional sorrows that do not properly come within
60 our lot. As if the natural calamities of life were not sufficient for it, we turn the most indifferent circumstances into
misfortunes and suffer as much from trifling accidents as
from real evils. I have known the shooting of a star spoil
a night's rest, and have seen a man in love grow pale
65 and lose his appetite upon the plucking of a merrythought.
A screech owl at midnight has alarmed a family more
than a band of robbers; nay, the voice of a cricket has

struck more terror than the roaring of a lion. There is nothing so inconsiderable that it may not appear dreadful to an imagination filled with omens and prognostics. A rusty nail, a crooked pin, shoot up into prodigies.

3. An old maid that is troubled with the vapors produces infinite disturbances of this kind among her friends and neighbors. I know a maiden aunt, of a great family, who is one of these antiquated sibyls that forebodes and prophesies from one end of the year to the other. She is always seeing apparitions and hearing deathwatches and was the other day almost frighted out of her wits by the great house dog that howled in the stable at a time when she lay ill of the toothache. Such an extravagant cast of mind engages multitudes of people not only in impertinent terrors but in supernumerary duties of life, and arises from that fear and ignorance which are natural to the soul of man. The horror with which we entertain the thoughts of death (or indeed of any future evil) and the uncertainty of its approach fill a melancholy mind with innumerable apprehensions and suspicions and consequently dispose it to the observation of such groundless prodigies and predictions. For as it is the chief concern of wise men to retrench the evils of life by the reasonings of philosophy, it is the employment of fools to multiply them by the sentiments of superstition.

4. I know but one way of fortifying my soul against these gloomy presages and terrors of mind, and that is by securing to myself the friendship and protection of that Being who disposes of events and governs futurity. He sees at one view the whole thread of my existence, not only that part of it which I have already passed through but that which runs forward into all the depths of eternity. When I lay me down to sleep, I recommend myself to His care; when I awake, I give myself up to His direction. Amidst all the evils that threaten me, I will look up to Him for help and question not but He will either avert them or turn them to my advantage. Though I know neither the time nor the manner of the death I am to die, I

am not at all solicitous about it, because I am sure that He knows them both and that He will not fail to comfort and support me under them.

※ ※ ※

1.   What is join-hand? (ll. 14-15.) Childermas day? (l. 16.) A merrythought? (l. 65) A sibyl? (l. 74.) A deathwatch? (l. 76.) What are the vapors? (l. 71.)

2.   Show the plan of the essay. In which paragraph does Addison explain why people are superstitious? In which is his main topic the ill effects of superstition? In which does he propose a sounder attitude? What is the function of the other paragraph? Of the three topics mentioned, which has the most emphatic position in the essay? Which is emphasized by reiteration?

3.   Put the thought of lines 82-87 ("The horror . . . predictions") into simpler language, such as could be understood by an intelligent child of twelve. You may have to use more words than Addison used, but let your explanation be as short as possible.

4.   Underline in red the six illustrations in Par. 2. Underline in black the abstract phrases which give the points of these two groups of illustrations.

5.   Underline in red the three omens named in Par. 3.

6.   Compare the effect of the text, lines 76-79, with that of the following version: . . . and the other day, as she lay ill of the toothache, was almost frighted out of her wits by the great house dog that howled in the stable.

7.   Before sermonizing his readers, Addison has provided them in Par. 1 with illustrations of five superstitions. Underline in red several words presenting each of these. (E.g., "strange dream portended misfortune.")

8.   Show that Par. 1 provides illustrations to support each of the charges which Addison later brings against superstitions: that they involve us in (a) imaginary afflictions and additional sorrows, (b) impertinent terrors, and (c) supernumerary duties. (You will first have to determine exactly what these phrases mean.)

9. The illustrations have, moreover, been woven into a pleasant little story. And the story is amusing largely because of the dramatic interplay between what two people? Point out the chief phrases or sentences which develop this dramatic element.

10. Before presenting expository narrative, it is good to indicate the topic or point of the story (cf. Fontenelle, *The Gold Tooth*) and to suggest to the reader the attitude you wish him to take toward it. In which phrases of the first three sentences has Addison done these things?

11. How does "next" (l. 36) contribute to the *reductio ad absurdum*?

12. Comment on the following changes of wording: *a trepidation* (l. 22) to *intrepidity; blank* (l. 25) to *pale; wench* (l. 35) to *maid; accidents* (l. 62) to *troubles; cricket* (l. 67) to *insect; prodigies* (l. 70) to *accomplishments; extravagant* (l. 79) to *costly; impertinent* (l. 80) to *impudent.*

A long step toward familiarity with the language is the recognition of those Latin roots and prefixes which appear in many English words. Certain living prefixes, such as dis-, mis-, re-, and un-, have been rather freely added to words in English, whether these words were ultimately derived from Latin or not: e.g., *dismount, mistake, rewrite, unfasten;* of such combinations the meaning is a simple sum of prefix and root, intelligible at once. But of older compounds, existing as such in Latin, a literal translation of the parts may give no clue to the sense. For instance, *sub-,* under, and *facere,* to make, do not very clearly add up to the meaning of our word *suffice.* (Older English compounds may be no plainer; e.g., *understand.*) The translation of Latin roots and prefixes is a roundabout and uncertain and indeed a preposterous way to discover the meanings of English words. A recognition of these elements does, nevertheless, enhance one's feeling for the texture of the language; it is a good thing to sense the kinship, however obscure, of *sufficient, efficient, deficient, deficit,* and *defect.* Such recognition may also enrich particular words: *dejected* (l. 3) becomes more vivid if read as a metaphor, literally "downcast."

13. Do the meanings of the prefixes and roots of any of the following words clearly suggest the meanings of these words as they are used in this passage? *Portend* (l. 5); *reflect* (l. 18);

confusion (l. 26); *commit* (l. 44); *suppose* (l. 45); *difficult* (l. 50); *conceive* (l. 51); *aversion* (l. 51); *aspect* (l. 53); *subject* (l. 57); *apprehension* (l. 85); *prediction* (l. 87); *protection* (l. 93).

14. For each of the words listed above, give as many other English words as you can in which the same Latin root appears, checking those of which the meanings are clearly suggested by the prefixes and roots.

15. What superstitious belief or practice is associated with the early history of each of the following words? *Augury, auspicious, contemplate, disaster, dismal.*

16. A warlike spirit was called *martial* in reference to the god rather than to the planet. What temperaments are named with reference to planetary influence? Why is there no such word derived from the planet Uranus? From Earth?

17. Write an essay on some folly, affectation, or petty vice which you have had opportunity to observe. There are the pretenders to sophistication, the ostentatious lovers of art, the obsessed radicals, the solicitous mothers, the procrastinators, the eternal clowns, the offensively red-blooded fellows—you will think of others—all needing to have their excess gently pointed out and analyzed. Rely upon what you have observed rather than upon what you suppose. Remember, too, that Addison gave no less than fourteen illustrations of the folly he was discussing.

LONDON[1]

THOMAS BABINGTON MACAULAY

•

1. THE COFFEE-HOUSE MUST NOT BE DISMISSED WITH A cursory mention. It might indeed at that time have been not improperly called a most important political institution. No Parliament had sat for years. The municipal council of the City had ceased to speak the sense of the citizens. 5 Public meetings, harangues, resolutions, and the rest of the modern machinery of agitation had not yet come into fashion. Nothing resembling the modern newspaper existed. In such circumstances the coffee-houses were the chief organs through which the public opinion of the metropolis 10 vented itself.

2. The first of these establishments had been set up, in the time of the Commonwealth, by a Turkey merchant, who had acquired among the Mohammedans a taste for their favorite beverage. The convenience of being able to 15 make appointments in any part of the town, and of being able to pass evenings socially at a very small charge, was so great that the fashion spread fast. Every man of the upper or middle class went daily to his coffee-house to learn the news and to discuss it. Every coffee-house had one 20 or more orators to whose eloquence the crowd listened with admiration, and who soon became, what the journalists of our time have been called, a fourth Estate of the realm. The court had long seen with uneasiness the growth of this new power in the state. An attempt had been made, 25 during Danby's administration, to close the coffee-houses. But men of all parties missed their usual places of resort so much that there was a universal outcry. The government

[1] From *The History of England from the Accession of James the Second.*

did not venture, in opposition to a feeling so strong and gen-
30 eral, to enforce a regulation of which the legality might
well be questioned. Since that time ten years had elapsed,
and during those years the number and influence of the
coffee-houses had been constantly increasing. Foreigners remarked that the coffee-house was that which especially dis-
35 tinguished London from all other cities, that the coffee-
house was the Londoner's home, and that those who wished
to find a gentleman commonly asked, not whether he lived
in Fleet Street or Chancery Lane, but whether he frequented the Grecian or the Rainbow. Nobody was excluded
40 from these places who laid down his penny at the bar.

3. Yet every rank and profession, and every shade of religious and political opinion, had its own headquarters.
There were houses near Saint James's Park where fops con-
gregated, their heads and shoulders covered with black or
45 flaxen wigs, not less ample than those which are now worn
by the Chancellor and by the Speaker of the House of
Commons. The wig came from Paris; and so did the rest
of the fine gentleman's ornaments, his embroidered coat,
his fringed gloves, and the tassel which upheld his panta-
50 loons. The atmosphere was like that of a perfumer's shop.
Tobacco in any other form than that of richly scented
snuff was held in abomination. If any clown, ignorant of
the usages of the house, called for a pipe, the sneers of the
whole assembly and the short answers of the waiters soon
55 convinced him that he had better go somewhere else. Nor,
indeed, would he have had far to go. For, in general, the
coffee-rooms reeked with tobacco like a guard-room; and
strangers sometimes expressed their surprise that so many
people should leave their own firesides to sit in the midst
60 of eternal fog and stench. Nowhere was the smoking more
constant than at Will's. That celebrated house, situated between Covent Garden and Bow Street, was sacred to polite
letters. There the talk was about poetical justice and the
unities of time and place. There was a faction for Perrault
65 and the moderns, a faction for Boileau and the ancients.
One group debated whether Paradise Lost ought not to

have been in rhyme. To another an envious poetaster demonstrated that Venice Preserved ought to have been hooted
from the stage. Under no roof was a greater variety of
figures to be seen. There were earls in stars and garters, 70
clergymen in cassocks and bands, pert Templars, sheepish
lads from the Universities, translators and index-makers in
ragged coats of frieze. The great press was to get near the
chair where John Dryden sat. In winter that chair was always in the warmest nook by the fire; in summer it stood 75
in the balcony. To bow to the Laureate, and to hear his
opinion of Racine's last tragedy or of Bossu's treatise on
epic poetry, was thought a privilege. A pinch from his
snuffbox was an honor sufficient to turn the head of a
young enthusiast. There were coffee-houses where the first 80
medical men might be consulted. Doctor John Radcliffe,
who, in the year 1685, rose to the largest practice in London,
came daily, at the hour when the Exchange was full, from
his house in Bow Street, then a fashionable part of the
capital, to Garraway's, and was to be found, surrounded 85
by surgeons and apothecaries, at a particular table. There
were Puritan coffee-houses where no oath was heard, and
where lank-haired men discussed election and reprobation
through their noses; Jew coffee-houses where dark-eyed
money-changers from Venice and from Amsterdam greeted 90
each other; and Popish coffee-houses where, as good Protestants believed, Jesuits planned, over their cups, another
great fire, and cast silver bullets to shoot the King.

4. These gregarious habits had no small share in forming the character of the Londoner of that age. He was in- 95
deed a different being from the rustic Englishman. There
was not then the intercourse which now exists between the
two classes. Only very great men were in the habit of di-
viding the year between town and country. Few esquires
came to the capital thrice in their lives. Nor was it yet the 100
practice of all citizens in easy circumstances to breathe the
fresh air of the fields and woods during some weeks of
every summer. A cockney, in a rural village, was stared at
as much as if he had intruded into a kraal of Hottentots.

105 On the other hand, when the lord of a Lincolnshire or
Shropshire manor appeared in Fleet Street, he was as easily
distinguished from the resident population as a Turk or a
Lascar. His dress, his gait, his accent, the manner in which
he gazed at the shops, stumbled in the gutters, ran against
110 the porters, and stood under the water-spouts, marked him
out as an excellent subject for the operations of swindlers
and banterers. Bullies jostled him into the kennel. Hack-
ney coachmen splashed him from head to foot. Thieves
explored with perfect security the huge pockets of his horse-
115 man's coat, while he stood entranced by the splendor of
the Lord Mayor's show. Money-droppers, sore from the
cart's tail, introduced themselves to him, and appeared to
him the most honest friendly gentlemen that he had ever
seen. Painted women, the refuse of Lewkner Lane and
120 Whetstone Park, passed themselves on him for countesses
and maids of honor. If he asked his way to Saint James's,
his informants sent him to Mile End. If he went into a
shop, he was instantly discerned to be a fit purchaser of
everything that nobody else would buy, of second-hand em-
125 broidery, copper rings, and watches that would not go.
If he rambled into any fashionable coffee-house, he became
a mark for the insolent derision of fops and the grave wag-
gery of Templars. Enraged and mortified, he soon returned
to his mansion, and there, in the homage of his tenants and
130 the conversation of his boon-companions, found consolation
for the vexations and humiliations which he had undergone. There he was once more a great man, and saw
nothing above himself except when at the assizes he took his
seat on the bench near the judge, or when at the muster
135 of the militia he saluted the lord-lieutenant.

※ ※ ※

Macaulay is a lively writer. In his third paragraph, he undertook to differentiate the coffee-houses, to create for each of
several specimens its own peculiar atmosphere. The reader looks
on, more or less aware that he is witnessing a demonstration of
literary dexterity, as Macaulay confidently adds one telling

stroke after another. He produces three somewhat full pictures, with that of Will's the most detailed; then he finishes off with three rapidly drawn single-line sketches; we almost hold our breath to watch him.

But if we pick up these sketches and scrutinize them, we may discover the method. It resembles the trick of the cartoonist or caricaturist: to indicate only the striking, characteristic features of the well-known personage. The trick in prose is to *particularize,* especially in illustrative statements. We are told, not simply that the frequenters of Will's talked about literature, but precisely what literary questions agitated them. Nor is this use of particulars invalidated by the possibility that the reader may not be familiar with such exact allusions: suppose the reader has never head of *Paradise Lost;* still Macaulay's sentence (ll. 66-67) is better than "One group discussed contemporary poetry." Of course, the reader's understanding of *either* sentence may be impaired by ignorance, but vagueness of reference doesn't make life easier for the ignorant. Again, we have no notion of where Lewkner Lane and Whetstone Park were, but the very names of these streets are more impressive than some such general term as "slums" or "disreputable neighborhoods."

The fourth paragraph, delightfully comic, may be compared with Par. 3 of "The Country Doctor." Both are imaginative reconstructions of typical situations, and both are full of particulars. McMaster has obviously studied the style of Macaulay. Which paragraph do you think more brilliant?

1. What word is to be emphasized in the second sentence? Why?

2. To which sentences does the phrase "in such circumstances" (l. 9) refer? Write a sentence summarizing these circumstances. Where might it be inserted in the paragraph?

3. Par. 2 is a narrative. Show that you understand its plan by giving it a title and by marking off five stages in its development, giving a title to each.

4. Under what headings is Par. 3 organized? Mark off its parts.

5. In lines 37-39, Macaulay might have written, "not where he lived, but which coffee-house he frequented." He preferred, however, to particularize the idea. Again, in lines 44-50, we

find a general term, "fine gentleman's ornaments," and a number of particularizations—"black or flaxen wigs," "embroidered coat," etc.

a) Underline the general term in black and the particularizations in red.

b) Enclose the section, "sacred . . . stage" (ll. 62-69), in brackets; underline the general term in black and the particularizations in red.

c) Do the same in the section, "Under no roof . . . frieze." (ll. 69-73.)

d) In the next section, "The great press . . . enthusiast" (ll. 73-80), no summary phrase is included; what general term is here implied?

6. What are the three divisions of the passage on Will's? (ll. 61-80.) Consider the arrangement of these three topics in another order, and compare it with the present order.

7. Why did not Macaulay *first* describe the perfumed atmosphere of the foppish coffee-houses and *then* the dress of the habitués? (Consider the relation of this section to the rest of the paragraph.)

8. What four phrases particularize the adjective "Puritan"? (l. 87.) What phrases particularize "Jew"? (l. 89.) "Popish"? (l. 91.) "Medical men"? (l. 81.) Enclose each section in brackets and underline in black and red.

9. The parts of Par. 2 could not logically have been presented in a different order; could those of Par. 3? (Assume, of course, that transitions can be adjusted to any desirable arrangement.) Why or why not?

10. Whatever your answer to Question 9, the description of Garraway's (ll. 80-86) should not be at the beginning or end of the paragraph; why not?

11. Could Pars. 1, 2, and 3 have been arranged in any other order? Suggest a feasible alternative plan or explain why the present sequence is necessary—i.e., why 1 before 2, 2 before 3.

12. Read the Britannica article "Bill of Rights"; to which article is the development of the coffee-house relevant?

13. The verb *intrude* is plainly related to the noun *intrusion;* what verbs are similarly related to *resolution, administration, reprobation, derision?*

14. Find cognates for *cursory, parliament, eloquence, congregate.*

15. Comment on the following changes of wording: *polite* (l. 62) to *courteous; demonstrated* (l. 67) to *claimed; election* (l. 88) to *politics; entranced* (l. 115) to *spellbound; rambled* (l. 126) to *ventured.*

16. Explain the derivations of *assizes, coffee, enthusiast, garter, harangue, pantaloons, Parliament, tobacco.*

17. Write an essay on some such topic as local lodges, fraternities, sewing circles, rival churches, pool rooms, hotels, movie houses. After some appropriate general remarks on the social institution, describe several species: appearance, activities, membership, patronage, etc.

SPARE THE ROD[1]

JEAN JACQUES ROUSSEAU

●

1. In setting my pupil free from all compulsions, I set
him free from children's greatest source of wretchedness:
books. Reading is the scourge of childhood; yet teachers
seem unable to think of any other activity with which to
5 occupy their charges. Until my pupil is twelve, he will
hardly know what a book is. But, my critics will say,
surely Émile must learn to read! I agree. He must learn
to read when reading is useful to him; until then, it is
a nuisance.

10 2. If children are not to be made to do things merely
for the sake of their obedience, it follows that they will
learn nothing until they recognize in it a real and immediate profit or pleasure. What other motive will induce
them to learn? The advantage of being able to communicate
15 with persons at a distance, transmitting our sentiments and
our desires, must be plain to persons of all ages. Why,
then, are the agreeable and useful arts of reading and
writing regarded by children as a torment? Because reading and writing have been forced upon them and have been
20 put to uses which children do not understand. A child is
hardly eager to perfect the instrument with which he is
tortured; only make that instrument serve his pleasure, and
he will apply himself in spite of you.

3. A great fuss is made to find the best method of teach-
25 ing children to read; the pedagogs have devised anagrams
and spelling boards; they have turned the nursery into a
printing shop. Locke would have children taught their
letters by means of alphabet dice. Is not this ingenious! An
agent surer than all of these, but invariably overlooked,

[1] From *Émile,* by Jean Jacques Rousseau.

is the desire to learn! Implant this desire in the child, and 30 you may forget your blocks and cards. Any method will serve.

4. The one sure motivation is the hope of immediate advantage. From time to time Émile receives from his family or his friends a letter inviting him to dinner or a picnic 35 or a boating party or a parade. These letters are short, neat, legibly written. But Émile must rely on someone else to read them for him. That someone, however, is not to be found— or proves as unobliging in the matter as was Émile himself in some affair of yesterday. When at last the letter is 40 read to him, the occasion has passed. Ah! if only he had been able to read it for himself! He gets other notes. They are quite short, and the contents are probably very interesting. He tries to make them out and with some casual assistance deciphers a part of them: something is going on 45 tomorrow . . . there will be refreshments . . . but he cannot tell where or when. What an effort he will make to read the rest! I do not believe that Émile will need the assistance of alphabet blocks.

5. Let me point out one important principle: a child 50 learns promptly and firmly those things which he is not driven to learn. Thus I am confident that Émile will be able to read and write before he is ten, precisely because I am in no hurry about it. Indeed, I had rather he never learned to read, if the act of learning were to strip the art 55 of all its possible value for him. What is the use of being able to read, if one has been made to loathe reading?

6. If you dare to disregard the conventional procedures, if, instead of stuffing the mind of your pupil with information about faraway countries and centuries, you try rather 60 to turn his attention to what immediately concerns him, then you will find him quite able to perceive, to remember, even to reason; this is nature's plan. As the sentient being becomes active, he acquires a power of discernment corresponding to his physical powers. And it is through a 65 superabundance of those very energies that are needed for self-preservation that he develops the speculative faculties

whereby he directs his energies to higher ends. Thus if you wish to make your pupil intelligent, develop in him a
70 physical vigor for intelligence to control. Continually exercise his body. Make him robust and healthy, so that he may become reasonable and wise. Let him work, run, shout; let him be always on the move. Develop in him a manly vigor, and he will soon develop for himself a
75 manly mentality.

7. This method will, of course, merely brutalize your pupil if you always direct him, if you forever order him about: "Go," "Come," "Stay," "Do this," "Don't do that." If it is your mind that governs his body, his mind will soon
80 become useless. But let us remember our first principles. If you are a mere pedant, you waste your time reading this.

8. There are two kinds of men whose bodies are constantly exercised—and both are quite unconcerned about the development of their souls. Peasants are loutish, clumsy,
85 stolid. Savages are renowned for the sharpness of their senses and for their subtlety of mind. No creature so dull as the peasant; none so keen as the savage. Why should there be such a difference? The peasant always does what he is commanded, what he has seen his father do, what he
90 did himself as a child; he plods in a rut, bound forever to the same routine of toil, and in his automatic life, habit and obedience take the place of reason. With the savage, things are otherwise. Tied down to no one place, having no prescribed task, obeying no master, knowing no law but
95 his own will, he must in every action of his life exercise reason. He makes no movement without first considering its consequences. In such conditions of freedom, the greater his physical activity, the greater his enlightenment of mind. Force and reason grow together, each enhancing
100 the other.

❋ ❋ ❋

1. Divide the passage into two sections, each containing a theoretical discussion and an illustrative paragraph.

2. Which two sentences in Par. 2 present the principal ideas illustrated in the corresponding narrative?

3. You are to write a similar story about Émile which will illustrate the ideas of Par. 6. As you will first have to understand precisely what these ideas are, you had better not guess at words of uncertain meaning. Underline those parts of Par. 6 —not more than seven lines—which outline the theory and which therefore must underlie the illustrative narrative. Then write the story.

4. To what does Rousseau attribute the excellence of his savage? Why is the peasant needed in Par. 8?

5. What principle of education is developed in *both* sections of the whole passage?

6. Suppose that social explorers after Rousseau's time have had to seek farther and farther for a savage who is not the slave of dark fears and iron custom; how do you think that would affect Rousseau's argument? Explain your conclusion.

7. Explain the derivations of *peasant, savage, intelligence*.

8. Write about a child some phase of whose education has been faulty. Let your essay contain an illustrative narrative, and develop the underlying theory in sufficient detail. For instance, do not be content merely to say that the child was reasoned with; why should not a child be reasoned with?

TALL TALK[1]

HENRY LOUIS MENCKEN

•

1. ALL HESITATIONS DISAPPEARED, AND THERE AROSE A NA-
tional consciousness so soaring and so blatant that it began
to dismiss every British usage and opinion as puerile and
idiotic. The new Republic would not only produce a civilization and a literature of its own; it would show the way
for all other civilizations and literatures. Rufus Wilmot Gris-
wold rose in his decorous Baptist pulpit to protest that so
much patriotism amounted to chauvinism and absurdity,
but there seems to have been no one to second the motion.
The debate upon the Oregon question gave a gaudy chance
to the new breed of super-patriots, and they raged un-
checked until the time of the Civil War. Thornton, in his
Glossary, quotes a typical speech in Congress, the subject
being the American eagle and the orator being the Hon.
Samuel C. Pomeroy, of Kansas. I give a few strophes:

The proudest bird upon the mountain is upon the American
ensign, and not one feather shall fall from her plumage there.
She is American in design, and an emblem of wildness and
freedom. I say again, she has not perched herself upon American
standards to die there. Our great Western valleys were never
scooped out for her burial place. Nor were the everlasting, un-
trodden mountains piled for her monument. Niagara shall not
pour her endless waters for her requiem; nor shall our ten
thousand rivers weep to the ocean in eternal tears. No, sir, no!
Unnumbered voices shall come up from river, plain, and mountain, echoing the songs of our triumphant deliverance; wild
lights from a thousand hill-tops will betoken the rising of the
sun of freedom.

[1] Reprinted from *The American Language*, by H. L. Mencken, by permission of and special arrangement with Alfred A. Knopf, Inc., authorized publishers.

2. This tall talk was by no means reserved for occasions of state; it decorated the everyday speech of the people, especially in the Jackson country to the southward and beyond the mountains. It ran, there, to grotesque metaphors and far-fetched exaggerations, and out of it came a great many Americanisms that still flourish. Thornton gives a specimen from a Florida newspaper, *c.* 1840, the speaker being a local fee-faw-fo-fum:

This is *me,* and no mistake! Billy Earthquake, Esq., commonly called Little Billy, all the way from the No'th Fork of Muddy Run! . . . Whoop! won't *nobody* come out and fight me? Come out, some of you, and die decently, for I'm spiling for a fight. . . . I'm a poor man, it's a fact, and smell like a wet dog, but I can't be run over. . . . Maybe you never heard of the time the horse kicked me, and put both his hips out of jint —if it ain't true, cut me up for catfish bait! W-h-o-o-p! I'm the very infant that refused its milk before its eyes were open, and called out for a bottle of old rye. . . . Talk about grinning the bark off a tree—'taint nothing; one squint of mine at a bull's heel would blister it. Oh, I'm one of your toughest sort—live forever, and then turn to a white-oak post. I'm the ginewine article, a real double-acting engine, and I can out-run, out-jump, out-swim, chaw more tobacco and spit less, and drink more whiskey and keep soberer than any man in these localities.

Another noble example comes from Mark Twain's *Life on the Mississippi,* the time being *c.* 1852:

Whoo-oop! I'm the old original iron-jawed, brass-mounted, copper-bellied corpse-maker from the wilds of Arkansaw! Look at me! I'm the man they call Sudden Death and General Desolation! Sired by a hurricane, dam'd by an earthquake, half-brother to the cholera, nearly related to the smallpox on the mother's side! Look at me! I take nineteen alligators and a bar'l of whiskey for breakfast when I'm in robust health, and a bushel of rattlesnakes and a dead body when I'm ailing. I split the everlasting rocks with my glance, and I squench the thunder when I speak! Whoo-oop! Stand back and give me room according to my strength! Blood's my natural drink, and the wails of the dying is music to my ear! Cast your eye on me, gentle-

men, and lay low and hold your breath, for I'm 'bout to turn
myself loose!

3. This extravagance of metaphor, with its naïve bom-
70 bast, had but little influence, of course, upon the more
decorous native literati. It was borrowed eagerly by the
humorous writers, and especially by those who performed
regularly in the newspapers, and at the end of the period it
was to leave its marks upon two literary artists of the high-
75 est quality, Whitman and Mark Twain, but the generality
of American authors eschewed it very diligently.

4. Thus, on the levels below the Olympians, a wild
and lawless development of the language went on, and
many of the uncouth words and phrases that it brought to
80 birth gradually forced themselves into more or less good
usage. "The *jus et norma loquendi,*" says W. R. Morfill,
the English philologian, "do not depend upon scholars." Particularly in a country where scholarship is strange, cloistered,
and timorous, and the overwhelming majority of the peo-
85 ple are engaged upon new and highly exhilarating tasks,
far away from schools and with a gigantic cockiness in their
hearts. The old hegemony of the Tidewater gentry, North
and South, had been shaken by the revolt of the frontier
under Jackson, and what remained of an urbane habit of
90 mind and utterance began to be confined to the narrowing
feudal areas of the South and the still narrower refuge of
the Boston Brahmins, who were presently recognized as a
definite caste of *intelligentsia,* self-charged with carrying the
torch of culture through a new Dark Age. The typical
95 American, in Paulding's satirical phrase, became " a bundling, gouging, impious" fellow, without either "morals,
literature, religion or refinement." Next to the savage
struggle for land and dollars, party politics was the chief
concern of the people, and with the disappearance of the
100 old leaders and the entrance of pushing upstarts from the
backwoods, political controversy sank to an incredibly low
level. Bartlett, in the introduction to the second edition of
his Glossary, described the effect upon the language. First
the enfranchised mob, whether in the city wards or along

the Western rivers, invented fantastic slang-words and 105
turns of phrase; then they were "seized upon by stump-
speakers at political meetings"; then they were heard in
Congress; then they got into the newspapers; and finally
they came into more or less good repute. Much contemporary evidence is to the same effect. W. C. Fowler, in 110
listing "low expressions" in 1850, described them as "chiefly
political." "The vernacular tongue of the country," said
Daniel Webster, "has become greatly vitiated, depraved and
corrupted by the style of the congressional debates." Thornton, in the appendix to his Glossary, gives some astounding 115
specimens of congressional oratory between the 20's and
60's, and many more will reward the explorer who braves
the files of the *Congressional Globe*. This flood of racy and
unprecedented words and phrases beat upon and finally
penetrated the austere retreat of the literati, but the dignity 120
of speech cultivated there had little compensatory influence
upon the vulgate. The newspaper was enthroned, and *belles
lettres* were cultivated almost in private, and as a mystery.
It is probable, indeed, that *Uncle Tom's Cabin* and *Ten
Nights in a Bar-room,* both published in the early 50's, 125
were the first contemporary native books, after Cooper's
day, that the American people, as a people, ever really read.
Nor did the pulpit, now fast falling from its old high
estate, lift a corrective voice. On the contrary, it joined the
crowd, and Bartlett denounced it specifically for its bad 130
example, and cited, among its crimes against the language,
such inventions as *to doxologize* and *to funeralize*.

5. This pressure from below eventually broke down the
defenses of the purists, and forced the new national idiom
upon them. Pen in hand, they might still achieve laborious 135
imitations of the hated English reviewers, but their mouths
began to betray them. "When it comes to *talking,*" wrote
Charles Astor Bristed for Englishmen in 1855, "the most
refined and best educated American, who has habitually
resided in his own country, the very man who would write, 140
on some serious topic, volumes in which no peculiarity
could be detected, will, in half a dozen sentences, use at

least as many words that cannot fail to strike the inexperienced Englishman who hears them for the first time."

. . . . .

145 6. Along with these new verbs came a great swarm of verb-phrases, some of them short and pithy and others extraordinarily elaborate, but all showing the national talent for condensing a complex thought, and often a whole series of thoughts, into a vivid and arresting image. To the first class belong *to fill the bill, to fizzle out, to make tracks, to peter out, to plank down, to go back on, to keep tab, to light out* and *to back water.* Side by side with them we have inherited such common coins of speech as *to make the fur fly, to cut a swath, to know him like a book, to keep a stiff upper lip, to cap the climax, to handle without gloves, to freeze on to, to go it blind, to pull wool over his eyes, to have the floor, to know the ropes, to get solid with, to spread oneself, to run into the ground, to dodge the issue, to paint the town red, to take a back seat* and *to get ahead of.* These are so familiar that we use them and hear them without thought; they seem as authentically parts of the English idiom as *to be left at the post.* And yet, as the labors of Thornton have demonstrated, all of them appear to be of American nativity, and the circumstances surrounding the origin of some of them have been accurately determined. Many others are as certainly products of the great movement toward the West, for example, *to pan out, to strike it rich, to jump* or *enter a claim, to pull up stakes, to rope in, to die with one's boots on, to get the deadwood on, to get the drop, to back and fill, to do a land-office business* and *to get the bulge on.* And in many others the authentic American flavor is no less plain, for example, in *to kick the bucket, to put a bug in his ear, to see the elephant, to crack up, to do up brown, to bark up the wrong tree, to jump on with both feet, to go the whole hog, to make a kick, to buck the tiger, to let it slide* and *to come out at the little end of the horn.*

7. It was not, however, among the verbs and adjectives

that the American word-coiners of the first half of the
century achieved their gaudiest innovations, but among the 180
substantives. Here they had temptation and excuse in plenty,
for innumerable new objects and relations demanded names,
and they exercised their fancy without restraint. As in the
colonial and revolutionary periods, three main varieties of
new nouns were thus produced. The first consisted of Eng- 185
lish words rescued from obsolescence or changed in meaning,
the second of compounds manufactured of the common
materials of the mother tongue, and the third of entirely
new inventions. Of the first class, good specimens are *deck*
(of cards), *gulch, gully,* and *billion*, the first three old Eng- 190
lish words restored to usage in America and the last a
sound English word changed in meaning. Of the second
class, examples are offered by *gum-shoe, mortgage-shark,
carpet-bagger, cut-off, mass-meeting, dead-beat, dug-out,
shot-gun, stag-party, wheat-pit, horse-sense, chipped beef,* 195
oyster-supper, buzz-saw, chain-gang and *hell-box*. And of
the third there are instances in *buncombe, conniption,
bloomer, campus, galoot, maverick, roustabout, bugaboo,*
and *blizzard*. Of these coinages perhaps those of the second
class are most numerous and characteristic. In them Amer- 200
ica exhibits one of its most marked tendencies, a habit of
achieving short cuts by bold combinations. Why describe
a gigantic rain storm with the lame adjectives of everyday?
Call it a *cloud-burst* and immediately a vivid picture of it
is conjured up. *Rough-neck* is a capital word; it is more 205
apposite and savory than any English equivalent, and it is
unmistakably American. The same instinct for the terse, the
vivid and the picturesque appears in *boiled-shirt, blow-out,
big-gun, claim-jumper, home-stretch, spread-eagle, come-
down, back-number, bed-spread, claw-hammer* (coat), 210
*bottom-dollar, poppycock, cold-snap, back-talk, back-taxes,
corn-belt, calamity-howler, fire-bug, grab-bag, grip-sack,
grub-stake, pay-dirt, tender-foot, stocking-feet, moss-back,
crazy-quilt, ticket-scalper, store-clothes, small-potatoes, cake-
walk, prairie-schooner, round-up, worm-fence, snake-fence,* 215
flat-boat and *jumping-off place*. Such compounds (there are

thousands of them) have been largely responsible for giving the American vulgate its characteristic tang and color. *Bell-hop, square-meal,* and *chair-warmer,* to name three
220 charming specimens, are as distinctively American as jazz or the quick-lunch.

❈ ❈ ❈

1. What was the Oregon question (l. 10) and when was it mooted? What was the "hegemony of the Tidewater gentry"? (l. 87.) What were the "Boston Brahmins"? (l. 92.) Explain "a new Dark age." (l. 94.) What were bundling and gouging? (ll. 95-96.) When was Cooper's day? (ll. 126-127.)

2. The thesis of each paragraph is stated in its first sentence. Show that you understand the argument of the essay by explaining, in one sentence, as compact as you can make it, the connection between Pomeroy's speech and such word-coinages as *horse-sense.*

3. Explain, in one sentence, the connection between Jackson (l. 89) and the thesis of Par. 4.

4. Explain, in one sentence, the relevance of *Uncle Tom's Cabin* (l. 124) to the thesis of Par. 4.

5. How do the explanations of Bartlett (ll. 102-109) and of Webster (ll. 111-114) differ? How are they "to the same effect"? Can both be correct?

6. Which tall talk do you think more successful, the Floridan's or the Arkansan's? (ll. 37-52, 55-68.) What phrases make one better, the other inferior? Now suggest one or two rules for excellence in this kind of performance.

7. Write a paragraph in the vein of Congressman Pomeroy. Must it be on a patriotic theme?

8. Write a paragraph in the self-assertive vein of the corpse-makers. Must the subject be one's physical prowess?

9. Select two verb phrases from Par. 7 and two noun phrases from Par. 8 which seem to you particularly vivid or which "condense a whole series of thoughts." Explain their origins and their implications.

10. We miss much of the flavor of American because we take our familiar phrasings for granted. H. W. Horwill's

Dictionary of Modern American Usage is a short survey of the divergence between English and American. Among its more interesting entries are across, allow, band, blind, casket, common, crowd, cute, eat, guess, hog, home, kick, light, low, muckrake, slush, work, you all.

a) Read in it fifteen pages at random and report briefly on several Americanisms.

b) Or report on several peculiarly English words or meanings.

c) Or take any ten consecutive words and classify them according to the scheme given on p. vi of the Preface.

11. Read at random in Thornton, *An American Glossary,* or in Craigie and Hulbert, *A Dictionary of American English,* and report on several words or phrases of interesting origin.

12. Give ten other vigorous compounds (cf. l. 219) from the American vulgate.

13. Write an essay on the contribution of baseball to the popular vocabulary. (Or pugilism, the automobile, finance, politics, movies, etc. But you had better not write about the words used in connection with dance music, most of which represent no natural development of language but are manufactured for an infantile market.) Distinguish between terms drawn from the general vocabulary and given new, technical applications (*diamond, dashboard*), terms strictly technical (*two-bagger*), and terms of which the technical sense has been figuratively extended (*not get to first base, step on it*). Or you may limit yourself to the third class, which is the most interesting.

WALTER HEADLAM[1]

E. F. BENSON

•

1. OF ALL THE CLASSICAL FELLOWS OF KING'S ABOUT THIS time there was just one who worked conformably to the spirit of the bounty of King Henry VI, for in return for his board and lodging and fellowship, he devoted himself en-
5 tirely to the study of Greek. Those who lectured, those who taught, those who, like Mr. Nixon, looked over our weekly efforts in Latin prose or Greek Iambics were not scholars at all in any real sense of the word: their knowledge of these languages was of the same class as that of the twenty
10 or twenty-five undergraduates who yearly took a first in the Classical Tripos. They knew the principal dates and main operations in the Peloponnesian war, they could translate passages of Greek and Latin into grammatical English, and they could turn passages of English prose
15 into Greek that probably bore the same relation to classical Greek, as written in the age of Pericles, as the best Baboo does to plain decent English prose of the day. Like the Baboo clerk, who, when asked by his employer for what reason he wanted a day's remission from office work, re-
20 plied "The hand that rocked the cradle has kicked the bucket" (the proper English for which is "My mother is dead"), so these admirable preceptors of ours would produce the most remarkable patchwork of recondite constructions and unusual words snipped from Thucydides and Plato
25 and neatly stitched together, and hand them to their pupils as models for classical composition. Their knowledge of Greek ended just about where Walter Headlam's began: his mind was Greek, and he kept on learning the lore of its

[1] From *As We Were,* by E. F. Benson; reprinted by permission of Longmans, Green and Co., Inc.

54

ancestors. The fragmentary mimes of Herondas had lately been discovered, and on this new text he poured out a 30 knowledge which was as far beyond that of the accredited tutors of the College as is some advanced treatise on mathematics beyond the scope of an ordinary schoolteacher of algebra. Though he was of a rich and boyish humanity, he had also that queer aloof quality which develops in those 35 whose life is centred on research, and he passed into regions where no calls or needs of the flesh could penetrate.

2. One morning, for instance, his water for shaving was not hot; so after breakfast he put a small kettle to boil over his spirit-lamp, and as he waited for that, he sat down 40 in the armchair where he worked and casually looked at a note he had made the evening before. It was about a change of rhythm in a Greek chorus, or perhaps it was a word in his Herondas which occurred in no dictionary but which he knew he had seen before in some scholiast on 45 Aristophanes. But where was the particular book he wanted? His room was lined with bookshelves, books that he was using paved the floor round his chair, and the table was piled high with them. There it was underneath a heap of others on the table, and he pulled it out: those on the top 50 of it tumbled to the ground. He put down his pipe on the edge of the table, and as he turned the leaves, he found not just that which he was looking for, but something else he had wanted yesterday. He made a note of this on a slip of paper and picked up his pipe, which had gone out. There 55 were no matches; so he folded up the paper on which he had made his note, thrust it into the flame of the spirit-lamp, and lit his pipe again. Then he found the passage he had originally started to hunt up. Awfully interesting: it was a slang word, not very polite, in use among the 60 daughters of joy in Corinth during the fifth century B.C. These intelligent ladies seemed to have an argot of their own; there were several other words of the sort which he had come across. He became lost in this pursuit, his pipe had to be relit several times, and presently a smell of roasting 65 metal brought him back for a brief moment to the surface

of life. His shaving-water had all boiled away, and so he put out the spirit-lamp. Later in the morning his gyp came to see if he wanted any lunch ordered for him: bread and butter and cheese would do, with a tankard of beer. These were laid and left in the next room, and he wandered there after another hour or two deep in his investigation. The sight of food aroused no association of desire, but he had a drink out of the tankard and carrying it back with him, put it in a nest of books on his table. Presently more books got piled up round the tankard; he absently laid a folio notebook on the top of it, and so it completely vanished. Then he wanted more books from his shelves; in one of these excursions he stepped on his pipe and broke the stem. It did not matter, for there were others about, but he forgot to look for them in the heat of this diverting chase. "I shall write a monograph on the slang current in Corinthian brothels," he said to himself.

3. It began to grow dark on this early close of the autumn afternoon. There was no electric light in those days, and he fetched a couple of candles and put them on the edge of his table. He was hungry now, and he gobbled up his bread and cheese, wondering what time it was, for his watch had stopped. Beer too: he felt sure he had ordered some beer, but where the devil was it? It should have been on his table with the bread and cheese. He looked everywhere for it, even in his bedroom, but it was nowhere to be seen. Then his razor lying ready on his dressing-table reminded him that he had not yet shaved. It was true there was no hot water, but cold water would do, and though it was rapidly getting dark, he had not yet found any matches to light his candles. But one ought to be able to shave in the dark, he thought, for an action, often repeated, became, as Aristotle said, an instinctive process, and it would be interesting to see if he could not make quite a good job of it. He made a fair job of it; there were a few negligible cuts; and finding that he had a box of matches in his pocket all the time, he lit his candles and went back to the ladies of Corinth. Then his gyp came in to see if he would go

into Hall for dinner or dine in his room: he settled to have 105
some cold meat here, but where was the beer he had ordered
for lunch? The gyp felt sure he had brought it, but evidently he was mistaken, for there was no sign of it. So he
brought the cold meat and another tankard, and with this
comfortless refreshment Walter Headlam pursued the 110
ladies of Corinth till the small hours of the morning. The
missing tankard came to light the next day.

4. He would work like this for several days on end;
then he was drained of scholarly energy and emerging as
from deep seas with some pearls of research, he busied him- 115
self with social concerns and diversions till he could dive
again.

5. One day he fell in love with an intelligent young lady
from Newnham, but he soon forgot about her, because he
went to a concert where he heard Schubert's "Unfinished 120
Symphony." Instantly all became dross except Schubert,
and though he could not read a note of music, nor play
a correct scale, he sat hour after hour at his piano, dabbing
at single notes till out of them he had extricated a short
melody of four bars, which I wrote down for him; it was 125
to be the air in the slow movement of "Headlam Op. 1."
Then he immersed himself in Greek again, and again rising
to the surface came across a pseudo-medical primer. The
study of this convinced him that he had diabetes, and so
sure was he of this that he never consulted a doctor at all. 130
He had a tragic collection of unmistakable insignia, head-
ache, fitful appetite, fatigue, and so there was no doubt
about it. He told me very seriously that he had not long
to live, and when I asked what was the matter with him,
he said in a hollow but resigned whisper "Sugar." So we 135
went to a race-meeting at Newmarket, and entirely bowled
over with adoration for the splendour and the speed of the
flying hooves and the rhythm of their galloping, he felt
that he must instantly learn to ride: for the moment the
whores of Corinth were pale to him. He ordered some 140
elegant riding breeches and hired a horse, and we set out
along the backs. One of his feet slipped out of its stir-

rup, but in these first moments of poise upon a horse's back, he did not think it wise, in spite of advice and 145 proffered assistance, to imperil his balance by recovering it, and in consequence when his horse decided to walk into the shallow water of the Grantchester mill-pool and drink, he slipped gently out of the saddle and fell in. Then he thought he would like to go for a drive, as a less 150 hazardous method of commerce with horses, and he asked a friend to come out for a spin with him. On arrival at the livery stables, a high dog-cart was made ready for them, and Walter Headlam asked his friend if he would do the driving. The friend very properly replied that he had never 155 done such a thing in his life, and so he said, "Nor have I," and was instructed that the reins went in the left hand and the whip in the right. A little way out of Cambridge, in trying to turn a corner, he drove up a bank at the side of the road, and the dog-cart upset. As he flew out of it (still with 160 the reins in his left hand) he was heard to observe, "Damn: I shall never finish Herondas," and alighted unharmed in a hedge.

※ ※ ※

1. How do lines 5-26 contribute to a description of Walter Headlam?

2. What is wrong with Baboo prose? Why, apart from the convenient similarity of style, is the Baboo clerk a good analogy for the "admirable preceptors"? (Better find out what "Baboo" means.) What comment on Headlam is illuminated by this discussion of style?

3. Paragraphs 2 and 3 are merely a chronicle of Headlam's movements about his rooms. The details of the narrative, though intrinsically unexciting, hang together and hold the attention because they develop a single plain theme. (Headlam's character, which, like most people's, must really have been very complex, has been quite simply defined.) The action, though never drastic, is always relevant and so at every step affords the reader the pleasure of recognizing a plausible, if not altogether admirable, species of humanity.

a) What is Headlam's motive throughout Pars. 2 and 3?

b) Where was this motive first—and more circumstantially —explained?

c) What is the chief trait of character expressed in the action?

d) Where was this character explicitly defined?

4. What are the four or five chief episodes in Pars. 2 and 3?

5. The smell of roasting metal (l. 65), which informs us that Headlam forgot to shave, has been prepared for in lines 39-40. Obviously it would have been clumsy to omit this preparation and then write: Presently a smell of roasting metal reminded him of the kettle of shaving water which he had previously set over a small spirit-lamp and which had now all boiled away.

Find several other such preparations for later episodes in Pars. 2 and 3.

6. The sudden appearance of a piano in line 123 is startling; unless Headlam bought it after the concert, it must have been all the while in his rooms, which, however, have been imagined without it.

a) Make some revision in Par. 2—as simple as possible— which will prepare the reader for lines 123-126.

b) Suppose you know that Headlam did acquire the piano after the concert; will your revision still be proper?

c) And what if the episode of the tankard of beer actually occurred after the work on Opus 1?

7. In Pars. 2 and 3 Benson has got in a number of incidental indications of character, not strictly required by the narrative but rounding out the portrait. E.g., *"his* Herondas" (l. 44) suggests the proprietorship involved in love and mastery; "awfully interesting" (l. 59) quotes Headlam's thoughts. Find several other such minor suggestions of character.

8. What chief trait of Headlam's character is exhibited in Par. 5? (Notice that this trait is reflected in the very structure of the paragraph.)

9. Point out four or five phrases in Par. 5 (apart from Headlam's last remark) which you find amusing.

10. Explain the following words in terms of their roots and prefixes, if any: *graduates* (l. 10); *principle* (l. 11); *operation* (l. 12); *admirable* (l. 22); *composition* (l. 26); *investigate*

(l. 72); *excursion* (l. 79); *extricate* (l. 124); *primer* (l. 128); *appetite* (l. 132).

11.   What other words can you think of in which the same roots appear?

12.   Comment on the following changes of wording: *snipped* (l. 24) to *chipped; scope* (l. 33) to *range; aloof* (l. 35) to *lofty; quality* (l. 35) to *excellence; tumbled* (l. 51) to *dropped; pearls* (l. 115) to *gems; observe* (l. 160) to *exclaim.*

13.   Read the Britannica article on Herodas and summarize what seems noteworthy in about fifty words.

14.   Benson admired Headlam, as appears in his account of archeological research at Athens: "The plane trees had perished from the bank of the Ilyssus and its stream was dwindled, and the washerwomen scolded and rinsed their linen by its shrunken pools, but it was here in very truth that Socrates had sat and told young Phaedrus of the chariots of the soul, and when his tale was done had prayed 'Beloved Pan, and all ye deities that haunt this place, give me inward beauty of soul, and may the outward and the inward man be at one.' My year of studying archaeology at Cambridge, and above all intercourse with Walter Headlam and Professor Middleton, who instead of lecturing gave me Greek gems and fragments of red-figured vases to examine, had begun the vivifying work, and now the dry bones of that arid valley of education were all astir, and they came together, bone to his bone, and were transformed into a host of swift and comely presences." [2]

What is your reaction to Headlam and his kind of life? What sort of moral do you draw from Benson's account of him? That it is silly to be moved by Schubert? Organize your opinions and present them as coherently and as forcefully as you can in a short essay.

[2] *As We Were;* by permission of Longmans, Green and Co.

THE GOOD DUKE[1]

NORMAN DOUGLAS

•

1. THE CANNON, TO BE HEREINAFTER DESCRIBED, IS NOT THE sole surviving relic of the Good Duke's rule. Turn where you please on his island domain, memories of that charming and incisive personality will meet your eye and ear; memories in stone—schools, convents, decayed castles and bathing chalets; memories in the spoken word—proverbs attributed to him, legends and traditions of his sagacity that still linger among the populace. *In the days of the Duke:* so runs a local saying, much as we speak of the "good old times." His amiable laughter-loving ghost pervades the capital to this hour. His pleasantries still resound among those crumbling theatres and galleries. That gleeful deviltry of his, compounded of blood and sunshine, is the epitome of Nepenthe. He is the scarlet thread running through its annals. An incarnation of all that was best in the age, he identified, for wellnigh half a century, his interests with those of his faithful subjects.

2. He meditated no conquests. It sufficed him to gain and to retain the affection of men in whose eyes he was not so much a prince, a feudal lord, as an indulgent and doting father. He was the ideal despot, a man of wide culture and simple tastes. "A smile," he used to say, "will sway the Universe." Simplicity he declared to be the keynote of his nature, the guiding motive of his governance. In exemplification whereof he would point to his method of collecting taxes—a marvel of simplicity. Each citizen paid what he liked. If the sum proved insufficient he was apprised of the fact the next morning by having his left hand amputated;

[1] From *South Wind*, by Norman Douglas. Used by permission of the publishers, Dodd, Mead and Company.

a second error of judgment—it happened rather seldom
30 —was rectified by the mutilation of the remaining member.
"Never argue with inferiors," was one of His Highness's
most original and pregnant remarks, and it was observed
that, whether he condescended to argue or not, he generally
gained his point without undue loss of time.

35   3. It was the Good Duke Alfred who, with a shrewd
eye to the future prosperity of his dominions, made the first
practical experiments with those hot mineral springs—
those healing waters whose virtues, up till then, had been
unaccountably neglected. Realizing their curative possibili-
40 ties, he selected fifty of the oldest and wisest of his Privy
Councillors to undergo a variety of hydrothermal tests on
their bodies, internal and external. Seven of these gentlemen
had the good luck to survive the treatment. They received
the Order of the Golden Vine, a coveted distinction. The
45 remaining forty-three, what was left of them, were cre-
mated at night-time and posthumously ennobled.

4. He was the author of some mighty fine dissertations
on falconry, dancing, and architecture. He wrote, further-
more, in the flamboyant style of his period, two dozen pas-
50 toral plays, as well as a goodly number of verses addressed,
for the most part, to ladies of his Court—a Court which
was thronged with poets, wits, philosophers and noble
women. The island was a gay place in those days! There was
always something doing. His Highness had a trick of cast-
55 ing favourites into dungeons, and concubines into the sea,
that endeared him to his various legitimate spouses; and
the rapidity with which these self-same spouses were be-
headed one after the other, to make room for what he mirth-
fully called "fresh blood," struck his faithful subjects as an
60 ever-recurring miracle of state-craft. "Nothing," he used to
say to his intimates, "nothing ages a man like living always
with the same woman." Well aware, on the other hand,
of the inequality of social conditions and keenly desirous
of raising the moral tone of his people, he framed iron laws
65 to restrain those irregularities of married life which had

been a disreputable feature of local society prior to his accession.

5. His high aspirations made him the precursor of many modern ideas. In educational and military matters, more especially, he ranks as a pioneer. He was a pedagogue by natural instinct. He took a sincere delight in the school-children, limited their weekly half-holidays to five, designed becoming dresses for boys and girls, decreed that lute playing and deportment should become obligatory subjects in the curriculum, and otherwise reformed the scholastic calendar which, before his day, had drifted into sad confusion and laxity. Sometimes he honoured the ceremony of prize-giving with his presence. On the other hand it must be admitted that, judged by modern standards, certain of his methods for punishing disobedience smack of downright pedantry. Thrice a year, on receiving from the Ministry of Education a list containing the names of unsatisfactory scholars of either sex, it was his custom to hoist a flag on a certain hill-top; this was a signal for the Barbary pirates, who then infested the neighbouring ocean, to set sail for the island and buy up these perverse children, at purely nominal rates, for the slave-markets of Stamboul and Argier. They were sold ignominiously—by weight and not by the piece—to mark his unqualified disapproval of talking and scribbling on blotting-pads during school hours.

6. It is recorded of the Good Duke that on one occasion he returned from the scene looking haggard and careworn, as though the sacrifice of so many young lives weighed on his fatherly spirit. Presently, envisaging his duties towards the State, he restrained these natural but unworthy emotions, smiled his well-known smile, and gave utterance to an apophthegm which has since found its way into a good many copy-books: "In the purity of childhood," he said, "lie the seeds of national prosperity."

7. His predecessors, intent only upon their pleasures, had given no thought to the possibility of a hostile invasion of their fair domain. But the Good Duke, despite his popularity, was frequently heard to quote with approval that

wise old adage which runs "In peace, prepare for war."
105 Convinced of the instability of all mundane affairs and
being, moreover, a man of original notions as well as something of an artist in costumery, he was led to create that
picturesque body of men, the local Militia, which survives
to this day and would alone entitle him to the grateful
110 notice of posterity. These elegant warriors, he calculated,
would serve both for the purpose of infusing terror into
the minds of potential enemies, and of acting as a decorative
body-guard to enhance his own public appearances on gala
days. He threw his whole soul into the enterprise. After
115 the corps had been duly established, he amused himself by
drilling them on Sunday afternoons and modelling new
buttons for their uniforms; to give them the requisite military stamina he over-fed and starved them by turns, wrapped
them in sheepskin overcoats for long route-marches in July,
120 exercised them in sham fights with live grapeshot and un-
blunted stilettos and otherwise thinned their ranks of unde-
sirables, and hardened their physique, by forcing them to
escalade horrible precipices at midnight on horseback. He
was a martinet; he knew it; he gloried in the distinction.
125 "All the world loves a disciplinarian," he was wont to say.

8. Nevertheless, like many great princes, he realized that
political reasons might counsel at times an abatement of
rigour. He could relent and show mercy. He could inter-
pose his authority in favour of the condemned.
130 9. He relented on one celebrated occasion which more
than any other helped to gain for him the epithet of "The
Good"—when an entire squadron of the Militia was condemned to death for some supposed mistake in giving the
salute. The record, unfortunately, is somewhat involved in
135 obscurity and hard to disentangle; so much is clear, however,
that the sentence was duly promulgated and carried into
effect within half an hour. Then comes the moot question
of the officer in command who was obviously destined for
execution with the rest of his men and who now profited,
140 as events proved, by the clemency of the Good Duke. It
appears that this individual, noted for a childlike horror of

bloodshed, had unaccountably absented himself from the
ceremony at the last moment—slipping out of the ranks in
order, as he said, to bid a last farewell to his two aged and
widowed parents. He was discovered in a wine-shop and 145
brought before a hastily summoned Court-martial. There his
old military courage seems to have returned to him. He
demonstrated by a reference to the instructions laid down
in the Militiaman's Yearbook that no mistake in saluting
had been made, that his men had therefore been wrong- 150
fully convicted and illegally executed and that he, *a fortiori,*
was innocent of any felonious intent. The Court, while ap-
proving his arguments, condemned him none the less to the
indignity of a double decapitation for the offence of leaving
his post without a signed permit from His Highness.   155

10. It was at this moment that the Good Duke inter-
posed on his behalf. He rescinded the decree; in other words,
he relented. "Enough of bloodshed for one day," he was
heard to remark, quite simply.

11. This speech was one of his happiest inspirations. 160
Instantly it echoed from mouth to mouth; from end to end
of his dominions. Enough of bloodshed for one day! That
showed his true heart, the people declared. Enough of bloodshed! Their enthusiasm grew wilder when, in an access of
princely graciousness, he repaired the lamentable excess of 165
zeal by pinning the order of the Golden Vine to the offend-
ing officer's breast; it rose to a veritable frenzy as soon as
they learned that, by Letters Patent, the entire defunct
squadron had been posthumously ennobled. And this is
only one of many occasions on which this ruler, by his in- 170
timate knowledge of human nature and the arts of government, was enabled to wrest good from evil, and thereby
consolidate his throne.

12. It is passing strange, on the face of it, that this vivid
personality, one of the most arresting figures in the history 175
of the country, should be so briefly dealt with in the pages
of Monsignor Perrelli. Doubly strange, and a serious disappointment to the reader, in view of the fact that the two men
were contemporaries, and that the learned writer must have

180 enjoyed exceptional facilities for obtaining first-hand knowledge of his subject. Almost inexplicable indeed, when one
remembers those maxims which he himself, in the Introduction to his *Antiquities*, lays down for the writing of history;
when one calls to mind his own gleams of exotic scholarship,
185 those luminous asides and fruitful digressions, those states-
manlike comments on things in general which make his
work not so much a compendium of local lore as a mirror
of the polite learning of his age. It is no exaggeration to
say that, compared with the ample treatment meted out to
190 inconspicuous rulers like Alfonso the Seventeenth or Florizel
the Fat, his account of the Good Duke Alfred is the baldest,
the most perfunctory and conventional of chronicles. Neither
good nor evil is related of him. There is nothing but a
monotonous enumeration of events.

195 13. It was the bibliographer who, poring over the pages
of the rival monk Father Capocchio, that audacious and
salacious friar already mentioned—it was the bibliographer
who hit upon a passage which suggested a solution of the
mystery and proved that, though Monsignor Perrelli lived
200 during the reign of the Good Duke, it would be stretching
unduly the sense of a plain word to say that he "flourished"
under his rule. Other persons may have flourished; not so
the kindly prelate.

14. "Nothing whatever," says this implacable enemy of
205 Nepenthe, "is to be recorded to the credit of the sanguinary
brigand—so he terms the Good Duke—nothing whatsoever:
save and except only this, that he cut off the ears of a certain prattler, intriguer, and snuff-taking sensualist called
Perrelli who, under the pretence of collecting data for an
210 alleged historical treatise, profited by his priestly garb to
play fast and loose with what little remained of decent
family life on that God-abandoned island. Honour to whom
honour is due! The ostensible reason for this unique act
of justice was that the said Perrelli had appeared at some
215 palace function with paste buckles on his shoes, instead of
silver ones. The pretext was well chosen, inasmuch as the
tyrant added to his other vices and absurdities the pose

of being an extravagant stickler for etiquette. We happen
to know, nevertheless, that the name of a young dancer, a
prime favourite at Court, cropped up persistently at the 220
time in connection with this malodorous but otherwise in-
significant episode."

15. It were idle, at this hour of the day, to pursue the
enquiry; the mutilation of Monsignor Perrelli's person,
however, would explain better than anything else his equiv- 225
ocal attitude as historian. Nor is the incident altogether
inconsistent with what we know of the Duke's cheerful
propensities. "Nose after ears!" was one of his blithest
watchwords. Faced with so dispiriting a prospect and aware
that His Highness was as good as his princely word, the 230
sympathetic scholar, while too resentful to praise his achievements, may well have been too prudent to disparage them.
Hence his reticence, his circumspection. Hence that monotonous enumeration of events.

❁ ❁ ❁

Such an impudent detractor as Father Capocchio could, by
his artful insinuation, make many of Duke Alfred's civic virtues appear to be imperfections or shortcomings. The one
chronicler from whom a distinguished portrait of the Duke
might have been expected, Monsignor Perrelli, maintained a
sulky silence, the reasons for which Mr. Douglas has ferreted
out and offered for our detached consideration. Lacking the
impartial eyewitness recommended by the Sieur de Fontenelle,
one can only make allowances to compensate for the known
prejudices of a reporter. Since few men are quite impartial, this
Quellenkritik or study of the bias of the sources of historical
information is one of the first and most perplexing problems of
the modern historian. But Mr. Douglas has not been content
with this; truly desirous to give "honor to whom honor is due,"
he has gone on to rehabilitate the Duke's régime. Through the
study of this interpretative portrait, you may learn to appreciate the benevolent insight whereby the modern biographer
may perceive nobility of motive and breadth of vision beneath
a businesslike and unpresuming exterior.

1. Alfred's temperament and administration have been illu-

minated by a variety of evidence, grouped under the following headings: collection of internal revenues, scientific researches, literary activities, domestic arrangements, social legislation, educational reforms, maintenance of school discipline, exercise of the militia, pardon of the condemned man. Mark off these sections in the text.

2. This evidence is of two kinds: *single, isolated actions* ("decreed that lute playing and deportment should become obligatory," ll. 73-74) and *repeated or habitual action* ("designed becoming dresses"—apparently a favorite pastime). Mr. Douglas surely felt no conscious concern to use both kinds of illustrative material; it often happens that a beginner, however, starting his collection of materials with one kind of evidence, forgets that the other kind is also available. To fix the two possibilities in your mind, classify each item of evidence and distinguish it by a line in the margin, red for unique actions, blue for repeated actions.

3. From these data, certain qualities of mind or character have been attributed to Alfred. In each section, underline in black those words or phrases in which the inferences are stated. If there is no such phrase in the text, formulate your own.

4. Is "faithful" (l. 17) restrictive or non-restrictive?

5. What is the effect of the phrase "judged by modern standards"? (l. 79.)

6. The clause "certain of his methods smack of downright pedantry" may be called an understatement. What notable instance of understatement do you find in Par. 11? Explain.

7. Explain the meanings of the following words in their context; remark the etymology if it is relevant. *Epitome* (l. 13), *incarnation* (l. 15), *pregnant* (l. 32), *condescended* (l. 33), *practical* (l. 37), *perfunctory* (l. 192), *"flourished"* (l. 201), *ostensible* (l. 213), *pretext* (l. 216), *reticence* (l. 233), *circumspection* (l. 233).

8. Comment on the following changes of wording: *incisive* (l. 4) to *strong; resound* (l. 11) to *are remembered; curative* (l. 39) to *therapeutic; two dozen* (l. 49) to *twenty-four; pedantry* (l. 81) to *cruelty; moot* (l. 137) to *debatable; ceremony* (l. 143) to *execution; sanguinary* (l. 205) to *cheerful; unique* (l. 213) to *remarkable; blithest* (l. 228) to *fiercest*.

9. In what other English words do the roots of the following words appear? *Incisive, incarnation, aspiration, precursor, domain, luminous, digression.*

10. Explain the derivations of *disparage, falcon, flamboyant, frenzy, lute, spouse, stiletto.*

11. *Martinet* was probably not derived, as has been supposed, from the name of a French general; cf., however, *bloomers, chesterfield, filbert, grog, macadam, shadrack, to bowdlerize, to boycott, to burke.* Do you know any other words of this kind?

12. Write a 1000-word portrait of some vivid personality; a sketch of a local dignitary or derelict is likely to be more successful than one of an international bogey-man.

ELIZABETH[1]

JOHN RICHARD GREEN

•

1. ENGLAND'S ONE HOPE LAY IN THE CHARACTER OF HER
Queen. Elizabeth was now in her twenty-fifth year. Personally she had more than her mother's beauty; her figure
was commanding, her face long but queenly and intelligent, her eyes quick and fine. She had grown up amidst
the liberal culture of Henry's court, a bold horsewoman, a
good shot, a graceful dancer, a skilled musician, and an
accomplished scholar. She studied every morning the Greek
Testament, and followed this by the tragedies of Sophocles
or orations of Demosthenes, and could "rub up her rusty
Greek" at need to bandy pedantry with a Vice-Chancellor.
But she was far from being a mere pedant. The new literature which was springing up around her found constant
welcome in her court. She spoke Italian and French as
fluently as her mother-tongue. She was familiar with
Ariosto and Tasso. Even amidst the affectation and love
of anagrams and puerilities which sullied her later years,
she listened with delight to the *Faerie Queene,* and found
a smile for "Master Spenser" when he appeared in her
presence. Her moral temper recalled in its strange contrasts
the mixed blood within her veins. She was at once the
daughter of Henry and of Anne Boleyn. From her father
she inherited her frank and hearty address, her love of
popularity and of free intercourse with the people, her
dauntless courage and her amazing self-confidence. Her
harsh, manlike voice, her impetuous will, her pride, her
furious outbursts of anger came to her with her Tudor
blood. She rated great nobles as if they were schoolboys;
she met the insolence of Essex with a box on the ear; she

[1] From *A Short History of the English People.*

would break now and then into the gravest deliberations 30
to swear at her ministers like a fishwife. But strangely in
contrast with the violent outlines of her Tudor temper
stood the sensuous, self-indulgent nature she derived from
Anne Boleyn. Splendor and pleasure were with Elizabeth
the very air she breathed. Her delight was to move in per- 35
petual progresses from castle to castle through a series of
gorgeous pageants, fanciful and extravagant as a caliph's
dream. She loved gaiety and laughter and wit. A happy retort or a finished compliment never failed to win her favor.
She hoarded jewels. Her dresses were innumerable. Her 40
vanity remained, even to old age, the vanity of a coquette
in her teens. No adulation was too fulsome for her, no
flattery of her beauty too gross. "To see her was heaven,"
Hatton told her, "the lack of her was hell." She would
play with her rings that her courtiers might note the deli- 45
cacy of her hands, or dance a coranto that the French am-
bassador, hidden dexterously behind a curtain, might report her sprightliness to his master. Her levity, her frivolous
laughter, her unwomanly jests gave color to a thousand
scandals. Her character in fact, like her portraits, was utterly 50
without shade. Of womanly reserve or self-restraint she
knew nothing. No instinct of delicacy veiled the voluptuous temper which had broken out in the romps of her
girlhood and showed itself almost ostentatiously throughout her later life. Personal beauty in a man was a sure 55
passport to her liking. She patted handsome young squires
on the neck when they knelt to kiss her hand, and fondled
her "sweet Robin," Lord Leicester, in the face of the court.

2. It was no wonder that the statesmen whom she out-
witted held Elizabeth almost to the last to be little more 60
than a frivolous woman, or that Philip of Spain wondered
how "a wanton" could hold in check the policy of the
Escurial. But the Elizabeth whom they saw was far from
being all of Elizabeth. The wilfulness of Henry, the trivial-
ity of Anne Boleyn played over the surface of a nature 65
hard as steel, a temper purely intellectual, the very type
of reason untouched by imagination or passion. Luxurious

and pleasure-loving as she seemed, Elizabeth lived simply and frugally, and she worked hard. Her vanity and caprice 70 had no weight whatever with her in state affairs. The co-quette of the presence-chamber became the coolest and hardest of politicians at the council-board. Fresh from the flattery of her courtiers, she would tolerate no flattery in the closet; she was herself plain and downright of speech 75 with her counsellors, and she looked for a corresponding plainness of speech in return. If any trace of her sex lingered in her actual statesmanship, it was seen in the simplicity and tenacity of purpose that often underlies a woman's fluctuations of feeling. It was this in part which gave 80 her her marked superiority over the statesmen of her time. No nobler group of ministers ever gathered round a council-board than those who gathered round the council-board of Elizabeth. But she was the instrument of none. She listened, she weighed, she used or put by the counsels of 85 each in turn, but her policy as a whole was her own. It was a policy, not of genius, but of good sense. Her aims were simple and obvious: to preserve her throne, to keep England out of war, to restore civil and religious order. Something of womanly caution and timidity perhaps backed 90 the passionless indifference with which she set aside the larger schemes of ambition which were ever opening before her eyes. She was resolute in her refusal of the Low Countries. She rejected with a laugh the offers of the Protestants to make her "head of the religion" and "mistress of the 95 seas." But her amazing success in the end sprang mainly from this wise limitation of her aims. She had a finer sense than any of her counsellors of her real resources; she knew instinctively how far she could go, and what she could do. Her cold, critical intellect was never swayed by 100 enthusiasm or by panic either to exaggerate or to underestimate her risks or her power.

❋ ❋ ❋

This portrait of Elizabeth served as a frontispiece to Green's account of Elizabethan England. But Green did not limit himself to a description of the Queen at the moment of her accession in 1558: he drew his illustrative material from her life at large. There was no dearth of materials; indeed, his constant problem in writing *A History of the English People* from the Anglo-Saxon conquest to Waterloo in less than 1500 pages was to select and to compress. Not knowing what Green rejected, one can only surmise the propriety of his choices. The technic of compression, however, may be studied in this portrait. Whereas Norman Douglas's account of Alfred is leisurely and expansive, Green had no room for lengthy episode; his illustrations are close packed. You will find this compactness hard to achieve.

The biographical data, though brief, are of three familiar kinds. Some sentences report a single episode: "she found a smile for 'Master Spenser' when he appeared in her presence." Others generalize a series of similar actions: "she studied every morning the Greek Testament." Here the reader still has sight of the occasions; but sometimes the inductive process is carried further, until the actions are resolved into an attribute: Elizabeth was a bold horsewoman; she spoke Italian fluently; her address was frank and hearty.

Such a rapid succession of diverse details may overwhelm the reader's assimilative power, each image obliterating its predecessor. In order that the biographical data, with their various implications for Elizabeth's character, might make sense rather than fall together in a chaotic heap, it was necessary for Green to arrange them in some rigorously schematic fashion. It is only the logical structure of Par. 1 that keeps the assortment of facts from melting into one blur.

1. Who were some of the makers of the new literature mentioned in lines 12-13? What have Ariosto and anagrams to do with pedantry? What *are* anagrams in this context? Identify Leicester, Hatton, and Essex.

2. Point out several illustrative items drawn from a period later than the opening years of Elizabeth's reign.

3. How may the use of materials drawn from a whole lifetime affect the accuracy of a portrait? What are the consequent limitations of the method? Illustrate your answers by reference to a possible biographical subject other than Elizabeth.

4. Underline, in Par. 1, those phrases reporting a single

action in red, those reporting a series of similar actions in blue, and those attributing to Elizabeth certain qualities or accomplishments or mannerisms in black.

5. Do the materials which you have underlined in red and blue usually precede or follow the corresponding summary statement? Always? Explain the rhetoric of this.

6. Outline Par. 1 under the headings: body, mind, spirit; mark off the sections. Subdivide section 2 under the formula: not only . . . but also. . . . Subdivide section 3 under the formula: both . . . and. . . . What words announce each section or subdivision?

7. Read the paragraph, omitting these key phrases and revising, where necessary, to avoid reference to the divisions. (E.g., in lines 23-24, read: Her address was frank and hearty; she loved popularity, etc.) Why?

8. It was convenient to group the traits of Elizabeth as paternal and maternal inheritances; consider each of these traits and decide whether or not you think it can be inherited. Does it matter?

9. The three hackneyed headings under which Par. 1 is organized may seem inevitable to any portrait or character analysis. Not so. Perhaps one man's character might better be discussed under the headings: at business, at home, at play. Or another woman's temperament might change as she came in contact with men, with children, and with other women. Draw up plans for two portraits, either of acquaintances or of historical personages or of characters in fiction, indicating under what headings each character might be presented and including some illustrative material under each heading.

10. Analyze Par. 2 without the help of hints and leading questions. What is it about? How is it related to Par. 1? What are its parts?

11. Explain the derivations of *caliph, caprice, coquette, dexterous, flattery, fondle, panic, romp, vanity.*

12. What other dances, like the coranto, are named from their characteristic movement? (Not *jig!*) How else are dances often named?

13. Write a brief portrait, 500-600 words. Perhaps one of the subjects worked up in Question 9 will serve. You are likely to write better about someone you do not altogether admire.

THE ROAD TO RICHES[1]

FREDERICK LEWIS ALLEN

•

1. IT WAS ALGER'S FORTUNE TO HAVE JUST THAT SIMPLICITY, that elementary directness of approach to fiction-writing, which would make his books a joy to immature minds. Some of the titles, such as *Bound to Rise, Luck and Pluck, Sink or Swim, Do and Dare, Strive and Succeed,* will evoke 5 nostalgic memories in many an older reader today. And almost all of the books were essentially the same—variations upon an invariable theme.

2. The standard Horatio Alger hero was a fatherless boy of fifteen or thereabouts who had to earn his way, 10 usually in New York City. Sometimes he had to help support a widowed mother with his bootblacking or peddling; sometimes his parentage was unknown and he lived with an aged and eccentric miser, or with a strange hermit who claimed to be his uncle. It might even be that his father was 15 living, but was having trouble with the mortgage on the old farm. Always, however, the boy had to stand on his own feet and face the practical problem of getting on.

3. This problem was set before the reader in exact financial detail. On the very first page of *Do and Dare,* for 20 example, it was disclosed that the young hero's mother, as postmistress at Wayneboro, had made during the preceding year just $398.50. Whenever "our hero" had to deal with a mortgage, the reader was told the precise amount, the rate of interest, and all other details. When our hero 25 took a job, the reader could figure for himself exactly how much progress he was making by getting $5 a week in wages at the jewelry store and another $5 a week tutoring

---

[1] From "Horatio Alger, Jr.," *The Saturday Review of Literature,* September 17, 1938, by permission of the author and publishers.

Mrs. Mason's son in Latin. Our hero was always a good
30 boy, honest, abstemious (in fact, sometimes unduly disposed to preach to drinkers and smokers), prudent, well-
mannered (except perhaps for the preaching), and frugal.
The excitement of each book lay in his progress toward
wealth.

35   4. Always there were villains who stood in his way—
crooks who would rob him of his earnings, sharpers who
would prey upon his supposed innocence. His battles with
these villains furnished plenty of melodrama. They tried to
sell him worthless gold watches on railroad trains, held
40 him up as he was buggy-driving home with his employer's
funds, kidnaped him and held him a prisoner in a New
York hide-out, chloroformed him in a Philadelphia hotel
room, slugged him in a Chicago alley-tenement. But always
he overcame them—with the aid of their invariable coward-
45 ice. (There must be many men now living who remember
the shock of outraged surprise with which they discovered
that the village bully did not, as in the Alger books, invariably run whimpering away at the first show of manly
opposition, but sometimes packed a nasty right.) The end
50 of the book found our hero well on his way toward wealth:
a fortune which might reach to more than a hundred thousand dollars, which, to the average boy reader of the
seventies and eighties, was an astronomical sum.

   5. When one considers that the period in which these
55 books were the delight of millions of American boys was
that very period when the economic expansion of the United
States was going on full tilt, to the accompaniment of every
sort of financial knavery and speculative excess, and when
one realizes that to most of these millions of young readers
60 the Alger books provided their first intelligible picture of
economic life and the making of an individual fortune,
one looks again, with an analytical eye, to see how the
Alger hero's fortune was achieved. And one notes, not
without amusement, that the boy never got rich from the
65 direct fruits of his industrious labor. How could he, start-

ing in at $5 a week, even with rapid increases in pay? No;
he got his hands on capital.

6. Sometimes this capital was inherited: the supposed
orphan, ragged though he was, proved to be the son of a
man whose supposedly worthless mining stock was good
for $100,000. Sometimes the capital was a gift: rich Mr.
Vanderpool was so impressed with the boy's pluck that he
made over to him the $50,000 that the boy had helped him
to save from the robbers. Or the boy was out in Tacoma,
buying lots as a real-estate agent (on his boss's inside information that the Northern Pacific was to be extended
to the Coast), and in a Tacoma hotel he befriended an
invalid gentleman, who out of gratitude gave him a part
interest in some lots that promptly soared in value and put
him on Easy Street. The method varied; but when the time
came for our hero to get into the money, it was a transaction in capital which won the day for him.

7. Yet always he was so good, and husbanded so prudently the $175 in his savings account (though he was
generous, too, to the poor washerwoman and to the other
bootblacks), that to the casual reader the lesson of these
stories was not that hard work brings in but a pittance, or
that the way to succeed is to stand in with the men who
have the capital, but something quite different. The lesson
was that capital comes as a reward from heaven to him
who labors mightily and uses his head all the time. Work,
save, be a good boy, shun the fleshpots, and presently the
mining stock will fall into your lap and all will be well.

8. Possibly this explains something about the Gilded Age
—when Americans worked furiously, and opened up the
West, and accomplished wonders in invention and manu-
facturing; when the average American of moderate means
was hard-headed, diligent, and on the whole fairly scrupulous; but when the ethical level of the big operations in
capital was often well-nigh barbaric. Once capital began to
fall into a man's lap, he did not inquire unduly whence
it came. He had labored meritoriously; merit was always

rewarded—was it not?—and now his reward was at hand;
obviously it must come from heaven. One remembers Rocke-
105 feller saying, "God gave me my money," and one knows
that other men of millions felt as he did. Who knows but
that to some of them—and to some of their successors in
more recent times—this conviction grew, in part at least,
out of early lessons in economics from *Andy Grant's Pluck*
110 or *Tom the Bootblack*—lessons learned when the man of
millions had been a farm boy reading in the shade of the
barn, or a grocer's clerk hiding under the counter the
latest enthralling volume in the "Brave and Bold" series?

❧ ❧ ❧

1. In Pars. 2-6, Mr. Allen tells a story—not the story of
Do and Dare or of *Bound to Rise,* but of what? (Which words
or phrases make you think so?)

2. Select from Pars. 2-6 just those sentences or parts of
sentences which, read consecutively, outline the story abstractly.
Underline these in black.

3. What is the function of the rest of Pars. 2, 3, 4, and 6?

4. The method of Pars. 2-6, which may be called composite
narrative, may be used to present materials of a certain kind.
  a) For which of the following groups of stories might
this treatment be suitable? The Lone Ranger radio episodes.
Sherlock Holmes stories. Several novels by Sinclair Lewis:
Main Street, Babbitt, Arrowsmith, It Can't Happen Here.
The Henry Aldrich radio episodes. Shakespeare's tragedies.
The adventures of Superman. Movies starring Bette Davis.
The tales of Edgar Allan Poe. The exploits of Don Quixote.
  b) Now formulate a general rule: a group of stories may
be presented as a composite narrative on what condition?
  c) May the method be applied to non-literary materials?
Could it, for instance, be used in the development of any of
the following topics? Roland's friendships, intense and brief.
My first week at college. The trials of amateur play production. Fraternity rushing. The launching of a ship. (Are you
sure?)
  d) When the method is suitable, what are its advantages?

5. Complete your analysis of the logical structure of the whole passage by defining the roles of Par. 7 and Par. 8.

6. "Mature," now applied to persons, as in line 3, contains a metaphor: the Latin word *matura* meant "ripe"; thus a person called mature was likened to ripened fruit. What metaphors are contained in *eccentric* (l. 14), *cowardice* (ll. 44-45), *scrupulous* (ll. 98-99), *enthrall* (l. 113)?

7. Comment on the following changes of wording: *claimed* (l. 15) to *alleged*; *face* (l. 18) to *tackle*; *Mrs. Mason's* (l. 29) to *a neighbor's*; *good* (l. 29) to *virtuous*; *innocence* (l. 37) to *guiltlessness*; *kidnaped* (l. 41) to *abducted*; *industrious* (l. 65) to *diligent*; *promptly* (l. 79) to *soon*; *prudently* (ll. 83-84) to *prudishly*; *diligent* (l. 98) to *hard-working*; *meritoriously* (l. 102) to *meretriciously*; *latest* (l. 113) to *last*.

8. Explain the derivations of *abstemious, astronomy, hermit, miser, nostalgia, pittance, pluck*.

9. Write an essay consisting largely of a composite narrative. Enough topics have been suggested to enable you to find suitable materials within your own experience.

THE PIKES[1]

CLARENCE KING

•

1. UNDER NOBLE GROUPS OF PINES SMOULDERED A GENEROUS heap of coals, the ruins of a mighty log. A little way from this lay a confused pile of bedclothes, partly old and half-bald buffalo-robes, but, in the main, thick strata of what is
5 known to irony as comforters, upon which, outstretched in wretched awkwardness of position, was a family, all with their feet to the fire, looking as if they had been blown over in one direction, or knocked down by a single bomb-shell. On the extremities of this common bed, with the air
10 of having gotten as far from each other as possible, the mother and father of the Pike family reclined; between them were two small children—a girl and boy—and a huge girl, who, next the old man, lay flat upon her back, her mind absorbed in the simple amusement of waving one foot (a
15 cowhide eleven) slowly across the fire, squinting, with half-shut eye, first at the vast shoe and thence at the fire, alternately hiding bright places and darting the foot quickly in the direction of any new display of heightening flame. The mother was a bony sister, in the yellow, shrunken, of
20 sharp visage, in which were prominent two cold eyes and a positively poisonous mouth; her hair, the color of faded hay, tangled in a jungle around her head. She rocked jerkily to and fro, removing at intervals a clay pipe from her mouth in order to pucker her thin lips up to one side, and spit
25 with precision upon a certain spot in the fire, which she seemed resolved to prevent from attaining beyond a certain faint glow.

2. I have rarely felt more in difficulty for an overture to

[1] From *Mountaineering in the Sierra Nevadas*, by Clarence King; reprinted by permission of Charles Scribner's Sons.

conversation, and was long before venturing to propose, "You seem to have a pleasant camp-spot here." The old 30 woman sharply, and in almost a tone of affront, answered, "They's wus, and then again they's better."

"Doos well for our hogs," inserted the old man. "We've a band of pork that make out to find feed."

"Oh! how many have you?" I asked. 35

"Nigh three thousand."

"Won't you set?" asked Madame; then, turning, "You, Susan, can't you try for to set up, and not spread so? Hain't you no manners, say?"

At this the massive girl got herself somewhat together, 40 and made room for me, which I declined, however.

"Prospectin'?" inquired Madame.

"I say huntin'," suggested the man.

"Maybe he's a cattle-feller," interrupted the little girl.

"Goin' somewhere, ain't yer?" was Susan's guess. 45

I gave brief account of myself, evidently satisfying the social requirements of all but the old woman, who at once classified me as not up to her standard.

3. The shouts which I heard proceeding from the direction of my camp were easily translatable into summons for 50 supper. Mr. Newty invited me to return later and be sociable, which I promised to do, and, going to my camp, supped quickly and left the men with orders about picketing the animals for the night, then, strolling slowly down to the camp of my friends, seated myself upon a log by 55 the side of the old gentleman.

4. The old woman was in the exciting dénouement of a coon-story, directed to her little boy, who sat clinging to her skirt and looking in her face with absorbed curiosity. "And when Johnnie fired," she said, "the coon fell and 60 busted open." The little boy had misplaced his sympathies with the raccoon, and having inquired plaintively, "Did it hurt him?" was promptly snubbed with the reply, "Of course it hurt him. What do you suppose coons is made for?" Then turning to me she put what was plainly enough 65 with her a test-question: "I allow you have killed your

coon in your day?" Instinct had taught her that I had never killed a coon, and she had asked me thus ostentatiously to place me at once and forever before the family in my true
70 light. "No, ma'am," I said; "now you speak of it, I realize that I never have killed a coon." This was something of a staggerer to Susan and her father; yet as the mother's pleasurable dissatisfaction with me displayed itself by more and more accurate salivary shots at the fire, they rose to the
75 occasion, and began to palliate my past. "Maybe," ventured Mr. Newty, "that they don't have coon round the city of York"; and I felt that I needed no self-defense when Susan firmly and defiantly suggested to her mother that perhaps I was in better business.

80 5. I ventured a few platitudes concerning pigs, not penetrating the depths of that branch of rural science enough to betray my ignorance. Such sentiments as "A little piece of bacon well broiled for breakfast is very good," and "Nothing better than cold ham for lunch," were received by Susan
85 and her father in the spirit I meant,—of entire goodwill toward pork generically. By half past nine the gates of conversation were fairly open, and our part of the circle enjoyed itself socially,—taciturnity and clouds of Virginia plug reigning supreme upon the other. The two little children
90 crept under comforters somewhere near the middle of the bed, and subsided pleasantly to sleep. The old man at last stretched sleepily, finally yawning out, "Susan, I do believe I am too tired out to go and see if them corral bars are down. I guess you'll have to go. I reckon there ain't no
95 bears round tonight." Susan rose to her feet and stretched herself. In the region of six feet tall, square-shouldered, of firm iron back and heavy mould of limb, she yet possessed that suppleness which enabled her as she rose to throw herself into nearly all the attitudes of the Niobe chil-
100 dren. As her yawn deepened, she waved nearly down to the ground, and then, rising upon tiptoe, stretched up her clenched fists to heaven with a groan of pleasure. Turning to me, she asked, "How would you like to see the hogs?" The old man added, as an extra encouragement, "Pootiest

band of hogs in Tulare County! There's littler of the real [105] sissorbill nor Mexican racer stock than any band I have ever seen in the State. I driv the original outfit from Pike County to Oregon in '51 and '52." By this time I was actually interested in them, and joining Susan we passed out into the forest. . . . [110]

6. When I had breakfasted I joined Mr. Newty in his trip to the corral, where we stood together for hours, during which I mastered the story of his years since, in 1850, he left his old home in Pike of Missouri. It was one of those histories common enough through this wide West, yet [115] never failing to startle me with its horrible lesson of social disintegration, of human retrograde.

7. That brave spirit of Westward Ho! which has been the pillar of fire and cloud leading on the weary march of progress over stretches of desert, lining the way with graves [120] of strong men, of new-born lives, of sad, patient mothers, whose pathetic longing for the new home died with them, of the thousand old and young whose last agony came to them as they marched with eyes strained on after the sunken sun, and whose shallow barrows scarcely lift over the drift- [125] ing dust of the desert,—that restless spirit which has dared to uproot the old and plant the new, kindling the grand energy of California, laying foundations for a State to be,— that is admirable, is poetic, is to fill an immortal page in the story of America; but when, instead of urging on to wresting [130] from new lands something better than old can give, it degenerates into mere weak-minded restlessness, killing the power of growth, the ideal of home, the faculty of repose, it results in that race of perpetual emigrants who roam as dreary waifs over the West, losing possessions, love of life, [135] love of God, slowly dragging from valley to valley till they fall by the wayside, happy if some chance stranger performs for them the last rites,—often less fortunate, as blanched bones and fluttering rags upon too many hillsides plainly tell. [140]

8. The Newtys were of this dreary brotherhood. In 1850, with a small family of that authentic strain of high-

bred swine for which Pike County is widely known, as
Mr. Newty avers, they bade Missouri and their snug farm
145 good-by, and, having packed their household goods into a
wagon drawn by two spotted oxen, set out with the baby
Susan for Oregon, where they came after a year's march,
tired, and cursed with a permanent discontent. There they
had taken up a rancho, a quarter-section of public domain,
150 which at the end of two years was "improved" to the extent
of the "neatest little worm fence this side of Pike," a barn,
and a smoke-house. "In another year," said my friend, "I'd
have dug for a house, but we tuck ager and the second baby
died." One day there came a man who "let on that he
155 knowed" land in California much fairer and more worthy
tillage than Oregon's best; so the poor Newtys harnessed
up the wagon and turned their backs upon a home nearly
ready for comfortable life, and swept south with pigs and
plunder. Through all the years this story had repeated itself:
160 new homes gotten to the edge of completion, more babies
born, more graves made, more pigs, who replenished as
only the Pike County variety may, till it seemed to me the
mere multiplication of them must reach a sufficient dead
weight to anchor the family; but this was dispelled when
165 Newty remarked: "These yer hogs is awkward about moving, and I've pretty much made my mind to put 'em all
into bacon this fall, and sell out and start for Montana."

9. Poor fellow! at Montana he will probably find a man
from Texas who in half an hour will persuade him that
170 happiness lies there.

10. As we walked back to their camp, and when Dame
Newty hove in sight, my friend ventured to say, "Don't
you mind the old woman and her coons. She's from Ar-
kansas. She used to say no man could have Susan who
175 couldn't show coonskins enough of his own killing to make
a bedquilt, but she's over that mostly." Regarding her as
a sad product of the disease of chronic emigration, her hard
thin nature, all angles and stings, became to me one of the
most depressing and pathetic spectacles, and the more when
180 her fever-and-ague boy, a mass of bilious lymph, came and

sat by her, looking up with great haggard eyes as if pleading for something, he knew not what, but which I plainly
saw only death could bestow.

❊ ❊ ❊

1. This sketch from the travel book of a great American
geologist is at first glance merely a humorous personal remi-
niscence. But King has so developed his account of a chance
meeting with curious folk as to make it rather more than
that. What?

2. Divide the passage into three main sections: Pars. 1-6,
Par. 7, and Pars. 8-10. Define briefly the content of each section and explain its function in the development of the essay
as a whole.

3. Justify the order of these three parts. That is, why was
not such a discourse as that in Par. 7 placed at the beginning of
the essay?—or at the end?

4. Underline those phrases or sentences which serve as
transitions between the sections. Analyze the transitional
sentences, showing that they take the reader from one level of
thought to another.

5. Compare the text, lines 1-9, with the following version:
The Pike family, when I first saw them, lay outstretched
in wretched awkwardness of position, all with their feet
toward the fire, looking as if they had been blown over in
one direction or knocked down by a single bombshell, upon
a confused pile of bedclothes, partly old and half-bald buffalo
robes, but, in the main, thick strata of what is known to irony
as comforters. Near them smoldered a generous heap of
coals, the ruins of a mighty log, and above towered noble
groups of pine trees. On the extremities of their common
bed. . . .

6. We may assume that King has adhered to the facts of
his experience with the Newtys, but he has also selected for the
reader such facts as are relevant to his theme. Why did he
mention the location of the individual Newtys on their bed?

7. Some of the conversation furthers the action (e.g.,
ll. 92-95); some conveys factual information (l. 36); some

characterizes the Newty family or its members. Or it may do several of these things. Mark off unified sections of the quoted conversation in Pars. 1-5, and note the function of each section. Where the conversation reveals character, explain briefly what the point is.

8. As we become more acquainted with these people, our impression of them changes. First determine the lines in which Susan is described, noticing the impression given by each comment on her; then outline the stages in the development of her full portrait. Do the same for the old woman. Where are we shown her through the eyes of another member of the family, and why?

9. Much of Newty's narrative in Par. 8 is paraphrased; why are certain speeches quoted directly?

10. In the eloquence of Par. 7 there may be distinguished two elements, imagery and metaphor. "Stretches of desert" and "graves" bring the historical actuality to mind and may be called imagery. "Pillar of fire and cloud" and "uproot and plant" are figurative expressions, metaphors. Point out several other instances of both imagery and metaphor. Which of the two types of pictorial phrase do you think more telling in this paragraph?

11. Explain the derivations of *ague, barrow, palliate, patient, picket, platitude, pucker, test.*

12. Write a sketch presenting and commenting on a social type: a refugee, the summer boarders, the family across the tracks, the Yankees who room at the other end of the hall, the members of the chess club, the Salvation Army squad, the bridge set, etc.

THE ROMAN FUNERAL[1]

THEODOR MOMMSEN

•

1. THE LIFE OF THE ROMAN WAS AUSTERE AND RESTRAINED, and the nobler he was, the less he knew of freedom or of impulse. The unquestioned authority of custom allowed him but a narrow range of action or, indeed, of thought; his ultimate worthiness was to have led a serious and strict 5 or, to use the characteristic Latin expressions, a sad and severe life. He had no more and no less to do than soberly to govern his household and manfully to bear his part of counsel and action in public affairs. Thus the individual had neither the power nor the desire to be aught else than a 10 member of the community. Yet the glory and the might of that community were felt by every individual burgess as a personal possession, to be transmitted along with his family name and his homestead to his posterity. As one generation after another was laid in the tomb, each having con- 15 tributed to the accumulating store of ancient honors, the collective sense of dignity in the noble families of Rome swelled into that mighty civic pride, the like of which the earth has never seen, and the traces of which, as strange as they are grand, seem to us to belong to another world. 20 For his intense pride of citizenship the Roman found little expression in his daily life; he was compelled, by the rigid simplicity and equality of Roman society, to keep it locked within his heart. This civic feeling was, however, vigorously and plainly manifest in the funeral rites of the man 25 of distinction. This ceremonial, more than any other phenomenon of Roman life, affords us who live in later times a glimpse of that wonderful spirit of the Romans.

[1] From *The History of Rome,* adapted from the translation by W. P. Dickson.

2. It was a remarkable procession, to which the burgesses
were summoned by the public crier: "Yonder warrior is
dead; whoever can, let him come to escort Lucius Aemilius;
he is borne forth from his house." It was opened by bands
of wailing women, musicians, and dancers. One of the
dancers was dressed up and furnished with a mask in the
likeness of the deceased; presumably his impersonation included gestures and actions; thus the appearance of the
well-known citizen was once more presented to the multitude. Then came the grandest and most peculiar part of
the solemnity: the procession of ancestors. This part of
the pageant so outshone the rest in splendor that noble-
men of the true Roman type enjoined their heirs to restrict
the funeral ceremony to that procession alone. The chief
ornament of a Roman house was the collection of masks
of those ancestors who had held the curule aedileship or any
higher magistracy. These masks, wrought in wax and
painted—usually modelled from life, but representing even
the ancestors of the earlier ages, before the time of the
kings—were placed in wooden niches along the walls of the
family hall. When a death occurred, suitable persons,
chiefly actors, wore these masks and the corresponding
official costumes in the funeral ceremony. Thus the ancestors, each in the principal dress worn by him in his lifetime—the triumphator in his gold-embroidered robe, the
censor in his purple, the consul in his robe with purple
border,—with their lictors and the insignia of their office,
and all in chariots, gave the final escort to the dead. He lay
upon the bier overspread with fine linen cloths and with
coverlets embroidered in purple and gold. Like his ancestors, he wore the full costume of his highest office. Around
him lay the armor of the enemies he had slain and the
chaplets he had won. Behind the bier came the mourners,
all in black, without ornament: the sons of the deceased
with heads veiled, the daughters without veil, the relatives
and clansmen, the friends, the clients and freedmen. Thus
the procession passed on to the Forum. There the corpse
was set erect; the ancestors descended from their chariots

and seated themselves in the curule chairs. The son or
nearest gentile kinsman of the deceased mounted the
rostrum and announced to the assembled multitude, in
simple recital, the names and deeds of each of the dead 70
men who sat in a circle around him and, last of all, the
name and deeds of him who had recently died.

3. This may be called a barbarous custom, and a nation
of artistic temperament would certainly not have persisted
in this odd resurrection of the dead down to an epoch of 75
fully developed civilization. But even Greeks who were
very dispassionate and little disposed to reverence, such
as Polybius, were greatly impressed by the naïve pomp of
this funeral ceremony. The conception was essentially in
keeping with the grave solemnity, the uniform movement, 80
and the proud dignity of Roman life, that departed genera-
tions should continue to walk among the living, and that,
when a burgess weary of labors and of honors was gathered
to his fathers, these fathers themselves should appear in
the Forum to receive him.   85

❋ ❋ ❋

1. Define aedile (l. 44), curule (ll. 67, 44), censor (l. 54),
consul (l. 54), lictor (l. 55), chaplet (l. 61), client (l. 64),
Forum (l. 65), gentile (l. 68), rostrum (l. 69). Identify Polybius
(l. 78). Show that *individual* is accurately used in line 9.

2. Why should the traces of civic pride seem strange to us?
Define briefly what you consider to be the modern conception
of honor, dignity, glory, the good life, in such a way as to
distinguish it from that of the Romans.

3. State, as briefly as possible, the relation Mommsen makes
between Roman family pride and civic pride.

4. Consider the logical organization of the whole passage.
Which paragraph presents fact? Which interprets it? (Which
element, that of Par. 1 or that of Par. 2, do you suppose came
first in the author's mind?) What are the functions of the
other paragraph?

5. Mommsen, having determined what qualities of the
Romans were expressed in their funeral ceremony, had to

manage his account of it in such a way as to exhibit these qualities. Show that he has done this.

6. Is the narrative an account of a particular event, or is it typical? Must it be so, in order to accomplish Mommsen's purpose? Explain.

7. The materials of Par. 2 are arranged according to what plan? Where is the pattern broken? Do the inserted sentences explain a *preceding* or a *following* part of the narrative? May Mommsen's practice be taken as a sound general rule for inserted explanations?

8. Divide Par. 3 into two parts: assertion and concession. Which part might be omitted? How would such omission change the tone of the essay? Of the two parts, which comes last? May this be established as a general rule?

9. The noun *procession* is plainly related to the verb *proceed;* what noun or verb is related to each of the following words? Impulse, distinction, conception, enjoin.

10. Explain the connection between the meanings of the following pairs: *civic* and *civility, gesture* and *jest, magistrate* and *master, pageant* and *page.*

11. What other ceremonies or customs, past or present, might be treated in this way? Confirmation, Passover Feast, Rain Dance, quilting party, alumni reunion, bank night—add to the list. Before selecting one as the subject of an essay, ask yourself whether the custom has any significance worth discussion and whether it is sufficiently uniform to be generalized.

THE FREE CITIZEN'S AMUSEMENT[1]

GEORGES DUHAMEL

•

1. "ALL THOSE LIGHTS," SAID PITKIN: "THAT'S WHERE WE'RE going. This is one of the biggest movies in the world, something really splendid. But you will see for yourself."

His air of detachment was unconvincing. It was plain that Pitkin, an intelligent and cultivated man, took personal 5 pride in the magnificence of this theatre, felt it an honor to belong to the great nation that can erect such extensive buildings.

2. "It's Sunday: we'll have to pay a dollar a seat. All these people in line pay the same admission. The moving 10 picture is democratic." •

Indeed all these people paid very dearly for their favorite pleasure and for the right to await, in clusters along the wall, under a sooty drizzle, their admittance to the sanctuary of the movies, the temple wherein the images move. 15 Thus aligned they hardly spoke, but stood patiently, with vague eyes, already submissive to the hypnosis that soon would seize them in the enchanted darkness. From time to time a portion of the queue was ingested into the lower orifices of the building; the line shuffled along, sprouted, 20 lengthened. Within the brilliant cavern the pilgrim presented his obolus, his dollar.

3. Flunkies in princely livery directed the crowd. As we raced through vast and desolate foyers, our footsteps were muffled by imitation oriental rugs; upon the walls were 25 canvases that might be recognized as copies of copies of originals notorious and ugly; hundreds of statues stood about on pedestals, apparently intended to resemble Greek

[1] Adapted from *America the Menace* (*Scènes de la Vie future*), by Georges Duhamel, by special permission of, and by arrangement with, the authorized publishers, Houghton Mifflin Company.

sculpture; they were made of some translucent material
and were ingeniously lighted up by electric bulbs concealed
within them.

"Gorgeous, eh?" remarked Pitkin, tentatively, in case I
admired it.

And so it was. The luxury of this interior was that of a
fashionable bourgeois brothel, an industrialized luxury,
designed for a public as insensitive as the machines by
which it was made, a standardized luxury which might be
enjoyed from one end of the democracy to the other. But
there was no time for such confusing meditations; with
the crowd we were shoved between lines of plush rope—
like animals in a slaughter house. Every five minutes the
doors opened to emit, in a gust of music, several scores of
amusement seekers. They seemed anesthetized, emerging
from their pleasures in a mournful stupor, quitting the
movie as one leaves a restaurant or an office. The satiated
were replaced by an equal number of the fresh, so that the
auditorium might remain filled.

4. Our turn came to be pushed into this shadowy pit of
oblivion. Within we found more cords, more barriers, more
disdainful flunkies to order us to further intermediary sta-
tions. But now we could see the pictures, glimmering far
off in the nether darkness; yet they seemed quite near.
Pitkin, an habitué, participated at once, named the flicker-
ing faces as they hovered and vanished. After more jostling,
we sat in excellently cushioned armchairs, enjoying American comfort, a comfort purely tactile and kinesthetic. My
escort promptly became absorbed in the pictures, which
presumably conveyed a story; as I did not know what had
gone before, their import was not obvious to me. Nor did
any detail of setting or gesture or grimace correspond with
any reality that I had ever observed. The crowd all around
was placid and somnolent; when it laughed I realized what
a multitude of people was there. Then I lifted my eyes to
a heaven where stars twinkled among gently drifting clouds.
It was, of course, a false heaven, fitted out with false stars
and false clouds, affording a false impression of freshness.

Everything here was false: the shadow-life on the screen, the music distributed by means of some miraculously blatant apparatus—even, perhaps, that human throng which seemed only to dream what it saw upon the screen, and which stirred heavily from time to time, as a man sleeping. It was disturbingly easy to doubt my own reality—to feel myself only the simulacrum of a man, an imitation of Duhamel.

"See, that brute of an officer has struck the peasant boy, but he won't stand for it."——

I retained indeed a complete physical consciousness, but I seemed to be losing any consciousness of my soul; I had known the experience in the dentist's office. The dwelling place of my soul had become indurate and grievously remote; was my soul to be extracted, as at the dentist's——

"Just as I said: the peasant comes to his senses; he will clear out of that foreign country and follow his elder brothers to America, the land of freedom. . . ."

5. In a panic-stricken effort toward intellectual autonomy —for the moving images were substituting themselves for my own thoughts—I tried to concentrate upon the music. But the music was elusive; one heard it without listening; it flowed continuous and intangible as the wind. By shutting my eyes and making a severe effort of the will, I succeeded; I could control my intelligence; I was not yet, like the helot mob around me, drowned in the muddy torrent of sensation. The music too proved false, a preserved stuff, manufactured like the breakfast sausages in some huge middle-western slaughter house of music and packed in discs for distribution. It was a kind of musical scrapple, consisting of a harmonic gelatine stuffed with morsels from well-known compositions, chosen for their supposed relevance to the cinematic text: ten measures from the wedding march from *Lohengrin,* as the lovers crossed the screen, a little of Haydn's *Military Symphony* when soldiers marched, the first allegro of Beethoven's *Symphony in A* for cavalry, a phrase from the *Unfinished,* that cherished victim of the movies. The sublime melodies which we, from our adolescence, have murmured rather with our hearts than with

105 our lips, which have been our daily bread, our study, our glory, which represent the flesh and blood of our master musicians, have been chopped and hacked and mutilated, and the wreckage has been cast into a stream of warm lard and molasses, flowing ceaselessly as the drowsy audience 110 chews its gum, belches, digests its food, stares at the hysterical pictures.

6. On what pretext had the butchers dared slip in four bars of *Tristan*? I glanced at the screen: two faces, hideous with enamel and vaseline, approached each other. As the 115 monstrous mouths were joined, Parker P. Pitkin whispered in my ear,

"There's a new law. Not more than seven feet of that."

"Of what?"

"Kissing on the mouth. The clinches used to last so long 120 they had to make a law. Safeguard public morals. Not more than seven feet—of film, of course—about two metres twenty. That's quite a lot, when you come to think of it."

7. But there was no opportunity for thought. The "feature" was followed by vaudeville and a series of "shorts." 125 The great organ uttered vaguely religious sonorities, for the cinema replaces and abridges all other institutions. Finally we saw the beginning of the movie. Again the faucet was turned on: music and imagery flowed aimless and swift. Whereas every work worthy to be called a work 130 strives for permanence and verity, these pictures, representing not life as we know it but another world, where all is false, arbitrary, and absurd, hurried past. At last Pitkin announced,

"This is where we came in. . . ."

135 To get the beginning after one has had the conclusion —this is the new fashion in life and letters; nor are American emotions compromised or inconvenienced by the inversion. The show goes on in a continuous round, like the spectacle of humanity itself, like the stars in their courses. 140 One gets in on it at any point, witnesses a complete revolution, and retires, sated. One has had one's dollar's worth; to withdraw is discreet. We stumbled past a rank of spec-

tators, thirty human beings feebly taking their pleasure, and
departed from the hall of lost hours and lost illusions.

8.   The movie is the diversion of slaves, the pastime of 145
illiterate wretches harried by wants and worries, the astutely
poisoned pabulum of a multitude condemned by the forces
of Moloch to this vile degradation.

9.   The movie demands no responsive effort on the part
of the beholder; it assumes no sequence of thought, poses 150
no problems, kindles no passion, awakens no understanding
within the heart, excites no hope save the pathetic yearning
to be some day a "star" at Hollywood. The dynamics of
the movie snatch from contemplation whatever images
might be pondered: its pleasures, like the most mercenary 155
caresses, are offered to a public which need participate only
by a flabby and casual adhesion; and these pleasures succeed one another with feverish rapidity, so that no one may
be bored. There is no room for any act of the intelligence,
no room for discussion, no room for any reaction or de- 160
liberate participation. Every work of art through which I
have achieved a greater maturity represents a conquest on
my part: I have had to struggle to understand such works;
I have had to merit them by the fervor of my passion. But
the movie need not be wooed and won: it prostitutes it- 165
self; it puts the mind and the heart to no test. It blurts out
at once the little all that it has to say; it is without mystery,
without intricacy, without depth, without reserve. It is intended to glut us, but it leaves us ill at ease; its nature is
movement, but it leaves us inert, depressed, paralyzed.   170

10.   This terrible machine, with its bedazzlements, its
luxury, its music, its human voices—so marvelously equipped
for the stultification and the brutalization of a populace—
is today one of the most menacing forces in the world. A
people dominated for fifty years by the American movie is 175
on its way to the worst kind of decadence. It is true that
America boasts many large-scale enterprises. But whereas
a skyscraper rises at the rate of two or three stories a week,
a work of art or of intellect is a more tedious achievement:
it took Wagner twenty years to complete his Tetralogy; 180

it took Littré a lifetime to compile his dictionary. And a
people stupefied by the fugitive, epidermal pleasures of the
movie, obtained without the slightest intellectual or aesthetic
effort, will one day find itself incapable of any sustained
185 endeavor, a protoplasmic mass unequal to any disciplined
mental activity.

❊ ❊ ❊

1.   Describe the organization of this essay; divide it into
two parts and explain the function of each part.

2.   Might the order of these parts be reversed? Is Duhamel's
plan like that of King's "Pikes" or like that of Mommsen's
"Roman Funeral"? Explain why Duhamel's plan should differ
from one of these.

3.   a) "The movie . . . assumes no sequence of thought."
(ll. 149-150.) In which of the preceding lines has this idea been
expressed or illustrated?

b) "It leaves us ill at ease . . . , inert," etc. (ll. 169-170.)
Where has this charge been illustrated?

c) Its pleasures are "fugitive, epidermal . . . , obtained
without the slightest . . . effort." (ll. 182-184.) In which lines
has Duhamel prepared for this charge?

4.   The narrative appears to record a single trip to a certain
theatre; do you think it was actually written from a single experience or from several? On what condition is it feasible to
present one instance as the evidence for a general indictment?
Has this condition been met by M. Duhamel's narrative? Is
there any advantage in making the narrative represent a single
occasion?

M. Duhamel's problem was to present sufficient evidence to
support the charges he wished to make. Instead of telling a
story, he might have sorted his data into paragraphs, under
such headings as Plot, Musical Accompaniment, Physical Environment. But such an analysis of the material would have been
a logical exercise leading nowhere in particular; one would
expect a German scholar to go at it that way. Narrative holds
the material together just as well. Moreover, narrative has an
impulse of its own: one thing leads to another, causally or

merely chronologically, and so the reader is carried along; the essay moves. Adopting the story form, the author had to make sure of three things: that the narrative did progress, i.e., that its details were set forth in prompt and plausible sequence; that it included enough details to justify the later comments; and that the descriptions of these details were vigorously phrased.

5. There were other ways of arranging the story.

a) Why did not Duhamel enter the theatre at the beginning of the picture and leave after the close-up described in lines 113-115?

b) Would it not have been better to describe the foyer on the way out?

c) Would it not have been better to describe the satiated amusement seekers after an account of the performance which had affected them?

6. Study the role of Pitkin.

a) Why did not Duhamel go to the movies by himself?

b) What is the purpose of Pitkin's two remarks on the plot of the movie? (ll. 74-75, 81-83.)

c) What is the point of the phrase, "about two metres twenty"? (ll. 121-122.)

7. Comment on the following changes of wording: *extensive* (l. 7) to *magnificent*; *images* (l. 15) to *pictures*; *hypnosis* (l. 17) to *visions*; *obolus* (l. 22) to *talisman*; *democracy* (l. 38) to *nation*; *autonomy* (l. 84) to *self-control*; *gelatine* (l. 96) to *treacle*; *arbitrary* (l. 132) to *pointless*; *pabulum* (l. 147) to *opiate*.

8. Explain lines 151-152 by an illustration from your own experience: what work of art has ever awakened an understanding in your heart? Or explain how one may achieve greater maturity through a work of art. (l. 162.) Do you think the process indeed as arduous as Duhamel claims?

9. "There is . . . no room for discussion, no room for any . . . deliberate participation." (ll. 159-161.) Might not these criticisms be urged against the legitimate theatre with equal validity?

10. Comment on the following retort: Duhamel has overlooked the fact that we Americans go to the movies only to be amused; we don't go there to learn culture.

Other topics for discussion: What do technicolor and stereoscopic effects add to *realism?* This involves a definition of realism. Is realism desirable in art?

Are historical pictures educational? This involves a definition of education; consider not only the subject matter of the historical movie but the change in the person so educated.

Duhamel, concerned with the reaction of the audience, makes no very thorough analysis of the movie itself; his sneer at the plot of his picture is unconvincing. Subtler critics have studied the aesthetics of the movie not in its plot but in its *method,* which, it is argued, seems designed to gratify man's "magic omnipotence wish"—to afford the pleasures of marihuana in a safer way. The presentation of every story embodies the same elements of style: "brightly reflected lighting; spacious interiors obviously without four walls; the ritual series of facial close-up and the follow-shot of the angelic person moving down halls and through walls, freed from the laws of matter; the music that sounds from nowhere; the continuity of fades; the scrambling montage in which all dissolves into kaleidoscopy." This style affords the spectator "freedom, ease, domination of obstacles, evaporation of solidity, speed, super-humanity, daydream, and the pleasant destruction of the universe." (Cf. Paul Goodman, "Griffith and the Technical Innovations," in *Partisan Review,* May-June, 1941.)

We may learn much from The Foreign Visitor, for his perceptions are not clouded by familiarity, and he is not usually prejudiced in our favor. (Cf. Allan Nevins, *American Social History as Recorded by British Travellers,* Henry Holt & Company, Inc., New York, 1931, and C. E. Andrews, "French Authors Take Revenge," in *The Bookman,* March, 1931.)

He is, too, a useful literary device: through him the social critic may report candidly and comment in accents purely reasonable. This device was congenial to the rationalism of the eighteenth century: cf. Montesquieu's *Lettres persanes* and Goldsmith's *Citizen of the World;* the *Spectator, Gulliver,* and *Candide* are variations on this method. The fictitious traveler may visit a Utopia and report on laws and customs which put his own civilization to shame; or the imaginary country may be a caricature of the author's own society: thus Gulliver's *Voyage to Lilliput,* Anatole France's *Penguin Island,* and André Maurois' *Voyage to the Land of the Articoles.* M. Duhamel called his American sketches *Scènes de la Vie future* because he feared that American business would impose its civilization upon the whole world, and Aldous Huxley has elaborated such criticisms as Duhamel's in the prophetic and premonitory novel, *Brave New World*.

11. Suppose yourself a Man from Mars or a Stranger from the Other Side of the Earth; record your observations of some phase of the life of these curious foreigners. (Do not waste time on the mechanics of your arrival. And do not try to cover too much ground.)

PAGAN PIETY[1]

WALTER PATER

•

1. ABOUT THE TIME WHEN THE DYING ANTONINUS PIUS ordered his golden image of Fortune to be carried into the chamber of his successor, there was a boy living in an old country-house, half farm, half villa, who, for himself, re-cruited that body of antique traditions by a spontaneous force of religious veneration such as had originally called them into being. The restoration of religious usages, and their retention where they still survived, was come to be the fashion through the influence of imperial example; and what had been in the main a matter of family pride with his father was sustained by a native instinct of devotion in the young Marius. A sense of conscious powers external to ourselves, pleased or displeased by the right or wrong conduct of every circumstance of daily life—that *conscience*, of which the old Roman religion was a formal habitual recognition, was become in him a powerful current of feeling and observance. The old-fashioned, partly puritanic awe, the power of which Wordsworth noted and valued so highly in a northern peasantry, had its counterpart in the feeling of the Roman lad, as he passed the spot, "touched of heaven," where the lightning had struck dead an aged laborer in the field: an upright stone, still with moldering garlands about it, marked the place. He brought to that system of symbolic usages, and they in turn developed in him further, a great seriousness—an impressibility to the sacredness of time, of life and its events, and the circumstances of family fellowship; of such gifts to men as fire, water, the earth, from labor on which they live, really un-

[1] From *Marius the Epicurean*, by Walter Pater. By permission of The Macmillan Company, publishers.

derstood by him as gifts—a sense of religious responsibility in the reception of them. It was a religion for the most 30
part of fear, of multitudinous scruples, of a year-long burden
of forms; yet rarely (on clear summer mornings, for instance) the thought of those heavenly powers afforded a
welcome channel for the almost stifling sense of health and
delight in him, and relieved it as gratitude to the gods.   35

2. The day of the "little" or private *Ambarvalia* was
come, to be celebrated by a single family for the welfare
of all belonging to it, as the great college of the Arval
Brothers officiated at Rome in the interest of the whole
state. At the appointed time all work ceases; the instru- 40
ments of labor lie untouched, hung with wreaths of flowers,
while masters and servants together go in solemn procession along the dry paths of vineyard and cornfield, con-
ducting the victims whose blood is presently to be shed
for the purification from all natural or supernatural taint 45
of the lands they have "gone about." The old Latin words
of the liturgy, to be said as the procession moved on its
way, though their precise meaning was long since become
unintelligible, were recited from an ancient illuminated
roll, kept in the painted chest in the hall, together with the 50
family records. Early on that day the girls of the farm had
been busy in the great portico, filling large baskets with
flowers plucked short from branches of apple and cherry,
then in spacious bloom, to strew before the quaint images
of the gods—Ceres and Bacchus and the yet more mysteri- 55
ous Dea Dia—as they passed through the field, carried in
their little houses on the shoulders of white-clad youths,
who were understood to proceed to this office in perfect
temperance, as pure in soul and body as the air they
breathed in the firm weather of that early summer-time. 60
The clean lustral water and the full incense-box were carried after them. The altars were gay with garlands of
wool and the more sumptuous sort of blossom and green
herbs to be thrown into the sacrificial fire, fresh-gathered
from a particular plot in the old garden, set apart for the 65
purpose. Just then the young leaves were almost as fragrant

as flowers, and the scent of the bean-fields mingled pleasantly with the cloud of incense. But for the monotonous
intonation of the liturgy by the priests, clad in their strange,
70 stiff, antique vestments, and bearing ears of green corn upon
their heads, secured by flowing bands of white, the procession moved in absolute stillness, all persons, even the
children, abstaining from speech after the utterance of the
pontifical formula, *Favete linguis!*—Silence! Propitious
75 Silence!—lest any words save those proper to the occasion
should hinder the religious efficacy of the rite.

3. With the lad Marius, who, as the head of his house,
took a leading part in the ceremonies of the day, there
was a devout effort to complete this impressive outward
80 silence by that inward tacitness of mind, esteemed so
important by religious Romans in the performance of these
sacred functions. To him the sustained stillness without
seemed really but to be waiting upon that interior, mental
condition of preparation or expectancy, for which he was
85 just then intently striving. The persons about him, certainly, had never been challenged by those prayers and
ceremonies to any ponderings on the divine nature: they
conceived them rather to be the appointed means of setting
such troublesome movements at rest. By them, "the religion
90 of Numa," so staid, ideal and comely, the object of so
much jealous conservatism, though of direct service as
lending sanction to a sort of high scrupulosity, especially in
the chief points of domestic conduct, was mainly prized as
being, through its hereditary character, something like a
95 personal distinction—as contributing, among the other ac-
cessories of an ancient house, to the production of that
aristocratic atmosphere which separated them from newly-
made people. But in the young Marius, the very absence
from those venerable usages of all definite history and dog-
100 matic interpretation had already awakened much speculative
activity; and today, starting from the actual details of the
divine service, some very lively surmises, though scarcely
distinct enough to be thoughts, were moving backwards
and forwards in his mind, as the stirring wind had done

all day among the trees, and were like the passing of some 105
mysterious influence over all the elements of his nature
and experience. One thing only distracted him—a certain
pity at the bottom of his heart, and almost on his lips, for
the sacrificial victims and their looks of terror, rising almost
to disgust at the central act of the sacrifice itself, a piece of 110
everyday butcher's work, such as we decorously hide out
of sight; though some then present certainly displayed a
frank curiosity in the spectacle thus permitted them on a
religious pretext. The old sculptors at Athens have de-
lineated the placid heads of the victims led in it to sacrifice, 115
with a perfect feeling for animals in forcible contrast with
an indifference as to their sufferings. It was this contrast
that distracted Marius now in the blessing of his fields,
and qualified his devout absorption upon the scrupulous
fulfillment of all the details of the ceremonial, as the pro- 120
cession approached the altars.

4. The names of that great populace of "little gods,"
dear to the Roman home, which the pontiffs had placed
on the sacred list of the *Indigitamenta*, to be invoked, because they can help, on special occasions, were not forgotten 125
in the long litany—Vatican who causes the infant to utter
his first cry, Fabulinus who prompts his first word, Cuba
who keeps him quiet in his cot, Domiduca especially, for
whom Marius had through life a particular memory and
devotion, the goddess who watches over one's safe coming 130
home. The urns of the dead in the family chapel received
their due service. They also were now become something
divine, a goodly company of friendly and protecting spirits,
encamped about the place of their former abode—above all
others, that father, dead ten years before, of whom, remem- 135
bering but a tall, grave figure above him in early childhood,
Marius habitually thought as a *genius* a little cold and
severe.

Candidus insuetum miratur limen Olympi,
Sub pedibusque videt nubes et sidera.—   140

Perhaps!—but certainly needs his altar here below. and

garlands today upon his urn. But the dead *genii* were satisfied with little—a few violets, a cake dipped in wine, or a
morsel of honeycomb. Daily, from the time when his child-
145 ish footsteps were still uncertain, had Marius taken them
their portion of the family meal, at the second course,
amidst the silence of the company. They loved those who
brought them their sustenance; but, deprived of these
services, would be heard wandering through the house, cry-
150 ing sorrowfully in the stillness of the night.

5. And those simple gifts, like other objects as trivial—
bread, oil, wine, milk—had regained for him, by their use
in such religious service, that poetic and as it were moral
significance, which surely belongs to all the means of daily
155 life, could we but break through the veil of our familiarity
with things by no means vulgar in themselves. A hymn
followed, while the whole assembly stood with veiled faces.
The fire rose up readily from the altars, in clean, bright
flame—a favorable omen, making it a duty to render the
160 mirth of the evening complete. Old wine was poured out
freely for the servants at supper in the great kitchen, where
they had worked in the imperfect light through the long
evenings of winter. The young Marius himself took but a
very sober part in the noisy feasting. A devout, regretful
165 after-taste of what had been really beautiful in the ritual
he had accomplished took him early away, that he might
the better recall in reverie all the circumstances of the cele-
bration of the day. As he sank into a sleep, pleasant with
all the influences of long hours in the open air, he seemed
170 still to be moving in procession through the fields, with a
kind of pleasurable awe. That feeling was still upon him
as he awoke amid the beating of violent rain on the shutters,
in the first storm of the season. The thunder which startled
him from sleep seemed to make the solitude of his chamber
175 almost painfully complete, as if the nearness of those angry
clouds shut him up in a close place alone in the world. Then
he thought of the sort of protection which that day's ceremonies assured. To procure an agreement with the gods—
Pacem deorum exposcere; that was the meaning of what

they had all day been busy upon. In a faith sincere but half- 180
suspicious, he would fain have those Powers at least not
against him. His own nearer household gods were all around
his bed. The spell of his religion as a part of the very
essence of home, its intimacy, its dignity and security, was
forcible at that moment; only, it seemed to involve certain 185
heavy demands upon him.

❋ ❋ ❋

Marius the Epicurean is an account of the spiritual explora-
tions of a young man in the Roman world of the latter second
century A.D. As Marius, bred in the aristocratic and conservative
paganism of ancient agrarian Rome, meets new people and
witnesses new aspects of life at school and in the metropolis,
he also extracts from the philosophies of the Epicureans, the
Stoics, and the Christians their fairest meanings. Thus the
novel was a device whereby Pater might evaluate these systems
of belief and set down what, to his appreciation, they could
offer to a man in quest of a good life; the narrative form
enabled Pater to translate the abstract formulas of the several
philosophies into terms of personal and inward experience. This
passage is offered for comparison with Mommsen's interpretation of a similar ceremony. Whereas Mommsen might adduce,
in explanation of the funeral, only those traits of thought and
behavior shared by all noble Romans, Pater, in the person of
Marius, might offer his conjectures as to what the *Ambarvalia*
meant to an unusually sensitive participant—what spiritual
significance it held for Pater as he imagined himself in the
place of his hero. Thus he indulged in subtler sympathies and
more subjective psychological analyses than did the historian.
Yet he was careful to indicate that Marius was exceptional; the
religious satisfactions of the rest of the Roman household are
shown to be simpler and more forthright than the moods of
Marius.

1. In which paragraph is the rite described? Where is the
description of custom continued and concluded? Is the rite
exhibited in its typical form, or does this account include details
not likely to have occurred in ordinary Roman practice?

2. What four parts of the ceremony are interpreted in terms

of their effect upon Marius? Mark off these sections in the text, and label them. Summarize briefly his response to each of these four parts of the ritual.

3. In which of these discussions has Pater described another Roman ceremonial observance and its meaning for Marius? Mark off this section.

4. Which of these responses anticipates a later sympathy on the part of Marius for Christianity? What probable future re-action of Marius to Christian doctrine is indicated by his medi-tation upon the lines from Vergil's *Eclogues*?

"In solemn white at Heaven's gate he marvels
    And sees beneath him clouds and constellations."

5. In which lines throughout the passage has Pater said what the symbolic usages may have meant to members of the household other than Marius?

6. Do you agree that ceremonies are ordinarily a "means of setting such troublesome movements at rest"? (ll. 88-89.) Explain your opinion.

7. What is the function of Par. 1 in the plan of the whole passage?

8. Point out the essential differences—if there are any—be-tween Pater's definition of *conscience* in lines 12-14 and that in your dictionary.

9. Why did Pater include a thunderstorm in his narrative? (ll. 172-176.)

10. In what English words do the elements of *Ceres, Vati-can, Fabulinus, Cuba,* and *Domiduca* appear?

LENSES[1]

DONALD CULROSS PEATTIE

●

1. THE STORM IS GONE, AND HERE IN THE COUNTRY A MILD sun has bit by bit argued the cold and snow away. There is the upheaval of a final thaw in the March lawns that are the color of old straw, and in the ponderous black velvet loam, this Illinois sod without a pea-sized pebble in it. 5 Across the roll and dip of the great plain I saw, as I went walking with my blackthorn, the distant woods as blue-black, rainy-looking islands upon the immense watery prairie, and near at hand the young yellow of the willow whips, first brilliance of the year. Now this was a scene a 10 midlander could love, but I went thinking, thinking, wagging that human tail my cane, how all that I saw came to me thus only because of a specified convexity in the cornea of my eye.

2. My sense of proportion, to say nothing of esthetics, 15 is really superbly egotistic. Matter, to regard it more exactly than humanly, is full of holes. The solidest thing is as a net; the space between the electronic particles is like unto the spaces between the sun and the planets. The trouble with our human concepts is that we are so pitifully small when 20 it comes to the great, and so unbearably gross when it comes to the small. We occupy a position in the scale of things that is somewhat on the trivial side of total mediocrity. Little wonder if our ideas are mediocre too.

3. A bee, the first of the year, went by with that direct 25 flight of hers—the most practical people in the world, bees, having no eye for scenery and hence no temptation either to wander or to wonder. A hawk cut a great circular glide

[1] From *Green Laurels*, by Donald Culross Peattie. Copyright, 1936, by Donald Culross Peattie and published by Simon and Schuster, Inc.

through the pale blue air above me, balanced, it seemed,
30 upon the tip of one wing, the other wing pointing almost
to the zenith. He takes the opposite view of things. He sees
all, for miles about, is curious about all, and much of the
time appears simply to be enjoying his perspective, save
when emotions incomprehensible to me suddenly shake
35 him, and set up a windy metallic clamor.

4. I cannot ever share the bee's-eye view or the hawk's-
eye view. Whatever their God-given lenses showed them of
reality, I would never know what it was. I saw the scene
in my human way—the roll and dip of the great plain, the
40 black-silver lakes of snow water seeking out unsuspected
dimples, the cottonwood stands, very white of bark as
they always are at winter's end, looking at a distance lofty
and thoughtful, but turning out — like literary lions on
closer acquaintance — to be talkative and flimsy.

45 5. My swinging cane struck something soft, was de-
layed in some yielding yet persistent medium. And I knew,
even through the blackthorn, that it was living tissue. There
is something about almost any living thing that is plasmic,
resilient, and in a way alarming. We say, "I touched some-
50 thing—and it was *alive!*" There is no such shock in touching
that which has never lived. The mineral world is vast, it
is mighty, rigid and brittle. But the hand that touches vital
matter infallibly recognizes the feel of life and recoils in
excitement.

55 6. What I had struck was nothing but a big, soggy
fungus, a giant puffball persistent from autumn. From the
wound I had made in it there was still curling on the airs
a smoke of mustard-green powder. I struck it again deliberately, and like a staked snake teased into spewing
60 venom, it coughed forth another belch of spores.

7. I unscrewed the crystal of my watch, caught a little
of the living dust in it, screwed the watch face down upon
the upturned glass, and pocketed the whole. At home, at
least, I had a pair of eyes that would deprive the infinitely
65 little of half its mystery. Eyes such as neither hawk nor
bee possesses, eyes for probing into the nature of Nature,

that man has made for himself with monstrous patience, intricate invention piled upon invention.

8. At my desk, I draw the microscope out of its case, and though it is heavy, it slides out to me, when I grasp 70 it by its middle, with an ease like a greeting. It is a matter of a moment to whisk the fungus spores on a glass slide, a moment more to find them in the lower magnification, and then with a triumphant click to swing the intense myopic gaze of the tinier lens upon them. 75

9. From a speck as fine as a particle of wandering cigarette smoke, a spore leaps suddenly up at my eyes as a sphere of gold meshed with vitreous green bands that cut up this tiny world, this planetesimal of sealed-up life, into latitude and longitude. Here a living plant has put its substance into 80 minutest compass and launched it upon the air, where only the most wildly improbable chances, really an unbroken series of lucky one-in-a-thousand hazards, would ever see it grow to a puffball. Here was the whole of heredity, here the past and future of a chain of lives. Intricate, formed to 85 a pattern and plan by the stresses within it, organized by the very fact that it had specific form, this frail and tiny speck of life differed, I saw, from the atom of cigarette smoke precisely as the cry of the hawk differed from the squeal of a rusty hinge which it so much resembled. 90

10. I would be at a loss to show the difference between the sound made by a living thing and an inorganic noise. But the lens takes soundings for us in the depths of optical dimensions. There is no shock, for the young mind with a bent for science, like the first look through a microscope. 95 I am not likely to forget the moment when I saw the green world of the algae come alive—delicate twisted bands of color in the glassy cell walls, diatoms like bits of carven glass, desmids like a trembling green lace, the hexagonal meshes of the water-net like the work of bobbins, and 100 *Oscillatoria,* that plant that swims with a slow eel-like motion. Under the lens I witnessed life's crucial event, when I saw the whip-tailed male cells escape from the sack of a sea kelp and assault the great, inert egg cell, like meteors

105 raining upon a ponderous planet. Under that purposeful attack the planet cell began to roll, with a great, a gentle but irresistible momentum, until one dart, predestined, broke through the surface tensions, dropped to the nuclear core like a solid thing descending through a gas, and then the 110 conquered planet ceased its rolling and the rejected meteors dropped away. Life had begun again.

11. By a coincidence which has no meaning—or perhaps it has every meaning—human fertilization is startlingly like that in the big red seaweed, and who has seen this latter 115 has in effect looked into the very bottom of the well of self.

12. Because the lens has left scant privacy to Nature, it is difficult for the modern mind to recall what battles were once waged over the subject of fertilization, the sexuality of plants, the structure of the cell. Men without the weapon 120 of the lens tussled then in bootless speculation as the Trojans and Greeks pulled the body of Patroclus this way and that.

13. One comes at last to feel that the invention of the microscope by Janssen of Holland in the seventeenth cen- 125 tury was the beginning of modern natural history, for the lens added a new dimension to our eyes and enabled us literally to see to the heart of many a problem. The sentence I have just written sounds good enough to pass unchallenged. But it sounds better than it is, for it seems to assert 130 that one man invented the microscope, and it leaves us to infer that, once it was invented, men, peering through it, saw truth at last. In fact, however, having seventeenth century minds, they did not in the least make of what they saw what we would. Except for a few larger minds, the 135 early microscopists were largely engaged in watching the antics of fleas.

14. And the revolution in biological thought consequent on the use of the microscope did not take place in the seventeenth century but in the unfinished century, 1850 to 140 our times. It is the modern technical improvements, coupled with the forward march of allied sciences, that have created the merciful triumphs of bacteriology, carried us into a deep

perspective of atomic structure and brought light into the
dark mystery of protoplasm itself. The seventeenth century
microscopy was necessarily limited by the imperfections of 145
the early instruments, and still more by the state of the allied
sciences at the time. But it was, none the less, an era of
high adventure in natural history, for the lens, however
faulty, gave to all greatly inquisitive minds the first rap-
turous look at the wonderworld of structure.

※ ※ ※

1. This passage, introducing a chapter on the discovery and
development of the microscope, is skillfully planned to that
end.

   a) Divide it into three sections. Summarize each of these
briefly—in one or two sentences—in such a way as to show
how each section prepares for the following one.

   b) Which sentences throughout the second and third sections are of chief importance in establishing the connection between them?

   c) Which in the first and second?

2. Why did Mr. Peattie take a blackthorn stick with him
in line 7?

3. Did the hawk appear in Par. 4 for the sake of lines 87-
89, or were these lines a happy utilization of a previous chance
remark? Explain.

4. Are "talkative" and "flimsy" (l. 44) the right words for
cottonwoods? The comparison of the trees to literary lions may
seem a strained witticism; what previous phrase in the paragraph
perhaps justifies it?

5. Explain "substance." (l. 80.) How are "past and future"
(l. 85) in the spore?

6. How is the quite literal term "sphere" (l. 77) developed
in other words and phrases in the paragraph?

7. Do Pars. 9-11 have a tone of girlish gushiness? Distinguish three types of statement: those which objectively report things seen, those which *imply* that these things were
marvelous (e.g., "sealed-up life"), and those which say *ex-*

plicitly that they were exciting and significant. Which type of statement is preponderant?

8. It is generally inadvisable to discuss one's own writing process, as has been done in Par. 13. Fix the reader's attention on the subject, not on the bubble in the glass. Revise the paragraph—or a part of it—so as to avoid this reference to the literary medium. Must the word "enabled" (l. 126) be changed?

9. Comment on the following changes of wording: *brilliance of the year* (l. 10) to *messenger softly whispering of the coming spring; egotistic* (l. 16) to *vain; shake* (l. 34) to *arouse; wonder* (l. 28) to *speculate; spewing* (l. 58) to *vomiting; probing* (l. 66) to *prying; whisk* (l. 72) to *place; myopic* (l. 75) to *optical; vitreous* (l. 78) to *shiny; launched* (l. 81) to *cast; crucial* (l. 102) to *dangerous; bootless* (l. 120) to *barefoot; created* (l. 141) to *made possible.*

10. Write an essay on your own introduction to a study—not necessarily a science—which proved fascinating—or which you were unfitted to appreciate.

THE INDUSTRIAL REVOLUTION[1]

WILLIAM BECKFORD

●

Falmouth, March 7, 1787

1. SCOTT CAME THIS MORNING AND TOOK ME TO SEE THE consolidated mines in the parish of Gwynnap; they are situated in a bleak desert, rendered still more doleful by the unhealthy appearance of its inhabitants. At every step one stumbles upon ladders that lead into utter darkness, 5 or funnels that exhale warm copperous vapours. All around these openings the ore is piled up in heaps waiting for purchasers. I saw it drawn reeking out of the mine by the help of a machine called a *whim*, put in motion by mules, which in their turn are stimulated by impish children hang- 10 ing over the poor brutes, and flogging them round without respite. This dismal scene of *whims*, suffering mules, and hillocks of cinders, extends for miles. Huge iron engines creaking and groaning, invented by Watt, and tall chimneys smoking and flaming, that seem to belong to old 15 Nicholas's abode, diversify the prospect.

2. Two strange-looking Cornish beings, dressed in ghostly white, conducted me about, and very kindly proposed a descent into the bowels of the earth, but I declined initiation. These mystagogues occupy a tolerable house, 20 with fair sash windows, where the inspectors of the mine hold their meetings, and regale upon beef, pudding, and brandy.

3. While I was standing at the door of this habitation, several woful figures in tattered garments, with pickaxes 25 on their shoulders, crawled out of a dark fissure and repaired to a hovel, which I learnt was a gin-shop. There they

[1] From *Italy: With Sketches of Spain and Portugal*, by the Author of *Vathek*.

pass the few hours allotted them above ground, and drink, it is to be hoped, an oblivion of their subterraneous exist-
30 ence. Piety as well as gin helps to fill up their leisure moments, and I was told that Wesley, who came apostolizing into Cornwall a few years ago, preached on this very spot to above seven thousand followers.

4. Since this period methodism has made a very rapid
35 progress, and has been of no trifling service in diverting the attention of these sons of darkness from their present condition to the glories of the life to come. However, some people inform me their actual state is not so much to be lamented, and that, notwithstanding their pale looks and
40 tattered raiment, they are far from being poor and unhealthy. Fortune often throws a considerable sum into their laps when they least expect it, and many a common miner has been known to gain a hundred pounds in the space of a month or two. Like sailors in the first effusion of
45 prize-money, they have no notion of turning their good luck to advantage; but squander the fruits of their toil in the silliest species of extravagance. Their wives are dressed out in tawdry silks, and flaunt away in ale-houses between rows of obedient fiddlers. The money spent, down
50 they sink again into damps and darkness.

5. Having passed about an hour in collecting minerals, stopping engines with my finger, and performing all the functions of a diligent young man desirous of information, I turned my back on smokes, flames, and coal-holes, with
55 a great pleasure.

6. Not above a mile and a half from this black bustling scene, in a sheltered valley, lies the mansion of Mr. Beauchamp, wrapped up in shrubberies of laurel and laurustine. Copses of hazel and holly terminate the prospect on al-
60 most every side, and in the midst of the glen a broad clear stream reflects the impending vegetation. This transparent water, after performing the part of a mirror before the house, forms a succession of waterfalls which glitter between slopes of the smoothest turf, sprinkled with daffodils:
65 numerous flights of widgeon and Muscovy ducks were

sprucing themselves on the edge of the stream, and two grave swans seemed highly to approve of its woody retired banks for the education of their progeny.

7. Very glad was I to disport on its "margent green," after crushing cinders at every step all the morning; had not the sun hid himself, and the air grown chill, I might have fooled away three or four hours with the swans and the widgeons, and lost my dinner.

※ ※ ※

In this candid and nonchalant record of a day's sightseeing, William Beckford reveals his own rococo temperament with appalling precision. Whether he reports what he saw or what he did or what somebody said, his prose is remarkable for its literal accuracy. There is little personal comment—no apology, no rationalization, no hypocrisy, no social cant. Nor is Beckford in the least concerned to exhibit a soul more noble than the next fellow's. He was extraordinarily wealthy.

1. The first sentence in Par. 3 might have been concluded: "repaired to a gin-shop in a hovel." What implications are added by "which I learnt"?

2. What is the force of "some people inform me"? (ll. 37-38.) Of "so much to be lamented"? (ll. 38-39.) Why not, for instance, "so wretched"?

3. The fourth sentence (ll. 8-12) might have been written: "a *whim*, driven by mules, which are tended by impish children." Why is Beckford's phrasing horrible? (If you find the idea fascinating, you may pursue it historically in Descartes' *Automatism of Brutes,* especially the "Letter to Henry More, 1649" and the "Letter to the Marquis of Newcastle." These have been conveniently reprinted in the selections from Descartes in the Modern Students Library, New York, 1927.)

4. Beckford tells us that he quit the mines "with a great pleasure"; but in Par. 5 he implies much more than this about his attitude toward his tour of inspection. Write several sentences to define this attitude.

5. Which phrases in Par. 6 suggest that Mr. B.'s estate was a conscious work of landscape art? (For eighteenth-cen-

tury theories of landscape, cf. Pope's *Epistle* to Burlington, *Of Taste,* and Elizabeth Manwaring, *Italian Landscape in Eighteenth Century England,* New York, 1925.)

6. Define as precisely as you can, after a careful study of the whole passage, Beckford's attitude toward the miners. Consider especially such phrases as "diverting the attention" and "mystagogues" (instead of the simpler "guides").

7. The description in Par. 1 is more successful in imparting a mood than in evoking a mental picture. This relative weakness of the paragraph may be accounted for by which of the following criticisms:

a) There is no preliminary characterization of the whole landscape before the details are filled in.

b) The details are not drawn with sufficient sharpness of sense impression.

c) Too many non-visual sense impressions (i.e., things heard, smelled, felt) are recorded.

d) The position in the landscape of the several details (whims, chimneys, etc.) is not precisely defined.

e) In the first sentence, the shift of perspective from panorama to close-up is too sudden.

f) The phrase "at every step" confuses the perspective.

g) The characterization of the animate objects diverts attention from the landscape.

8. Explain the derivations of *apostle, collect, flog, imp, purchase, tawdry, woe.*

9. You perhaps remember the famous explanation in *Ivanhoe* of how the Saxon serfs applied an Anglo-Saxon word, *ox* or *cow,* to the animal in the fields, while the Norman gentry gave the dressed meat the French name of the animal, *beef* (Fr. *bœuf,* L. *bovis*). What other pairs of words are analogous to *ox* and *beef?*

10. Starting with *copper,* work up a list of names of metals or elements having interesting derivations. Classify them.

UNHAPPINESS[1]

BERTRAND RUSSELL

•

1. THE CAUSES OF UNHAPPINESS LIE PARTLY IN THE SOCIAL system, partly in individual psychology—which, of course, is itself to a considerable extent a product of the social system. To prevent the perpetuation of poverty is necessary if the benefits of machine production are to accrue in any 5 degree to those most in need of them; but what is the use of making everybody rich if the rich themselves are miserable? Education in cruelty and fear is bad, but no other kind can be given by those who are themselves the slaves of these passions. These considerations lead us to the problem of the individual: what can a man or woman, here and now, in the midst of our nostalgic society, do to achieve happiness for himself or herself? In discussing this problem, I shall confine my attention to those who are not subject to any extreme cause of outward misery. I shall assume 15 a sufficient income to secure food and shelter, sufficient health to make ordinary bodily activities possible. I shall not consider the great catastrophes, such as loss of all one's children, or public disgrace. My purpose is to suggest a cure for the ordinary day-to-day unhappiness from which 20 most people in civilized countries suffer, and which is all the more unbearable because, having no obvious external causes, it appears inescapable. I believe this unhappiness to be very largely due to mistaken views of the world, mistaken ethics, mistaken habits of life, leading to destruction of 25 that natural zest and appetite for possible things upon which all happiness ultimately depends. These are matters which lie within the power of the individual.

[1] From *The Conquest of Happiness,* by Bertrand Russell, published by Liveright.

2. I was not born happy. As a child, my favorite hymn was "Weary of earth and laden with my sin." At the age of five, I reflected that, if I should live to be seventy, I had only endured, so far, a fourteenth part of my whole life, and I felt the long-spread-out boredom ahead of me to be almost unendurable. In adolescence, I hated life and was continually on the verge of suicide, from which, however, I was restrained by the desire to know more mathematics. Now, on the contrary, I enjoy life; I might almost say that with every year that passes I enjoy it more. This is due partly to having discovered what were the things that I most desired, and having gradually acquired many of these things. Partly it is due to having successfully dismissed certain objects of desire—such as the acquisition of indubitable knowledge about something or other—as essentially unattainable. But very largely it is due to diminishing preoccupation with myself. Like others who had a Puritan education, I had the habit of meditating on my sins, follies, and shortcomings. I seemed to myself—no doubt justly—a miserable specimen. Gradually I learned to be indifferent to myself and my deficiencies; I came to center my attention increasingly upon external objects: the state of the world, various branches of knowledge, individuals for whom I felt affection. External interests, it is true, bring each its own possibility of pain: the world may be plunged in war, knowledge in some direction may be hard to achieve, friends may die. But pains of these kinds do not destroy the essential quality of life, as do those that spring from disgust with self. And every external interest inspires some activity which, so long as the interest remains alive, is a complete preventive of *ennui*. Interest in oneself, on the contrary, leads to no activity of a progressive kind. It may lead to the keeping of a diary, to getting psychoanalyzed, or perhaps to becoming a monk. But the monk will not be happy until the routine of the monastery has made him forget his own soul. The happiness which he attributes to religion he could have obtained from becoming a crossing-sweeper, provided he were compelled to remain one. Ex-

ternal discipline is the only road to happiness for those un-
fortunates whose self-absorption is too profound to be
cured in any other way.

3. Self-absorption is of various kinds. We may take the 70
sinner, the narcissist, and the megalomaniac as three very
common types.

4. When I speak of "the sinner," I do not mean the man
who commits sins: sins are committed by every one or no
one, according to our definition of the word. I mean the 75
man who is absorbed in the consciousness of sin. This man
is perpetually incurring his own disapproval, which, if
he is religious, he interprets as the disapproval of God.
He has an image of himself as he thinks he ought to be,
which is in continual conflict with his knowledge of himself 80
as he is. If, in his conscious thought, he has long since discarded the maxims that he was taught at his mother's knee,
his sense of sin may be buried deep in his unconscious, and
only emerge when he is drunk or asleep. Nevertheless it
may suffice to take the savor out of everything. At bottom 85
he still accepts all the prohibitions he was taught in infancy.
Swearing is wicked; drinking is wicked; ordinary business
shrewdness is wicked; above all, sex is wicked. He does not,
of course, abstain from any of these pleasures, but they are
all poisoned for him by the feeling that they degrade him. 90
The one pleasure that he desires with his whole soul is that
of being approvingly caressed by his mother, which he can
remember having experienced in childhood. This pleasure
being no longer open to him, he feels that nothing matters; since he *must* sin, he decides to sin deeply. When he 95
falls in love, he looks for maternal tenderness, but cannot
accept it, because, owing to the mother-image, he feels no
respect for any woman with whom he has sexual relations.
Then, in his disappointment, he becomes cruel, repents of
his cruelty, and starts afresh on the dreary round of imag- 100
ined sin and real remorse. This is the psychology of very
many apparently hard-boiled reprobates. What drives them
astray is devotion to an unattainable object (mother or
mother-substitute) together with the inculcation, in early

105 years, of a ridiculous ethical code. Liberation from the tyranny of early beliefs and affections is the first step towards happiness for these victims of maternal "virtue."

5. Narcissism is, in a sense, the converse of an habitual sense of sin; it consists in the habit of admiring oneself 110 and wishing to be admired. Up to a point it is, of course, normal, and not to be deplored; it is only in its excesses that it becomes a grave evil. In many women, the capacity for feeling love is completely dried up, and is replaced by a powerful desire that all men should love them. When a 115 woman of this kind is sure that a man loves her, she has no further use for him. When vanity is carried to this height, there is no genuine interest in any other person, and therefore no real satisfaction to be obtained from love. Other interests fail even more disastrously. A narcissist, for 120 example, inspired by the homage paid to great painters, may become an art student; but, as painting is for him a mere means to an end, the technique never becomes interesting, and no subject can be seen except in relation to self. The result is failure and disappointment, with ridicule in- 125 stead of the expected adulation. The same thing applies to those novelists whose novels always have themselves idealized as heroines. All serious success in work depends upon some genuine interest in the material with which the work is concerned. The tragedy of one successful poli- 130 tician after another is the gradual substitution of narcissism for an interest in the community and the measures for which he stands. The man who is only interested in himself is not admirable, and is not felt to be so. Consequently the man whose sole concern with the world is that it shall ad- 135 mire him is not likely to achieve his object. But even if he does, he will not be completely happy, since human instinct is never completely self-centered, and the narcissist is limiting himself artificially just as truly as is the man domi- nated by a sense of sin. The primitive man might be proud 140 of being a good hunter, but he also enjoyed the activity of the chase. Vanity, when it passes beyond a point, kills pleasure in every activity for its own sake, and thus leads

inevitably to listlessness and boredom. Often its source is diffidence, and its cure lies in the growth of self-respect. But this is only to be gained by successful activity inspired by objective interests.

6. The megalomaniac differs from the narcissist by the fact that he wishes to be powerful rather than charming, and seeks to be feared rather than loved. To this type belong many lunatics and most of the great men in history. Love of power, like vanity, is a strong element in normal human nature, and as such is to be accepted; it becomes deplorable only when it is excessive or associated with an insufficient sense of reality. Where this occurs, it makes a man unhappy or foolish, if not both. The lunatic who thinks he is a crowned head may be, in a sense, happy, but his happiness is not of a kind that any sane person would envy. Alexander the Great was psychologically of the same type as the lunatic, though he possessed the talent to achieve the lunatic's dream. He could not, however, achieve his own dream, which enlarged its scope as his achievement grew. When it became clear that he was the greatest conqueror known to fame, he decided that he was a god. Was he a happy man? His drunkenness, his furious rages, his indifference to women, and his claim to divinity suggest that he was not. There is no ultimate satisfaction in the cultivation of one element of human nature at the expense of all the others, or in viewing all the world as raw material for the magnificence of one's own ego. Usually the megalomaniac, whether insane or nominally sane, is the product of some excessive humiliation. Napoleon suffered at school from inferiority to his schoolfellows, who were rich aristocrats, while he was a penurious scholarship boy. When he allowed the return of the *émigrés,* he had the satisfaction of seeing his former schoolfellows bowing down before him. What bliss! Yet it led to the wish to obtain a similar satisfaction at the expense of the Czar, and this led to Saint Helena. Since no man can be omnipotent, a life dominated wholly by love of power can hardly fail, sooner or later, to meet with obstacles that cannot be overcome. The knowledge

that this is so can be prevented from obtruding on consciousness only by some form of lunacy. And wherever psycho-
analytic repression in any marked form takes place, there is
no genuine happiness. Power kept within its proper bounds
185 may add greatly to happiness, but as the sole end of life it
leads to disaster, inwardly if not outwardly.

7. The psychological causes of unhappiness, it is clear,
are many and various. But all have something in common.
The typical unhappy man is one who, having been deprived
190 in youth of some normal satisfaction, has come to value this
one kind of satisfaction more than any other, and has therefore given to his life a one-sided direction, together with a
quite undue emphasis upon the achievement as opposed
to the activities connected with it. There is, however, a
195 further development which is very common in the present
day. A man may feel so completely thwarted that he seeks
no form of satisfaction, but only distraction and oblivion.
He then becomes a devotee of "pleasure." That is to say, he
seeks to make life bearable by becoming less alive. Drunken-
200 ness, for example, is temporary suicide: the happiness that
it brings is merely negative, a momentary cessation of unhappiness. The narcissist and the megalomaniac believe
that happiness is possible, though they may adopt mistaken
means of achieving it; but the man who seeks intoxication,
205 in whatever form, has given up hope except in oblivion.

※ ※ ※

1. Any very elaborate definition ordinarily includes both
positive and negative statements: what the thing is and what
it is not. Indeed, *to define* means, etymologically, to set limits.
In his preceding paragraphs, not given here, Russell has described the "day-to-day unhappiness" he intends to discuss in
his book. What exclusions does he make in Par. 1, and in what
lines? In what positive statement does he summarize his subject thus limited?

2. Par. 2 contains a personal narrative. The topic of this
narrative is stated in the first sentence; what *thesis* is the story

intended to develop? At what point in the story is this thesis first plainly suggested?

3. Par. 5 contains four samples of narcissism and one sample of a kind of man not so afflicted, the savage. These illustrations are set forth in very general terms, not individualized, and not imaged. Each illustration does, however, reiterate two important characteristics of the narcissist: what he does and what he fails to do. What are these two phases of his error? Show that they are presented in each of the illustrations.

4. Russell might have made his primitive man (ll. 138-141) more picturesque by alluding to the lion skin proudly displayed in his hut, his fierce shout as he cast his spear, etc. Write a more highly imaged version of one of the four samples of narcissism—or a new sample of your own invention. Do you think the paragraph might be improved by this more graphic rhetorical method? Explain.

5. There are in Par. 5, along with the illustrations, a number of explanations of the consequences of narcissism. What are they? Which do you think the most serious?

6. Whereas in Par. 4 the career of "the sinner" is presented chronologically, beginning with the cause of his troubles, it is not until the end of Par. 5 that Russell suggests diffidence as a source of vanity. Why should not this be discussed at the beginning of Par. 5?

7. In Par. 6, Alexander and Napoleon illustrate what two different points?

8. Compare the illustrations of Par. 5 with those of Par. 6. Which set do you think more likely to make a reader recognize similar faults in himself? Why?

9. Suppose you are to describe not a kind of unhappiness, but an unhappy individual. Make a tentative outline for such an essay.

10. This passage raises a number of questions which may afford materials for an essay. What is "education in cruelty and fear"? Is it envy that makes one want to save other people from their vices, or an interest in the state of the world? Does religion make people feel guilty or relieve them of their sense of guilt? How do children ever escape the desire to please

their parents? Is love a discovery of oneself or of others? What is the distinction between vanity and self-respect? How does diffidence lead to vanity? Or humiliation to a yearning for power? What forms of power afford happiness? Which forms of competition are unprofitable? Is there a cure for boredom? For pleasure-seeking? Which of Russell's assertions or implications do you think wrong? (You may be interested to see how Harry Emerson Fosdick treats similar topics in his *On Being a Real Person,* Harper & Brothers, 1943.)

Do not write your essay simply to give a quick answer to one of these questions—some of which are not worded in an answerable way. Rather let the question start you on your preliminary meditations; test your ideas by applying them to people you know; turn them over in your mind for several days before sorting out the materials of which your essay is to be made.

THE DISCOVERY OF LANDSCAPE[1]

JACOB BURCKHARDT

•

1. BUT, OUTSIDE THE SPHERE OF SCIENTIFIC INVESTIGATION, there is another way to draw near to nature. The Italians are the first among modern peoples to see and feel the outward world as something beautiful.

2. The power to do so is always the result of a long and complicated development, and its origin is not easily detected, since a dim feeling of this kind may exist long before it shows itself in poetry and painting, and thereby becomes conscious of itself. Among the ancients, for example, art and poetry had gone through the whole circle of human interests, before they turned to the representation of nature, and even then the latter filled always a limited and subordinate place. And yet, from the time of Homer downwards, the powerful impression made by nature upon man is shown by countless verses and chance expressions. The Germanic races, which founded their states on the ruins of the Roman Empire, were thoroughly and specially fitted to understand the spirit of natural scenery; and though Christianity compelled them for a while to see in the springs and mountains, in the lakes and woods, which they had till then revered, the working of evil demons, yet this transitional conception was soon outgrown. By the year 1200, at the height of the Middle Ages, a genuine, hearty enjoyment of the external world was again in existence, and found lively expression in the minstrelsy of different nations, which gives evidence of the sympathy felt with all the simple phenomena of nature—spring with its flowers, the green fields and the woods. But these pictures are all

[1] From *The Civilization of the Renaissance in Italy*, by Jacob Burckhardt, translated by S. G. C. Middlemore; reprinted by permission of George Allen and Unwin, Ltd., Publishers.

foreground without perspective. The epic poetry, which de-
30 scribes armour and costumes so fully, does not attempt
more than a sketch of outward nature; and even the great
Wolfram von Eschenbach scarcely anywhere gives us an
adequate picture of the scene on which his heroes move.
From these poems it would never be guessed that their
35 noble authors in all countries inhabited or visited lofty
castles, commanding distant prospects. Even in the Latin
poems of the wandering clerks, we find no traces of a distant view—of landscape properly so called—but what lies
near is sometimes described with a glow and splendour
40 which none of the knightly minstrels can surpass. What picture of the Grove of Love can equal that of the Italian poet
—for such we take him to be—of the twelfth century?

> Immortalis fieret
> Ibi manens homo;
> 45 Arbor ibi quaelibet
> Suo gaudet pomo;
> Viae myrrha, cinnamo
> Fragrant, et amomo—
> Conjectari poterat
> 50 Dominus ex domo,[2] etc.

To the Italian mind, at all events, nature had by this time
lost its taint of sin, and had shaken off all trace of de-
moniacal powers. Saint Francis of Assisi, in his Hymn to
the Sun, frankly praises the Lord for creating the heavenly
55 bodies and the four elements.

3. But the unmistakable proofs of a deepening effect of
nature on the human spirit begin with Dante. Not only
does he awaken in us by a few vigorous lines the sense
of the morning airs and the trembling light on the distant
60 ocean, or of the grandeur of the storm-beaten forest, but
he makes the ascent of lofty peaks, with the only possible
object of enjoying the view[3]—the first man, perhaps, since

---

[2] Carmina Burana, p. 162, *De Phyllide et Flora,* str. 66.

[3] It would be hard to say what else he had to do at the top of the
Bismantova in the province of Reggio, *Purgat.,* iv, 26. The precision with
which he brings before us all the parts of his supernatural world shows
a remarkable sense of form and space.

the days of antiquity who did so. In Boccaccio we can do
little more than infer how country scenery affected him;[4]
yet his pastoral romances show his imagination to have
been filled with it. But the significance of nature for a
receptive spirit is fully and clearly displayed by Petrarch—
one of the first truly modern men.

4. Petrarch was not only a distinguished geographer—
the first map of Italy is said to have been drawn by his
direction[5]—and not only a reproducer of the sayings of the
ancients,[6] but felt himself the influence of natural beauty.
The enjoyment of nature is, for him, the favourite accompaniment of intellectual pursuits; it was to combine the
two that he lived in learned retirement at Vaucluse and
elsewhere, that he from time to time fled from the world
and from his age.[7] We should do him wrong by inferring
from his weak and undeveloped power of describing natural
scenery that he did not feel it deeply. His picture, for instance, of the lovely Gulf of Spezia and Porto Venere, which
he inserts at the end of the sixth book of the *Africa,* for
the reason that none of the ancients or moderns had sung
of it,[8] is no more than a simple enumeration, but Petrarch
is also conscious of the beauty of rock scenery, and is perfectly able to distinguish the picturesqueness from the utility
of nature.[9] During his stay among the woods of Reggio, the

[4] Besides the description of Baiae in the *Fiammetta,* of the grove in the
Ameto, etc., a passage in the *De genealogia deorum,* xiv, 11, is of importance, where he enumerates a number of rural beauties—trees, meadows, brooks, flocks and herds, cottages, etc.—and adds that these things
"animum mulcent"; their effect is "mentem in se colligere."

[5] Libri, *Hist. des Sciences Mathématiques,* ii, 249.

[6] He is fond of referring to them: e.g. *De vita solitaria,* esp. p. 241,
where he quotes the description of a vine-arbour from St. Augustine.

[7] *Epist. famil.,* vii, 4, page 675. "*Interea utinam scire posses, quanta
cum voluptate solivagus ac liber, inter montes et nemora, inter fontes et
flumina, inter libros et maximorum hominum ingenia respiro, quamque
me in ea, quae ante sunt, cum Apostolo extendens et praeterita oblivisci
nitor et praesentia non videre.*" Comp. vi. 3, p. 665.

[8] "*Jacuit sine carmine sacro.*" Comp. *Itinerar. Syriacum,* p. 558.

[9] He distinguishes in the *Itinerar. Syr.,* p. 557, on the Riviera di Levante:
"*colles asperitate gratissima et mira fertilitate conspicuos.*" On the port
of Gaeta, see his *De remediis utriusque fortunae,* i, 54.

sudden sight of an impressive landscape so affected him that
he resumed a poem which he had long laid aside.[10] But
the deepest impression of all was made upon him by the
ascent of Mont Ventoux, near Avignon.[11] An indefinable
longing for a distant panorama grew stronger and stronger
in him, till at length the accidental sight of a passage in
Livy, where King Philip, the enemy of Rome, ascends
the Haemus, decided him. He thought that what was not
blamed in a grey-headed monarch might be well *excused*
in a young man of private station. The ascent of a mountain for its own sake was unheard of, and there could be
no thought of the companionship of friends or acquaintances. Petrarch took with him only his younger brother
and two country people from the last place where he halted.
At the foot of the mountain an old herdsman besought
him to turn back, saying that he himself had attempted to
climb it fifty years before, and had brought home nothing
but repentance, broken bones, and torn clothes, and that
neither before nor after had anyone ventured to do the
same. Nevertheless, they struggled upward, till the clouds
lay beneath their feet, and at last they reached the top. A
description of the view from the summit would be looked
for in vain, not because the poet was insensible to it, but, on
the contrary, because the impression was too overwhelming.
His whole past life, with all its follies, rose before his mind;
he remembered that ten years ago that day he had quitted
Bologna a young man, and turned a longing gaze towards
his native country; he opened a book which then was his
constant companion, the *Confessions of St. Augustine,* and
his eye fell on the passage in the tenth chapter, "and men
go forth, and admire lofty mountains and broad seas, and
roaring torrents, and the ocean, and the course of the stars,
and forget their own selves while doing so." His brother,
to whom he read these words, could not understand why
he closed the book and said no more.

❈ ❈ ❈

[10] *Letter to Posterity: "Subito loco specie percussus."*
[11] *Epist. fam.,* ed., Fracassetti, i, 193 *seq.*

Burckhardt's *Renaissance* may be classified as *Kulturgeschichte,* that is to say, the description of the culture of a period or a people and the analysis of its evolution. Culture comprises such aspects of human life as moral and religious ideas, domestic and social manners, taste, sensibilities, and amusements. When you say, "City people are always in a hurry," or "Americans are politically backward," or "The movie habit has made us forget how to play," you are dabbling in *Kulturgeschichte.* There is nothing wrong in that.

Your analyses, however, are likely to be wrong—and entertaining. For such analysis necessarily involves a good deal of generalization and interpretation. Burckhardt supported his theses by the citation of notable and representative documents, and his conclusions are no less interesting for being somewhat abstract.

1. Burckhardt distinguishes three stages in the development of nature appreciation among modern Europeans (i.e., excluding the ancients, ll. 9-15). Mark off the sections in the text, and briefly define each stage.

2. Explain, in one sentence if possible, what the loftiness of medieval castles (l. 35) has to do with Burckhardt's argument concerning the epic poets.

3. List the items of evidence intended to demonstrate that Petrarch "felt the influence of natural beauty." Some of these items are more convincing as evidence than others; indicate their relative value as evidence by numbering them, beginning with the least persuasive. (You may have to make arbitrary decisions as to which of any two should stand higher; be able, however, to justify the general order of your ratings.)

4. Now with this series as a scale, evaluate the evidence for Boccaccio.

5. The reference in lines 59-60 is to a passage in the *Purgatorio,* canto I:

> "L'alba vinceva l'ora mattutina
>   che fuggia innanzi, si che di lontano
>   conobbi il tremolar della marina."

(The dawn was vanquishing the breath of morn which fled before her, so that from afar I recognized the trembling of the sea.—Trans. Mr. Thomas Okey.)

A few brief passages of this sort may seem hardly to demon-strate a poet's sensibilities. The lines from the *Purgatorio, iv,* 25 f., are translated:

> One can walk at Sanleo and get down to Noli; one can mount Bismantova to its summit, with feet alone; but here a man must fly, I mean with the swift wings and with the plumes of great desire, behind that Leader, who gave me hope, and was a light to me. (Okey.)

Evaluate each of the two Dante exhibits, again using the Pe-trarch evidence as a scale.

6. Which do you think harder to prove, that the wandering clerks *did not* have a feeling for landscape or that Dante *did?* Why?

7. What is implied in lines 7-9 to be the function of art? Explain this function in terms broad enough to include paint-ing as well as literature, and do not limit it to landscape painting and landscape poetry.

8. Burckhardt, though remarking that certain races may be "specially fitted to understand the spirit of natural scenery," is here chiefly concerned to chronicle the development of a conscious feeling for nature. In the two following passages there are attempts to account for that development.

> Classical mythology, instead of embellishing nature, falsi-fies it, minimizes it, and destroys its true charm. Thus the ancients had no descriptive poetry; although Hesiod, Theoc-ritus, and Vergil depicted the labors, the customs, and the pleasures of rural life, their works contain hardly a sug-gestion of that landscape poetry which enriches our literature, visions of the countryside, the seasons, the skies. These men were surely sensitive enough to have observed nature and skillful enough to have described it, had they not been blinded by their mythology, which, peopling the universe with elegant phantoms, excluded seriousness, grandeur, soli-tude. The poet wandering by grove or stream encountered only the faun and the dryad, saw Priapus leering from the fork of an olive tree or Vertumnus and the zephyrs gliding in their endless dance. In sunset light athwart a forest or gleaming golden across the surging sea, in the daybreak splendors which daily remind us of the miracle of creation,

the ancients could see only an ingenious stage machinery, manipulated by their ridiculous troops of comic opera deities. Naiads and sylvans are pleasant fancies, but what have they to offer the heart and the mind?

How much more fortunate the Christian poet in the solitudes, where God walks with him! For Christianity banished these fauns and nymphs and satyrs, and so restored silence to the caverns, to the forests their reveries. The wilderness became melancholy and sublime, the heavens more vastly arched; the little urns of the river nymphs were broken, and the torrents plunged from mountain crag down to the ultimate abyss. The true God, reappearing in His handiwork, imparted something of His own immensity to nature.

Yet were man to reject God, remaining but a thinking thing, unattended, unobserved, he would be more august in his loneliness than surrounded by the trivial deities of classic fable. For the empty wilderness would respond in harmony to the vastness of his thought, the weariness of his passions, his loathing of a life without illusion and without hope.

There is in man an instinct which finds its correspondence in nature. Who has not sat for hours by a river, watching the movement of the waves? Who has not rejoiced, by the seashore, at the white foam flung by a distant reef? One may pity the ancients, whose Ocean was but the palace of Neptune, the grotto of Proteus, and who saw only the escapades of Tritons and Nereids in that vast tumult of waters which seems to us a turbulent echo of our souls, filling us with vague desire to quit our own life, to lose ourselves in nature, and to mingle with its Author.—Chateaubriand.[12]

The appreciation of natural scenery is closely connected with the progress of political and material civilisation. As soon as the western traveller had decent roads, and was relieved from the fear of robbery and murder whenever he passed by a wood, he began to look about him with relish. For obvious reasons this stage was reached at widely separated dates in various countries. In primitive phases of development man saw with pleasure, and therefore wished to be reminded of

[12] Adapted from *Le Genie du Christianisme*, by Chateaubriand, Part 2, Book 4, Chapter 1.

only what Ruskin called "the available and useful"—fertile
meadows, prosperous towns, vineyards, still waterways, young
isolated trees. The very sight of mountain and rock was
horrible, recalling arduous journeys and robbers; the forest
was similarly connected with wild beasts and outlaws, old
trees with goblins, the sea with shipwreck. Landscape in the
Homeric epoch and in the Middle Ages is therefore confined
to references to "smiling" scenes, gardens, and sheltered
nooks.—Christopher Hussey.[13]

Write an essay comparing Burckhardt, Chateaubriand, and
Mr. Hussey. There may be several ways to organize such an
essay; a bad one would be simply to summarize each passage,
one at a time. Review the subject itself with reference to the
ideas of the three men, noting how they differ as to facts or in
their explanations of them. Comment on the soundness of
their methods or their conclusions.

9.   In this passage Burckhardt has argued from the sensibilities of certain individual Italians to the sensibilities of the
Italians as a people. (Cf. ll. 2-4.) Do you think such reasoning
is sound? This question cannot be answered with a plain "yes"
or "no"; since it involves other postulates, as to the nature of
history, the relation of the individual to his society, etc., you
will have to explain your position, for or against, at some length.

10.   In the preceding pages of his chapter on "The Discovery
of the World and of Man," Burckhardt has discussed the new
scientific interests of the Italian Renaissance, as revealed in geographical treatises, the popular knowledge of astronomy, bo-
tanical collections, menageries, and studs. Compare the "nature" to which the scientist draws near with the "nature"
whose discovery Burckhardt traces in this passage. Write up
your definitions in a short essay; you should be able to make
the two concepts plain in something between 100 and 500 words.
Support your abstract terms with illustrations. (Does one
"nature" include the other, or are they mutually exclusive?
What have the two concepts in common? How do they differ? Definition involves setting limits: what is *not* "nature"?
These questions are intended to direct your thought, not to outline your essay. Dictionary definitions will start your ideas;

[13] From *The Picturesque,* by Christopher Hussey; reprinted by permission of Putnam and Company, Ltd.

they may not take you very far and need not be quoted in your essay.)

11. *Nazi* is a cognate of *nature;* what other, more comely cognates can you find?

12. Explain the derivations of *clerk, folly, German, knight, minstrel, monarch, perspective, taint.*

HAWKINS[1]

JAMES ANTHONY FROUDE

•

1. THE SALE OF NEGROES IN THE WEST INDIES BEING THE
very thing which Philip was most desirous to prevent, it was
not very clear how it could be prosecuted as innocently as
Hawkins pretended. His arguments, however, or the great-
5 ness of the temptation, satisfied Elizabeth's scruples. In
October, 1567, he sailed from Plymouth with five well-ap-
pointed vessels, one of them the Queen's ship *Jesus*, which
carried his flag on his first voyage; and among those who
went with him was the after-hero of English history, his
10 young "kinsman," Francis Drake.

2. The voyage, though commencing with a storm, was
prosperous beyond the most glittering hopes which he had
formed upon his past successes. Hawkins ran down to
Sierra Leone, where he formed an alliance with a tribe
15 which were at war with a neighbouring tribe. He sacked a
densely peopled town, and was rewarded with as many
prisoners as he could stow; and by the spring of the following year he was among the Spanish settlements, doing
a business which realised the wildest dreams of Eldorado.
20 Where the ports were open he found an easy market; where
the governor attempted to keep him out he forced an
entrance as usual, and found the planters no less willing
to deal with him. Stray ships were stopped and plundered
where their cargoes were worth the seizure. And thus before
25 the summer was over he had amassed, in bars of gold and
silver, in precious stones and other commodities, property
worth more than a million pounds. Before he could sail for
England the ships' bottoms required a scouring. Their spars

[1] From *History of England from the Fall of Wolsey to the Death of
Elizabeth.*

had suffered in a gale of wind in the gulf of Mexico. At
the beginning of September, therefore, he put into St. Jean 30
de Luz to refit, take in water and provisions, and dispose of
four hundred Negroes, "the best and choicest" which he
had, that still remained unsold.

3. The halcyon weather was about to close in a tornado.
The small harbour of St. Jean de Luz is formed by a 35
natural breakwater which lies across the mouth of the bay.
The day after the English ships entered, a Spanish fleet
appeared outside, consisting of thirteen men-of-war, the
smallest of them larger than the *Jesus*, a force from which
in the open sea escape might have been possible, but with 40
which, under the fairest conditions, it would have been
madness to have sought an engagement. If Hawkins could
have made up his mind to dispute the entrance of a Spanish
admiral into one of his own harbours, he believed that he
could have saved himself, for the channel was narrow, and 45
the enemy's numbers would give him no advantage. But
neither his own nor Elizabeth's ingenuity could have invented a pretext for an act of such desperate insolence. At
best he would be blockaded, and sooner or later would
have to run. The Spaniards passed in and anchored close 50
on board the Englishmen. For three days there was an in-
terchange of ambiguous courtesies. On the fourth Philip's
admiral had satisfied himself of Hawkins' identity. He had
been especially sent upon this coast to look for him; and
by the laws of nations he was unquestionably justified in 55
treating the English commander as a pirate. The form of
calling on him to surrender was dispensed with. The name
of Hawkins was so terrible that the Spaniards dared not
give him warning that he was to be attacked. They took
possession of the mole in the dark, and mounted batteries 60
upon it; and then from shore and sea every gun which
could be brought to bear opened upon the *Jesus* and her
comrades. Taken by surprise, for many of their boats'
crews were in the town, the English fought so desperately
that two of the largest of the Spanish ships were sunk, and 65
another set on fire. The men on shore forced their way

on board to their companions; and, notwithstanding the tremendous odds, the result of the action still seemed uncertain, when the Spaniards sent down two fireships, and then 70 Hawkins saw that all was over, and that vessels and treasures were lost. The only hope now was to save the men. The survivors of them were crowded on board two small tenders, one of fifty tons, the other rather larger, and leaving the *Jesus* and the other ships, the gold and silver bars, the 75 Negroes, and their other spoils to burn or sink, they crawled out under the fire of the mole and gained the open sea. There their position scarcely seemed less desperate. They were short of food and water. Their vessels had suffered heavily under the fire; they were choked up with men, and 80 there was not a harbour west of the Atlantic where they could venture to run; a hundred seamen volunteered to take their chance on shore some leagues distant down the coast, and after wandering miserably in the woods for a few days, they were taken and carried as prisoners to 85 Mexico. Hawkins and Drake, and the rest, made sail for the English Channel, which in due time, in torn and wretched plight, they contrived to reach.

※ ※ ※

Most of the narrative you have previously considered has been expository: the story was told in order to develop a thesis. Expository narrative is supported by the thesis, which gives it its point. (You may wonder whether the passages by King and Duhamel are exceptions to this principle.) The interest of Froude's narrative, however, remains within the story itself. There is no external point, no lurking argument, no droll or pathetic characterization to compel the reader's attention, which must thus be held by the action itself, the succession of events. This pure narrative, though logically simpler than expository narrative, is probably harder to write well. You may recognize in Froude's yarn a certain urgency of movement; one goes briskly through it and wants to get along; one feeds and is yet in appetite. This impetus has nothing to do with suspense of the who-done-it sort; nor may it be achieved in sheer violence of subject matter: a massacre may be the dullest thing. It derives technically from the construction of the whole narrative and from the handling of the single sentences.

A narrative may cover the events of a year in one paragraph, the events of a day in another, the events of an hour in another. The principle is plain enough; in practice the beginner, especially if he spins his tale as he goes along, may overlook the possibility of his changing his stride. Having got his hero to Sierra Leone in two sentences, he will take him to the Gulf in two more and home with a thud halfway down the first page. Or, more cautiously, he will chronicle each particular plunder and so spend five pages and his reader's patience getting to St. Jean de Luz. The shift of time perspective, from broad summary to minute detail or the other way around, comes naturally enough, however, if one first marks out the story in sections.

1. Give a title to each of the following parts: a) lines 11-33, b) lines 34-52, c) lines 52-76, d) lines 77-87. How much time, by calendar or clock, is covered in each?

2. A whole series of military actions is contained in "forced an entrance as usual"; another action is given in part of a sentence (ll. 15-16); a third is described at length (ll. 59-76). Justify this inequality.

3. Are we to assume that Hawkins first entered all the open ports, then all the closed ports, and that he then plundered ships?

4. The urgency of the narrative is due in part to Froude's knack of making us look ahead: by forecasts ("The voyage . . . was prosperous," ll. 11-12) or by statements of plans ("Before he could sail for England . . . ," ll. 27-28). Find several other such anticipatory phrases or sentences.

Moreover, a certain forward impetus is achieved in the movement of the thought of the sentences. Compare the following alternative with lines 37-43:

A Spanish fleet appeared outside the harbor the day after the English ships had entered. It consisted of thirteen men-of-war, all larger than the *Jesus,* a force with which it would have been madness to have sought an engagement under the fairest conditions, but from which escape might have been possible in the open sea.

In the first sentence, the reversal of the time order brakes the thought. The second, although here there is no question of time order, moves in the wrong direction. As Hawkins is not in the open sea, the possibility of escape there is hypothetical; but an engagement, which it would have been madness to have sought, is impending. Thus Froude's sentence points toward the future action.

5. Using the principles of *time order* and *logical direction* as criteria, compare the following alternatives with the text. The changes may not all be for the worse.

a) Hawkins ran down to Sierra Leone, where, finding two tribes at war, he formed an alliance with one against the other. (Cf. ll. 13-15.)

b) Here he acquired as many prisoners as he could stow, by helping in the sack of a densely populated town. (Cf. ll. 15-17.)

c) Sales were lively in the open ports; nor were the planters less willing to deal with him when, as usual, he had forced an entrance against the governor's attempt to exclude him. (Cf. ll. 20-23.)

d) When the cargoes promised to be worth seizing, stray ships were stopped and plundered. (Cf. ll. 23-24.)

e) Hawkins' reputation was too terrible for the Spaniards to indulge in the formality of demanding his surrender. Not daring to warn him that he was to be attacked, they took possession of the mole in the dark and mounted batteries upon it. When every gun which could be brought to bear upon the *Jesus* and her comrades opened fire, from shore and sea, the English were taken by surprise, for many of their boats' crews were in town. Yet the English fought so desperately that . . . (Cf. ll. 56-65.)

f) They dared not seek refuge in any harbor west of the Atlantic; nor would they venture upon the high seas in vessels so choked up with men and so badly damaged by the Spanish fire. (Cf. ll. 78-81.)

6. Do you think the length of sentences has anything to do with the rapidity of narrative? Compare the following alternative with lines 13-18:

Hawkins ran down to Sierra Leone. Here he formed an alliance with a tribe which were at war with a neighboring tribe. He sacked a densely peopled town. He was rewarded

with as many prisoners as he could stow. By the spring of the
following year . . .

Find the notably short sentences in Froude's passage; can you
detect any method in their use?

7. Comment on the following changes of wording: *glittering* (l. 12) to *audacious; realized* (l. 19) to *comprehended; other
commodities* (l. 26) to *Negroes; desperate* (l. 48) to *reckless;
ambiguous* (l. 52) to *equivocal; terrible* (l. 58) to *awful; choked
up* (l. 79) to *overburdened*.

8. Which do you think the most forceful word in lines 11-
27? (Try several; then decide.)

9. Explain the derivations of *pirate, buccaneer, corsair,
rover*.

10. Write a narrative based upon a personal experience.
(How you were caught on the bay in a storm, if you like,
or the fight at Adelaide's birthday party, or how you got even
with the deacon—but *not* the time it turned out to be only the
cat!)

[Source materials for historical narrative may be found in
such works as Hakluyt's *Principal Navigation;* the Publications
of the Hakluyt Society; *Purchas His Pilgrims,* 20 vols., Glas-
gow, 1905-1907; *Voyages and Travels,* 2 vols., ed., C. R. Beaz-
ley, in An English Garner; *Narratives of the Indian Wars,* ed.,
Charles Henry Lincoln, New York, 1913; the Original narratives of early American history series, gen. ed., J. Franklin
Jameson, New York, 1906-1917. The assigned material should
contain fairly active narrative and not merely reports of things
seen; Marco Polo, for instance, is not suitable for the sort of
theme that might be modeled on this passage by Froude.]

A JESUIT IN THE WILDERNESS[1]

FRANCIS PARKMAN

•

1. NOW, LEAVING THE RIVER BEHIND, THEY ENTERED THOSE savage highlands whence issue the springs of the St. John, —a wilderness of rugged mountain-ranges, clad in dense, continuous forests, with no human tenant but this troop of
5 miserable rovers, and here and there some kindred band, as miserable as they. Winter had set in, and already dead Nature was sheeted in funereal white. Lakes and ponds were frozen, rivulets sealed up, torrents encased with stalactites of ice; the black rocks and the black trunks of the
10 pine-trees were beplastered with snow, and its heavy masses crushed the dull green boughs into the drifts beneath. The forest was silent as the grave.

2. Through this desolation the long file of Indians made its way, all on snow-shoes, each man, woman, and child
15 bending under a heavy load, or dragging a sledge, narrow, but of prodigious length. They carried their whole wealth with them, on their backs or on their sledges,—kettles, axes, bales of meat, if such they had, and huge rolls of birch-bark for covering their wigwams. The Jesuit was loaded
20 like the rest. The dogs alone floundered through the drifts unburdened. There was neither path nor level ground. De-scending, climbing, stooping beneath half-fallen trees, clam-bering over piles of prostrate trunks, struggling through matted cedar-swamps, threading chill ravines, and crossing
25 streams no longer visible, they toiled on till the day began to decline, then stopped to encamp. Burdens were thrown down, and sledges unladen. The squaws, with knives and hatchets, cut long poles of birch and spruce saplings; while the men, with snow-shoes for shovels, cleared a round or

[1] From *The Jesuits in North America.*

square space in the snow, which formed an upright wall 30
three or four feet high, inclosing the area of the wigwam.
On one side, a passage was cut for an entrance, and the
poles were planted around the top of the wall of snow,
sloping and converging. On these poles were spread the
sheets of birch-bark; a bear-skin was hung in the passage- 35
way for a door; the bare ground within and the surrounding snow were covered with spruce boughs; and the work
was done.

3. This usually occupied about three hours, during
which Le Jeune, spent with travel, and weakened by pre- 40
carious and unaccustomed fare, had the choice of shivering
in idleness, or taking part in a labor which fatigued, without warming, his exhausted frame. The sorcerer's wife was
in far worse case. Though in the extremity of a mortal sickness, they left her lying in the snow till the wigwam was 45
made,—without a word, on her part, of remonstrance or
complaint. Le Jeune, to the great ire of her husband, sometimes spent the interval in trying to convert her; but she
proved intractable, and soon died unbaptized.

4. Thus lodged, they remained so long as game could be 50
found within a circuit of ten or twelve miles, and then,
subsistence failing, removed to another spot. Early in the
winter, they hunted the beaver and the Canada porcupine;
and, later, in the season of deep snows, chased the moose
and the caribou.   55

5. Put aside the bear-skin, and enter the hut. Here, in a
space some thirteen feet square, were packed nineteen savages, men, women, and children, with their dogs, crouched,
squatted, coiled like hedgehogs, or lying on their backs,
with knees drawn up perpendicularly to keep their feet out 60
of the fire. Le Jeune, always methodical, arranges the griev-
ances inseparable from these rough quarters under four
chief heads,—Cold, Heat, Smoke, and Dogs. The bark
covering was full of crevices, through which the icy blasts
streamed in upon him from all sides; and the hole above, 65
at once window and chimney, was so large, that, as he lay,
he could watch the stars as well as in the open air. While

the fire in the midst, fed with fat pine-knots, scorched him
on one side, on the other he had much ado to keep himself
70 from freezing. At times, however, the crowded hut seemed
heated to the temperature of an oven. But these evils were
light, when compared to the intolerable plague of smoke.
During a snow-storm, and often at other times, the wigwam
was filled with fumes so dense, stifling, and acrid, that all
75 its inmates were forced to lie flat on their faces, breathing
through mouths in contact with the cold earth. Their
throats and nostrils felt as if on fire; their scorched eyes
streamed with tears; and when Le Jeune tried to read, the
letters of his breviary seemed printed in blood. The dogs
80 were not an unmixed evil, for, by sleeping on and around
him, they kept him warm at night; but, as an offset to this
good service, they walked, ran, and jumped over him as he
lay, snatched the food from his birchen dish, or, in a mad
rush at some bone or discarded morsel, now and then
85 overset both dish and missionary.

6. Sometimes of an evening he would leave the filthy
den, to read his breviary in peace by the light of the moon.
In the forest around sounded the sharp crack of frost-riven
trees; and from the horizon to the zenith shot up the silent
90 meteors of the northern lights, in whose fitful flashings the
awe-struck Indians beheld the dancing of the spirits of the
dead. The cold gnawed him to the bone, and, his devotions
over, he turned back shivering. The illumined hut, from
many a chink and crevice, shot forth into the gloom long
95 streams of light athwart the twisted boughs. He stooped
and entered. All within glowed red and fiery around the
blazing pine-knots, where, like brutes in their kennel, were
gathered the savage crew. He stepped to his place, over
recumbent bodies and leggined and moccasined limbs, and
100 seated himself on the carpet of spruce boughs. Here a tribulation awaited him, the crowning misery of his winter-
quarters,—worse, as he declares, than cold, heat, and dogs.

7. Of the three brothers who had invited him to join the
party, one, we have seen, was the hunter, Mestigoit; another,
105 the sorcerer; and the third, Pierre, whom, by reason of his

falling away from the Faith, Le Jeune always mentions as
the Apostate. He was a weak-minded young Indian, wholly
under the influence of his brother, the sorcerer, who, if not
more vicious, was far more resolute and wily. From the
antagonism of their respective professions, the sorcerer hated 110
the priest, who lost no opportunity of denouncing his in-
cantations, and who ridiculed his perpetual singing and
drumming as puerility and folly. The former, being an
indifferent hunter, and disabled by a disease which he had
contracted, depended for subsistence on his credit as a 115
magician; and, in undermining it, Le Jeune not only outraged his pride, but threatened his daily bread. He used
every device to retort ridicule on his rival. At the outset, he
had proffered his aid to Le Jeune in his study of the Algonquin, and palmed off upon him the foulest words in the 120
language as the equivalent of things spiritual. Thus it happened, that, while the missionary sought to explain to the
assembled wigwam some point of Christian doctrine, he
was interrupted by peals of laughter from men, children,
and squaws. And now, as Le Jeune took his place in the 125
circle, the sorcerer bent upon him his malignant eyes, and
began that course of rude bantering which filled to overflowing the cup of the Jesuit's woes. All took their cue from
him, and made their afflicted guest the butt of their inane
witticisms. "Look at him! His face is like a dog's!"—"His 130
head is like a pumpkin!"—"He has a beard like a rabbit's!"
The missionary bore in silence these and countless similar
attacks; indeed, so sorely was he harassed, that, lest he
should exasperate his tormentor, he sometimes passed whole
days without uttering a word. 135

8. There was one point touching which Le Jeune and his
Jesuit brethren had as yet been unable to solve their doubts.
Were the Indian sorcerers mere impostors, or were they in
actual league with the Devil? That the fiends who possess
this land of darkness make their power felt by action direct 140
and potential upon the persons of its wretched inhabitants
there is, argues Le Jeune, good reason to conclude; since

it is a matter of grave notoriety, that the fiends who infest Brazil are accustomed cruelly to beat and otherwise tor- 145 ment the natives of that country, as many travellers attest. "A Frenchman worthy of credit," pursues the Father, "has told me that he has heard with his own ears the voice of the Demon and the sound of the blows which he discharges upon these his miserable slaves; and in reference to this a 150 very remarkable fact has been reported to me, namely, that, when a Catholic approaches, the Devil takes flight and beats these wretches no longer, but that in presence of a Hugue- not he does not stop beating them."

9.   Thus prone to believe in the immediate presence of 155 the nether powers, Le Jeune watched the sorcerer with an eye prepared to discover in his conjurations the signs of a genuine diabolic agency. His observations, however, led him to a different result; and he could detect in his rival nothing but a vile compound of impostor and dupe. The 160 sorcerer believed in the efficacy of his own magic, and was continually singing and beating his drum to cure the dis- ease from which he was suffering. Towards the close of the winter, Le Jeune fell sick, and, in his pain and weakness, nearly succumbed under the nocturnal uproar of the sor- 165 cerer, who, hour after hour, sang and drummed without mercy,—sometimes yelling at the top of his throat, then hissing like a serpent, then striking his drum on the ground as if in a frenzy, then leaping up, raving about the wigwam, and calling on the women and children to join him in sing- 170 ing. Now ensued a hideous din; for every throat was strained to the utmost, and all were beating with sticks or fists on the bark of the hut to increase the noise with the charitable object of aiding the sorcerer to conjure down his malady, or drive away the evil spirit that caused it.

175   10.   He had an enemy, a rival sorcerer, whom he charged with having caused by charms the disease that afflicted him. He therefore announced that he should kill him. As the rival dwelt at Gaspé, a hundred leagues off, the present execution of the threat might appear difficult; but distance

was no bar to the vengeance of the sorcerer. Ordering all 180
the children and all but one of the women to leave the
wigwam, he seated himself, with the woman who remained,
on the ground in the centre, while the men of the party,
together with those from other wigwams in the neighborhood, sat in a ring around. Mestigoit, the sorcerer's brother, 185
then brought in the charm, consisting of a few small pieces
of wood, some arrowheads, a broken knife, and an iron
hook, which he wrapped in a piece of hide. The woman
next rose, and walked around the hut, behind the company.
Mestigoit and the sorcerer now dug a large hole with two 190
pointed stakes, the whole assembly singing, drumming, and
howling meanwhile with a deafening uproar. The hole
made, the charm, wrapped in the hide, was thrown into it.
Pierre, the Apostate, then brought a sword and a knife to
the sorcerer, who, seizing them, leaped into the hole, and, 195
with furious gesticulation, hacked and stabbed at the charm,
yelling with the whole force of his lungs. At length he
ceased, displayed the knife and sword stained with blood,
proclaimed that he had mortally wounded his enemy, and
demanded if none present had heard his death-cry. The 200
assembly, more occupied in making noises than in listening
for them, gave no reply, till at length two young men declared that they had heard a faint scream, as if from a great
distance; whereat a shout of gratulation and triumph rose
from all the company. . . . 205

11. ' Nowhere was his magic more in requisition than in
procuring a successful chase to the hunters,—a point of vital
interest, since on it hung the lives of the whole party. They
often, however, returned empty-handed; and, for one, two,
or three successive days, no other food could be had than 210
the bark of trees or scraps of leather. So long as tobacco
lasted, they found solace in their pipes, which seldom left
their lips. "Unhappy infidels," writes Le Jeune, "who spend
their lives in smoke, and their eternity in flames!"

12. As Christmas approached, their condition grew des- 215
perate. Beavers and porcupines were scarce, and the snow

was not deep enough for hunting the moose. Night and
day the medicine-drums and medicine-songs resounded
from the wigwams, mingled with the wail of starving chil-
220 dren. The hunters grew weak and emaciated; and, as after
a forlorn march the wanderers encamped once more in
the lifeless forest, the priest remembered that it was the
eve of Christmas. "The Lord gave us for our supper a porcupine, large as a sucking pig, and also a rabbit. It was
225 not much, it is true, for eighteen or nineteen persons; but
the Holy Virgin and St. Joseph, her glorious spouse, were
not so well treated, on this very day, in the stable of
Bethlehem."

13. On Christmas Day, the despairing hunters, again
230 unsuccessful, came to pray succor from Le Jeune. Even the
Apostate had become tractable, and the famished sorcerer
was ready to try the efficacy of an appeal to the deity of
his rival. A bright hope possessed the missionary. He composed two prayers, which, with the aid of the repentant
235 Pierre, he translated into Algonquin. Then he hung against
the side of the hut a napkin which he had brought with
him, and against the napkin a crucifix and a reliquary, and,
this done, caused all the Indians to kneel before them, with
hands raised and clasped. He now read one of the prayers,
240 and required the Indians to repeat the other after him,
promising to renounce their superstitions, and obey Christ,
whose image they saw before them, if he would give them
food and save them from perishing. The pledge given, he
dismissed the hunters with a benediction. At night they
245 returned with game enough to relieve the immediate necessity. All was hilarity. The kettles were slung, and the feasters
assembled. Le Jeune rose to speak, when Pierre, who, having killed nothing, was in ill humor, said, with a laugh,
that the crucifix and the prayer had nothing to do with
250 their good luck; while the sorcerer, his jealousy reviving as
he saw his hunger about to be appeased, called out to the
missionary, "Hold your tongue! You have no sense!" As
usual, all took their cue from him. They fell to their repast

with ravenous jubilation, and the disappointed priest sat dejected and silent.

※ ※ ※

For the glory of God, the Jesuits entered a wilderness truly demon-haunted. Nor were these demons the romantically conceived woodland spirits who smiled from grassy glens upon fair-haired Teutons and whose expulsion by the Cross Burckhardt lamented. These demons—or their equivalent—enslaved the savages of North America, and Le Jeune, leaving a civilization in which one was never very far from the sight of a church steeple, undertook a life so bestial, so inadequately clothed and fed and sheltered, that none of us who have no cross to guard our souls could withstand it. One begins to comprehend that the old word "Christendom" was more than a territorial designation.

Such was the expedition which Parkman, the historian of French discovery and colonization in the New World, has here described. The two cultures, that of the Algonquins and that of Le Jeune, are drawn in firm clear lines. The first and easiest condition of Parkman's success was his sympathetic reading of Le Jeune's narrative. Then he had to plot his own story, and some of the following questions may help you to understand how this was done.

But the final requirement was his mastery of prose; in the editor's opinion, this is the most beautiful prose you are likely to read this year or next. It has the elegance of seeming far simpler than it is. Parkman did not avoid rhetoric or affect a colloquial idiom, but his rhetoric calls no attention to itself and exists only to express what he has to say. And this prose is graceful: its movement reflects the movement of its thought. Every sentence, it will appear on close examination, was planned to present its words and their concepts to the reader's intelligence in precisely the right order; yet there is no awkwardness. The beauty of Parkman's prose may be compared to that of the fleur-de-lis: white lilies gold-encircled.

1. Locate on a map the territory in which Le Jeune and the Algonquins passed the winter. Define its situation.

2. Parkman found in Le Jeune's narrative of his winter with the Algonquins a certain dramatic quality which he

enhanced in his presentation of the story. Two antagonists are at cross-purposes. Who are they? What are the motives and aims of each of them? How do their purposes conflict?

3. Before exhibiting the conflict, Parkman had to convey preliminary information: the general locale or background; the foreground or stage-setting proper; the character of each of the two main actors. Where has he done each of these four things?

4. In lines 3-20, the range of vision is gradually narrowed until the reader's attention is focused, as in a "close-up," upon Le Jeune. Distinguish four stages in this process, marking them off in the text and naming them. Which phrases act as transitions between these several stages?

5. Compare the description in lines 6-12 with that in lines 21-25. Which is more pictorial? Why do the half-fallen trees, the swamps, and the ravines belong in Par. 2 rather than in Par. 1?

6. Although the four discomforts described in Par. 5 fell upon all the inmates of the hut, they were most grievous to Le Jeune. Which phrases apply exclusively to Le Jeune? What do they reveal of his character?

7. By the end of Par. 7 the reader—almost without realizing it—is into the thick of the conflict. Parkman has exhibited this conflict in a series of episodes, as follows: lines 118-125, lines 125-135, lines 160-174, Par. 10, Par. 11, Par. 12, Par. 13. For convenience of reference, give a brief title to each of these episodes.

Give a decision on each episode: whose round was it? Or was it a draw? Explain your decision on Pars. 10, 11, and 12.

8. Some of these episodes, like Par. 6, are generalized from a series of similar events; others represent particular occasions. Which are of each kind? Whereas generalized episodes may be arranged in any order without regard to time sequence, a report of a single occasion may contain some clue as to chronology. How has Parkman departed from strict time order in presenting the seven rounds of the contest?

9. Account for his arrangement. Why should the first two episodes (ll. 118-125, 125-135) be at the beginning? The next two are obviously an inseparable group, and so are the last

three; what would be the effects of reversing the position of the two groups?

10. Wishing to include Le Jeune's theological speculations somewhere in his narrative, Parkman has managed to introduce this material in Par. 8, without digressing from his main line. What is the significance of the question raised in Par. 8 with reference to the dramatic conflict? (Perhaps you are not accustomed to regard evil as the result of a supernatural and personal agency, but Le Jeune, who was neither stupid nor unconcerned, found this assumption plausible.) Why is this a good point to insert the discussion of theology, rather than earlier or later in the story?

11. What is the dramatic function of lines 43-49?

12. Divide Par. 6 into two sections; what elements of contrast, physical and spiritual, can you find between them? The paragraph is beautiful; has it any point?

13. Explain why each of the following alternatives is inferior to the text:

a) Here nineteen savages, men, women, and children, crouched, squatted, coiled like hedgehogs, or lying on their backs, with knees drawn up perpendicularly to keep their feet out of the fire, were packed, with their dogs, in a space some thirteen feet square. (Cf. ll. 56-61.)

b) Long streams of light shot forth into the gloom from the many chinks and crevices of the illumined hut and fell athwart the twisted boughs. (Cf. ll. 93-95.)

c) Within the hut, the savage crew, like brutes in a kennel, were gathered around the blazing pine-knots, which glowed red and fiery. (Cf. ll. 96-98.)

d) Thus peals of laughter from men, children, and squaws interrupted the missionary when he sought to explain some point of Christian doctrine to the assembled wigwam. (Cf. ll. 121-125.)

14. Make similar rearrangements of four other sentences, and use your alternatives to demonstrate the felicity of Parkman's phrasing.

15. What was Le Jeune's crowning tribulation (l. 101), and why was it the crowning one?

16. Memorize Par. 6.

17. Read Chapter III, "Sympathetic Magic," of Sir James Frazer's *The Golden Bough*, one volume edition; then write a paragraph analyzing the procedure described in Par. 10.

18. Explain the derivations of *awe, charm, demon, devil, diabolic, doctrine, missionary, precarious, slave, sorcerer, tribulation*.

19. *Caribou* is an Algonquin word of interesting derivation; how many other words of Indian origin can you find in the passage?

THE SEA[1]

ALFRED ZIMMERN

•

1. EVERY ENGLISHMAN IS FAMILIAR WITH "THE SEA"; BUT the sea of the Greeks is not the sea that we know. Landlocked on all sides, as its name implies, except for the narrow exits at Gibraltar and the Dardanelles, the Mediterranean seems in summer as gentle as an inland lake. Yet to call it a lake 5 is to belie its possibilities. It is in fact double-natured, sometimes a lake far better adapted to oars than to sails, sometimes an ocean, not adapted, as a timid Greek navigator might say, for either: or to put it in his own language, a lake when the gods are kind, and an ocean when they are 10 spiteful. This double-natured sea has its own peculiarities, some of which have interesting bearings upon the life of those who dwell round it.

2. To begin with, it is not self-sufficing. It is a warm inland sea subject to constant shrinkage by evaporation, 15 and its supplies of fresh water are not enough to make up the deficiency. Only three large rivers—the Nile, the Po, and the Rhone—flow into it, and there is comparatively little rain.

3. If the Mediterranean were entirely landlocked, this 20 constant evaporation would gradually dry up parts of it altogether and reduce it to a chain of salt lakes, as some geologists say it once has been. As it is, it is considerably more salt than the outer ocean and becomes increasingly salt in its more eastern portions. Hence the collection of 25 salt in salt-pans or "salt-fixings," as the Greeks called them, is a simple process, and a trade in salt from the coast to the saltless people of the hinterland went on all through

[1] From *The Greek Commonwealth*, by Alfred Zimmern; reprinted by permission of the Clarendon Press, Oxford.

antiquity; salt was commonly exchanged for slaves, so com-
30 monly that a certain kind of cheap slave was known as a
"saltling." Only two of the Roman roads were not called
after their constructors: the Via Latina and the Via *Salaria*,
the old highway by which salt was conveyed up the Tiber
valley from Ostia to the interior.

35   4. The deficiency of water is, of course, made up at both
ends—from the outer ocean and from the big fresh-water
supplies brought by the Russian rivers and the Danube into
the Black Sea. But the straits of Gibraltar narrow to a little
over seven miles and are comparatively shallow; and in
40 antiquity they were a little narrower and shallower still.
They do not let in nearly enough water to equalize the
levels of the Mediterranean and the Atlantic. The Dardanelles and the Bosporus are still narrower. Hence there is
a strong current at both exits of the Mediterranean, and
45 this, together with the rush of wind through the straits,
made both the Atlantic and the Black Sea passages difficult
for seamen before the days of steam.

  5. The Greeks as a whole, before the Hellenistic age,
knew little of the Atlantic. For a long time their knowledge
50 ceased absolutely at Gibraltar or, as the Greeks named it,
the Pillars of Heracles. The name itself suggests the first
impression made upon a mariner from the East: for the
long ridge of the Rock, throwing out a tongue, or, as the
Greeks called it elsewhere, a Dog's Tail, into the strait,
55 looks anything but a pillar to seamen approaching from
the West. Then stray traders were blown by the Levanter
through the funnel of the straits, past Trafalgar, into the
bay of Cadiz, and discovered the "virgin market" of Tarshish
on the Guadalquivir. But beyond Cape St. Vincent they
60 knew nothing at all; even Heracles got no further than
Geryon's island in Cadiz Bay; "man cannot sail into the
darkness West of Cadiz; turn back the ship to the land of
Europe," says Pindar, as one of his many ways of breaking
off a long tale. Herodotus had heard stories of tin being
65 brought from the Tin Islands, but he could find out nothing
definite. Moreover, it is significant that he tells us of two

different pioneering companies who found their way to Tartessus—the Phocaeans and the Samian Colaeus. This was probably not because, as with the North Pole, there was a competition for the honour of discovery, but because the 70 route was so hazardous that communications had not been properly kept up.

6. It was, however, not only the difficulty of the Gibraltar passage but the competition of Carthage which kept Greeks out of the Atlantic. The Carthaginians traded all along the 75 nearer coasts of the Atlantic, both in Spain and Africa. They had rounded the Cape of Good Hope and sailed far into the Northern sea for the tin of Cornwall and the Scillies. A Carthaginian account of the West African route is extant in Greek—the so-called Itinerary of Hanno. Rud- 80 yard Kipling seems to have made use of it for his story "The Joyous Venture" in *Puck of Pook's Hill*: it speaks of reaching an island inhabited by shaggy women who bit and scratched and whom the interpreters called "Gorillas."

7. It was of course to the interest of the Carthaginians, 85 as of all pioneer sea powers, to keep their voyages secret and to exaggerate their danger. It was a long time before their next rivals, the Romans, found their way to the British tin mines. The geographer Strabo has an interesting passage about this British trade and how its monopoly was safe- 90 guarded:—

The Tin Islands, he says, are ten in number. . . . One of them is desert, but the others are inhabited by men in black cloaks, clad in tunics reaching to the feet, girt about the breast and walking with sticks, like Furies in a tragedy. They subsist 95 by their cattle, leading for the most part a wandering life. Of the metals they have tin and lead, which with skins they barter with the merchants for earthenware, salt, and brazen vessels. Formerly the Phoenicians alone carried on this traffic from Gades, concealing the passage from every one; and when the 100 Romans followed a certain skipper in order to discover the mar- ket for themselves, the skipper purposely ran his vessel on to a shoal, luring the Romans to the same fate. He himself escaped on a piece of wreckage and received from the State the value of

105 the cargo he had lost. Nevertheless the Romans persevered
until they discovered the passage.

8. Parallels to this story could be found in the annals
of early Dutch and English seamanship, when the passage
into perilous and monopolized seas was being made in the
110 opposite direction.

9. Two other results follow from the nature of the
straits of Gibraltar. They are too shallow for the cold deep-
sea water, which circulates from polar regions through the
oceans of the world, to make its way in, and the bottom
115 temperature of the Mediterranean is thus almost the same as
that just below the surface. How warm that is every traveller knows who has disregarded local warnings and braved
it when "it is far too cold to bathe." Here the naturalist
would add a section on the curious effects of this on the
120 deep-sea life of the Mediterranean, which we will omit.

10. Secondly, the Mediterranean has nothing that the
Northerner would call a tide. It has a small ebb and flow
of its own, which can be measured everywhere and is just
noticeable in some places, but our big ocean tides scarcely
125 penetrate beyond the entrance. The absence of tides is convenient in many ways. It simplifies the use of harbours and
landing-places, the construction of docks, and the laying out
of seaport towns. It is no more difficult to put to sea or put
ashore in the Mediterranean than on an English river.
130 Small Greek boats, and even triremes and merchant-vessels,
were just run ashore and hauled up a few feet out of the
water, ready for embarkation. Hence the many "Battles at
the Ships" we read of in Greek history and legend, in which,
like Aeschylus's brother at Marathon, men could get their
135 hands chopped off while hanging on to the stern of a warship
which was being pushed into the water. Hence, too, a Greek
port looks very different from an English one. There are
no high quays or sea-wall with a long expanse of shingle and
seaweed below. Everything is much neater and more closely
140 packed. The villa dwellers on the Bosporus can have their
bow-windows over the sea, and Aeginetan fishermen tumble

out their sponges straight on to the high road. Nausicaa, who liked things tidy, thus describes the arrangement of her father's model port in Phaeacia. "There is a fine harbour on each side of the city; the entrance between them is 145 narrow, and the curved ships are drawn up along the road: for each man has a special slip assigned to him." And there too, she goes on, is the market-place, with the stores of the ship chandlers and the workshops for the oars near by. The same arrangement is found today in many an island port, 150 where there is just room to squeeze the town between the harbour and the hills; and the effect of neatness given by the orderly arrangement of the ships along the low quay is heightened by the sharpness of the coast-line and by the edging that seems drawn so boldly and clearly along it 155 where red-brown rocks and brimming water meet.

11. On the other hand, a tide brings with it advantages of its own which the Greeks would have known how to appreciate. It supplies a perpetual motive power upon which the seaman can reckon with complete assurance in order 160 to save himself trouble: and he can counteract it in a moment by the use of that oldest of all brakes, the anchor. Putting out to sea from a windless harbour was always a trouble to the Greeks. They would have gazed with envy on the shipping that glides lazily with the tide up and down 165 our northern estuaries.

12. However, if the Mediterranean has not tides, it makes up, to some extent, for the deficiency by its currents. These the navigator has continually to reckon with, particularly in narrow waters. "Currents have more than one way 170 of running through a strait," as Strabo remarks, and their different peculiarities were a constant source of preoccupation. The two best known are those at the Straits of Messina and in the Euripus.

13. Scylla and Charybdis present no difficulty to modern 175 steamships; and the little whirlpool off the harbour of Messina which has been identified as Charybdis can never by itself have been very alarming. But the currents set up by the meeting of the two seas, together with the wind,

180 made the passage an awkward one for ancient ships, and
Thucydides, who had observed it, and always makes sense
of a legend when he can, wisely extends the name Charybdis
to the entire strait. In any case, Charybdis, wherever the
exact scene of her operations, made the fortune of one of
185 the richest towns of antiquity. For skippers who feared the
straits, and perhaps too the strong arm of the Chalcidian
colonists at Rhegium and Messina who commanded them,
preferred to deliver their Western-bound goods in a port
on the Eastern coast and have them conveyed across the toe
190 of Italy by land. The shortest and most convenient way of
doing this was up the valley of the Crathis from Sybaris;
and the wealth of Sybaris, which became proverbial, was
due mainly to her command and use of this "isthmus" road,
which led across in two days' journey to her colony of Laos
195 on the Western Coast. Here the goods were re-embarked for
the ports of Etruria on the further West. That is why, when
Sybaris had been destroyed by her neighbour Croton, "the
Milesians of every age shaved their heads and displayed
marks of deep mourning: for these two cities had been
200 more closely befriended than any others we know of."
Miletus was the chief Greek trading city at that time. Man-
chester would be as sorry, though she might show it differently, if the Cape were in foreign hands and we then
lost control of the Suez Canal.

※ ※ ※

1. Draw a map of the Mediterranean in sufficient detail to
illustrate this essay; include all the places here referred to—
the Po, Carthage, Marathon, etc.

2. Why is the Mediterranean "increasingly salt in its more
eastern portions"? (l. 25.)

3. The footnotes, in which Professor Zimmern referred to
the relevant passages in Hesiod, Thucydides, Pindar, etc., have
been omitted. The note to Par. 3, however, deserves quotation:
"Teiresias in *Od.* xi. 123 speaks of inland people who eat their
food without salt. He is probably talking (as a prophet should)
not without good information; for hunting and pastoral people,

who live on meat and milk, do not need salt. It is only the eating of cereals that makes salt indispensable. Hence even in Greece traditions survived of a time when no salt was eaten, and meat offered to the gods was always unsalted." What may be inferred from the phrasing *"even* in Greece"? Why should sacrificial customs be mentioned here?

4. Suppose the long ridge of rock at Gibraltar looked from the West as it does from the East; how would that modify the argument of Par. 5?

5. Lines 198-200 are quoted from Herodotus vi, 21: "When the Milesians suffered thus at the hands of the Persians, the Sybarites, who inhabited Laos and Scydrus, having been deprived of their country, did not show equal sympathy; for when Sybaris was taken by the Crotonians, all the Milesians of every age shaved their heads . . ." etc. Comment on the behavior of the Sybarites.

6. What do you take to be the purpose of this investigation? In other words, of what use is such an essay as this?

7. Outline the essay, omitting Pars. 6-8. What is its logical structure?—i.e., what is the relation of each topic to its subtopics? How do Pars. 6-8 fit into this structure? Why did not the author discuss first the currents at the exits and then shrinkage by evaporation?

8. Even a strictly technical statement of the information contained in this essay would have been readable, for most of the circumstances here discussed have an intrinsic human interest which needs no enhancement. But frequently Professor Zimmern, at no great expense of words, by means of a brief allusion or the turn of a phrase, has given his material a human relevance which the reader might otherwise have overlooked. Find half a dozen of these picturesque or humorous or humane touches, and comment on the two you like best.

9. Which of the following words are cognates of "navigator"? *Naïve, nave, naughty, nausea, nautical, nautilus, navel, navvy, navy.* Which of the following are cognates of "mariner"? *Mare, maritime, marsh, mermaid, mire, morass.*

10. Explain the connection, if any, between *pioneer, pawn,* and *peon.* Between *strait, straight,* and *strict.*

11. Which of the following words are cognates? *Canal, canary, canine, channel, chant, kennel.*

12. In what parts of the world did the following winds first blow, and why were they so named? *Levanter, hurricane, monsoon, simoom, sirocco, tornado, typhoon, zephyr, blizzard, breeze, cyclone.*

13. What inference as to the nature of Roman settlements may be drawn from the derivation of *colony?*

14. Cognates of *salt* appear in what languages? What inferences may be drawn from this fact? What English words beginning with *sal-* are cognates of *salt?*

15. Explain the derivations of *anchor, cargo, harbor, port, tide.*

THE TRADING FRONTIER[1]

FREDERICK JACKSON TURNER

•

1. The Atlantic frontier was compounded of fisher-man, fur-trader, miner, cattle-raiser, and farmer. Excepting the fisherman, each type of industry was on the march toward the West, impelled by an irresistible attraction. Each passed in successive waves across the continent. Stand at 5 Cumberland Gap and watch the procession of civilization, marching single file—the buffalo following the trail to the salt springs, the Indian, the fur-trader and hunter, the cat-tle-raiser, the pioneer farmer—and the frontier has passed by. Stand at South Pass in the Rockies a century later and 10 see the same procession with wider intervals between. The unequal rate of advance compels us to distinguish the frontier into the trader's frontier, the rancher's frontier, or the miner's frontier, and the farmer's frontier. When the mines and the cow pens were still near the fall line the 15 traders' pack trains were tinkling across the Alleghenies, and the French on the Great Lakes were fortifying their posts, alarmed by the trader's birch canoe. When the trappers scaled the Rockies, the farmer was still near the mouth of the Missouri. 20

2. Why was it that the Indian trader passed so rapidly across the continent? What effects followed from the trader's frontier? The trade was coeval with American discovery. The Norsemen, Vespucius, Verrazani, Hudson, John Smith, all trafficked for furs. The Plymouth pilgrims 25 settled in Indian cornfields, and their first return cargo was of beaver and lumber. The records of the various New England colonies show how steadily exploration was car-

[1] From *The Frontier in American History*, by Frederick Jackson Turner; reprinted by permission of Henry Holt & Company, Inc., Publishers.

ried into the wilderness by this trade. What is true for
30 New England is, as would be expected, even plainer for
the rest of the colonies. All along the coast from Maine to
Georgia the Indian trade opened up the river courses.
Steadily the trader passed westward, utilizing the older
lines of French trade. The Ohio, the Great Lakes, the Mis-
35 sissippi, the Missouri, and the Platte, the lines of western
advance, were ascended by traders. They found the passes
in the Rocky Mountains and guided Lewis and Clark,
Frémont, and Bidwell. The explanation of the rapidity of
this advance is connected with the effects of the trader on
40 the Indian. The trading post left the unarmed tribes at the
mercy of those that had purchased fire-arms—a truth which
the Iroquois Indians wrote in blood, and so the remote and
unvisited tribes gave eager welcome to the trader. "The
savages," wrote La Salle, "take better care of us French
45 than of their own children; from us only can they get guns
and goods." This accounts for the trader's power and the
rapidity of his advance. Thus the disintegrating forces of
civilization entered the wilderness. Every river valley and
Indian trail became a fissure in Indian society, and so
50 that society became honeycombed. Long before the pioneer
farmer appeared on the scene, primitive Indian life had
passed away. The farmers met Indians armed with guns.
The trading frontier, while steadily undermining Indian
power by making the tribes ultimately dependent on the
55 whites, yet, through its sale of guns, gave to the Indian
increased power of resistance to the farming frontier.
French colonization was dominated by its trading frontier;
English colonization by its farming frontier. There was
an antagonism between the two frontiers as between the
60 two nations. Said Duquesne to the Iroquois, "Are you
ignorant of the difference between the king of England
and the king of France? Go see the forts that our king has
established and you will see that you can still hunt under
their very walls. They have been placed for your advantage
65 in places which you frequent. The English, on the contrary,
are no sooner in possession of a place than the game is

driven away. The forest falls before them as they advance, and the soil is laid bare so that you can scarce find the wherewithal to erect a shelter for the night."

3. And yet, in spite of this opposition of the interests of the trader and the farmer, the Indian trail pioneered the way for civilization. The buffalo trail became the Indian trail, and this became the trader's "trace"; the trails widened into roads, and the roads into turnpikes, and these in turn were transformed into railroads. The same origin can be shown for the railroads of the South, the Far West, and the Dominion of Canada. The trading posts reached by these trails were on the sites of Indian villages which had been placed in positions suggested by nature; and these trading posts, situated so as to command the water systems of the country, have grown into such cities as Albany, Pittsburgh, Detroit, Chicago, St. Louis, Council Bluffs, and Kansas City. Thus civilization in America has followed the arteries made by geology, pouring an ever richer tide through them, until at last the slender paths of aboriginal intercourse have been broadened and interwoven into the complex mazes of modern commercial lines; the wilderness has been interpenetrated by lines of civilization growing ever more numerous. It is like the steady growth of a complex nervous system for the originally simple, inert continent. If one would understand why we are today one nation, rather than a collection of isolated states, he must study this economic and social consolidation of the country.

❊ ❊ ❊

1. Locate the Cumberland Gap and South Pass on a map, and define their situation.

2. A frontier may be defined as "the most remote settled part of a country, facing an unexplored region." What three ideas has Turner added to this concept in Par. 1?

3. In Par. 1 Turner addressed the reader's imagination—and hence his understanding—in two ways: first he explained the American frontier in a kind of diagram; then he described it pictorially.

a) Mark off the two sections; what lines are in each?

b) Which phrases are most important in the creation of the diagram?

c) Which four words do you think most effective in making the picturesque description vivid?

4. In the second sentence (ll. 2-4) there is what amounts to a mixed metaphor, a contradiction in terms; suggest a simple revision which will avoid this.

5. Show that you understand the actual nature of the trading frontier by explaining the movements of the individual trader with respect to his advancing frontier. Explain the movements of the individual farmer with respect to his advancing frontier.

6. The two questions opening Par. 2 forecast the paragraph.

a) The first is developed and answered in what lines?

b) What is the point of lines 23-29?

c) Answer Turner's first question in one sentence.

d) Which lines explain the effects of the trader's frontier? What were those effects?

7. Perhaps it would have been better to devote a separate paragraph to each of the questions. How might this have been done? (The change may involve some rewordings for accuracy or for smoothness of transition; include these details in your answer.) Which plan do you prefer?

8. Perhaps Par. 2 could have been opened with assertions rather than with questions. Write such a positive introduction to the paragraph; you must forecast the thought and still allow some room for its development. Which method do you think easier, question or assertion? Have you been able to improve on Turner?

9. The quotations from La Salle and Duquesne (ll. 43-46, 60-69) are summarized in what statements? Does it matter, rhetorically, whether the quotation or its point is put first?

10. "Yet the trader, although he impeded the farmer, pioneered the way for civilization." Compare this with Turner's introduction to Par. 3; which do you think better? Would the alternative be improved by the omission of the dependent clause?

11. "Arteries" carrying "an ever richer tide" (l. 84)—"complex nervous system for . . . inert continent" (ll. 89-91). Do these diverse metaphors conflict with each other? If you think so, suggest an alternative phrasing.

12. The following paragraphs are from Harold Frederic's historical novel *In the Valley* and are reliably documented. The speaker is a young Dutchman from the Mohawk Valley.

"From the Straits west I saw the Frenchman for the first time, and read the reasons for his failure to stand against the English. Even while we suspected grounds for fearing his hostility, we found him a more courteous and affable man than the Englishman or Yankee. To be pleasant with us seemed a genuine concern, though it may really have been otherwise. The Indians about him, too, were a far more satisfactory lot than I had known in the Valley. Although some of our Mohawks could read, and some few write, and although the pains and devotion of my friend Samuel Kirkland had done much for the Oneidas, still the French-spoken, Jesuit-taught Indians seemed a much better and soberer class than my neighbors of the Iroquois. They drank little or no rum, save as English traders furtively plied them with it, for the French laws were against its sale. They lived most amicably with the French, too, neither hating nor fearing them; and this was in agreeable contrast to the wearisome bickering eternally going on in New York between the Indians striving to keep their land, and the English and Dutch forever planning to trick them out of it. So much for the good side.

"The medal had a reverse. The Frenchman contrived to get on with the Indian by deferring to him, cultivating his better and more generous side, and treating him as an equal. This had the effect of improving and softening the savage, but it inevitably tended to weaken and lower the Frenchman—at least, judged by the standard of fitness to maintain himself in a war of races. No doubt the French and Indians lived together much more quietly and civilly than did the English and Indians. But when these two systems came to be tested by results, it was shown that the Frenchman's policy and kindliness had only enervated and emasculated him, while the Englishman's rough domineering and rule of force had hardened his muscles and fired his resolution. To be sure, measured by the received laws of humanity, the Frenchman was right and the other wrong.

But is it so certain, after all, that the right invariably wins?" [2]

Does Frederic support Turner in matters of fact? How do their interpretations correspond and how do they differ?

13. *Gun* may be short for *Lady Gunhild,* apparently a pet name for a certain fourteenth-century weapon. (Cf. *Big Bertha.*) Other types of firearm have been given names perhaps intended to terrify the enemy, as *dragon.* (Whence *dragoon.*) Work up a classified list of weapons having interesting derivations.

14. Explain the connection, in meaning and etymology, between *corn* and *grain.* (Compare *barley—farina.*)

15. Explain the derivations of *birch, cargo, farmer, fort, inert, pilgrim, post, scale, trader.*

[2] From *In the Valley,* by Harold Frederic; reprinted by permission of Charles Scribner's Sons, Publishers.

CHARDIN[1]

EDMOND AND JULES DE GONCOURT

•

1. CHARDIN WAS OF THE PETTY BOURGEOISIE, AND HE painted the domestic life of his own class. His daily habits, his thoughts, his affections were all contained within this humble society; nor did he rove beyond it in his art. He was content to depict his own household and the homes of [5] his neighbors; the accessory objects of his pictures were things he himself handled, the people those he saw from day to day. These are not the great bourgeoisie, a class which already, in the early eighteenth century, had grown ambitious and aloof from the common people, assuming [10] the luxury, the pride, and the pomp of a lesser order of nobility; in Chardin's paintings we see the simple, inno- cent faces of the lower middle class, a sober, hard-working folk, yet happy in their peace, their daily toil, their ob- scurity. His genius was the genius of the hearth. [15]

2. The sturdy mother of the Third Estate lives forever upon his canvas. Here the matron of Paris might with astonishment have recognized herself, meticulously and sincerely mirrored, from head to foot, from the fashion of her garments to the virtues of her heart. Chardin records [20] every detail of her costume: her sleeves rolled above the elbows, her bibbed apron, her neckerchief, the cross hung from a slender chain about her neck, her skirt of striped calamanco. Her colors are seemly and sober, and the painter has caught the austerity of her bearing. She is busy [25] about her household chores, those menial occupations which the petty bourgeoisie had retained in their emergence from the social depths. In the kitchen she peels vegetables for the soup. She returns from market with a leg of mutton in her basket, under the napkin. She washes and scrubs. The busy [30]

[1] Adapted from *L'Art du XVIIIme siècle,* by Edmond and Jules de Goncourt.

165

housewife appears again and again in Chardin's pictures.
Through the doorways of his immaculate interiors, remi-
niscent of Peter de Hooch, we catch a shadowy glimpse of
her, sweeping or drying clothes, or she steps into the
35 lighted foreground from the bakehouse, where we descry
the woodbin, the meat hanging from hooks, the store of
candles for the sconces, old casks redolent of wine. Or she
plies her needle, or bends over her basket of yarn, or ad-
monishes the little girl who has taken careless stitches in
40 her fancywork. She brushes the three-cornered hat of a
lad with books under his arm, about to set off for school.
Thus faithfully Chardin exhibits the domestic life of the
middle-class matron: her round of duties, hour by hour,
her serenity and patience, her modest pleasures, the joys
45 and duties of her motherhood.

3.   Chardin's pictures are suffused with a winsome and
familiar piety, bestowing a benediction upon the household.
In one, a mother, with a platter in one hand, and about to
plunge her ladle into a steaming pewter soup-kettle, pauses
50 until her little girl has said grace; the child, perched on the
edge of her stool, her eyes fixed upon her mother's, her
hands clasped, hastily murmurs her little prayer. In another, a somewhat older girl, who must recite her gospel lesson to her mother, stands awkwardly, staring at the floor
55 as though seeking the answer there. Again, the mother—
to whom Chardin always returns—gives the finishing
touches to the daughter's preparations for church. On the
cluttered dressing table burns the candle by which the child
arose, its curlicues of smoke floating in the pallid air. From
60 the window, morning light falls upon the parquet floor
and casts a silvery reflection upon the far corner cupboard,
where a clock marks the hour of seven. In the background
are a great kettle of hot water and the stool where mamma
has laid her big prayerbook. While the mother, in her
65 black hood and tucked up skirts, knots her child's kerchief,
the little one, impatient to be off, her muff already in one
hand, turns to glance a sidelong smile of satisfaction at her
reflection in the mirror. All the charm of the middle-class
Sunday breathes in this picture.

4. These domestic scenes have a radiant comeliness, a 70
naïve coquetry, an air of truthfulness. This wholesome
charm was peculiar to Chardin, unique in an age when
painting was wanton, voluptuous, roguish in its very execution. His work, like the social class it represents, was immune to the corruptions of the eighteenth century; it re- 75
tained the soundness and the sincerity of bourgeois virtue.
Chardin loved what he painted. Moreover, he respected
it. That is why his people are authentic, and why the per-
fume of honesty permeates his interiors; we sense it in the
very arrangement of the furniture and the simplicity of its 80
design, in the bareness of the walls, in the tranquillity of
his line, reaffirming the tranquillity of his people. Chardin
knew the peacefulness of homely things, harmoniously ordered under a calm light. This insight was his secret and his
strength, the source from which he drew a poetry at once 85
rare and familiar.

※ ※ ※

As one may often criticize a novel merely by telling the story,
so there are many painters of whose work one may give a good
report merely in terms of the subject matter. In this portion of
their essay the Goncourts have said little about Chardin's painting as painting. There are but a few casual references to his
lighting and his line. So in your report on a painter, you had
better leave the discussion of coloring, chiaroscuro, perspective,
composition, brushwork, and such strictly pictorial matters to
the professional critics, or at least make them incidental to the
narrative elements of the painting.

1. Compare Pars. 2 and 3.

a) About how many pictures have been used as evidence
in each?

b) How does the treatment of single pictures differ in the
two paragraphs?

c) Whereas a painting is looked at all at once, prose exists
in time, phrase by phrase. Thus the reporting of a picture involves a certain difficulty—especially when which method is
employed? Show by an analysis of part of the paragraph that
the difficulty exists and that the Goncourts have met it.

d) What other deftnesses of reporting, possibly worth emulat-
ing, do you find in either paragraph?

2.   What is the topic or thesis of Par. 2? Of Par. 3?

3.   Account for the order of the two paragraphs. Why should they not be reversed? Does this order depend upon the topic or upon the treatment?

4.   What are the functions of Par. 1 and Par. 4 in the plan of the whole passage? "To introduce" and "to conclude" are hardly satisfactory answers to this question. What in their content makes them properly introductory and conclusive? What important idea of Par. 1 is reiterated in Par. 4? How is this idea differently applied or further developed, so that the essay moves?

5.   Some difficulties may be forestalled by observing the management of the verbs.

a) On what principles do the Goncourts use the present tenses? The past tenses?

b) Account for the past perfect "had grown" (l. 9), the present perfect "has caught" (l. 25), "has taken" (l. 39), the past "arose" (l. 59).

6.   For your essay, select a painter who can be profitably discussed in terms of his subject matter. Although madonnas, flights into Egypt, and martydoms are by no means all alike, the differences are of detail and treatment; thus the individuality of the painters of standard religious subjects will elude the unpracticed art critic. Moreover, your painter should have produced a number of pictures on the same theme. Thus, even if Van Gogh is your favorite and you can recognize his work without looking at the label, you had better not try to generalize sunflowers and rustic bridges; nor can you write more than two sentences about squiggly brush strokes. More promising painters are Hogarth, Daumier, Canaletto, Peter Breughel, Jan Steen, Peter de Hooch, Vermeer of Delft, and indeed most of the Dutch school, Goya, Fragonard, Millet, Degas, Diego Rivera, etc. Perhaps you can find in the library a volume of pictures by one of these men. Or you might write about a popular magazine artist, such as Norman Rockwell. Some of the *New Yorker* cartoonists have a characteristic subject matter and style, and their work is a consistent comment on some phase of life, quite independent of the quips which make it salable. Whatever your choice, try to appreciate the mood and attitude of the artist, so that your selection of details for your essay may have some point.

MADAME BOVARY[1]

RICHARD PENNY

•

1. In *Madame Bovary,* FLAUBERT CONTEMPLATES WITH compassionate cynicism the romantic pursuit of happiness. Emma Bovary, an imaginative young woman who yearns for the emotional adventures promised by romantic fiction, is disappointed in her marriage and in a series of liaisons, 5 each more practical than the last, hence more sordid and sentimentally unsatisfying, more dangerously compromising.

2. As a child in her early 'teens at a convent school, Emma Rouault formed her ideas of what life offers the 10 ardent soul. Her heart was quickened by the fragrant mysteries of theology and sweetly stirred by pictures of the suffering Jesus, allusions in sermons to the celestial bridegroom, the melancholy prose of Chateaubriand. More exciting were the smuggled novels full of "persecuted ladies 15 fainting in lonely pavilions, . . . sombre forests, heartaches, vows, sobs, tears and kisses, little skiffs by moonlight, nightingales in shady groves, gentlemen brave as lions, gentle as lambs, virtuous as no one ever was, always well dressed, and weeping like fountains." Under the spell 20 of Sir Walter Scott she adored and envied the unhappy heroines of history; in satin-bound "keepsakes" she read Byronic verses and mused over the engravings of exotic landscapes, England or the Orient, far-away places. Returning thus educated to her father's farm, she found house- 25 hold chores disgusting and willingly married the first stranger who appeared: Charles Bovary, a dull, plodding country doctor, who, lacking the confidence to prescribe

[1] From *Studies in Nineteenth Century Literature,* by Richard Penny; reprinted by permission of Harper & Brothers, Publishers.

anything more drastic than a sedative or a purge, had
30 managed not to kill off his patients. Charles was in love
with Emma, and he settled down to enjoy the blessings of
marriage. But Emma missed something: waterfalls and
precipices, minarets and lemon trees, the Swiss chalet or
the Scottish cottage—in a word, the raptures she had longed
35 for. Her husband, who would have understood nothing of
this, told her about his day's visits, gaped in admiration
as she jangled the piano, and snored in his armchair. Her
discontent was sharpened by a visit to the chateau of a
neighboring marquis; the country couple dined among
40 noble folk, in rooms resplendent with gleaming silver, wax
candles, crystal ware, and flowers; at the head of the table
heaped with rare viands sat the old Duke de Laverdière.
His napkin tied round his neck like a child's, he bent over
his plate with bloodshot eyes, dripping gravy from the
45 corners of his mouth, stammering as he pointed at the
foods; Emma, knowing what a dashing figure he had cut
before the Revolution, gazed at him in reverent fascination: "He had lived at court and slept in the bed of queens!"
After dinner, Charles stood for hours watching whist, a
50 game he did not understand, and Emma waltzed with a
viscount. Ravished by her brief experience of aristocratic
luxury, Emma subscribed to a Paris magazine and moped
about the house. She complained of the neighborhood, and
Charles, when valerian and camphor baths had proved
55 futile, agreed to move to another district.

3. At Yonville, a dull provincial village twenty-four
miles from Rouen, Emma made her extra-marital experiments in passion. When the Bovarys arrived at the inn,
the new doctor was promptly engaged in conversation by
60 the local apothecary, Homais, a blatant and absurd champion of progress, while Emma chatted with a young lawyer's clerk named Leon. These two soon discovered a common admiration for sunsets and the sea, which elevate the
soul, and for German music, which makes one dream. The
65 sentimental affinity ripened, until both were painfully in
love. Emma, thus aroused, expanded in domestic tenderness

to Charles, whose banality made her feel the more virtuous, and her sorrows made her beautiful. Leon, tremulous
with adoration, thought her inaccessible and fled to Paris,
leaving her to relapse into her vapors. Rodolphe, a coarse 70
and cynical squire, understood better how to amuse himself with the doctor's pretty wife. Charles agreed that horseback riding would be good for Emma's health, and although Emma was reluctant, foreseeing sin, the thought
of wearing a riding habit decided her. Once expertly se- 75
duced by a man without compunction about romantic
little lies, Emma carried on the intrigue with abandon,
writing daily letters to be tossed into Rodolphe's biscuit box
with his other souvenirs, recklessly crossing the ploughed
fields at dawn to fling herself into his arms. She exchanged 80
locks of hair with him and asked for a ring; she spoke
of their departed mothers looking down from heaven. The
energies released by her passion involved her in practical
affairs of the village. In a lull in Rodolphe's attentions, she
helped Homais persuade her husband to win glory in the 85
fight against reaction and superstition by operating on the
club-footed errand boy; the operation was bungled, and
when the gangrened leg had been amputated at the thigh,
Emma despised Charles more than ever. Another reality
entered her life in the person of the drygoods merchant and 90
money-lender, Lheureux, who plied Emma with elegant little luxuries on credit, gifts for her lover, atoning adorn-
ments for her own house; Lheureux gladly discounted new
notes as the old ones fell due. When Emma at last would
have realized her dreams by flying with Rodolphe to some 95
delightful distant place, that practical adulterer wrote explaining that destiny and duty forbade him the pleasure
of ruining her life and absented himself from the district.
Emma, felled by this blow, languished through the winter;
in the spring a fit of religion engrossed her passions without 100
relieving them, and Homais at last persuaded Charles
that a trip to Rouen to hear the opera would revive in
Emma a taste for the joys of life.

4. There the Bovarys met Leon, who, having sampled

105 the student life in Paris, felt magnificently bold in the company of the provincial couple. Emma resisted him only vigorously enough to be romantic, then plunged into desperate adultery. Entangling herself in elaborate deceptions, she kept a weekly rendezvous in a Rouen hotel room, cosy, 110 luxurious, a little world apart; the sea shells on the mantel whispered of the sea, and the cupid on the clock hid his head coyly under an upraised arm, smirking at her raptures. The coach that carried her back to Yonville was invariably accosted by a blind beggar, loathsomely dis- 115 figured, who sang a ditty of summer love and thrust his filthy hat in at the window for alms, and Emma slumped shivering in her corner, feeling "death in her soul." At home she pined the week out, patching her lies and staving off Lheureux, signing more notes and wandering deeper 120 into his web. Wretched and unappeased, she promised herself a profound felicity on her next excursion; but a savage wantonness only brought her the sooner to find in adultery all the platitudes of marriage. Reality had failed her at every turn; humiliated in her lust, she clung to it 125 in corruption. Only when she wrote love letters she could imagine a lover who climbed to her fragrant balcony by moonlight and enraptured her with a kiss. Then the notes fell due, and there were no more renewals.

5. It is not Flaubert's intention to scold Emma or to 130 make fun of her. She is not inherently vicious, and it would be hard to say at what precise point, with her education, she might have found a more satisfying conduct of life. Her romantic notions are ridiculous to us, for they are of an old fashion. But Flaubert does not limit his question to 135 her particular scheme of folly: he finds the world full of equally fantastic delusions. "Every bourgeois in the flush of his youth . . . has believed himself capable of immense passions, of lofty enterprises. The most mediocre libertine has dreamed of sultanas; every notary bears within him the 140 debris of a poet." These illusions, which man evolves in an effort to transcend the meagreness of life, are therefore false in perspective, so out of keeping with reality that they

cannot be realized. They remain mawkish or grotesque affectations, pathetic and absurd; any serious attempt to enact them may be disastrous. Charles Bovary's naïve dreams 145 of fireside tranquillities, much in the vein of our Eddie Guest, are banal, touching, and doomed to disappointment. When he is infected by Homais and Emma with grandiose notions of himself as a master-surgeon, Charles horribly tortures the poor clubfoot who falls into his clutches. But 150 may one not admire old Binet, who spends his hours harmlessly at his lathe, enjoying the pride of craftsmanship? He devotes his life to the production of a roomful of napkin rings! The illusions of Homais are in keeping with his times: he is a positivist and a liberal, a comic species 155 akin to our own pompous and vaguely benevolent "fellow travellers" of the late 'thirties. He recommends Voltaire and wears a magnetic belt; he writes turgid letters to the press in praise of progress; he harries the clergy at every oppor- tunity. Over the corpse of Emma, he enjoys a round of 160 theological bickering with the priest who drills the cate- chism into snivelling village urchins. Those few persons in the novel who have an altogether practical understand- ing of reality are odious: Rodolphe and Lheureux, whose highest calculation is to establish a rival coach service 165 through Yonville and so eventually to control the whole commerce of that municipality. In this profoundly sombre book there is pity as well as disdain for the hungry souls who would find dignity in one tawdry illusion or another. And man's aspirations are the more pathetic because they 170 are perennial: when Emma has expiated her foolish quest of ecstasy, the romantic process begins anew as little Justin, the apothecary's drudge, who has worshipped this beau- tiful lady, kneels in devotion at her grave.

※ ※ ※

Most of us flee the person who offers to tell us the plot of a movie or a novel, for such narratives are likely, we know, to wander aimlessly among a multitude of trivial and superficial details, irrelevant to whatever inward meanings the novelist may have intended to convey. And so we may think of the mere retelling of a story as a procedure useless to the serious critic and below his dignity—a chore devised only for high school children, who must, in their book reports, prove that they have done their outside reading. Yet the plot summary, although elementary, is thereby fundamental to the study of fiction.

For the author of a novel conceives of his plot as the embodiment, in concrete and plausible circumstance, of a *theme;* or, if you prefer, the theme is the *essence* of the action. This theme may be a moral or rule for proper human conduct; it may be a philosophical or political thesis; it may be a comment upon the customary behavior of man or society. It may be asserted universally or of a particular time and place. If the commentator fails to find any theme underlying the story, or if his retelling of the story obscures this theme, then he is dull indeed; but if he can condense the story in such a way as to make the theme stand out in sharp relief, then, as this passage shows, he can reveal much about the author and his work.

(He may even neglect to say that the description was excellent but tiresome, that the characterization was fine—especially the villain—and that he thinks everybody would derive enjoyment from a perusal of this book.)

In connection with this study, it would be helpful to read *Madame Bovary,* in order to see better how Mr. Penny has gone about summarizing it.

1. Observe the plan of the essay; divide it into three parts and explain the function of each. Justify the order of these parts. (Try putting them in some other order; what are the advantages of the present arrangement?)

2. What are the several stages in the action of *Madame Bovary* as indicated in Mr. Penny's statement of the theme and in his telling of the story?

3. Of a 400-page edition of the novel, pp. 1-78 are covered in Par. 2, pp. 79-253 in Par. 3, and pp. 254-400 in Par. 4. Is the essay a scale-model of the novel?

4. The first part of the novel may be outlined as follows:

pp. 1-22   Charles's education and first marriage, to a widow supposed wealthy. He sets old Rouault's broken leg.

Compare Par. 2 with this outline.

a) Which part of the novel is omitted? Why?

b) Which part is presented out of its original order? Why?

c) Which parts are treated at proportionally greater length? Why?

5. The following passage is an accurate report and might be substituted for lines 99-101:

When Emma had planned to elope with Rodolphe, she had secretly purchased expensive luggage from Lheureux. Now in order to stave him off before he appealed to Charles, and incidentally to get possession of some ready money, she persuaded her husband to sign a paper giving her the power of attorney to manage his business affairs. It was on the pretense of consulting Leon, who was a lawyer's clerk, on this matter that she made her first trip to Rouen. Later she pretended to be taking piano lessons from a Mademoiselle Lempereur; this ruse became dangerous, however, when Charles, happening to meet the supposed teacher, inquired about Emma's progress; but by forging a receipt for three months' lessons, she was able to dispel any suspicions. On the death of Charles's father, the Bovarys inherited some property which Emma used as security in order to borrow still more money, at outrageous interest, from Lheureux.

What is wrong with it?

An obviously wrong way to condense a novel would be to report the successive chapters in one or two sentences each. Such a procedure would spread the story too thin; the result would be both tedious and colorless. On the one hand, it would be overloaded with accounts of incidental movements of the characters; on the other, it would lack the sharp, picturesque detail of gesture or circumstance which gave substance to the original novel.

In writing an essay of this sort, you will be strongly tempted to explain all the *machinery* of the plot. It will require a bold resolution on your part not to identify all your characters in terms of their family connections, etc. Here, for instance, a beginner would have felt obliged at least to explain how Emma met Charles and how she came to be invited to the chateau and how she met Rodolphe; Mr. Penny has omitted even to say how she learned where Homais kept the arsenic with which she committed suicide.

This reduction of the plot to a simple outline leaves room for more effective details. There are glimpses of the characters in significant poses or gestures: Charles gapes as Emma jangles the piano. Other details stir the imagination and suggest the local color of the original: the satin-bound "keepsakes," the armchair, the wax candles, the camphor baths. Sometimes a novelist makes of his stage properties more than setting or equipment for the action; an object may become a symbol for one of the dominant ideas of the story. The clock mentioned in line 111, adorned with a grimacing cupid, yet marking the inexorable flight of time, has this symbolic quality. It is not mere furniture; it is a metaphor charged with meaning. The skillful novelist thus embodies his ideas in concrete images the better to convey them to the reader's mind and heart; a skillful summarizer, recognizing such symbols, will make use of them in his own work. Thus Penny, instead of taking the inlaid rosewood table or the gleaming andirons—also in Flaubert's description—to illustrate the cosy luxury of the room, preferred the clock. (He might have made more of it: e.g., "and while time moved relentlessly, the cupid on the clock . . . " etc.)

6.　Select from Pars. 2-4 three or four good examples of each of these kinds of imaginative detail: symbols, characteristic gestures, local color. Briefly indicate the significance or aptness of each.

7.　Compare the text, ll. 9-11 and 24-26, with the following: When Emma Rouault was a child in her early 'teens at a convent school, her heart was quickened by . . . Returning to her father's farm, she found household chores disgusting.—How do these revisions affect the reading of the paragraph? Where else in Par. 2 do you find the same rhetorical device?

8.　However effective the details, one must not bog down in them. While the story may be enriched with much illustrative material, many sentences should take long strides through the narrative, summarizing a good deal of action in a phrase. E.g., "She married the first stranger who appeared" (ll. 26-27), "he settled down" (l. 31), "Emma moped" (l. 52). Underline ten such narrative summaries in Pars. 3-4.

9. The formulation of the theme raises problems of a different order.

a) Suppose the second sentence (ll. 3-8) written: Emma Bovary, an imaginative young woman, disappointed in her marriage, seeks the emotional adventures promised by romantic fiction in a series of liaisons . . . etc.—How does this differ from the text in meaning? Show why one is more accurate than the other, according to Penny's telling of the story.

b) How does Penny's narrative justify the wording: "each more practical . . . , more sordid and sentimentally unsatisfying"?

c) What do "cynicism" and "compassionate" mean in the first sentence? (This involves a consideration of the whole essay.)

d) Which do you suppose more difficult to write, Par. 1 or Pars. 2-4? Why?

10. Of some novels the theme is universal, asserted of human beings everywhere and always; of others, it is historical, asserted of a particular time and place.

a) In which class is *Madame Bovary,* as Mr. Penny reads it?

b) The critic trying to determine the theme of a novel may be helped by recalling these two possibilities. Perhaps you have read some of the following novels; in which class are they? John Steinbeck's *The Grapes of Wrath;* Pearl Buck's *The Good Earth;* Stevenson's *Dr. Jekyll and Mr. Hyde;* Sinclair Lewis's *Babbitt;* Howells's *The Rise of Silas Lapham;* Stephen Crane's *The Red Badge of Courage;* Dostoievsky's *Crime and Punishment;* Hawthorne's *The Scarlet Letter;* Hugo's *Les Miserables;* Marjorie Rawlings' *The Yearling;* Cervantes' *Don Quixote;* Hardy's *Tess of the D'Urbervilles.*

c) Formulate the theme of any of these novels.

d) Of the novels which you have recently read, name two of each class, and formulate the themes of two of them.

11. Write an essay summarizing the plot of a novel or short story.

ENGLISH TYPES IN DICKENS[1]

HIPPOLYTE TAINE

•

1. THE EARLIEST FRUIT OF ENGLISH SOCIETY IS HYPOCRISY, ripened by the double breath of religion and morality. In a country where Sunday laughter is frowned on, where melancholy Puritanism is still distrustful of gaiety, where 5 scholars include in their ancient histories dissertations on the precise extent of Nebuchadnezzar's virtue, it is natural that the appearance of morality should be useful. Those who lack this necessary coin make false money, and the more precious it is declared by public opinion, the more 10 assiduously it is counterfeited. This is an English fault. Mr. Pecksniff cannot be met with in France. His phrases would disgust us. If we have an affectation, it is of vice rather than of virtue; one succeeds not by asserting his principles but by confessing his weaknesses; our impostors 15 boast of their immorality. We had our hypocrites once, when religion was popular, but since Voltaire, Tartufe is impossible. We no longer affect a sanctity which deceives no one and leads nowhere. Hypocrisy varies with local custom, religion, the intellectual fashion; that of Peck- 20 sniff is adapted to his environment. English religion is little concerned with dogmas and much with morals: whereas Tartufe let fall theological phrases, Pecksniff expands in philanthropic tirades. He has marched with the times; he has become a humanitarian philosopher. He has 25 named his daughters Mercy and Charity. He does not conceal his tenderness; he abandons himself to domestic effusions of good will. To visitors he innocently exhibits charming family scenes; he displays the heart of a father, the sentiments of a husband, the benevolence of a good

[1] From *Histoire de la Littérature Anglaise.*

178

master. Now that family virtues are in style, he must be 30
draped in them. Orgon, coached by Tartufe, rose above
the relationships of this earth, learned to wave aside his
mother, his children, his wife; but modern English piety
would not approve of this. We must not despise this world
for the sake of the next; we must improve it. Tartufe al- 35
luded to his hairshirt and his scourge; Mr. Pecksniff
prattles of his comfortable little parlor, of the joys of home,
of the beauties of nature. He wants all mankind to live
in harmony; in the accents of the Peace Society, he holds
forth on the benefits of concord with such evident emotion 40
that the listener must respond. Much reading of elegiac
poetry has refined and quickened the sensibilities of men;
they are no longer to be deceived by the gross effronteries
of a Tartufe. But Mr. Pecksniff's gestures of sublime patience, his smiles of ineffable compassion, his enthusiasms, 45
his tokens of affection—these may seduce the most exact-
ing of his countrymen and ravish the most sentimental. The
English, in their parliaments and public meetings, their
societies and ceremonials, have learned the oratorical phrase-
ology, the lofty abstractness, and the jargon of the political 50
economist, the newspaper editor, the prospectus writer. Mr.
Pecksniff talks like a prospectus. He has its obscurity, its
verbosity, its fervor. He seems to soar above the earth, into
the ether of pure idea, to nestle in the bosom of truth. He
might be one of the twelve apostles—brought up in the 55
Times office. He can utter a generalization upon any occasion. He discovers a moral lesson in the ham and eggs
he has just eaten. Eggs come and go; so transitory is the
world; let us remember our frailty and the accounting we
must one day render. As he folds his napkin, he rises to 60
lofty contemplations:

The process of digestion . . . is one of the most wonderful
works of nature. I do not know how it may be with others,
but it is a great satisfaction to me to know, when regaling on
my humble fare, that I am putting in motion the most beautiful 65
machinery with which we have any acquaintance. I really feel
at such times as if I was doing a public service. When I have

wound myself up, if I may employ such a term, . . . and know
that I am Going, I feel that in the lesson afforded by the works
70 within me, I am a Benefactor to my Kind!

This you perceive to be a new species of hypocrisy. Vices
change from age to age, to consort with the virtues.

2. The practical temperament, like the moral temperament, is English; through commerce, industry, and self-
75 government, the nation has acquired a taste for business
and a talent for it. In excess, this practicality destroys
imagination and sensibility, turns man into a calculating
machine registering only facts and figures. He abjures the
life of the mind and the joys of the heart; he recognizes
80 in the world only profit and loss; hardened, bitter, avari-
cious, he treats his fellows as so much machinery; eventually he becomes pure merchant, pure banker, pure statis-
tician. He ceases to be a man. Dickens has drawn many of
these pragmatic men: Ralph Nickleby, Scrooge, Antony
85 and Jonas Chuzzlewit, Alderman Cute, Mr. Murdstone and
his sister, Bounderby, Tom Gradgrind—there are such in
all his novels. Whether practical by instinct or by education, they are hateful, for they make it their business
to ridicule and to destroy kindness, sympathy, compassion,
90 altruism, religious feeling, imaginative fervor—all that is
fair in mankind. They grind down children, they strike
women, they starve the poor, they insult the unfortunate.
The best of them, like automatons of polished brass, fulfill their legal obligations and remain ignorant of the suf-
95 fering they cause. England has produced a philosophy to
justify and glorify such men. French authors have depicted
misers, financiers, shopkeepers; Balzac is full of them; but
he accounts for them by their imbecility, or he makes them
curious monsters like Grandet and Gobseck. Those of
100 Dickens constitute an actual social type and represent a
national vice. Read this passage from *Hard Times*, and
say whether Mr. Gradgrind is not, body and soul, wholly
English:

"Now, what I want is Facts. Teach these boys and girls noth-

ing but Facts. Plant nothing else, and root out everything else. 105
You can only form the minds of reasoning animals upon Facts:
nothing else will ever be of any service to them. This is the
principle on which I bring up these children. Stick to Facts,
Sir!"

The scene was a plain, bare, monotonous vault of a school- 110
room, and the speaker's square forefinger emphasized his observations by underscoring every sentence with a line on the
schoolmaster's sleeve. The emphasis was helped by the speaker's
mouth, which was wide, thin, and hard set. The emphasis was
helped by the speaker's voice, which was inflexible, dry, and 115
dictatorial. The emphasis was helped by the speaker's hair,
which bristled on the skirts of his bald head, a plantation of firs
to keep the wind from its shining surface, all covered with
knobs, like the crust of a plum-pie, as if the head had scarcely
warehouse room for the hard facts stored inside. The speaker's 120
obstinate carriage, square coat, square legs, square shoulders,—
nay, his very neckcloth, trained to take him by the throat with
an unaccommodating grasp, like a stubborn fact, as it was,—
all helped the emphasis.

"In this life, we want nothing but Facts, Sir; nothing but 125
Facts!"

The speaker and the schoolmaster backed a little and swept
with their eyes the inclined plane of little vessels then and there
arranged in order, ready to have imperial gallons of facts poured
into them until they were full to the brim. . . .   130

"Thomas Gradgrind, Sir! A man of realities. A man of facts
and calculations. A man who proceeds upon the principle that
two and two are four, and nothing over, and who is not to be
talked into allowing for anything over. . . . With a rule and
a pair of scales, and the multiplication table always in his pocket, 135
Sir, ready to weigh and measure any parcel of human nature,
and tell you exactly what it comes to. It is a mere question of
figures, a case of simple arithmetic."

3.   Another fault generated by habitual domineering and
conflict is pride. It flourishes in an aristocratic nation, and 140
no one has derided the aristocracy more harshly than
Dickens. Every portrait is a sarcasm: James Harthouse, a
dandy disgusted with everything, chiefly himself, and
rightly so; Lord Frederick Verisopht, a gullible sot, whose

145 wit consists in staring at people and sucking the end of his
cane; Lord Feenix, a slot-machine for parliamentary
phrases, now out of order and hardly able to conclude the
absurd orations into which he launches on the slightest
pretext; Mrs. Skewton, a hideous old ruin, coquetting to
150 the last, parading her daughter through the salons of England in order to sell her to some vain husband, and insist-
ing that her own deathbed be draped in rose-colored curtains; Sir John Chester, a rascal in high life, who, lest he
be compromised, refuses, with an exquisite grace as he
155 finishes his chocolate. to help his bastard son. But the most
complete and the most English portrait of the aristocratic
temperament is that of Mr. Dombey, the business man.

4.   This London merchant is as vigorous a type as may
be found in our haughtiest châteaux. Like a true nobleman,
160 Dombey identifies his personal interests with those of his
house. If he disdains his daughter and yearns for a son, it
is that the ancient name of his banking house may be
perpetuated. His ancestors were commercial men; he wishes
to transmit their traditions and their power. In his opulence
165 and in the scope of his operations, he is a prince, and he
has princely sentiments. Such a character could be produced
only in a country whose commerce encircles the globe,
where merchants are potentates, whence a band of traders
has exploited continents, conducted wars, overthrown king-
170 doms, and established empire over a hundred million men.
There is no meanness in the arrogance of such a man as
Mr. Dombey, but a terrible tranquillity and aloofness. To
find his like, one must reread the *Memoirs* of Saint-Simon.
Mr. Dombey has always commanded; that he should yield
175 to anything or anyone never enters his mind. He accepts
flattery as his due tribute. From his eminence he looks
down upon an inferior race created to beseech and to obey.
His second wife, the high-spirited Edith Skewton, scorns
him; as the arrogance of the merchant is pitted against
180 the arrogance of a daughter of the nobility, their unspoken
antipathies rise to an intensity of hatred such as only souls
thus born and thus nurtured could contain. Upon her

wedding anniversary, Edith, to avenge her pride, leaves
Dombey's house, as though she were an adulteress. Then
Dombey's cold pride stiffens. Suspecting his daughter of
complicity, he drives her away too and prohibits communication with either. He lays an interdict upon the very
mention of their names in his presence; even to his guests
he manifests the same austerity. Desperate, his heart
gnawed by the insult, the chagrin of defeat, the shame of
public ridicule, he remains nevertheless firm, haughty, impassive. Ever more audacious business enterprises bring
him to ruin and the verge of suicide. Yet the bronze column
stands unbroken. Now the exigencies of public morality
pervert the theme: Dombey's daughter arrives just in time;
she entreats; he softens; she leads him off; he becomes the
best of fathers—and spoils a fine novel.

5. Let us consider some other characters. Set against
these wicked and unnatural products of the national institutions are people good as nature made them.

6. First the children. We have none of them in our literature. Racine's *petit Joas* could have been born only for
the edification of the young ladies of Saint-Cyr; the poor
child speaks only in his rôle of princeling, uttering noble
phrases as though he repeated his catechism. Nowadays
these portraits are found only in our gift-books, written
as models for proper little boys and girls. Dickens did not
intend his child-portraits to be instructive, and they are
charming. All his children are sensitive, loving and needing to be loved. To understand his choice and his warmth
of treatment, one must think of the physical type. English
children have so fresh a complexion, so delicate a coloring,
such transparent skin, and such clear blue eyes that they
are like flowers; no wonder the novelist loves them and
fears lest such frail roses be bruised by the callous hands
that would bend them. One must think, too, of the soil
in which they grow. When at five o'clock the merchant
and his clerks leave the office, they hasten to pretty little
cottages where their children have played all day upon

220 the lawn. The evening fireside is their sanctuary, and domestic caresses are their sufficient poetry. Deprived of this atmosphere of affection, a child is stifled, and the novelist will need a whole book to explain its wretchedness; Dickens has recorded it in ten volumes, and at last 225 he has written the story of David Copperfield. David is loved by his mother and a faithful servant girl, Peggotty; he plays with her in the garden, watches her sew, reads her the natural history of the crocodile; he fears the geese and chickens that strut formidably in the courtyard; he 230 is perfectly happy. When his mother marries again, everything changes. The step-father, Mr. Murdstone, and his sister Jane are harsh, methodical, frigid; their stern words continually wound the poor little fellow. He dares not speak or stir or kiss his mother; he feels the leaden gaze of these 235 new inmates of the household like a constant weight upon him. He shrinks into himself; he studies the lessons heaped upon him so mechanically and so fearfully that he cannot remember them; whipped and shut up in a lonely room on bread and water, he is terrified by night, asks himself 240 whether he is not indeed wicked, weeps. This terror without respite and without hope, the stupefying of David's intelligence and the bruising of his tender heart, his watchful anxiety, his wretchedness in his solitary prison, his passionate longing to kiss his mother or to sob against the 245 bosom of his nurse,—these things make sad reading. These childish sorrows are as profound as grown-up grief. A delicate plant blossomed in sunshine; suddenly transplanted to snow, it drops its leaves and withers.

7. The common people are like children, dependent, 250 unpolished, close to nature, subject to oppression; in short, Dickens has glorified them. This is not new to us: witness the novels of M. Eugène Sue; the theme derives from Rousseau. But the British novelist restates it with unusual force. His heroes have an admirable delicacy and devotion. 255 They are vulgar only in their dialect; otherwise they are all nobility and generosity. A circus performer gives up his

daughter, his one joy in life, lest he sully her in some way. A young woman devotes herself to the care of the worthless wife of the man she loves and by whom she is loved; when this man dies, she continues, in sheer abnegation, 260 to nurse the degraded creature. A poor waggoner, believing his wife unfaithful, loudly proclaims her innocence; his only vengeance is to overwhelm her with kindness. It is only the common people, according to Dickens, who feel so intensely the happiness of mutual love, the innocent 265 joys of family life. Theirs is the keenest compassion for those deformed and invalid creatures they so often bring into the world. No other class has so strict a moral sense. Indeed, the heroes of Dickens bear an unfortunate likeness to the outraged fathers of French melodrama. Old Peg- 270 gotty, on learning that his niece has been seduced, takes his staff and sets off across France, Germany, and Italy, to find her and bring her back to her duty. But above all, these people have one English sentiment which we lack: they are Christians. In France, the women take refuge in 275 the idea of another world; in England even the men think of heaven. There, where there are so many sects and each man chooses his own, everyone believes. And this noble sentiment still further exalts the righteousness of their will and the delicacy of their hearts.   280

8. So the novels of Dickens may be summed up in a phrase: Be good, and love; true happiness dwells in the heart; feeling is the whole of man. Leave science to the savants, pride to the gentry, luxury to the rich; compassionate the lowly and wretched; the least of these is worth 285 more than thousands of the mighty in their pride. Take care not to bruise the delicate souls, young or old, which bloom in all classes of society, in rags and in fine raiment. Believe that humanity, pity, and forgiveness are man's fairest virtues; believe that friendship, confidences, tender- 290 ness, and tears are the sweetest things in the world. To exist is nothing; to be powerful, learned, or famous is little; to be useful is not enough. He alone has lived and is

a man who has wept at the memory of a kindness performed or received.

❊ ❊ ❊

You have seen, in Mr. Penny's treatment of Flaubert, how the critic may exhibit the theme of a novel in terms of its action. Taine makes use of the plot summary and of several other procedures, all quite simple; they may be listed:

   a) summary of plot
   b) series of brief plot summaries
   c) portrait of an individual character
   d) series of brief character sketches
   e) composite description of a character type.

This is certainly not an elaborate repertory of technical devices; yet the critic who knows when and how to use these methods is equipped for any ordinary analysis of fiction.

   1. Give Pars. 1, 2, 3, 4, 6, and 7 general titles—e.g., "hypocrisy," "the lower classes"—and say what method or combination of methods Taine has used in each.

   2. An effective analysis of character is likely to comprise a) the abstract labeling of qualities, b) illustration in terms of habitual behavior, and c) illustration in terms of single actions. Show that Pecksniff's hypocrisy is developed in these three ways.

   3. a) Do lines 73-83 refer to the economic man as he appears in English society or as he is drawn by Dickens? What about lines 87-95?

   b) Scrooge, of *The Christmas Carol,* never struck a woman. Justify lines 84 and 91-92, and explain the heightening effected by the rhetorical method employed in the paragraph.

   4. a) In Par. 4 Taine has combined two methods; at what point does he shift from one to the other?

   b) Show that he has stated the theme before outlining the plot.

   c) Why is the version of the text, lines 189-192, better than the following: "He remains impassive, haughty, and firm, although he is desperate, his heart gnawed by the shame of public ridicule, the chagrin of defeat, the sting of the insult"? (There are three changes to be criticized.)

d) Lines 171-177 ("There is no meanness . . . obey") might have preceded lines 159-170 ("Like a true nobleman . . . men.") This would have been inferior to the arrangement of the text for which reason?

1) Dombey's arrogance should come at the end of the character sketch because it leads into the outline of the plot.

2) The more precise references—to his children, his banking house, and his ancestors—should precede the more abstract qualifications, "arrogance" and "aloofness."

3) As Saint-Simon did not write his *Memoirs* until after the English had established their world empire, the transposition would violate chronological order.

4) The logical connection between "our haughtiest chateaux" and "nobleman" would be lost over the intervening lines.

5. a) In his account of *David Copperfield* (Par. 6), Taine has disregarded such memorable characters as Mr. Peggotty, Uriah Heep, Mr. Micawber, and Dora, the child wife; why?

b) Has Taine stated the theme of the novel *before* outlining the plot? If not, write a sentence which does this, and indicate where it should be inserted.

c) How does Taine state the theme *after* he has outlined the plot?

d) Show that he has used the same device in his treatment of *Dombey and Son*.

6. a) Of the five items in lines 142-145, which do you think the most vividly drawn? The feeblest?

b) Taine enlivens these sketches by means of striking metaphor, graphic detail, and quip. In which words or phrases do you find each of these resources?

c) Which is the most effective, and which is the last resource?

7. a) What statement of theme supports lines 256-263? ("A circus performer . . . kindness.")

b) In which of the four items in lines 256-263, 270-273, has Taine made use of the graphic detail?

c) Which of the four is feeblest? What in the nature of the material made it difficult to handle effectively?

8. Which is more likely to allow picturesque treatment, the brief plot summary or the brief portrait?

9. Write four one-sentence sketches of characters from Dickens's novels—or from fictions fresher in memory.

10. At what point in Par. 8 do you discover that Taine does not altogether admire Dickens?

11. Review the essay and note in the margin those places in which Taine has explained Dickens's work by reference to race, moment, or milieu. Suggest several other writers to whom you think Taine's critical principles might be applied, and indicate the argument for each.

THE TITANESS[1]

THOMAS BEER

•

1. THIS QUESTION OF AMERICAN WOMAN AND LETTERS seems to have been much debated just then and Charles Nolan fell foul of the shrewd Julian Ralph in an argument on a steamer. Ralph assured him that editors were really bothered and often insulted by notes from women and when the lawyer hooted the idea Ralph proved his point by collecting twenty-five specimens of abuse addressed to *Harper's,* the *Century* and, it seems, to *Lippincott's.* Three letters are dated from New York. The rest came from Ohio, Illinois, Indiana and Kentucky. The main topics of objurgation are three. A nice woman has been killed or failed of marrying the right man in some story. Liquor, including beer and claret, has been drunk by otherwise respectable people or has been mentioned without assault in an article. The story teaches nothing. In six of these letters the name of Louisa Alcott is cited as a proper writer and to one of them is signed the name of Frances Willard. By way of minor complaint one learns that John Fox's *A Cumberland Vendetta* has ungrammatical passages and contains coarse language unsuited to growing boys, that Lester Raynor's tale of the intriguing Mrs. Deepwater who arranged her dinners by getting one celebrity to meet another is an insult to "Western womanhood," that it is "disgusting and unmanly" to mention the Pope in an article containing the name of Edward McGlynn, author of *The Pope in Politics,* and that the words "breasts," "belly," "damn," "vomit," and "rape" are unfit for Christian women to read.

[1] Reprinted from *The Mauve Decade,* by Thomas Beer, by permission of and special arrangement with Alfred A. Knopf, Inc., authorized publishers.

The one attack on *Trilby* is signed by Ada Channing Walker, whose activities are now ending. She had lately discovered that William Whitney was a horse-racer and had written Grover Cleveland to oust him from the Democratic Party without getting satisfaction. So she drew up a document on marriage for her niece, advising her to marry only a man resembling "our precious Saviour, Jesus Christ, in manners and appearance." Unable to do so, from lack of data, the girl mourned her aunt two months and married a sugar broker, six feet three inches long.

2. A trait binds these letters: they are dated directly on the offence. Emotion took up a pen and wrote on the best paper. There is not a trace of intellectual process. They were annoyed; etiquette had been battered or an opinion expressed that they didn't like. It is the voice of the porch shaded by dusty maples along Grand Avenue in a hundred towns, a resolute violence of the cheapest kind, without breeding, without taste. And there comes, too, a hint of the slow battle between the city and the small town. "You people in New York" are doing thus and so. "I suppose," said Mrs. Janette B. Frobisher, "the society women in New York like to read swear words, but—" . . . And yet in Bucyrus, Ohio, a copy of Zola's *Nana* went from soft hand to soft hand until it came back to its owner in the state of a worn Bible and slim fingers stained the pages of a tall *Salammbo* opposite to the plate of Matho squatting with his head against the knees of the Princess, who cried out: "Moloch, thou burnest me!" while the kisses of the warrior, Gustave Flaubert said, seared her body, more biting than flames. However, he was French.

3. But if you were a proper editor, bred in the society of Newark or of Hartford, you did not trifle with the Titaness and for her sake you issued tales of women, by women, for women, in which one discovers the strangest things about that duel of the sexes, a deal discussed in the '90's. The voice of Louisa Alcott echoes in these tales: Alice Perrine on a trip to Boston found that her betrothed had once tried to

kiss the pretty wife of a professor during a dance. He is 65
given no chance to explain. Tears dribble on a box which
takes his ring back to him: Miss Cornwall finds that her
lover once wooed a girl who scorned him. The other girl is
now very sorry. Miss Cornwall, allegedly fond of her swain,
simply packs him off to his former fancy. The gentleman 70
gulps and goes to his doom. Another Miss Cornwall finds
her affianced once lived, ten years before, in Rome, with "a
woman." He is dispatched to find and marry the girl, and
"with bowed head, he faced the long path of his duty."
Charles Milton's lungs have sent him to California, orange- 75
growing, and he is very comfortable and prosperous. But
his wife yearns for Boston, the scene of her girlhood, and
on finding that out he simply sells the orange grove and
takes her home, "for he had learned what he owed to her
womanhood at last." And again you hear Louisa Alcott in 80
tales of Aunt Semanthy and Cousin Hetty from the country
who set the frivolous city folk to rights with advice and
chicken broth, flatteries of the farm against the triumphant
urban women whose photographs spotted the *New York
Herald,* whose balls were detailed in a dozen journals of 85
widest circulation.

4. Now too there appeared, sparsely, another fictional
flattery of women, often written by men, in which young
girls decide the winning of great football matches by sending some player a violet at the right second, in which 90
maidens repel and crush a male animal in high lust by a
simple stare of wonder, in which the female principal is
risen above romance and becomes an opalescent cloud, dripping odours which had nothing to do with the processes of
childbearing at all . . . and concurrently in Chicago a liv- 95
ing lawyer was consulted by a young woman of fashion
about a marriage contract in which her husband would
pledge himself not to consummate the marriage. He reported this to a friend of his calling in New York, and
on March 9, 1898, found that the metropolitan lawyer had 100
already been consulted about a dozen such contracts. A few
months before, in England, George Bernard Shaw had

inquired whether it was true that American women really liked to be worshipped on false pretences.

❧ ❧ ❧

1. What does "letters" mean in line 1? Identify Louisa Alcott, Frances Willard, and Trilby in sufficient detail to point the references in Par. 1. Why is the chapter from which this passage is taken called "The Titaness"?

2. Classify the illustrative material used in this essay as published documents, unpublished documents, and oral anecdotes. Counting Ralph's collection as a unit, you should find at least six items in the last two classes.

3. Mark off in the text the several stories which are summarized in lines 58-80. Frame a single statement of theme which will apply to all these stories. How can "another" (l. 87) be justified? I.e., how does the fictional flattery illustrated in Par. 4 differ from that of the first group of stories in Par. 3?

4. Why was the collection of twenty-five letters presented and analyzed before the discussion of magazine fiction rather than after it?

5. In which paragraph has Mr. Beer exhibited these letters as specimens of literary criticism? In which has he discussed the psychology of their authors? Justify or criticize the order in which these two topics were taken up.

6. What difference does it make where the letters came from? (ll. 8-10.) Where in the essay is the significance of this geographical circumstance indicated?

7. Explain the force of the following words: *otherwise* (l. 13), *learns* (l. 18), *discovered* (l. 30), *so* (l. 32). The phrase "six feet three inches long" is fiercely contemptuous of Ada Channing Walker; explain this.

8. In lines 50-52 there might have been written: " . . . a copy of Zola's *Nana* was loaned about until it was dog-eared and limp with exhaustion. . . ." Compare these phrasings with the text.

9. Is "Gustave Flaubert said" inserted to let the reader know who wrote *Salammbo*? Read the sentence aloud; you may be able to discover the point of the phrase by testing several

possible intonations of it. What difference does Flaubert's nationality make?

10. What is explained by the clause, "whose balls were detailed in a dozen journals of widest circulation"? (ll. 85-86.)

11. Compare the series of plot summaries in lines 63-80 with that in Taine's essay on Dickens, Par. 7. (p. 185.) Which is more sprightly written, and what words make it so?

12. Summarize as fully as you can in one sentence what this selection says about the influence of women upon magazine fiction of the 'nineties.

13. Write an essay discussing a class of contemporary fiction (e.g., *Gruesome Stories*, confession stories, "family" movies) with references to the tastes of the readers for which they are intended. You may find it helpful to compare new fashions with older ones: Superman with Tom Swift, or Tom Swift with Horatio Alger's heroes; or the desperate wives of the radio serials with the women in the stories described by Mr. Beer. Or compare modern children's books with Miss Alcott's, or with such tales as the Grimms collected.

14. If you might find in the garret a bundle of letters of whatever nature you wished, barring lucre, what would you choose? Explain your choice in a short essay.

THE SOCIAL GENIUS OF BOSWELL[1]

CHAUNCEY BREWSTER TINKER

•

1. I SUPPOSE THAT THE SIMPLEST MANIFESTATION OF SOCIAL genius is a desire of getting people together and exposing them to one another. Our interest in drama and novel consists largely in seeing people whom we know brought into 5 contact with strange or hostile persons, so that they may exhibit or develop new sides of themselves. It is hard to interest a reader in the unbroken serenities of family life. It is hard for social genius to content itself with the domestic circle. A man endowed with such a genius is perpetually 10 hankering after "new faces, other minds"; he finds in clubs and crowded drawing-rooms a varied and coloured life which puts to shame the modest pleasures of solitude and meditation.

2. All intellectual improvement arises, perhaps, from 15 submitting ourselves to men and to ways of life that are originally alien to us; if, in time, they get the better of our conservatism, our life is clearly the better for the enrichment they have given it; but if, on the other hand, we are in the end obliged to repudiate them, we retire with 20 the renewed strength that arises from opposition, and our second state is better than our first. If you happen, for example, to dislike Frenchmen, it would, according to this philosophy, be well for you to go and live among Frenchmen until you discover whether you are right. If you find 25 yourself becoming a snob or a Pharisee, it might be well for you to go among criminals and mendicants, until you realise the fascination of the irregular life. An hour's experience in such matters is worth more than a year of meditations.

[1] From *Young Boswell*, by Chauncey Brewster Tinker; reprinted by permission of Little, Brown and Company, Publishers.

3. Of this philosophy of exposure James Boswell was ever an ardent disciple. He loved friction—the excitement which arises from the sudden contact of rivals, the collision of opponents, ill-assorted companies: Jove among peasants, Samuel Johnson in the Hebrides. He let his imagination play with the thought of bringing Rousseau and Voltaire together. In his youth he went into the company of actors and of Roman Catholics, because actors and Roman Catholics were not approved of by the stern society in which he had been reared; in his maturer years he courted the acquaintance of the notorious Mrs. Margaret Caroline Rudd, who had barely escaped from the fangs of the law when the Perreau brothers were hanged for forgery; and he rode to the place of execution with the Reverend Mr. Hackman, the murderer.

4. Over these incidents the biographers and critics of Boswell have made merry, or wagged their heads with indignation. There is, however, something to be said for knowing human nature, even in its most unpopular, or even criminal, manifestations; one may hazard the opinion that the critics themselves would be the wiser for some knowledge of the unconventional life. What if Boswell did write an amatory song to Mrs. Rudd? It was because he felt her charm; and I do not doubt that she had more of it than all the bluestockings and dowagers in Scotland. Johnson himself envied Boswell his acquaintance with Mrs. Rudd.

5. There were, Boswell discovered, easy ways of introducing into conversation this necessary friction. One can always take the other side, whether he belongs on it or not. One can always affect ignorance or prejudice. This was, from the beginning, one of his favourite methods of drawing a man out. "I ventured," he writes of Paoli, "to reason like a libertine, that I might be confirmed in virtuous principles by so illustrious a preceptor. I made light of moral feelings. I argued that conscience was vague and uncertain; that there was hardly any vice but what men might be found who have been guilty of it without remorse." This

from the man who wrote reams of the most excellent counsel to Zélide! Yet, in the midst of his sermon to Zélide, he had cried out, "Defend yourself. Tell me that I am the severe Cato."

6. The record of Johnson's conversation teems with illustrations of Boswell's skill in starting or directing the flow of talk. When Johnson expatiated on the advantages to Scotland of the union with England, Boswell himself was delighted with the "copious exaggeration" of the talk, but he feared the effect of it on the Scotch listeners. "I therefore," says he, "diverted the subject." He talked with Mr. Gerard on the "difference of genius," for the express purpose of engaging him and Johnson in a discussion of the subject. On another occasion he wrote: "A strange thought struck me, to try if he knew anything of . . . the trade of a butcher. I enticed him into the subject."

7. Again, he was eternally asking questions. How else, pray, is one to discover the extent of another's conversation? Recall that fascinating vision which he summoned up, of Johnson shut into a tower with a new-born baby. "Sir, what would you do? Would you take the trouble of rearing it? Would you teach it anything?" And (doubtless as growing out of this very subject), "Is natural affection born with us? Is marriage natural to man?" Here is an interlocutor by no means profound, but eager and curious, full of novel expedients for waking his subject into activity, spurring, enticing, decoying him, and playing the fool before him.

8. I also (he wrote) may be allowed to claim some merit in leading the conversation. I do not mean leading, as in an orchestra, by playing the first fiddle; but leading as one does in examining a witness—starting topics, and making him pursue them.

It is a felicitous comparison. Boswell had the ingenuity of a lawyer trained in cross-examination and in wringing a subject dry. There is much also in the musical metaphor which he abandons. He *is* very like a performer on a

musical instrument. By skilful manipulation, he plays upon
men so as to display all that is most characteristic in them. 105
Of this peculiar skill he was fully aware, and loved to
analyse it. He had learned, for example, how to play upon
John Wilkes, and he so far divulged the secret as to write
thus to the man himself:—

Philosophy can analyze human nature, and from every man 110
of parts can extract a certain quantity of good. Dare I affirm
that I have found chearfulness, knowledge, wit, and generosity
even in Mr. Wilkes? I suppose few crucibles are so happily
constructed as mine, and I imagine that I have a peculiar talent
for finding the gold in your Honour's composition. Certain it 115
is that the process must be performed very delicately.

Another passage on the same theme makes use of a
metaphor much less felicitous, but is certainly of value in
showing the conscious art of which Boswell was the master.
It is drawn from the Commonplace Book, and reads:—   120

My friends are to me like the cinnamon tree, which produces nutmeg, mace, and cinnamon; not only do I get wisdom
and worth out of them, but amusement. I use them as the
Chinese do their animals; nothing is lost; there is a very good
dish made of the the poorest parts. So I make the follies of 125
my friends serve as a dessert after their valuable qualities.

9. Of the splendour of this endowment it is perhaps
hardly necessary to speak. To influence men in such a
way as to bring into life whatever is most characteristic;
to appreciate and elicit whatever is best in the man before 130
you; to make his true qualities triumph over his inertia
and his conventionality, is, in the fullest sense, surely a
creative act. Boswell could almost boast that he taught men
to know themselves.

10. Because of this more serious purpose, he cared but 135
little for mere pyrotechnical display in conversation. There
were, in his immediate circle, three men famous for epigrams and *bons mots,*—Beauclerk, Garrick, and Richard
Brinsley Sheridan,—yet he never cared to make a collec-

140 tion of their witty remarks. Wit, of course, he delighted in; but the highest form of wit is that in which it blends with wisdom, and in which it leads the enquirer on to a subtler consideration of the subject, or provides a sharp summary of it in some flash of inspiration. In Corsica, 145 Paoli had said to him, *"Je ne puis souffrir longtemps les diseurs de bons mots";* whereupon Boswell comments:—

How much superior is this great man's idea of agreeable conversation to that of professed wits, who are continually straining for smart remarks and lively repartee. They put 150 themselves to much pain in order to please, and yet please less than if they would just appear as they naturally feel themselves. A company of professed wits has always appeared to me like a company of artificers employed in some very nice and difficult work, which they are under a necessity of per- 155 forming.

11. It is because of this neglect of mere repartee that the conversation recorded by Boswell never impresses the reader as a jest-book or a collection of unset jewels. There is plenty of relief. It is his glory to have given us the gem in its setting.

※ ※ ※

1. Divide the essay into four sections: Pars. 1-4, 5-7, 8-9, and 10-11; put the essential thought of each in a sentence.

2. Justify the order in which these four ideas are presented.

3. In which paragraphs has Professor Tinker defined or illustrated elements of Boswell's social genius, and in which has he vindicated or appraised them?

4. Why, in the second section, should Tinker have presented Paoli and Zélide—a young woman of the Enlightenment whom Boswell had met while studying law at Utrecht—before Johnson rather than after?

5. Just what was included under the topic "difference of genius"? (l. 78.)

6. Professor Tinker has called Boswell an "interlocutor by no means profound"; yet elsewhere (*Young Boswell,* p. 59) he

has shown Boswell drawing out Voltaire by "a question which well indicates the skill with which he ensnared his destined prey. . . . 'I asked him if he could give me any notion of the situation of our ideas which we have totally forgotten at the time, yet shall afterwards recollect.'" To answer such a question is to define the nature of the soul. On this occasion, Voltaire avoided the bait and, after some meditation, retorted with a line from Thomson's *Seasons:* "Where sleep the winds when it is calm?" What must be the deeper significance of any answer Johnson might make to the question, "Would you take the trouble of rearing it?"—To, "Sir, would you teach it anything?"

7. Observe in lines 61-66 how succinctly Boswell could summarize a moral philosophy. Write a refutation of his argument.

8. Find out who John Wilkes was—the article by R. W. Postgate in the *Britannica* will prove useful—and write a paragraph explaining how Boswell's letter was adapted to its recipient.

9. Find three or four metaphors which Tinker himself has used to characterize the arts of conversation. Which do you think most felicitous? Phrase a simile of your own which might be applied to Boswell's conversation.

10. Comment on the following changes of wording: *hankering after* (l. 10) to *yearning for; fascination* (l. 27) to *attractiveness; fangs* (l. 40) to *arm; hazard* (l. 48) to *venture; affect* (l. 59) to *feign; novel* (l. 91) to *literary; spurring* (l. 92) to *luring; appreciate* (l. 130) to *enjoy; inertia* (l. 131) to *laziness; smart* (l. 149) to *fresh; nice* (l. 153) to *pleasant.*

11. Explain the derivations of *ardent, bluestocking, butcher, Catholic, decoy, drawing-room, Pharisee, remorse, snob.*

12. Read at least fifty pages in the *Life of Johnson* (any portion after 1763) or the *Tour to the Hebrides,* and write an essay on Johnson's conversation.

JOHNSON WITHOUT BOSWELL[1]

WALTER RALEIGH

•

1. IT IS PLAIN THAT JOHNSON WAS OFTEN AMUSED, AND often irritated, by the habits of his scribe. He disliked, above all, being put to the question. Boswell prided himself on his talent in drawing people out, and certainly was both
5 courageous and skilful at the business. The directness of his assault when he talked to Johnson has this excuse, that Johnson, on the testimony of his friends, never started a topic of conversation. He left others to put up the game, and was content to shoot it. "No one," says Mrs. Thrale, "was
10 less willing to begin any discourse than himself: his friend Mr. Thomas Tyers said, he was like the ghosts, who never speak till they are spoken to: and he liked the expression so well that he often repeated it. He had, indeed, no necessity to lead the stream of chat to a favourite channel, that
15 his fullness on the subject might be shewn more clearly, whatever was the topic; and he usually left the choice to others." Boswell tells, in *The Journal of a Tour to the Hebrides,* how, when they were shown the military stores at Fort George, Johnson made a very good figure in con-
20 versation with the officers on the various stages of the manufacture of gunpowder.

2. This is how it comes about that Johnson's retorts are sometimes not fully expressive of himself, and must not be taken to convey his most deeply cherished convic-
25 tions. He did not choose the subject, and when others chose it he was often displeased by the choice.

3. Boswell, for instance, attributes to him in many passages an almost sentimental horror of the very name of

[1] From *Six Essays on Johnson,* by Walter Raleigh; reprinted by permission of the Clarendon Press, Oxford.

200

death. It is true that Johnson thought often of death; but he did not think of it sentimentally. "When we were alone," says Boswell, under the year 1769, "I introduced the subject of death, and endeavoured to maintain that the fear of it might be got over." After some exchange of argument, Johnson answered, in a passion, "No, Sir, let it alone. It matters not how a man dies, but how he lives. The act of dying is not of importance, it lasts so short a time. . . . A man knows it must be so and submits. It will do him no good to whine." "I attempted," says Boswell, "to continue the conversation. He was so provoked, that he said, 'Give us no more of this'; and was thrown into such a state of agitation that he expressed himself in a way that alarmed and distressed me; showed an impatience that I should leave him, and when I was going away, called to me sternly, 'Don't let us meet tomorrow.'"

4. Is it not easy to imagine the scene? The pleasant, excitable, insistent voice of Boswell,—"With regard to death, Sir"; Johnson's brief, wise verdict, and dismissal of the topic; Boswell's mosquito-like return, and Johnson's outburst of wrath. It was not death that he feared; it was Boswell on death. He did not always shun the subject. His friend, John Hoole, tells how on November 30th, 1784, less than a fortnight before his death, "Frank bringing him a note, as he opened it he said an odd thought struck him, that one should receive no letters in the grave." Grim fancies on death were natural to him; tittle-tattle about it he could not bear.

5. If Boswell is sometimes all unconscious of the meaning of Johnson's reproofs, so is Mrs. Thrale. Mrs. Thrale was a lively, feather-headed lady, with a good deal of natural wit, and a perfect confidence in the exercise of it. Boswell disliked her, as his most highly-favoured competitor, but it is impossible to read her *Anecdotes* without falling under the spell of her easy, irresponsible charm. There is no sufficient reason to challenge her good faith, but her code of truth is not severe, and many of the facts that she narrates become lies under her touch. So, in

speaking of Johnson's expressions of contempt, she gives
as an instance a retort that he made to her. "He was no
gentler with myself, or those for whom I had the greatest
70 regard. When I one day lamented the loss of a first cousin
killed in America—'Prithee, my dear (said he), have done
with canting: how would the world be worse for it, I may
ask, if all your relations were at once spitted like larks,
and roasted for Presto's supper?' Presto was the dog that
75 lay under the table while we talked."

6. One story is good till another is told. Joseph Baretti,
who had been for some years a tutor in the Thrales' house,
was fortunately present at this conversation, and gave his
version, which, on the face of it, is the true one. "Mrs.
80 Thrale," he says, "while supping very heartily upon larks,
laid down her knife and fork, and abruptly exclaimed, 'O,
my dear Mr. Johnson, do you know what has happened?
The last letters from abroad have brought us an account
that our poor cousin's head was taken off by a cannon-ball.'
85 Johnson, who was shocked both at the fact, and her
light, unfeeling manner of mentioning it, replied, 'Madam,
it would give *you* very little concern if all your relations
were spitted like those larks and drest for Presto's supper.'"

7. Is not this a live piece of drama? Mrs. Thrale, quite
90 unaware of any cause in herself, and her flow of pleasant
chatter, for Johnson's reproof, took it as a gratuitous display of surliness and rudeness, showing how a great philosopher can be deficient in humane feeling. She does not
even mention that she was eating larks, so that the larks,
95 which were her own supper, become, under her light hand,
a merely rhetorical adornment of Johnson's invective. Yet
it is strange that she did not see what he meant, for she
understood and put on record several similar reproofs. Here
is one of them: "I was saying to a friend one day that I
100 did not like goose; one smells it so while it is roasting,
said I. 'But you, Madam (replies the Doctor), have been
at all times a fortunate woman, having always had your
hunger so forestalled by indulgence, that you never experienced the delight of smelling your dinner beforehand.'

'Which pleasure,' answered I pertly, 'is to be enjoyed in 105
perfection by such as have the happiness to pass through
Porridge-Island[2] of a morning.' 'Come, come (says he
gravely), let's have no sneering at what is so serious to
so many: hundreds of your fellow-creatures, dear Lady,
turn another way, that they may not be tempted by the 110
luxuries of Porridge-Island to wish for gratifications they
are not able to obtain: you are certainly not better than all
of them; give God thanks that you are happier.' "

8. These retorts, to Boswell and to Mrs. Thrale, show
Johnson as he was, unfailingly serious and sympathetic and 115
imaginative about the great elemental things. Boswell had
not thought deeply about death, Mrs. Thrale had not experienced poverty or imagined it in its effects; Boswell
was argumentative, like a Scottish philosopher, on death;
Mrs. Thrale was flippant, like a fashionable lady, on pov- 120
erty—hence the fierceness of Johnson's replies.

9. It would be easy to show how each of the biographies
of Johnson is limited and coloured by the predilections of
the writer, and by the nature of his, or her, relationship
to the great man. Johnson's talk, even though it be faith- 125
fully recorded, loses most of its value when it is taken out
of its setting. No one says all that he thinks in talk. He
selects only what has some relation to the company and
the circumstances. We must know the company and the
circumstances before we can understand the talk. It is one 130
of Boswell's greatest merits that he is careful of his background; wherever it is possible he gives us a full and true
account of the persons present, and the incidents and remarks that prompted Johnson's speech.

10. Another cause of Boswell's superiority is his care for 135
truth, even in the minutest details. Some part of this care
he may have learned from his master; like Reynolds, he was
"of Johnson's school." Perhaps no book so rich in opportunities for error has ever come through a century of mi-

---

[2] Mrs. Thrale's note on Porridge-Island describes it as "a mean street
in London, filled with cook-shops for the convenience of the poorer
inhabitants."

140 nute study and criticism with so little damage to its reputation as Boswell's *Life*. The author invented nothing and
suppressed nothing, and his book stands. Yet in the main
his details contribute to the portrait, and that portrait is
Boswell's Johnson. A little emphasis here and there, a judi-
145 cious management of the light, a lively touch of the brush
or of the pen,—these are enough for the painter or the
biographer who wishes to convey his own meaning. All
later writers on Johnson are copyists of Boswell. Macaulay
exaggerated the picture and vulgarized it, but suggestions
150 for his caricature are already to be found in Boswell. Take,
for instance, the question of Johnson's manner of eating.
Boswell's description is well known. "I never knew any
man who relished good eating as he did. When at table, he
was totally absorbed in the business of the moment; his
155 looks seemed rivetted to his plate; nor would he, unless
when in very high company, say one word, or even pay
the least attention to what was said by others, till he had
satisfied his appetite, which was so fierce, and indulged
with such intenseness, that while in the act of eating, the
160 veins of his forehead swelled, and generally a strong perspiration was visible." No doubt Boswell had seen Johnson on one or more occasions as he here describes him.
Hawkins says, "It was, at no time of his life, pleasing to
see him at a meal." On the other hand, Bishop Percy, under
165 whose roof Johnson lived for many weeks, says that Boswell's description is extremely exaggerated. "He ate heartily, having a good appetite, but not with the voraciousness
described by Mr. Boswell; all whose extravagant accounts
must be read with caution and abatement." And Richard
170 Cumberland says, "He fed heartily but not voraciously, and
was extremely courteous in his commendations of any dish
that pleased his palate." In *The Journal of a Tour to the
Hebrides* Boswell himself had remarked, "I observed that
he was disgusted whenever he met with coarse manners."
175   11. These quotations make it plain that here is a question of degree, to be determined "not dogmatically, but
deliberately." It is perhaps fair to conclude that Johnson

ate zealously, and with conviction. The fervour of his temper expressed itself in a hundred ways, and this no doubt
was one of them. Boswell's account is probably a little exag- 180
gerated; the most vivid of his memories of Johnson at table
is imposed upon the reader as if it were a daily experience.
Then came Macaulay; he seized upon the most picturesque
of Boswell's scattered descriptive phrases, joined them in a
single sentence, and heightened the picture out of all human 185
recognition. "The old philosopher is still among us, in the
brown coat with the metal buttons and the shirt which
ought to be at wash, blinking, puffing, rolling his head,
drumming with his fingers, tearing his meat like a tiger,
and swallowing his tea in oceans."

❧ ❧ ❧

In the long essay from which this passage is drawn, Sir Walter
Raleigh evaluates Boswell's account of Johnson, testing it against
the evidence of other biographers and defining Boswell's virtues
and limitations. Thus the essay is also a further portrait of
Johnson and an exercise in the critical use of testimony. (Within
this short excerpt, the point of the paragraphing is not always
plain, but the present divisions give a proper emphasis within
the essay as a whole.)

1. The episodes presented in Pars. 2 and 3 bear on what
question about Johnson? From a comparison of them, what
may be inferred about Boswell?

2. What does "canting" mean? (l. 72.) If Baretti's version
is the true one, could Mrs. Thrale have been properly accused
of canting? What do you take to have been Mrs. Thrale's
attitude toward canting? Explain.

3. Is Johnson's reproof *gratuitous* in both versions?

4. Why do you think Baretti's version more plausible than
Mrs. Thrale's? Or why not?

5. The two versions of the episode of the larks bear on what
question about Johnson? What inferences about Mrs. Thrale
may be drawn from them? With which of these inferences is
Raleigh chiefly concerned?

6. Precisely what did Johnson accuse Mrs. Thrale of sneering at? (l. 108.)

7. Is Johnson exhibited as surly or rude in lines 99-113?

8. Justify each of the terms applied to Johnson in lines 115-116: serious, sympathetic, imaginative.

9. What would Johnson say to each of the following maxims? Man ought to seek happiness and to shun pain. Virtue is the sure source of human happiness. Happiness is to be found in indifference to pleasure or pain.

10. Do you think that Raleigh's analysis of Macaulay's method (ll. 183-190) applies to his description of London manners? Illustrate your answer.

11. Compare Raleigh's sentence, lines 17-21, with the following alternative:

In *The Journal of a Tour to the Hebrides,* Boswell tells how good a figure Johnson made in conversation on the various stages of the manufacture of gunpowder with the officers who showed them the military stores at Fort George.

12. Compare lines 62-67 with the following:

. . . it is impossible to read her *Anecdotes* without being deceived by her charming manner. She is, in effect, an irresponsible liar, whether she knows it or not. So in speaking . . .

13. Comment on the following changes of wording: *put to the question* (l. 3) to *questioned; pleasant* (l. 45) to *urgent; not severe* (l. 65) to *loose; deficient* (l. 93) to *wanting; elemental* (l. 116) to *elementary; circumstances* (l. 129) to *conditions; judicious* (ll. 144-145) to *judicial; vulgarized* (l. 149) to *popularized; temper* (ll. 178-179) to *anger.*

14. Find cognates of *assault, cant, disgust, gratification, philosopher, retort, voracious.*

15. Explain the derivations of *alarm, code, deliberate, exaggerate, forestall, horror.*

ON BEING BUSY[1]

HENRY DAVID THOREAU

•

1. THIS WORLD IS A PLACE OF BUSINESS. WHAT AN INFINITE bustle! I am awaked almost every night by the panting of the locomotive. It interrupts my dreams. There is no sabbath. It would be glorious to see mankind at leisure for once. It is nothing but work, work, work. I cannot easily 5 buy a blank-book to write thoughts in; they are commonly ruled for dollars and cents. An Irishman, seeing me making a minute in the fields, took it for granted that I was calculating my wages. If a man was tossed out of a window when an infant, or scared out of his wits by the In- 10 dians, it is regretted chiefly because he was thus incapacitated for—business! I think that there is nothing, not even crime, more opposed to poetry, to philosophy, ay, to life itself, than this incessant business.

2. There is a coarse and boisterous money-making fel- 15 low in the outskirts of our town, who is going to build a bank-wall under the hill along the edge of his meadow. The powers have put this into his head to keep him out of mischief, and he wishes me to spend three weeks digging there with him. The result will be that he will perhaps 20 get some more money to hoard, and leave for his heirs to spend foolishly. If I do this, most will commend me as an industrious and hard-working man; but if I choose to devote myself to certain labors which yield more real profit, though but little money, they may be inclined to look on 25 me as an idler. Nevertheless, as I do not need the police of meaningless labor to regulate me, and do not see anything absolutely praiseworthy in this fellow's undertaking any

[1] From *Life Without Principle,* by Henry David Thoreau; reprinted by arrangement with Houghton Mifflin Company, Publishers.

more than in many an enterprise of our own or foreign
30 governments, however amusing it may be to him or them,
I prefer to finish my education at a different school.

3. If a man walk in the woods for love of them half of
each day, he is in danger of being regarded as a loafer; but
if he spends his whole day as a speculator, shearing off those
35 woods and making earth bald before her time, he is
esteemed an industrious and enterprising citizen. As if a
town had no interest in its forests but to cut them down!

4. Most men would feel insulted if it were proposed to
employ them in throwing stones over a wall, and then in
40 throwing them back, merely that they might earn their
wages. But many are no more worthily employed now. For
instance: just after sunrise, one summer morning, I noticed
one of my neighbors walking beside his team, which was
slowly drawing a heavy hewn stone swung under the
45 axle, surrounded by an atmosphere of industry,—his day's
work begun,—his brow commenced to sweat,—a reproach
to all sluggards and idlers,—pausing abreast the shoulders
of his oxen, and half turning round with a flourish of his
merciful whip, while they gained their length on him. And
50 I thought, Such is the labor which the American Congress
exists to protect,—honest, manly toil,—honest as the day is
long,—that makes his bread taste sweet, and keeps society
sweet,—which all men respect and have consecrated; one
of the sacred band, doing the needful but irksome drudgery.
55 Indeed, I felt a slight reproach, because I observed this
from a window, and was not abroad and stirring about a
similar business. The day went by, and at evening I passed
the yard of another neighbor, who keeps many servants,
and spends much money foolishly, while he adds nothing
60 to the common stock, and there I saw the stone of the morning lying beside a whimsical structure intended to adorn
this Lord Timothy Dexter's premises, and the dignity forth-
with departed from the teamster's labor, in my eyes. In my
opinion, the sun was made to light worthier toil than this.
65 I may add that his employer has since run off, in debt to a
good part of the town, and, after passing through Chancery,

has settled somewhere else, there to become once more a patron of the arts.

5. The ways by which you may get money almost without exception lead downward. To have done anything by which you earned money *merely* is to have been truly idle or worse. If the laborer gets no more than the wages which his employer pays him, he is cheated, he cheats himself. If you would get money as a writer or lecturer, you must be popular, which is to go down perpendicularly. Those services which the community will most readily pay for, it is most disagreeable to render. You are paid for being something less than a man. The State does not commonly reward a genius any more wisely. Even the poet-laureate would rather not have to celebrate the accidents of royalty. He must be bribed with a pipe of wine; and perhaps another poet is called away from his muse to gauge that very pipe. As for my own business, even that kind of surveying which I could do with most satisfaction my employers do not want. They would prefer that I should do my work coarsely and not too well, ay, not well enough. When I observe that there are different ways of surveying, my employer commonly asks which will give him the most land, not which is most correct. I once invented a rule for measuring cord-wood, and tried to introduce it in Boston; but the measurer there told me that the sellers did not wish to have their wood measured correctly,—that he was already too accurate for them, and therefore they commonly got their wood measured in Charlestown before crossing the bridge.

6. The aim of the laborer should be, not to get his living, to get "a good job," but to perform well a certain work; and, even in a pecuniary sense, it would be economy for a town to pay its laborers so well that they would not feel that they were working for low ends, as for a livelihood merely, but for scientific, or even moral ends. Do not hire a man who does your work for money, but him who does it for love of it. . . .

7. The community has no bribe that will tempt a wise
105 man. You may raise money enough to tunnel a mountain,
but you cannot raise money enough to hire a man who is
minding *his own* business. An efficient and valuable man
does what he can, whether the community pay him for it or
not. The inefficient offer their inefficiency to the highest
110 bidder, and are forever expecting to be put into office. One
would suppose that they were rarely disappointed.

8. Perhaps I am more than usually jealous with respect
to my freedom. I feel that my connection with and obligation to society are still very slight and transient. Those slight
115 labors which afford me a livelihood, and by which it is allowed that I am to some extent serviceable to my contemporaries, are as yet commonly a pleasure to me, and I
am not often reminded that they are a necessity. So far I am
successful. But I foresee that if my wants should be much
120 increased, the labor required to supply them would become
a drudgery. If I should sell both my forenoons and afternoons to society, as most appear to do, I am sure that for
me there would be nothing left worth living for. I trust
that I shall never thus sell my birthright for a mess of
125 pottage. I wish to suggest that a man may be very industrious, and yet not spend his time well. There is no more
fatal blunderer than he who consumes the greater part of
his life getting his living. All great enterprises are self-
supporting. The poet, for instance, must sustain his body
130 by his poetry, as a steam planing-mill feeds its boilers with
the shavings it makes. You must get your living by loving.
But as it is said of the merchants that ninety-seven in a
hundred fail, so the life of men generally, tried by this
standard, is a failure, and bankruptcy may be surely
135 prophesied.

❈ ❈ ❈

1. Explain the phrases:
a) "the police of meaningless labor" (ll. 26-27)
b) "to finish my education at a different school" (l. 31)

c) "more than the wages which his employer pays him" (ll. 72-73)

d) "get your living by loving" (l. 131).

2. In itself, this excerpt might be regarded either as a statement of private views or as social criticism; and, indeed, one usually involves the other, so that the difference between self-portraiture and homily is one of emphasis. Because Americans approved of preaching and because his own urge to justify himself was vigorous, Thoreau proceeded, in the rest of his essay, to censure the commercialism and superficiality of spirit manifested in the gold rush, newspaper reading, slave-owning, and other activities of the time.

Although Thoreau's argument is not developed as a logical demonstration, it is consistent as the expression of a personality. Determine the several leading ideas of the passage, and state them in your own sentences to make a coherent summary of Thoreau's thought.

3. The anecdotes presumably represent the personal experience out of which Thoreau had developed his ideas, and when he came to write his essay, he might use these episodes as illustrations. To make such narratives effective, he had to point the moral. In Par. 2, underline several phrases intended to indicate *the futility of mere industry*. Which of these most impresses you as skillful writing? What in this paragraph might as well have been omitted, and why?

4. Each of the first four paragraphs develops much the same opposition between the public view of industry and Thoreau's own. What in the style of Par. 1, as compared with the others, makes it introductory?

5. Par. 4 must come last in the group; the position of Pars. 2 and 4 could not, for instance, be effectively interchanged. Consider the tone and content of Par. 4, and give at least two reasons why it is climactic.

6. Rewrite lines 9-12, hypothecating two more pathetic causes of incapacitation. Compare your version with Thoreau's; which do you think better and why?

7. The panting locomotive of lines 2-3 interrupts dreams; thus by insight and a turn of phrase, a familiar circumstance is shown to contain a general truth. Where else in Par. 1 do you

find this device? Should the steam planing-mill of Par. 8 be classed with these, or is it merely a simile?

8. In thus presenting a personal philosophy, the writer may embody some of his views in anecdote; but he will also, from time to time, formulate his ideas more explicitly, in more or less aphoristic sentences. There are many such sentences in Pars. 5-8. Select two of the most effective and two of the least effective, and explain briefly why one is better than another.

9. Do you find any weaknesses in Thoreau's attitude as it is revealed in this passage? Write an essay retorting to Thoreau or qualifying his argument or developing it in terms of your own temperament and circumstance.

Or write a similar essay presenting your personal philosophy of studies, food, worship, the opposite sex, entertainment, sports, book-reading, etc. Choose some notion in which you stand apart from the vulgar mob. It will not be difficult to find some body of opinion to serve as foil to your own views.

10. Explain the derivations of *boisterous, bribe, idle, minute* (l. 7), *mischief*.

A FOLK HERO[1]

VERNON LOUIS PARRINGTON

•

1. GREATEST OF ALL THE HEROES OF THE AGE WAS THE VICtor of Appomattox. His fame was in all men's mouths, and his reputation was substantial enough to withstand the attacks of enemies and the gross shortcomings of his own character. It was not for any singular or remarkable quali- 5 ties of mind or personality that General Grant was taken to the heart of his generation, but rather because he was so completely a product of the times, so strikingly an embodiment of its virtues and weaknesses. In his spectacular career were the sharp contrasts that appealed to a plebeian people 10 wanting in fine and discriminating standards of appraisal. He had come up from the people, and the marks of his origins—the slovenly manners and uncritical force of frontier folk-ways—were stamped on him as indelibly as they were stamped on his fellow soldiers who proclaimed his 15 greatness. To a later generation he seems an odd and unaccountable figure for the high rôle of national hero; yet he was as native and homespun as Lincoln, like him sprung from the common stock and learning his lessons from harsh experience, a figure blown to huge dimensions by the pas- 20 sions of civil war. A generation that discovered something praiseworthy in the "smartness" of Jim Fisk, in the burly acquisitiveness of Commodore Vanderbilt, or in the clever humbuggery of Barnum the Showman, certainly would judge with no very critical eyes the claims to greatness of a 25 grim leader of armies who succeeded where so many before had failed.

---

[1] From *The Beginnings of Critical Realism in America*, by Vernon L. Parrington; reprinted by permission of Harcourt, Brace & Company, Inc., Publishers.

2. General Grant was no conventional military hero. It was not the gold stars on his epaulets that dazzled his generation. The people of the North had seen too many gold stars rise and set on the military horizon, they had been stricken too sorely by the bitter struggle, to be caught by military popinjays. They had gone through the fire and any hero of theirs must himself have passed through the fire. It was something veracious in the man, something solid and unyielding in the soldier, something plain as an old shoe in the field marshal of bloody battles, that caught the imagination of the North and made Grant a hero—this together with a certain gift of pungent phrase, befitting the leader of democratic hosts, that served to spread his fame amongst the common people. Vicksburg did much for his reputation, but the demand for "unconditional surrender," sent to a Confederate leader, did far more. The words fixed his character in the popular mind. Here at last was a fighting man who instead of planning how to fall back, as other generals did, thought only of going ahead; so the popular judgment shut its eyes to his dull plebeian character and set a wreath on his brows. It rested there somewhat grotesquely. In spite of a deep unconscious integrity and a stubborn will that drove him forward along whatever path his feet were set on, he was the least imposing of military heroes. Short, stooped, lumpish in mind and body, unintellectual and unimaginative, devoid of ideas and with no tongue to express the incoherent emotions that surged dully in his heart, he was a commonplace fellow that no gold braid could set off. He hated war and disliked soldiering; yet accepting life with a stolid fatalism he fought his bloody way to ultimate victory.

3. Graduated from West Point after four sterile years of drill, quite uneducated and unread even in his profession, he served for a time at different army posts, went through the Mexican War—which he looked upon as a stupid imperialistic debauch—as quartermaster without gaining distinction, and eventually, oppressed by the eventless routine of garrison life, he fell into the habit of solitary drinking

and was dismissed from the service. Misfortune that it
seemed, it was his making. Only as a volunteer could he
have risen so quickly to high command; as a captain or
major in the regular army he would have been detailed as
drill-master to the raw troops and have had no chance. 70
Nevertheless hard times came with his dismissal. Indolent
by nature and inclined to drift, he was as incompetent a
man in practical affairs as one could find in a frontier
township. But with a wife and children to support he must
turn his hand to something; so he tried his luck at farming, 75
selling real estate, and various odd jobs, yet all the time
growing poorer and seedier, till the war came and picking
him up flung him to mountain heights of popularity and
reputation. Thereafter till his death he was accounted the
greatest American of his generation. No accumulating evi- 80
dence of his well-meaning but witless incapacity in civic
and political affairs could pluck from his brows the wreath
that had been thrust upon him.

4. In his spectacular career Grant was an embodiment of
the dreams of all the Beriah Sellerses of the Gilded Age. He 85
was a materialistic hero of a materialistic generation. He
was dazzled by wealth and power, and after years of bitter
poverty he sat down in the lap of luxury with huge content.
He took what the gods sent; and if houses and fast horses
and wines and cigars were showered upon him he accepted 90
them as a child would accept gifts from a fairy godmother.
He had had enough of skimping meanness; with his generation he wanted to slough off the drabness of the frontier;
he wanted the good things of life that had so long been
denied him, and he was not scrupulous about looking a gift 95
horse in the mouth. He sought out the company of rich
men. He was never happier than when enjoying the luxury
of Jay Cooke's mansion in Philadelphia or riding with A. T.
Stewart in Central Park. As he grew fat and stodgy the
vulgar side of his plebeian nature was thrown into sharper 100
relief. He accepted gifts with both hands, and he seems
never to have suspected the price that would be exacted of
the President for the presents to the General. He never real-

ized how great a bill was sent to the American people for
the wine he drank or the cigars he smoked with his wealthy
hosts; yet if the wine had been molten gold and the cigars
platinum they would have been far cheaper. In return for a
few boxes of choice Havanas, Jay Cooke laid his hands on
millions of western lands for the Northern Pacific Railway.
It was the way of the Gilded Age, and Grant was only doing
what all his friends and associates were doing. If he accepted a fifty-thousand-dollar house in Philadelphia, his
comrade General Sherman accepted a hundred-thousand-
dollar house at Washington. Such gifts were not bribes; they
were open and aboveboard; it was the free and easy way
of the times. What the age was careless about is the fact
that it is hard to refuse a reasonable request from one's
fairy godmother, and what the General never understood
is that if one is President such a godmother is certain to be
a very dangerous member of the family.

5. There was far too much of that sort of thing all about
him for Grant to serve as President with credit to himself
or profit to the country. Honest himself, he was the source
of more dishonesty in others than any other American
President. His eight years in the White House marked the
lowest depths—in domestic affairs at least—to which any
American administration has fallen. They were little better
than a national disgrace. All the festering evils of post-war
times came to a head and pock-marked the body politic
from head to foot. Scandal and corruption whispered all
about him; the hands of his closest advisers were dirty; yet
he stubbornly refused to hear the whispers or see the dirt.
In judging men and policies he was no more than a child.
He could never distinguish between an honest man and a
rascal. He was loyal to his friends, and open-handedness
he regarded as a mark of friendship. In the end his blatant
followers despoiled him of pretty nearly everything.

6. In what must pass for his political views Grant was
as naïvely uninformed as a Wyoming cowboy. Utterly wanting in knowledge of political principles, he was a fit leader
for the organized mob that called itself the Republican

party, whose chief objective was the raiding of the treasure-
box of which it was the responsible guardian. He had been
nominally a Democrat, and the first vote he cast for President he cast for Buchanan. After Lincoln's death he turned 145
naturally to President Johnson and was one of his supporters till the wily Radical group got his ear and carried
him over to the rival camp. They wanted his reputation to
hide under, and they took possession of it with no great
credit to the General's reputation. Thereafter he was a 150
Republican of the Whig wing. It was where he belonged.
He was swayed politically by his emotional reactions, and
it was natural for him to drift into the opulent camp of
money and power. His frontier democracy sloughed away,
and with his generation he went over easily to a buccaneer 155
capitalism. No social conscience obtruded itself to give him
trouble. His millionaire friends were Whig Republicans,
and with his respect for rich men, his admiration for material success, he found himself in congenial company
amongst the Whig group. About the only political policy 160
he ever interested himself in was the policy of a protective
tariff, and his Whig associates took care that his interest did
not wane. Yet so completely did the naïve General reflect
the spirit of the Gilded Age that his noisy followers, con-
spiring to confuse in the public mind southern reconstruc- 165
tion and capitalistic expansion, and hiding a precious set of
rascals in the folds of the bloody flag, came near to making
him President for a third term. The General was bitterly
disappointed at their failure, and the General's wife, who
liked to live in the White House, was even more disap- 170
pointed. To millions of Americans Grant was an authentic
hero, to Mark Twain he was a very great man, and to Jay
Cooke he was a pawn to be used in the noble strategy of
fortune-seeking. What a comedy it all seems now—yet one
that leaves an unpleasant taste in the mouth. 175

7. Yet to dismiss the stolid General thus is scarcely to
do justice to the substantial core of the man. There remains
the work written in pain during his last days, the two volumes of *Memoirs* that in their plain directness—as unin-

180 spired, says a late biographer, as "a bale of hay"—laid bare
his honest simplicity and rugged meagerness. No black-
guard and no charlatan could have written such pages. If
General Grant was not the great man so many thought, he
was a native growth from American soil, endowed like his
185 age with a dogged will and a plodding energy, and he gave
his country what he had. Though the branches of the tree
were ungainly and offered too hospitable shelter to un-
seemly birds of the night, the gnarly trunk was sound at the
heart.

※ ※ ※

This portrait is concerned not so much with Grant's life as
with his popularity. Its thesis has been suggested in the introduction to the section "Folk Heroes," of which this essay forms
a part: "It is our own secret desires we attribute to our gods,
and if from the muck of the times a queer lot of heroes was
singled out, if an undisciplined generation rioting in its new
freedom chose to honor men who had scrambled upward in
uncouth ways, it only suggests that such figures were a composite picture of the secret desires of an age vastly concerned
with getting on." To put it briefly, Grant's admirers saw in
him, accurately enough, a glorified version of themselves.
Parrington's purpose is presumably to treat Grant's career and
character as a symbol of the age.

1. Outline the passage, by summarizing in single sentences
what seems to be the point of each paragraph.

2. In what respects is Grant shown to represent his generation? Let your tentative list be rather full; then revise it so that
it covers the ground without saying the same thing twice and
without making trivial distinctions. Give references to lines
in the text.

3. Parrington's prose is adorned with figures at once ingenious and perspicuous. Thus the double metonymy of "gold
stars" (ll. 28-31) enlivens the thought of both sentences; the
venerable personification, "lap of luxury" (l. 88), is rejuvenated
by the verb "sat down in." Select from the whole essay the ten
most effective figures of speech.

4. In amplifying his essay, Parrington made frequent use

of words in pairs: "It was not for any *singular or remarkable* qualities of *mind or personality* . . ." (ll. 5-6.) "Mind or personality" is more extensive than either term alone. But it is hard to see enough difference between singular qualities and remarkable qualities to justify the alternative. "Fine" and "discriminating" merely duplicate each other as qualifiers of "standards of appraisal." (l. 11.) Note all such pairs of words or phrases throughout the essay, and decide in each instance whether the doubling is justified.

5. The language of Par. 6 is very vigorous: Parrington seems mightily to approve or disapprove of something. Of what? "Frontier democracy"? "Capitalistic expansion"? The political views of cowboys? There are other interesting phrases in the paragraph. Say as briefly as possible what seems to have been the writer's implication.

6. Explain the derivations of *burly, charlatan, debauch, fatalism, marshal, pungent, soldier.*

THE AUTOCRAT[1]

OLIVER WENDELL HOLMES

•

1. I WANT TO MAKE A LITERARY CONFESSION NOW, WHICH
I believe nobody has made before me. You know very well
that I write verses sometimes, because I have read some
of them at this table. (The company assented,—two or
5 three of them in a resigned sort of way, as I thought, as if
they supposed I had an epic in my pocket, and were going
to read half a dozen books or so for their benefit.)—I continued. . . . Now I never wrote a "good" line in my life,
but the moment after it was written it seemed a hundred
10 years old. Very commonly I had a sudden conviction that
I had seen it somewhere. Possibly I may have sometimes
unconsciously stolen it, but I do not remember that I ever
once detected any historical truth in these sudden convictions of the antiquity of my new thought or phrase. I have
15 learned utterly to distrust them, and never allow them to
bully me out of a thought or line.

2. This is the philosophy of it. (Here the number of
the company was diminished by a small secession.) Any
new formula which suddenly emerges in our consciousness
20 has its roots in long trains of thought; it is virtually old
when it first makes its appearance among the recognized
growths of our intellect. Any crystalline group of musical
words has had a long and still period to form in. Here is
one theory.

25 3. But there is a larger law which perhaps comprehends
these facts. It is this. The rapidity with which ideas grow
old in our memories is in a direct ratio to the squares of
their importance. Their apparent age runs up miraculously,

[1] From *The Autocrat of the Breakfast-Table*, by Oliver Wendell Holmes;
reprinted by arrangement with Houghton Mifflin Company, Publishers.

like the value of diamonds, as they increase in magnitude. A great calamity, for instance, is as old as the trilobites an hour after it has happened. It stains backward through all the leaves we have turned over in the book of life, before its blot of tears or of blood is dry on the page we are turning. For this we seem to have lived; it was fore-shadowed in dreams that we leaped out of in the cold sweat of terror; in the "dissolving views" of dark day-visions; all omens pointed to it; all paths led to it. After the toss-ing half-forgetfulness of the first sleep that follows such an event, it comes upon us afresh, as a surprise, at waking; in a few moments it is old again,—old as eternity.

4. (I wish I had not said all this then and there. I might have known better. The pale schoolmistress, in her mourning dress, was looking at me, as I noticed, with a wild sort of expression. All at once the blood dropped out of her cheeks as the mercury drops from a broken barom-eter-tube, and she melted away from her seat like an image of snow; a slung-shot could not have brought her down better. God forgive me!

5. After this little episode, I continued, to some few who remained balancing teaspoons on the edges of cups, twirling knives, or tilting upon the hind legs of their chairs until their heads reached the wall, where they left gratuitous advertisements of various popular cosmetics.)

6. When a person is suddenly thrust into any strange, new position of trial, he finds the place fits him as if he had been measured for it. He has committed a great crime, for instance, and is sent to the State Prison. The traditions, prescriptions, limitations, privileges, all the sharp condi-tions of his new life, stamp themselves upon his conscious-ness as the signet on soft wax;—a single impression is enough. Let me strengthen the image a little. Did you ever happen to see that most soft-spoken and velvet-handed steam-engine at the Mint? The smooth piston slides back-ward and forward as a lady might slip her delicate finger in and out of a ring. The engine lays one of *its* fingers calmly, but firmly, upon a bit of metal; it is a coin now,

and will remember that touch, and tell a new race about it, when the date upon it is crusted over with twenty centuries. So it is that a great silent-moving misery puts a
70 new stamp on us in an hour or a moment,—as sharp an impression as if it had taken half a lifetime to engrave it.

7. It is awful to be in the hands of the wholesale professional dealers in misfortune; undertakers and jailers magnetize you in a moment, and you pass out of the individual
75 life you were living into the rhythmical movements of their horrible machinery. Do the worst you can, or suffer the worst that can be thought of, you find yourself in a category of humanity that stretches back as far as Cain, and with an expert at your elbow who has studied your case all out
80 beforehand, and is waiting for you with his implements of hemp or mahogany. I believe if a man were to be burned in any of our cities tomorrow for heresy, there would be found a master of ceremonies who knew just how many fagots were necessary, and the best way of
85 arranging the whole matter.

❈ ❈ ❈

Holmes's essays were shaped as the discourse of the Autocrat at a boarding-house; his table-mates were of diverse walks of American life.

His essays are familiar or informal. This one begins with the qualms of a versifier and ends with the heretic's fagots and is chiefly concerned with neither. Most of the essays you have read in this collection are ostensibly designed to explain some particular historical event or class of events, and this focusing of interest appears in their structure. Yet it may be argued that the ultimate value of history is its illumination of human behavior in general; historical studies do not so much provide us with rules of thumb for future situations as they enlarge our understanding of man's nature and his position in the universe, whereby we may conduct our lives in the best way given us to desire. The informal essay is another means to the same intelligence.

1. The essay though discursive is coherent. The thought moves conversationally from point to point; only the points do

not lie in a straight line. Sometimes Holmes proceeds from a general principle to a particular human experience which illustrates it; sometimes he proceeds from the human experience to an illuminating principle or law. Outline the logic of the essay by tracing these movements; there are some six or seven steps in all.

2. The mood of the essay is varied; intense moments are punctuated with somewhat carefully calculated drolleries. What are the several chief jests? Weigh their effect; do you think that any might advantageously have been omitted or modified?

3. Holmes's imagery is striking: he has the knack of embodying in a succinct metaphor an idea or a feeling which could be more literally defined only laboriously if at all. E.g., the roots of thought, in lines 18-22; again, the still, cold crystallization of a beautiful phrase—like ice on the lake, of a winter's night—in lines 22-23.

a) Indicate the notable metaphors by marginal checkmarks.

b) Select the three most effective and comment on them; try to account for their effectiveness.

c) Select the two least effective; try to account for their weakness.

d) Do you think Holmes's figures of speech as good as those which Professor Parrington was able to think up? What seems to be the difference between the figurative styles of the two writers?

4. Work up some metaphors of your own. Do you think novels are like ships or photographs or blindfolds? Is time your isthmus footing between two eternities, or the endless serpent of the past swallowing the endless serpent of the future, or a stream down which we float, or a parade which we watch go by, or a moving shadow under a ring of light? Now you try.

WITCHCRAFT[1]

GEORGE LYMAN KITTREDGE

•

1. THE ACCESSIBLE MATERIALS FOR A HISTORY OF ELIZA-
bethan witchcraft are scattered and fragmentary. Much is
lost, and much remains inedited. Yet we cannot hope to
understand the prosecutions of the last sixty years of the
5 seventeenth century, whether in Old England or in New,
until we arrive at a substantially accurate comprehension
of what was thought and done at the close of the great
Queen's reign. It is not only the dogmas of the theologians,
the tenets of the physicians, and the rules of the law that
10 we need to know, but, above everything else, the beliefs
and feelings of the populace—of the folk itself.

2. For it is in this matter of witchcraft, if anywhere, that
public opinion is supreme. The populace may, perhaps, be
restrained by the more enlightened part of the community,
15 but the so-called governing classes cannot prosecute with success if the populace does not approve. Witch-hunting never
flourishes unless the common people are eager for it. It is to
them that the officers of the law must look for testimony,
and it is the jury of the vicinage that renders the verdict.
20 Experience has taught over and over again, how hard it is
for the most skeptical judge to bring about an acquittal in
a particular case when the neighborhood from which the
jury comes is convinced of the reality of the crime in
general. There was a famous witch-trial at Exeter, England,
25 in 1682. Roger North was present, and here is his account
of the state of public opinion:

The women were very old, decrepit, and impotent, and were
brought to the assizes with as much noise and fury of the

[1] From *Witchcraft in Old and New England,* by G. L. Kittredge; reprinted by permission of Harvard University Press.

rabble against them as could be shewed on any occasion. The stories of their arts were in everyone's mouth, and they were 30 not content to belie them in the country, but even in the city where they were to be tried miracles were fathered upon them, as that the judge's coach was fixed upon the castle bridge, and the like. All which the country believed, and accordingly persecuted the wretched old creatures. A less zeal in a city 35 or kingdom hath been the overture of defection or revolution, and if these women had been acquitted, it was thought that the country people would have committed some disorder.

This was a case in which it seems clear that the judges 40 would have preferred a verdict of "not guilty" if they had been left to themselves. Another striking example is that of Jane Wenham, who was condemned to death for witchcraft in 1712. Her trial is notable for its recent date. By that time there was much incredulity on the subject in the minds of 45 educated men. Chief Justice Powell, who presided, made open fun of the evidence and summed up strongly in the defendant's favor, but in vain. He was obliged to sentence the woman to death and to content himself with procuring her pardon from the crown. Nor was it until 1736 that the 50 English and Scottish statutes against witchcraft were repealed.

3. In considering the tenacity of the popular belief on this subject, we should never forget that the essence of witchcraft is *maleficium*. The hatred and terror which a witch evokes 55 is due to her will and her power to inflict bodily injury. Compacts with the devil, the suckling of imps, the violation of graves, the abominations of the Witches' Sabbath—these are mere incidentals, the paraphernalia of the art. They aggravate the offence, to be sure, and proof that a woman 60 is implicated in such horrors may send her to the scaffold or the stake. But, in the last analysis, every witch is prosecuted, not because she amuses herself with riding a broomstick or because she has taken a fiend for a lover: she is hunted down like a wolf because she is an enemy to man-65 kind. Her heart is full of malignity. For a harsh word, or

the refusal of a bit of bread, she becomes your mortal foe.
And her revenge is out of all proportion to the affront,
for she is in league with spirits of evil who are almost
70 infinite in strength. She sends blight upon your crops,
the rot upon your sheep, the murrain on your cattle; your
house takes fire; your ship is cast away. She visits you and
your family with strange wasting diseases—with palsy, with
consumption, with raging fever, with madness, with death.
75 Witch-trials are not prompted by theological hair-splitting,
by systems of devil-lore, by the text, "Thou shalt not suffer
a witch to live." *These all come after the fact.* It is self-
protection that incites the accuser. His cause is fear—and
fear of bodily harm. The witch is a murderer, or may
80 become a murderer on the slightest provocation. She cannot be spared, for there is no safety for life, body, or estate
until she is sent out of the world.

4. Now the mere creed—the belief that witches exist
and that they can work supernaturally to the injury and
85 even to the destruction of their enemies—is the heritage of
the human race. The Englishman of the sixteenth or seventeenth century did not excogitate or dream it for himself,
or borrow it from the Continent, or learn it from his
spiritual advisers whether before the Reformation or after.
90 He inherited it in an unbroken line from his primeval
ancestors. And along with it came another dogma, likewise
of abysmal antiquity—the theory that all diseases are of
supernatural origin. This dogma had, to be sure, been
somewhat limited in scope as the shaman developed into
95 the physician, but it was still extant and still vigorous.
Every malady that baffled the doctors was ascribed to witchcraft, often by the doctors themselves; and all sudden or
virulent or wasting maladies lay under suspicion. These
things are truisms, but they are continually lost sight of
100 by the investigators of English witchcraft. There is a constant assumption that such beliefs are abnormal, a persistent
tendency to ignore the fact that it was rather a mark of
exceptional enlightenment in popular diagnosis to look to
natural causes than a mark of positive credulity or super-

stition to look to supernatural causes. In brief, the ordinary [105]
Elizabethan, in this essential particular—the doctrine of
maleficium and its application to disease—had not yet
emerged from barbarism. And it was the doctrine of
maleficium, and nothing else, that made the witch-creed
terrible. [110]

5. After a witch had been arrested, it is true, she often
fell into the hands of the learned who asked her questions
based on an elaborate system of demonology, and, when
so interrogated, she often confessed strange things, which
the industry of scholars may trace to foreign creeds or [115]
imported philosophies. Some of this erudite material, through
the pulpit or otherwise, did certainly attach itself to the
native and popular beliefs. And thus we may easily be
led to fancy that judges, philosophers, divines—and even
King James I—were to blame for the prevalence of Eng- [120]
lish witchcraft in the seventeenth century. But such elabora-
tions were merely incidental. They came into a particular
case, if at all, only when the witch had once been cried
out upon. Somebody falls sick, and the doctors cannot
cure him; a child has hysterical fits and is grievously tor- [125]
mented. There are aged women in the village at whom we
have long looked askance. They are foul-mouthed, perhaps,
and prone to curse when we offend them; or they have
laid claim to occult power, and have traded on the terror
they inspire. They may even imagine themselves to hold [130]
intercourse with Satan, for they share the current superstitions and are not very strong in their wits. One of these
beldames is mentioned as the bewitcher, perhaps because
the patient's distempered fancy has seen a face and called
a name. Then old rumors are revived: Smith's cattle died [135]
year before last, or Jones's little son. For there is ever at hand
a huge mass of such latent evidence, all connected with
the primitive doctrine of *maleficium*, and only waiting for
a prosecution to bring it before the courts. When the trial
begins, we may hear of compacts with Satan, of flights [140]
through the air, of sordid and hideous revels at the Witches'
Sabbath. But such things are mere confirmatory details.

The essential point, the really efficient impulse, is always *maleficium*—injury to goods or body or life through super-
145 natural means.

6. For England, the worst period of witch-persecution is, by common consent, the seventeenth century—the century of the Lancashire witches, of Matthew Hopkins and John Stearne, of Glanvil's *Saducismus Triumphatus*. The
150 reign of James, we remember, covers exactly twenty-two years, from March, 1603, to March, 1625. In 1604 Parliament enacted a famous statute against witchcraft, usually called the statute of James I. The idea has been prevalent that the delusion was dying out at the close of Elizabeth's
155 reign, and that the advent of the British Solomon gave it fresh vigor.

7. My purpose is to report an extremely interesting case of alleged witchcraft which occurred in Devonshire in 1601 and 1602, just before James came to the throne. This
160 alone would make it significant enough. But it is still further noteworthy because it exhibits the phenomena in what we may call a pure form. We have only the testimony of voluntary, and for the most part aggrieved, witnesses. There are no arguments, no confessions, no comments from
165 the bench. There is nothing but the beliefs and experiences of the witnesses themselves, honestly detailed according to their lights. Hence the documents afford us a perfect picture of the witchcraft creed as held by the common people. And we find, as we should expect, that the sum and sub-
170 stance of it all was *maleficium*—injury to the property and the health of the victims, amounting even to ruin and death.

8. The documents consist of eleven "examinations," taken before a Devon justice of the peace, Sir Thomas Ridge-
175 way, in 1601 and 1602. The scene of the trouble was Hardness, a village close to Dartmouth. Here lived Michael Trevisard, a fisherman, with his wife Alice and his son Peter. All were defamed for witchcraft, and suspicion against Michael and Alice was of long standing. The wit-
180 nesses against them were persons of their own humble

condition, belonging in Hardness or the vicinity. There is no trace of influence from the clergy or the gentry. It was the villagers themselves who appealed to the magistrate for protection. One witness speaks of a number of them as going to Tunstall, to the house of Sir Thomas Ridgeway, [185] to make a complaint, and as meeting Alice Trevisard on the way back. Whether the accused persons were ever brought to trial we do not know, but it is clear that Ridgeway had these documents prepared for eventual use at the assizes. [190]

9. The whole essential body of the witchcraft doctrine occurs, in a highly condensed form, in the examination of Alice Butler, of Hardness.

Devon Th' examination of Alice Butler of Hardness, in the County aforesaid, widow, taken before Sir Thomas Ridgeway, [195] Knight, the second of October, 1601.

1. This examinate saith that she, sitting at a door or bench in Hardness aforesaid about Christide last was twelvemonth with one Michael Trevysard of Hardness aforesaid, used these words: "I would my child were able to run as well as any of [200] these children that run here in the street!" Then said Trevysard, "It shall never run!" "No? That's hard!" says this examinate again. "No, it shall never run," answered Trevysard, "till thou hast another," repeating the same words a dozen several times at the least with great vehemency. Whereupon this examinate, [205] being much troubled in mind, especially upon a fear conceived by her before through the general bad report that went of him, departed from him. And the very same week the same child sickened, and consumed away, being well one day and ill another, for the space of seventeen weeks or thereabout, and then died. [210]

2. This examinate further saith, that Peter Trevysard, son of the said Michael Trevisard, came to this examinate's house to borrow a hatchet, which Alice Beere, servant to this examinate, denied, to whom the said Michael answered, "Shall I not have it? I will do thee a good turn ere twelvemonth be at an end." [215] And shortly the said Alice Beere sickened, continuing one day well and another day ill, for the space of eleven weeks, and then died. In which case both the husband of this examinate and another child of theirs fell sick, and so continued seventeen or eighteen weeks, and then died. [220]

Th: Ridgway.

10. The regular fashion of commenting on such utterances as these is to cry out against the malicious folly of the accuser and to lament the hard lot of the accused. May I be permitted, for once, to abandon custom, and to express my sympathy with poor Alice Butler, who had lost her husband and two of her children by some strange wasting sickness, for which she had no name, and who could only revert to the primeval tenets of savage man in her attempt to explain so dreadful a visitation? Few utterances in any records are more artlessly pathetic.

11. To the student of English witchcraft the document is very valuable on account of the purity and simplicity of type which it exemplifies. *Maleficium* is the gist of the whole matter, and the process described is perfectly accordant to rule. We have the *damnum minatum* and the *malum secutum*. That is all. There are no complications whatever. There is not a trace of those foreign and learned elements that are often thought to constitute the bulk of the English witchcraft doctrine after the Reformation. There is no Black Man, no book to sign, no compact with Satan. There are no infernal revels, no fiendish lovers. In short, there is nothing that is non-essential. Alice Butler's evidence is precisely the kind of testimony that might have been offered against a witch in any land and in any stage of civilization, from the Stone Age to day-before-yesterday. It would be quite pertinent at the trial of a witch of Ashantee or Congo or the Australian bush. It exhibits the primitive and universal creed of the whole human race, preserved without the contamination of culture or education, and surviving every religious vicissitude, to the beginning of the seventeenth century, in one of the most enlightened countries in the world. Incidentally, it was quite enough to send Michael Trevisard to the scaffold if he came to trial and the jury believed Alice's story. Finally, nobody was to blame. The responsibility lay not upon the jurists or the theologians or the neighborhood: it was the burden of the human race as a whole.

12. An equally distressing case was that of Joan Badda-

ford. Alice Trevisard, it appears, had fallen out with John 260
Baddaford, Joan's husband, and had "said unto him that
he should go to Pursever Wood and gather up his wits."
The precise meaning of this railing speech escapes me, but
I fancy it was equivalent to calling John a scatter-brained
fool. It was manifestly possible, if the sequel should warrant, 265
to interpret Alice's jeering words as a threat that John
should lose his mind. The sequel did so warrant.

Within three weeks after [Joan alleged] the said John Baddaford made a voyage to Rochelle, in the Hope of Dittsham,
and returned home again out of his wits, and so continued by 270
the space of two years, tearing and renting his clothes, in such
sort as four or five men were hardly able to bind him and keep
him in order.

13. On the occasion of the same quarrel, Joan averred,
Alice Trevisard had "further threatened this examinate 275
that within seven years after she should not be worth a
groat, nor have a house to dwell in, nor a coat to her back."
And these threats came true, for "whereas she had at that
time the fee simple of an house worth one hundred pounds,
now is she worth nothing." 280

14. Let us bear in mind that the things to which poor
Joan Baddaford bore witness must have been facts. Her insane husband and her fallen fortunes were neither delusions nor superstitions. We cannot ridicule or denounce;
we can only pity. If Joan was a bad logician—if she reasoned 285
post hoc ergo propter hoc—so do we, every day of our lives.
And as to threats, they are still admissible as evidence
against an accused murderer.

※ ※ ※

1. What parts of the argument of Par. 2 are illustrated by
the quotation from Roger North? Refer to particular lines in the
quotation.

2. What does "the mere creed" (l. 83) exclude? Does it
include the doctrine of *maleficium*?

3. Before presenting the main body of evidence—the Devonshire depositions—Kittredge gave his argument in full in Pars. 1-5. Summarize the thesis of each of these paragraphs in one sentence—which may contain both an assertion and a denial or a concession.

4. Pars. 3 and 5 are quite similar in thought; how do they differ in emphasis or tone or point of view?

5. Summarize the ideas which Kittredge seems chiefly concerned to oppose.

6. Do Hopkins, Stearne, and Glanvil (ll. 148-149) represent the populace or the more enlightened part of the community? Why are they introduced here?

7. Kittredge's preliminary comments on the depositions call attention to their circumstances. What is the significance of each of the following facts?
   a) the date (l. 159)
   b) that the witnesses were voluntary (l. 163)
   c) that the witnesses were aggrieved (l. 163)
   d) that there were no confessions (l. 164)
   e) that there were no comments from the bench (ll. 164-165)
   f) that the witnesses were of humble condition (ll. 180-181)
   g) what one witness said of the trip to and from Tunstall (ll. 184-187)
   h) Ridgway's purpose in preparing the documents (ll. 189-190).

8. What do *damnum minatum* and *malum secutum* mean? (ll. 236-237.) Which lines of the deposition come under each heading?

9. What does *post hoc ergo propter hoc* mean?

10. Perhaps it would have been better, in organizing the essay, first to present the depositions to the unprejudiced reader, and then to develop the argument (Pars. 1-5) based upon that evidence. Decide whether you think such a procedure would have been feasible or not, and explain several of its advantages or difficulties.

11. The compound narrative in Par. 5 is skillfully managed. Summarize it, omitting the specific details, using the general terms of the text or phrasing your own.

12. Compare the behavior and the psychology of the Trevi-sards (Pars. 9, 12, 13) with that of the old women in lines 126-132.

13. Read Pars. 3 and 5 aloud; in which do you find the more felicitous or striking effects of rhythm? Just where?

14. Comment on the following changes of wording: *evokes* (l. 55) to *provokes*; *incidentals* (l. 59) to *trifles*; *malignity* (l. 66) to *evil* or *malice*; *abysmal* (l. 92) to *vast*; *curse* (l. 128) to *swear*; *mentioned* (l. 133) to *accused*; *a face, a name* (ll. 134-135) to *her face, her name*; *truisms* (l. 99) to *platitudes*; *barbarism* (l. 108) to *barbarity*; *visitation* (l. 230) to *misfortune*; *responsibility* (l. 256) to *guilt*.

15. Explain the derivations of *abomination, beldame, murrain, palsy, paraphernalia, revel.*

16. *Woolgathering* may be analogous to Alice Trevisard's retort of lines 261-262. Make a list of popular terms alluding to mental weakness or aberration; work this material into a short essay.

17. Or make a list of terms applied to dealers in the black art (*witch, hag, necromancer*, etc.) with their derivations; work this material into a short essay.

THE FLORENTINE PAINTER[1]

FRANK JEWETT MATHER

•

1. FLORENCE WAS THEN AS NOW A LITTLE CITY, ITS POPULA-
tion about 100,000 souls, but it was growing. The old second wall of about two miles' circuit was already condemned
in favor of a turreted circuit of over six. Up the Arno the
5 forest-clad ridge of Vallombrosa was much as it is today;
down the valley the jagged peaks of the Carrara mountains
barred the way to the sea. The surrounding vineyards and
olive orchards by reason of encroaching forest were less
extensive than they are now, but through every gate and
10 from every tower one could see smiling fields guarded by
battlemented villas. In the city, the fortress towers of the
old nobility, partizans mostly of the foreign Emperor, rose
thickly, but already dismantled at their fighting tops, for
the people, meaning strictly the ruling merchant and manu-
15 facturing classes, had lately taken the rule from the old
nobles. Many of these had fled; some had been banished,
as was soon to be that reckless advocate of the Emperor,
Dante Alighieri, an excellent poet of love foolishly dabbling
in politics. Other patricians sulked in their fortress palaces.
20 Some shrewdly got themselves demoted and joined the
ruling trade guilds. Of these guilds a big four, five, or six
governed the city, while a minor dozen had political privilege. Only guild members voted for the city officers. The
guilds combined the function of a trade union and an
25 employer's association, including all members of the craft
from the youngest apprentice to the richest boss-contractor.
Such a guild as the notaries' must have been much like a
bar association, while the wholesale merchants' guild must

[1] From *A History of Italian Painting*, by F. J. Mather; reprinted by
permission of Henry Holt & Company, Inc., Publishers.

have resembled a chamber of commerce. The guild folk had early allied themselves with the Pope, the only perma- 30 nent representative of the principle of order in Italy. The Pope was also the bulwark of the new free communes against the claims of the Teutonic Emperors. So in Florence piety, liberty, and prosperity were convertible terms.

2. Within the narrow walls was a bustling, neighborly, 35 squabbling and making-up life. Everybody knew everybody else. The craftsman worked in the little open archways you may still see in the Via San Gallo, in sight and hearing of the passing world. Of weavers' shops alone there were 300. No western city was ever prouder than Florence in 40 those days. Her credit was good from the Urals to the Pentland Hills. Her gold florin was everywhere standard exchange. She had secret ways of finishing the fine cloths that came in ships and caravans from Ghent, Ypres, and Arras; she handled the silks of China and converted the 45 raw pelts of the north into objects of fashion.

3. Her civic pride was actively expressing itself in build- ing. Between 1294 and 1299 she had projected a new cathe- dral, the great Franciscan church of Santa Croce, a new town hall, and the massive walls we still see. For stately 50 buildings she had earlier had only the Baptistry, in which every baby was promptly christened, and the new church of the Friars Preachers (Dominicans), Santa Maria Novella. In considering this Florence you must think of a hard- headed, full-blooded, ambitious community, frankly de- 55 voted to money-making, but desiring wealth chiefly as a step towards fame. Since the painter could provide fame in this world and advance one's position in the next, his estate was a favored one.

4. The painter himself was just a fine craftsman. He 60 kept a shop and called it such—a *bottega*. He worked only to order. There were no exihibitions, no museums, no academies, no art schools, no prizes, no dealers. The paint- ers modestly joined the guild of the druggists (*speziali*), who were their color makers, quite as the up-to-date news- 65 paper reporter affiliates himself with the typographical

union. When a rich man wanted a picture, he simply went
to a painter's shop and ordered it, laying down as a matter
of course the subject and everything about the treatment
70 that interested him. If the work was of importance, a contract and specifications were drawn up. The kind of colors,
pay by the job or by the day, the amount to be painted by
the contracting artist himself, the time of completion, with
or without penalty—all this was precisely nominated in the
75 bond. Naturally the painter used his shop-assistants and apprentices as much as possible. Often he did little himself
except heads and principal figures. But he made the designs
and carefully supervised their execution on panel or wall.
A Florentine painter's *bottega* then had none of the precious-
80 ness of a modern painter's studio. It was rather like a
decorator's shop of today, the master being merely the business head and guiding artistic taste. When we speak of a
fresco by Giotto, we do not mean that Giotto painted much
of it, any more than a La Farge window implies that our
85 great American master of stained-glass design himself cut
and set the glass. The painter of Florence had to be a jack-
of-all-trades, a color grinder, a cabinet maker, and a wood
carver; a gilder; to be capable of copying any design and
of inventing fine decorative features himself. He must be
90 equally competent in the delicate methods of tempera
painting as in the resolute procedures of fresco.

5. These two methods set distinct limits to the work
and its effects. The colors were ground up day by day in
the shop. Each had its little pot. There was no palette.
95 Hence only a few colors were used, and with little mixing.
For tempera painting a good wooden panel—preferably
of poplar—was grounded with successive coats of finest
plaster of Paris in glue and rubbed down to ivory smoothness. The composition was then copied in minutely from
100 a working drawing. The gold background inherited from
the workers in mosaic was laid on in pure leaf. The composition was first lightly shaded and modelled either in
green or brown earth, and then finished up a bit at a
time, in colors tempered with egg or vegetable albumen.

The paints were thick and could not be swiftly manip- 105
ulated; the whole surface set and so hardened that re-
touching was difficult. How so niggling a method produced
so broad and harmonious effects will seem a mystery to
the modern artist. It was due to system and sacrifice.
Though the work was done piecemeal, everything was 110
thought out in advance. Dark shadows and accidents of
lighting which would mar the general blond effect were
ignored. The beauty desired was not that of nature, but
that of enamels and semi-precious stones. These panels
are glorious in azures, cinnabars, crimsons, emerald-greens, 115
and whites partaking of all of these hues. Their delicacy
is enhanced by carved frames, at this moment, 1300, simply
gabled and moulded; later built up and arched and fretted
with the most fantastic gothic features.

6. If the painter in tempera required chiefly patience 120
and delicacy, the painter in fresco must have resolution and
audacity. He must calculate each day's work exactly, and
a whole day's work could be spoiled by a single slip of the
hand in the tired evening hour. For fresco, the working
sketch was roughly copied in outline on a plaster wall. 125
Then any part selected for a day's work was covered with
a new coat of fine plaster. The effaced part of the design
must be rapidly redrawn on the wet ground. Then the
colors were laid on from their little pots, and only the
sound mineral colors which resist lime could be employed. 130
The vehicle was simply water. The colors were sucked deep
into the wet plaster, and united with it to form a surface
as durable as the wall itself. Generally the colors were
merely divided into three values,—light, pure colors, and
dark. Everything was kept clear, rather flat, and blond, 135
highly simple and beautifully decorative. One of the later
painters, Cennino Cennini (active about 1400), tells us
that a single head was a day's work for a good *frescante*.
The touch had to be sure, for a misstroke meant scraping
the wet plaster off, relaying it, and starting all over again. 140
The fresco painter accordingly needed discipline and
method. Nothing could be farther from modern inspira-

tional methods. Where everything was systematized and
calculated in advance, you will see it was quite safe for
145 a master to entrust his designs to pupils who knew his
wishes. Every fresco when dry was more or less retouched
in tempera, but the best artists did this sparingly, knowing
that the retouches would soon blacken badly or flake off.

7. So much for the shop methods. Now for him who,
150 makes shops possible—the patron. A wealthy Florentine as
naturally wanted to invest in a frescoed chapel as a wealthy
American does in a fleet of motor cars. Considering the
changed value of money, one indulgence was about as
costly as the other. But the Florentine never quite regarded
155 paintings as luxuries. They were necessary to him. He
loved them. They enhanced his prestige in this world and
improved his chances in the next. Then to beautify a
church was really to magnify the liberty and prosperity of
Florence, which largely derived from the Holy See. Recall
160 that every Florentine was born a Catholic, baptized in the
fair Church of St. John with the name of a saint. This
saint, he believed, could aid him morally and materially,
was in every sense his celestial patron. It paid to do the
saint honor, and that could best be done through the
165 painter's art. The poorest man might have a small portrait
of his patron, a rich man might endow a chapel and cause
all his patron's miracles to be pictured on the wall. Think
also that every altar—a dozen or more in every large church
—was a shrine, containing the bread and wine that by the
170 never-ceasing miracle of the Mass became the Saviour's
body and blood; and was also a reliquary or tomb, containing in whole or part the body of some saint. Every
altar then, and every chapel inclosing one, cried out for a
twofold interpretation of its meaning. Everything about the
175 Eucharist had to be explained (involving pretty nearly all
of Biblical history), and the particular relic required similar
illumination. Since many of the faithful could not read,
and the Catholic Church has ever been merciful as regards
sermonizing, these explanations of the altar as miracle

shrine of Our Lord and as tomb of a particular saint were 180
best made pictorially, and generally were so made.

※ ※ ※

Professor Mather's *History of Italian Painting* grew out of
lectures, "only slightly retouched and amplified." The prose is
colorful, conversational in its idiom and rhythms, and well
knit. Before discussing individual painters of the Florentine
school, Professor Mather has presented certain preliminary general information: a) the spirit of the commune in which the
artists worked, Pars. 1-3; b) commercial practice, technics, and
the market, Pars. 4-7; c) the subject matter, influenced by the
recent religious and literary revivals; and d) the previous style
—whence there is a natural transition to the work of particular
artists. Only the first two sections are printed here. The
rhetoric of this arrangement is plain enough; broadly, it proceeds from the general to the more specific and more immediately pertinent.

1. Demonstrate the validity of placing a) before b) by
noting those remarks concerning the painter and his trade in
Pars. 4-7 that have been anticipated and prepared for in Pars.
1-3. You should find at least five such references.

2. Supply a set of three labels, of one word each, which will
distinguish the special topics of Pars. 1, 2, and 3.

3. Explain the conclusion that "piety, liberty, and prosperity were convertible terms." Are they always so?

4. With what apparent ease Mather got from "Florence"
in line 1 to "the painter" in line 57, developing his survey
coherently, yet managing to include a diversity of preliminary
information. Analyze the rhetorical coherence of this section.

   a) By what phrase or reference is Par. 2 linked to Par. 3?
   b) How is Par. 3 linked to Par. 2?
   c) Trace Mather's steps through Par. 1 by means of a phrase
outline, each item of which will have some relation to the preceding one: Florence growing—walls too narrow—view outside walls—etc.
   d) At what point in the first three paragraphs are they
summarized?
   e) Where is the last sentence of Par. 3 reiterated?

5. What are the linking phrases in Pars. 5, 6, and 7?

6. What three topics are treated in each of the paragraphs on technic? (Pars. 5, 6.) Mark off the parts in the text. Can you see any reason for the different arrangement of these topics in the two paragraphs?

7. Which lines in Par. 7 explain the demand for tempera paintings, and which the demand for frescoes?

8. Often the conditions of Florentine life or painting have been made plainer by comparisons or contrasts with modern times. Find ten such allusions.

9. What is the literary allusion in lines 74-75? Is it appropriate?

10. Find half a dozen phrasings, throughout the essay, which you think in one way or another give the prose an easy, conversational tone.

11. The growth of Florence was made apparent by the inadequacy of the second wall; where else in Par. 1 do you find an historical circumstance presented in architectural terms? What changes in the life of your own city might be illustrated by changes in its physical aspect? Write them up in several good sentences.

12. The patron, we are told, made shops possible, and he laid down such specifications of subject and treatment as interested him. In what other ways have artists turned their paintings or writings into bread and butter? How do you suppose that these various marketing arrangements may have affected their work? Which do you think most salutary for the artist?

13. The Italian *speziale,* a druggist, a French *épicerie,* a grocer's shop, and English *spice* are cognates; how do you account for this?

14. The derivation of *florin* is obvious. Work up a list of coins (ducat, bezant, heller, lira, etc.), with their derivations. What are the chief principles by which coins have been named?

15. Explain the derivations of *azure, gothic, guild, orchard, patron.*

THE CLASSICAL MYTH IN AMERICAN ARCHITECTURE[1]

LEWIS MUMFORD

•

1. THESE EDUCATED EIGHTEENTH-CENTURY GENTLEMEN, these contemporaries of "Junius" and Gibbon, who had read Horace and Livy and Plutarch, had one foot in their own age, and the other in the grave of Rome. Thomas Jefferson exemplified this whole culture at its best and gave it a definite stamp: he combined in almost equal degrees the statesman, the student, and the artist. Not merely did Jefferson design his own Monticello; he executed a number of other houses for the surrounding gentry—Shadwell, Edgehill, Farrington—to say nothing of the Virginia State Capitol and the church and university at Charlottesville. It was Jefferson who in America first gave a strict interpretation to classicism; for he had nothing but contempt for the free, Georgian vernacular which was making its way among those who regarded the classical past as little more than a useful embellishment.

2. The contrast between the classical and the vernacular, between the architecture of the plantation and the architecture of the village, between the work of the craftsman and the work of the gentleman and the professional architect, became even more marked after the Revolutionary War. As a result of that re-crystallization of American society, the conditions of classical culture and classical civilization were for a short time fused in the activities of the community, even in the town. One may express the transformation in a crude way by saying that the carpenter-builder had been content with a classical finish; the architects of

---

[1] From *Sticks and Stones*, by Lewis Mumford; reprinted by permission of W. W. Norton & Company, Inc.

the early republic worked upon a classical foundation. It was the Revolution itself, I believe, that turned the classical taste into a myth which had the power to move men and mold their actions.

3. The merchant who has spent his hours in the counting house and on the quay cannot with the most lofty effort convert himself into a classical hero. It is different with men who have spent long nights and days wrangling in the State House, men who have ridden on horseback through a campaign, men who have plotted like Catiline and denounced like Cicero, men whose daily actions are governed with the fine resolution of a Roman general or dictator. Unconsciously, such men want a stage to set off and magnify their actions. King Alfred can perhaps remain a king, though he stays in a cottage and minds the cakes on the griddle; but most of us need a little scenery and ritual to confirm these high convictions. If the tailors had not produced the frock-coat, Daniel Webster would have had to invent one. The merchant wants his little comforts and conveniences; at most, he desires the architect to make his gains conspicuous; but the hero who has drawn his sword or addressed an assembly wants elbow room for gestures. His parlor must be big enough for a public meeting, his dining room for a banquet. So it follows that whereas under pre-Revolutionary conventions even civic buildings like Independence Hall in Philadelphia are built on a domestic scale, the early republican architecture is marked by the practice of building its domestic dwellings on a public scale. The fine houses of the early republic all have an official appearance; almost any house might be the White House.

4. Even when Dickens made his first visit to America, the classical myth and the classical hero had not altogether disappeared: one has a painful memory of the "mother of the modern Gracchi," and one sees how the republican hero had been vulgarized into a Jacksonian caricature like General Cyrus Choke. For a whole generation the classical

myth held men in its thrall; the notion of returning to a 65
pagan polity, quaintly modified by deism, was a weapon
of the radical forces in both America and France. Jean
Jacques himself preached the virtues of Sparta and Rome in
Le Contrat Social, as well as the state of nature which he
praised in *Émile*; and, in general, "radicalism" associated 70
itself with the worship of rule and reason, as opposed to the
caprice, the irrationality, the brute traditionalism of what
the children of that age then characterized as "Gothic superstition." Almost within his lifetime Washington became
Divus Caesar, and if a monument was not built to him im- 75
mediately, a city was named after him, as Alexandria had
been named after Alexander. Did not the very war-veterans
become the Society of the Cincinnati; did not the first pio-
neers on the westward march sprinkle names like Utica and
Ithaca and Syracuse over the Mohawk trail; and did not a 80
few ex-soldiers go back to their Tory neighbor's plow? As
Rome and Greece embodied the political interests of the
age, so did classical architecture provide the appropriate
shell. Even those who were not vitally touched by the dominant interests of the period were not immune to the fashion, 85
once it had been set.

5. The dominant designs of the early republican period
proceeded directly or indirectly from such books as Stuart's
Antiquities of Athens, and from such well-known examples
of temple architecture in southern Europe as the Maison 90
Carrée at Nîmes. In one sense, there was a certain fitness
in adapting the Greek methods of building to America.
Originally, the Greek temple had probably been a wooden
building. Its columns were trees, its cornices exposed beams;
and the architect's new opportunity to fabricate mightily in 95
wood may have furnished an extra incentive to the erection
of these colossal buildings. The fact that the Greek mode in
America was well under way before the first example of it
had appeared in Edinburgh, London, or Paris, shows perhaps that time and place both favored its introduction on 100
this side of the Atlantic: for the availability of certain ma-

terials often, no doubt, directs the imagination to certain forms.

6.   On the whole, however, the Greek temple precedent was a bad one. For one thing, since the Greek *cella* had no source of light except the doorway, it was necessary to introduce modifications in the elevation, and to break up the interior; and it was only in the South that the vast shadowed retreats formed by porches and second-story balconies proved a happy adaptation to the climate. Again: Greek architecture was an architecture of exteriors, designed for people who spent the greater part of the year out of doors. With no temple ritual comparable to the services of the church or cathedral, the Greeks lavished their attention upon externals, and as a great admirer of the Greeks, Sir Reginald Blomfield, well says, "may have been more successful with the outside of their buildings than with the inside." To fail with the interior in a northern climate is to fail with the essentials of a habitation; and these vast rooms, for all their ornament, too often remained bleak.

7.   Even on the esthetic side, the Greek style of building was not a full-blown success. With all their strict arrangement of the classic orders, with all their nice proportions, the muted white exteriors resembled a genuine Greek temple in the way that a sepia photograph would represent a sunrise—the warm tones, the colors, the dancing procession of sculptures were absent; it was a thinned and watered Greece that they called to mind. Indeed, the disciples of the Age of Reason and white perukes would have been horrified, I have no doubt, at the "barbarism" of the original Greek temples, as they would doubtless also have been at the meanness of the dwellings in which Pericles or Thucydides must have lived. Once the temple-house ceased to be a stage upon which the myth of classicism could be enacted, it ceased also to be a home. For who wishes to live in a temple? That is a spiritual exercise we do not demand even of a priest. Small wonder that the temple lingered longest in the South, where, down to the Civil War, gangs

of slaves supported the dignity of the masters and a large
household diminished the chilly sense of solitude.   140

❈ ❈ ❈

In this passage from a survey of American architecture,
"myth" has a rather special sense. Much as an individual may
understand himself in terms of a legendary character, fancying
himself a bold bad man like Mr. Bogart in the pictures, or a
neglected scientific genius, or an early Christian beset with
temptations and tribulations, or a campus Machiavelli or Lenin,
so a social group may conceive of themselves and their role in
history in terms of some supposed parallel. Thus the Puritan
sects, poring over the English Bible, often saw a likeness between the situation of the Israelites and their own: God's
chosen harassed by carnal Canaanites and Philistines. Such fancies, whether or not they fit the facts, have a real force in human
affairs. Public movers have attempted to make levers of such
myths: Germans were urged to think of themselves as a race
of blond barbarians, like their Teutonic ancestors, mighty,
loyal to their chieftain, ruthless, imposing their will on feebler
peoples; American mechanics have been advised to emulate
Daniel Boone or the Russian proletariat. A myth or motivating
belief does not necessarily rest upon an historical parallel. The
social myth is often summarized, for convenient distribution, in
a single phrase: "the class struggle," "manifest destiny," "the
white man's burden," "Armageddon" (the war to end war,
1914-18), "the managerial revolution." The validity of such
myths is not readily disputed, for what men sincerely believe
about themselves and their situation, however inaccurate, has
some consequence in their action. (Perhaps the truth of a belief
can be tested only by its consequences; cf. the Britannica article
on "Pragmatism," by F. C. S. Schiller.)

1. Mr. Mumford is here concerned with the "classical myth"
primarily as an influence on architecture. What other manifestations of the myth does he mention? List them. Why
does he include these in his essay?

2. Explain the allusions made in the following phrases:
a) King Alfred . . . griddle. (ll. 41-43.)
b) If the tailors . . . invent one. (ll. 44-46.)

3. What is the difference between the classical style of archi-

tecture and the vernacular, so far as you can gather from Pars. 1 and 2?

4. In the first sentence of Par. 2, which terms apply to which style? Improve the sentence.

5. It would be incorrect to say that the classical myth *created* a style of architecture; nor is the last sentence of Par. 2 very plain. Define more accurately—and in one sentence—the part which that myth played, according to Mumford, in the evolution of American architecture.

6. Par. 3 is written in the present tense. The merchant is presumably colonial, the hero republican; between them is the Revolution. (The two attitudes may, of course, have appeared successively in the same individual.) This time difference might have been indicated by putting the hero's actions in the past tense, the merchant's in the past perfect. Compare the analogous lines 25-28. Revise the verbs of Par. 3 in this way. (Not all the verbs will be changed.) What advantages or disadvantages do you find in such a revision?

7. Perhaps Par. 3 could have been clarified—for freshmen, at any rate—by an explanatory introductory sentence. Write it.

8. Consult Chapter XXI of *Martin Chuzzlewit* and report on the vulgarization of the republican hero. (For the "mother of the Gracchi," cf. Chapter XXII.)

9. It is implied in lines 121-128 that the republican architects did not imitate Greek models very accurately. Find out what you can about Greek architecture from an encyclopedia, and explain the nature of the error and why it was made.

10. Reread the essay, noting every sentence or passage in which Mumford indicates a way in which architecture may be influenced by physical environment, culture, historical circumstance, etc.

11. Classify your findings and write an essay explaining several factors which may influence architectural style. In this you need not, of course, confine yourself to ideas drawn from Mumford.

12. Explain the derivations of *cathedral, parlor, porch*. Work up a list of other architectural terms having interesting derivations. (*Louver, nave, vault, window,* etc.)

13. What other classical place-names are to be found in New York State? What other *types* of place-name do you find there? How do you account for such place-names as Bethlehem, Nazareth, Egypt, Zionsville, Bethel, Emaus, and Lebanon in the farming country of eastern Pennsylvania? What classical place-names do you find in Virginia? Compare Virginia with New York in this respect, and explain.

14. Explain the derivations of *banquet, caricature, crystal, grave, vernacular, vulgar, wrangle.*

THE MIRACLES OF OUR LADY[1]

HENRY ADAMS

•

1. THE VIRGIN WAS A REAL PERSON, WHOSE TASTES, WISHES,
instincts, passions, were intimately known. Enough of the
Virgin's literature survives to show her character and the
course of her daily life. We know more about her habits
5 and thoughts than about those of earthly queens. The
collection of the Virgin's miracles put in verse by Gaultier
de Coincy, monk, prior, and poet, between 1214 and 1233,
—the precise moment of the Chartres sculpture and glass,
—contains thirty thousand lines. Another great collection,
10 narrating especially the miracles of the Virgin of Chartres,
was made by a priest of Chartres Cathedral about 1240.
The miracles themselves, indeed, are not very numerous.
In Gaultier de Coincy's collection they number only about
fifty. The Chartres collection relates chiefly to the horrible
15 outbreak of what was called leprosy—the "mal ardent,"—
which ravaged the north of France during the crusades,
and added intensity to the feelings which brought all
society to the Virgin's feet. Recent scholars are cataloguing
and classifying the miracles, as far as they survive, and
20 have reduced the number within very moderate limits.
As poetry Gaultier de Coincy's are the best.

2. Of Gaultier de Coincy and his poetry, Gaston Paris
has something to say which is worth quoting:—

It is the most curious, and often the most singular mon-
25 ument of the infantile piety of the Middle Ages. Devotion to
Mary is presented in it as a kind of infallible guarantee not

[1] From *Mont St. Michel and Chartres*, by Henry Adams; reprinted by
permission of Houghton Mifflin Company, Publishers.

only against every sort of evil, but also against the most
legitimate consequences of sin and even of crime. In these
stories which have revolted the most rational piety, as well as
the philosophy of modern times, one must still admit a gentle 30
and penetrating charm; a naïveté; a tenderness and a simplicity
of heart, which touch, while they raise a smile. There, for
instance, one sees a sick monk cured by the milk that Our
Lady herself comes to invite him to draw from her "douce
mamelle"; a robber who is in the habit of recommending 35
himself to the Virgin whenever he is going to "embler," is
held up by her white hands for three days on the gibbet where
he is hung, until the miracle becomes evident and procures
his pardon; an ignorant monk who knows only his Ave Maria
and is despised on that account, when dead reveals his sanctity 40
by five roses which come out of his mouth in honour of the
five letters of the name Maria; a nun, who has quitted her
convent to lead a life of sin, returns after long years, and finds
that the Holy Virgin, to whom, in spite of all, she has never
ceased to offer every day her prayer, has, during all this time, 45
filled her place as sacristine, so that no one has perceived her
absence.

3. Gaston Paris inclined to apologize to his "bons
bourgeois de Paris" for reintroducing to them a character
so doubtful as the Virgin Mary, but, for our studies, the 50
professor's elementary morality is eloquent. Clearly, M.
Paris, the highest academic authority in the world, thought
that the Virgin could hardly, in his time, say the year 1900,
be received into good society in the Latin Quarter. Our
own English ancestors, known as Puritans, held the same 55
opinion, and excluded her from their society some four
hundred years earlier, for the same reasons which affected
M. Gaston Paris. These reasons were just and showed the
respectability of the citizens who held them. In no well-
regulated community, under a proper system of police, 60
could the Virgin feel at home, and the same thing may be
said of most other saints as well as sinners. Her conduct
was at times undignified, as M. Paris complained. She condescended to do domestic service, in order to help her friends,

65 and she would use her needle, if she were in the mood, for the same object. The "Golden Legend" relates that:—

A certain priest, who celebrated every day a mass in honour of the Holy Virgin, was brought up before Saint Thomas of Canterbury who suspended him from his charge, judging him 70 to be short-witted and irresponsible. Now Saint Thomas had occasion to mend his hair-cloth shirt, and while waiting for an opportunity to do so, had hidden it under his bed; so the Virgin appeared to the priest and said to him: "Go find the archbishop and tell him that she, for love of whom you celebrated masses, 75 has herself mended his shirt for him which is under his bed; and tell him that she sends you to him that he may take off the interdict he has imposed on you." And Saint Thomas found that his shirt had in fact been mended. He relieved the priest, begging him to keep the secret of his wearing a hair-shirt.

80   4. Mary did some exceedingly unconventional things, and among them the darning Thomas A' Becket's hair-shirt and the supporting a robber on the gibbet were not the most singular, yet they seem not to have shocked Queen Blanche or Saint Francis or Saint Thomas Aquinas so 85 much as they shocked M. Gaston Paris. You have still to visit the cathedral at Le Mans for the sake of its twelfth-century glass, and there, in the lower panel of the beautiful window of Saint Protais, you will see the full-length figure of a man, lying in bed, under a handsome blanket, watching, 90 with staring eyes, the Virgin, in a green tunic, wearing her royal crown, who is striking him on the head with a heavy hammer and with both hands. The miracle belongs to local history, and is amusing only to show how little the Virgin cared for criticism of her manners or acts. She was above 95 criticism. She made manners. Her acts were laws. No one thought of criticising, in the style of a normal school, the will of such a queen; but one might treat her with a degree of familiarity, under great provocation, which would startle easier critics than the French. Here is an instance:—

100   A widow had an only child whom she tenderly loved. On hearing that this son had been taken by the enemy, chained,

and put in prison, she burst into tears, and addressing herself
to the Virgin, to whom she was especially devoted, she asked
her with obstinacy for the release of her son; but when she saw
at last that her prayers remained unanswered, she went to the 105
church where there was a sculptured image of Mary, and there,
before the image, she said: "Holy Virgin, I have begged you to
deliver my son, and you have not been willing to help an unhappy mother! I've implored your patronage for my son, and
you have refused it! Very good! just as my son has been taken 110
away from me, so I am going to take away yours, and keep
him as a hostage!" Saying this, she approached, took the statue
child on the Virgin's breast, carried it home, wrapped it in
spotless linen, and locked it up in a box, happy to have such a
hostage for her son's return. Now, the following night, the 115
Virgin appeared to the young man, opened his prison doors, and
said: "Tell your mother, my child, to return me my Son now
that I have returned hers!" The young man came home to his
mother and told her of his miraculous deliverance; and she,
overjoyed, hastened to go with the little Jesus to the Virgin, say- 120
ing to her: "I thank you, heavenly lady, for restoring me my
child, and in return I restore yours!"

5. For the exactness of this story in all its details, Bishop
James of Voragio could not have vouched, nor did it
greatly matter. What he could vouch for was the relation 125
of intimacy and confidence between his people and the
Queen of Heaven. The fact, conspicuous above all other
historical certainties about religion, that the Virgin was
by essence illogical, unreasonable, and feminine, starts
a number of questions that history has shown itself clearly 130
afraid to touch. No one has ventured to explain why the
Virgin wielded exclusive power over poor and rich, sinners
and saints, alike. Why could not the Holy Ghost—the spirit
of Love and Grace—equally answer their prayers? Why
was the Son powerless? Why was Chartres Cathedral in 135
the thirteenth century—like Lourdes today—the expression
of what is in substance a separate religion? Why did the
gentle and gracious Virgin Mother so exasperate the Pilgrim Father? Why was the Woman struck out of the

140 Church and ignored in the State? These questions are not antiquarian or trifling in historical value; they tug at the very heart-strings of all that makes whatever order is in the cosmos.

6. Although certain to be contradicted by every pious
145 churchman, a heretic must insist on thinking that the Mater Dolorosa was the logical Virgin of the Church, and that the Trinity would never have raised her from the foot of the Cross, had not the Virgin of Majesty been imposed, by necessity and public unanimity, on a creed which was
150 meant to be complete without her. The true feeling of the Church was best expressed by the Virgin herself in one of her attested miracles: "A clerk, trusting more in the Mother than in the Son, never stopped repeating the angelic salutation for his only prayer. Once as he said
155 again the 'Ave Maria,' the Lord appeared to him, and said to him: 'My Mother thanks you much for all the Salutations that you make her; but still you should not forget to salute me also: tamen et me salutare memento.'" The Trinity feared absorption in her, but was compelled to
160 accept, and even to invite her aid, because the Trinity was a court of strict law, and, as in the old customary law, no process of equity could be introduced except by direct appeal to a higher power. She was imposed unanimously by all classes, because what man wanted most in the
165 Middle Ages was not merely law or equity, but also and particularly favour. Strict justice, either on earth or in heaven, was the last thing that society cared to face. All men were sinners, and had, at least, the merit of feeling that, if they got their deserts, not one would escape worse
170 than whipping. The instinct of individuality went down through all classes, from the count at the top, to the jugleors and menestreus at the bottom. The individual rebelled against restraint; society wanted to do what it pleased; all disliked the laws which Church and State were trying to
175 fasten on them. They longed for a power above law,—or above the contorted mass of ignorance and absurdity

bearing the name of law; but the power which they longed
for was not human, for humanity they knew to be corrupt and incompetent from the day of Adam's creation
to the day of the Last Judgment. They were all criminals; 180
if not, they would have had no use for the Church and
very little for the State; but they had at least the merit
of their faults; they knew what they were, and, like children, they yearned for protection, pardon, and love. This
was what the Trinity, though omnipotent, could not give. 185
Whatever the heretic or mystic might try to persuade himself, God could not be Love. God was Justice, Order,
Unity, Perfection; He could not be human and imperfect,
nor could the Son or the Holy Ghost be other than the
Father. The Mother alone was human, imperfect, and could 190
love; she alone was Favour, Duality, Diversity. Under any
conceivable form of religion, this duality must find embodiment somewhere, and the Middle Ages logically insisted that, as it could not be in the Trinity, either separately
or together, it must be in the Mother. If the Trinity was 195
in its essence Unity, the Mother alone could represent whatever was not Unity; whatever was irregular, exceptional,
outlawed; and this was the whole human race. The saints
alone were safe, after they were sainted. Every one else
was criminal, and men differed so little in degree of sin 200
that, in Mary's eyes, all were subjects for her pity and
help.

7. This general rule of favour, apart from law, or the
reverse of law, was the mark of Mary's activity in human
affairs. Take, for an example, an entire class of her mira- 205
cles, applying to the discipline of the Church! A bishop
ejected an ignorant and corrupt priest from his living, as
all bishops constantly had to do. The priest had taken
the precaution to make himself Mary's *man*; he had devoted himself to her service and her worship. Mary instantly 210
interfered,—just as Queen Eleanor or Queen Blanche would
have done,—most unreasonably, and never was a poor
bishop more roughly scolded by an orthodox queen! "Moult
airieement," very airily or angrily, she said to him:—

215 Ce saches tu certainement   Now know you this for sure and true,

Se tu li matinet *bien main*   Unless tomorrow this you do,
Ne rapeles mon chapelain   —And do it very early too,—
A son servise et a s'enor,   Restore my chaplain to his due,
L'ame de toi a desenor   A much worse fate remains for you!

220 Ains trente jors departira   Within a month your soul shall go

Et es dolors d'infer ira.   To suffer in the flames below.

8. The story-teller—himself a priest and prior—caught the lofty trick of manner which belonged to the great ladies of the court, and was inherited by them, even in England, 225 down to the time of Queen Elizabeth, who treated her bishops also like domestic servants;—"matinet bien main!" To the public, as to us, the justice of the rebuke was nothing to the point; but that a friend should exist on earth or in heaven, who dared to browbeat a bishop, caused the 230 keenest personal delight. The legends are clearer on this point than on any other. The people loved Mary because she trampled on conventions; not merely because she could do it, but because she liked to do what shocked every well-regulated authority. Her pity had no limit.

235 9. One of the Chartres miracles expresses the same motive in language almost plainer still. A good-for-nothing clerk, vicious, proud, vain, rude, and altogether worthless, but devoted to the Virgin, died, and with general approval his body was thrown into a ditch:—

240   Mais cele ou sort tote pities
     Tote douceurs tote amisties
     Et qui les siens onques n'oublie
     Son pecheor n'oblia mie.

"*Her* sinner!" Mary would not have been a true queen 245 unless she had protected her own. The whole morality of the Middle Ages stood in the obligation of every master to protect his dependent. Mary was the highest of all the feudal ladies, and was the example for all in loyalty to her own, when she had to humiliate her own Bishop of Chartres

for the sake of a worthless brute. "Do you suppose it 250
doesn't annoy me," she said, "to see my friend buried in
a common ditch? Take him out at once! I command! Tell
the clergy it is my order, and that I will never forgive them
unless tomorrow morning without delay, they bury my
friend in the best place in the cemetery!"   255

10. Naturally, her order was instantly obeyed. Mary's
wish was absolute law, on earth as in heaven. For her,
other laws were not made. Intensely human, but always
Queen, she upset, at her pleasure, the decisions of every
court and the orders of every authority, human or divine; 260
interfered directly in the ordeal; altered the processes of
nature; abolished space; annihilated time. Like other queens,
she had many of the failings and prejudices of her humanity. In spite of her own origin, she disliked Jews, and
rarely neglected a chance to maltreat them. She was not in 265
the least a prude. To her, sin was simply humanity, and
she seemed often on the point of defending her arbitrary
acts of mercy, by frankly telling the Trinity that if the
Creator meant to punish man, He should not have made
him. The people, who always in their hearts protested 270
against bearing the responsibility for the Creator's arbitrary
creations, delighted to see her upset the law and reverse
the rulings of the Trinity. They idolized her for being
strong, physically and in will, so that she feared nothing,
and was as helpful to the knight in the mêlée of battle as to 275
the young mother in child-bed. The only character in which
they seemed slow to recognize Mary was that of bourgeoise.
The bourgeoisie courted her favour at great expense, but
she seemed to be at home on the farm, rather than in the
shop. She had very rudimentary knowledge, indeed, of the 280
principles of political economy as we understand them, and
her views on the subject of money-lending or banking were
so feminine as to rouse in that powerful class a vindictive
enmity which helped to overthrow her throne.

11. Even in anger Mary always remained a great lady, 285
and in the ordinary relations of society her manners were
exquisite, as they were, according to Joinville, in the court

of Saint Louis, when tempers were not overwrought. The
very brutality of the brutal compelled the courteous to
290 exaggerate courtesy, and some of the royal family were
as coarse as the king was delicate in manners. In heaven
the manners were perfect, and almost as stately as those
of Roland and Oliver. On one occasion Saint Peter found
himself embarrassed by an affair which the public opinion
295 of the Court of Heaven, although not by any means puritanic, thought more objectionable—in fact, more frankly
discreditable—than an honest corrupt job ought to be; and
even his influence, though certainly considerable, wholly
failed to carry it through the law-court. The case, as re-
300 ported by Gaultier de Coincy, was this: A very worthless
creature of Saint Peter's,—a monk of Cologne,—who had
led a scandalous life, died, and in due course of law was
tried, convicted, and dragged off by the devils to undergo
his term of punishment. Saint Peter could not desert his
305 sinner, though much ashamed of him, and accordingly
made formal application to the Trinity for a pardon. The
Trinity, somewhat severely, refused. Finding his own interest insufficient, Saint Peter tried to strengthen it by
asking the archangels to help him; but the case was too
310 much for them also, and they declined. The brother
apostles were appealed to, with the same result; and finally
even the saints, though they had so obvious interest in
keeping friendly relations with Peter, found public opinion
too strong to defy. The case was desperate. The Trinity
315 were—or was—emphatic, and—what was rare in the Middle Ages—every member of the feudal hierarchy sustained
its decision. Nothing more could be done in the regular
way. Saint Peter was obliged to divest himself of authority, and place himself and his dignity in the hands of
320 the Virgin. Accordingly he asked for an audience, and
stated the case to Our Lady. With the utmost grace, she
instantly responded:—

> "Pierre, Pierre," our Lady said,
> "With all my heart I'll give you aid,
325   And to my gentle Son I'll sue

Until I beg that soul for you."
God's Mother then arose straightway,
And sought her Son without delay;
All her virgins followed her,
And Saint Peter kept him near,   330
For he knew his task was done
And his prize already won,
Since it was hers, in whom began
The life of God in form of Man. . . .
When He saw His Mother's face   335
He rose and said with gentle grace:
"Well are you come, my heart's desire!"
Like loving son, like gracious sire;
Took her hand gently in His own;
Gently placed her on His throne,   340
Wishing her graciously good cheer:—
"What brings my gentle Mother here,
My sister, and my dearest friend?"

12. One can see Queen Blanche going to beg—or command—a favour of her son, King Louis, and the stately 345
dignity of their address, while Saint Peter and the virgins
remain in the antechamber; but, as for Saint Peter's lost
soul, the request was a mere form, and the doors of paradise were instantly opened to it, after such brief formalities
as should tend to preserve the technical record of the law- 350
court.

13. We tread here on very delicate ground. Gaultier de
Coincy, being a priest and a prior, could take liberties
which we cannot or ought not to take. The doctrines of
the Church are too serious and too ancient to be wilfully 355
misstated, and the doctrines of what is called Mariolatry
were never even doctrines of the Church. Yet it is true that,
in the hearts of Mary's servants, the Church and its doctrines were at the mercy of Mary's will. Gaultier de Coincy
claimed that Mary exasperated the devils by exercising a 360
wholly arbitrary and illegitimate power:—

"In this law-suit," say the devils,
"Since it is a choice of evils,
We had best appeal on high

365 To the Judge Who does not lie.
What is law to any other,
'Tis no use pleading with His Mother;
But God judges us so true
That He leaves us all our due.
370 His Mother judges us so short
That she throws us out of court
When we ought to win our cause. . . .
In heaven and earth she makes more laws
By far, than God Himself can do,
375 He loves her so, and trusts her so,
There's nothing she can do or say
That He'll refuse, or say her nay.
Whatever she may want is right,
Though she say that black is white,
380 And dirty water clear as snow:—
My Mother says it, and it's so!"

14. If the Virgin took the feelings of the Trinity into consideration, or recognised its existence except as her Son, the case has not been reported, or, at all events, has been
385 somewhat carefully kept out of sight by the Virgin's poets. The devils were emphatic in denouncing Mary for absorbing the whole Trinity. In one sharply disputed case in regard to a villain, or labourer, whose soul the Virgin claimed because he had learned the "Ave Maria," the devils be-
390 came very angry, indeed, and protested vehemently:—

The ugly demons laugh outright
And grind their teeth with envious spite;
Crying:—"Marvel marvellous!
Because that flat-eared ploughman there
395 Learned to make your Dame a prayer,
She would like to kill us all
Just for looking toward his soul.
All the world she wants to rule!
No such Dame was ever seen!
400 She thinks that she is God, I ween,
Or holds Him in her hollow hand.
Not a judgment or command
Or an order can be given

Here on earth or there in heaven
That she does not want control. 405
She thinks that she ordains the whole,
And keeps it all for her own profit.
God nor Devil share not of it."

15. As regards Mary of Chartres, these charges seem
to have been literally true. Gaultier de Coincy saw no 410
impropriety in accepting, as sufficiently exact, the allega-
tions of the devils against the Virgin's abuse of power.
Down to the death of Queen Blanche, the public saw no
more impropriety in it than Gaultier did. Nevertheless
there were points in the royal policy and conduct of Mary 415
which thoughtful men even then hesitated to approve.
Mary's tastes were too popular; some of the uglier devils
said they were too low; many ladies and gentle men of the
"siècle" thought them disreputable, though they dared not
say so. As usual, one must go to the devils for the exact 420
truth, and in spite of their outcry, the devils admitted that
they had no reason to complain of Mary's administration:—

All the great dames and ladies fair
Who costly robes and ermine wear,
Kings, queens, and countesses and lords 425
Come down to hell in endless hordes;
While up to heaven go the lamed,
The dwarfs, the humpbacks, and the maimed;
To heaven goes the whole riff-raff;
We get the grain and God the chaff. 430

16. True it was, although one should not say it jestingly,
that the Virgin embarrassed the Trinity; and perhaps this
was the reason, behind all the other excellent reasons, why
men loved and adored her with a passion such as no other
deity has ever inspired; and why we, although utter stran- 435
gers to her, are not far from getting down on our knees
and praying to her still. Mary concentrated in herself the
whole rebellion of man against fate; the whole protest
against divine law; the whole unutterable fury of human
nature beating itself against the walls of its prison-house, 440

and suddenly seized by a hope that in the Virgin man
had found a door of escape. She was above law; she took
feminine pleasure in turning hell into an ornament; she
delighted in trampling on every social distinction in this
445 world and the next. She knew that the universe was as
unintelligible to her, on any theory of morals, as it was to
her worshippers, and she felt, like them, no sure conviction
that it was any more intelligible to the Creator of it. To
her, every suppliant was a universe in itself, to be judged
450 apart, on his own merits, by his love for her,—by no means
on his orthodoxy, or his conventional standing in the
Church, or according to his correctness in defining the
nature of the Trinity. She cared not a straw for conventional morality, and she had no notion of letting her friends
455 be punished for the sins of their ancestors or the pecca-
dilloes of Eve.

17. So Mary filled heaven with a sort of persons little
to the taste of any respectable middle-class society, which
has trouble enough in making this world decent and pay
460 its bills, without having to continue the effort in another.
Mary stood in a Church of her own, so independent that
the Trinity might have perished without much affecting
her position; but, on the other hand, the Trinity could look
on and see her dethroned with almost a breath of relief.
465 Mary's treatment of respectable and law-abiding people
who had no favours to ask and were reasonably confident
of getting to heaven by the regular judgment, without expense, rankled so deeply that three hundred years later
the Puritan reformers were not satisfied with abolishing her,
470 but sought to abolish the woman altogether as the cause
of all evil in heaven and on earth. The Puritans abandoned
the New Testament and the Virgin in order to go back
to the beginning and renew the quarrel with Eve.

18. Mary was rarely harsh to any suppliant or servant,
475 and she took no special interest in humiliating the rich or
the learned or the wise. For them, law was made; by
them, law was administered; and with their doings Mary
never arbitrarily interfered; but occasionally she could not

resist the temptation to intimate her opinion of the manner
in which the Trinity allowed their—the regular—Church to 480
be administered. She was a queen, and never for an instant forgot it, but she took little thought about her divine rights, if she had any,—while she was scandalised at
the greed of officials in her Son's Court. The administration of heaven was very like the administration of France; 485
the Queen Mother saw many things of which she could
not wholly approve; but her nature was pity, not justice,
and she shut her eyes to much that she could not change.
Her miracles, therefore, were for the most part mere evidence of her pity for those who needed it most, and these 490
were rarely the well-to-do people of the siècle, but more
commonly the helpless. Every saint performed miracles,
and these are standard, not peculiar to any one intermedia-
tor; and every saint protected his own friends; but beyond
these exhibitions of power, which are more or less common 495
to the whole hierarchy below the Trinity, Mary was the
mother of pity and the only hope of despair. One might go
on for a volume, studying the character of Mary and the
changes that time made in it, from the earliest Byzantine
legends down to the daily recorded miracles at Lourdes; 500
no character in history has had so long or varied a development, and none so sympathetic.

19.   One story is that of a tumbler—tombeor, street-acro-
bat—who was disgusted with the world, as his class has had
a reputation for becoming, and who was fortunate enough 505
to obtain admission into the famous monastery of Clairvaux, where Saint Bernard may have formerly been blessed
by the Virgin's presence. Ignorant at best, and especially
ignorant of letters, music, and the offices of a religious
society, he found himself unable to join in the services:— 510

> For he had learned no other thing
> Than to tumble, dance and spring:
> Leaping and vaulting, that he knew,
> But nothing better could he do.
> He could not say his prayers by rote;   515
> Not "Pater noster"; not a note;

Not "Ave Mary," nor the creed;
Nothing to help his soul in need.

20. Tormented by the sense of his uselessness to the
520 society whose bread he ate without giving a return in
service, and afraid of being expelled as a useless member,
one day while the bells were calling to mass he hid in
the crypt, and in despair began to soliloquize before the
Virgin's altar, at the same spot, one hopes, where the
525 Virgin had shown herself, or might have shown herself, in
her infinite bounty, to Saint Bernard, a hundred years before:—

"Ha!" said he, "how I am ashamed!
To sing his part goes now each priest,
530 And I stand here, a tethered beast,
Who nothing do but browse and feed
And waste the food that others need.
Shall I say nothing, and stand still?
No! by God's mother, but I will!
535 She shall not think me here for naught;
At least I'll do what I've been taught!
At least I'll serve in my own way
God's mother in her church today.
The others serve to pray and sing;
540 I will serve to leap and spring."
Then he strips him of his gown,
Lays it on the altar down;
But for himself he takes good care
Not to show his body bare,
545 But keeps a jacket, soft and thin,
Almost a shirt, to tumble in.
Clothed in this supple woof of maille
His strength and health and form showed well,
And when his belt is buckled fast,
550 Toward the Virgin turns at last:
Very humbly makes his prayer;
"Lady!" says he, "to your care
I commit my soul and frame.
Gentle Virgin, gentle dame,
555 Do not despise what I shall do,

For I ask only to please you,
To serve you like an honest man,
So help me God, the best I can.
I cannot chant, nor can I read,
But I can show you here instead,   560
All my best tricks to make you laugh,
And so shall be as though a calf
Should leap and jump before its dam.
Lady, who never yet could blame
Those who serve you well and true,   565
All that I am, I am for you."

Then he begins to jump about,
High and low, and in and out,
Straining hard with might and main;
Then, falling on his knees again,   570
Before the image bows his face:
"By your pity! by your grace!"
Says he, "Ha! my gentle queen,
Do not despise my offering!"

21. In his earnestness he exerted himself until, at the 575
end of his strength, he lay exhausted and unconscious on
the altar steps. Pleased with his own exhibition, and satisfied that the Virgin was equally pleased, he continued
these devotions every day, until at last his constant and
singular absence from the regular services attracted the 580
curiosity of a monk, who kept watch on him and reported
his eccentric exercise to the Abbot.

22. The medieval monasteries seem to have been gently
administered. Indeed, this has been made the chief reproach on them, and the excuse for robbing them for the 585
benefit of a more energetic crown and nobility who tolerated
no beggars or idleness but their own; at least, it is safe
to say that few well-regulated and economically administered
modern charities would have the patience of the Abbot of
Clairvaux, who, instead of calling up the weak-minded 590
tombeor and sending him back to the world to earn a living by his profession, went with his informant to the crypt,
to see for himself what the strange report meant. We have

seen at Chartres what a crypt may be, and how easily one
595 might hide in its shadows while mass is said at the altars.
The Abbot and his informant hid themselves behind a
column in the shadow, and watched the whole performance
to its end when the exhausted tumbler dropped unconscious
and drenched with perspiration on the steps of the altar,
600 with the words:—

> "Lady!" says he, "no more I can,
> But truly I'll come back again!"

23. You can imagine the dim crypt; the tumbler lying
unconscious beneath the image of the Virgin; the Abbot
605 peering out from the shadow of the column, and wondering what sort of discipline he could inflict for this unfore-
seen infraction of rule; when suddenly, before he could
decide what next to do, the vault above the altar, of its own
accord, opened:—

610
> The Abbot strains his eyes to see,
> And, from the vaulting, suddenly,
> A lady steps,—so glorious,—
> Beyond all thought so precious,—
> Her robes so rich, so nobly worn,—
615
> So rare the gems the robes adorn,—
> As never yet so fair was born.
>
> Along with her the angels were,
> Archangels stood beside her there;
> Round about the tumbler group
620
> To give him solace, bring him hope;
> And when round him in ranks they stood,
> His whole heart felt its strength renewed.
> So they haste to give him aid
> Because their wills are only made
625
> To serve the service of their Queen,
> Most precious gem the earth has seen.
> And the lady, gentle, true,
> Holds in her hand a towel new;
> Fans him with her hand divine
630
> Where he lies before the shrine.
> The kind lady, full of grace,

Fans his neck, his breast, his face!
Fans him herself to give him air!
Labours, herself, to help him there!
The lady gives herself to it;   635
The poor man takes no heed of it;
For he knows not and cannot see
That he has such fair company.

24. Beyond this we need not care to go. If you cannot
feel the colour and quality—the union of naïveté and art, the 640
refinement, the infinite delicacy and tenderness—of this little
poem, then nothing will matter much to you; and if you
can feel it, you can feel, without more assistance, the majesty
of Chartres.

� ✻ ✻ ✻

This essay is a study of the mediaeval thought and feeling
implicit in the legends of the Virgin. Paragraphs 1-5 are introductory: after describing the documentary sources, Adams illustrates the character attributed to Mary, the unconventionality
of which presents an historical problem. In Par. 6 he explains,
in terms of theology and psychology, why society conceived of
Mary in such a way; he develops and illustrates his thesis in
Pars. 7-18, indicating, too, why the conception was ultimately
renounced.

1. What is it to catalogue and to classify miracles, and
how can the number be reduced? (ll. 18-21.)

2. Would it not have been more accurate for Gaston Paris
to have written "infantile piety of *Gaultier de Coincy*" in line
25 and for Adams to have written "to *the story-teller*" in line
227? Explain.

3. Make a list of the legends used in the essay. To the four
cited by M. Paris, Adams has added nine, counting the three
quotations from the devils as one item. Give each legend a
title, for convenience, and say what Adams intended each to
illustrate.

4. Precisely who is referred to as "the feudal hierarchy" in
line 316? Why should these persons have been organized as a
feudal hierarchy—rather, for instance, than as a council of

Athenian citizens, or a soviet of workers' and peasants' deputies, or a house of representatives?

5. In what several ways did Mary resemble earthly queens? Why should this have been so?

6. Do you think, in view of the available evidence, that the Virgin did right in the affair of the robber? (ll. 35-39.) Of the wayward nun? (ll. 42-47.) Of the ejected priest? (Par. 7.) Of the monk of Cologne? (Par. 11.) Of the ploughman? (Par. 14.) Give your reasons for each decision.

7. To what extent are you in sympathy with the attitudes imputed to Mary in lines 266-270 and in lines 445-456? You need not answer point by point, as you may not care to accept the Virgin's formulation of the issues; but understand the validity of the questions raised, and answer in sufficient detail to make your own views plain.

8. Adams thinks the Virgin becomes intelligible when she is viewed in relation to the Trinity, as the Trinity was understood in the thirteenth century.

a) What earthly institution is suggested, in Par. 6, as the pattern from which the medieval conception of the Trinity was derived?

b) What human need is expressed in such a conception?

c) Adams writes that the Trinity "feared absorption" in Mary (l. 159) and was embarrassed by her activities (l. 432); in plain historical terms, what does this mean?

d) Why do you suppose that we in the twentieth century get along without such a conception of the Trinity? Or do we not?

9. How do you reconcile, in terms of literary history, the miracle described in lines 152-158 with lines 402-408?

10. Find out what "original sin" means, and point out what theological error Adams has made in Par. 6. Show that in Par. 16 he has avoided this error.

11. What kind of man objected to Mary and what she stood for? Explain the objections in practical terms.

12. "If the Creator *meant to punish* man. . . ." (l. 269.) Whereas the Virgin Mary was merely perplexed by God's behavior, John Milton undertook to justify it. Consult *Paradise Lost,* Book iii, lines 80-128, and Book v, lines 224-247. Why is

there a logical contradiction between Divine Omniscience and Human Responsibility? What is the practical or human contradiction between the two doctrines? How did Milton hope to reconcile them? Which doctrine do you think more important to man?

13. Adams is inclined to poke fun at Gaston Paris; notably in which phrases? What is his rhetorical purpose in doing so?

14. Comment on the poem about the Tumbler of Our Lady. First decide which lines make it charming, and then try to define the nature of its charm. What does Adams add to the story by his interpolated comments?

FREEDOM OF THE PRESS[1]

JOHN MILTON

•

1. GOOD AND EVIL WE KNOW IN THE FIELD OF THIS WORLD grow up together almost inseparably; and the knowledge of good is so involved and interwoven with the knowledge of evil, and in so many cunning resemblances hardly to be
5 discerned, that those confused seeds which were imposed upon Psyche as an incessant labor to cull out and sort asunder were not more intermixed. It was from out the rind of one apple tasted that the knowledge of good and evil, as two twins cleaving together, leaped forth into the
10 world. And perhaps this is that doom which Adam fell into of knowing good and evil; that is to say, of knowing good by evil.

2. As therefore the state of man now is, what wisdom can there be to choose, what continence to forbear, with-
15 out the knowledge of evil? He that can apprehend and consider vice with all her baits and seeming pleasures, and yet abstain, and yet distinguish, and yet prefer that which is truly better, he is the true warfaring Christian. I cannot praise a fugitive and cloistered virtue, unexercised and
20 unbreathed, that never sallies out and seeks her adversary, but slinks out of the race where that immortal garland is to be run for, not without dust and heat. Assuredly we bring not innocence into the world; we bring impurity much rather; that which purifies us is trial, and trial by
25 what is contrary.

3. Since therefore the knowledge and survey of vice is in this world so necessary to the constituting of human virtue, and the scanning of error to the confirmation of truth, how can we more safely, and with less danger, scout into

[1] Condensed from *Areopagitica*, by John Milton.

the regions of sin and falsity than by reading all manner 30 of tractates and hearing all manner of reason? And this is the benefit which may be had of books promiscuously read. And again, if it be true that a wise man, like a good refiner, can gather gold out of the drossiest volume, and that a fool will be a fool with the best book, yea, or with- 35 out book, there is no reason that we should deprive a wise man of any advantage to his wisdom, while we seek to restrain from a fool that which being restrained will be no hindrance to his folly.

4. If we think to regulate printing, thereby to rectify 40 manners, we must regulate all recreations and pastimes, all that is delightful to man. No music must be heard, no song be set or sung, but what is grave and doric. There must be licensing dancers, that no gesture, motion, or deportment be taught our youth, but what by their allow- 45 ance shall be thought honest. It will ask more than the work of twenty licensers to examine all the lutes, the violins, and the guitars in every house; they must not be suffered to prattle as they do, but must be licensed what they may say. And who shall silence all the airs and madri- 50 gals that whisper softness in chambers? The windows also and the balconies must be thought on; these are shrewd books, with dangerous frontispieces, set to sale: who shall prohibit them, shall twenty licensers? The villages also must have their visitors to inquire what lectures the bag- 55 pipe and the rebec read, even to the balladry and the gamut of every municipal fiddler.

5. Next, what more national corruption, for which England hears ill abroad, than household gluttony? Who shall be the rectors of our daily rioting? And what shall be 60 done to inhibit the multitudes that frequent those houses where drunkenness is sold and harbored? Our garments also should be referred to the licensing of some more sober workmasters, to see them cut into a less wanton garb. Who shall regulate all the mixed conversation of our youth, 65 male and female together, as is the fashion of this country? Who shall still appoint what shall be discoursed, what

presumed, and no further? Lastly, who shall forbid and separate all idle resort, all evil company? These things 70 will be, and must be; but how they shall be least hurtful, how least enticing, herein consists the grave and governing wisdom of a state.

6. To sequester out of the world into Atlantic and Utopian politics, which never can be drawn into use, will 75 not mend our condition; but to ordain wisely as in this world of evil, in the midst whereof God hath placed us unavoidably. Nor is it Plato's licensing of books will do this, but those unwritten or at least unconstraining laws of virtuous education, religious and civil nurture, which 80 will bear chief sway in such matters as these, when all licensing will be easily eluded. Impunity and remissness for certain are the bane of a commonwealth; but here the great art lies, to discern in what the law is to bid restraint and punishment, and in what things persuasion only is to 85 work. If every action which is good or evil in man at ripe years were to be under pittance, prescription, and compulsion, what were virtue but a name, what praise could be then due to well-doing, what gramercy to be sober, just, or continent?

90 7. Many there be that complain of divine Providence for suffering Adam to transgress. Foolish tongues! when God gave him reason, He gave him freedom to choose, for reason is but choosing; he had been else a mere artificial Adam, such an Adam as he is in the motions. We ourselves 95 esteem not of that obedience or love or gift which is of force; God therefore left him free, set before him a provoking object ever almost in his eyes; herein consisted his merit, herein the right of his reward, the praise of his abstinence. Wherefore did He create passions within us, pleasures 100 round about us, but that these rightly tempered are the very ingredients of virtue? They are not skilful considerers of human things who imagine to remove sin by removing the matter of sin. Though ye take from a covetous man all his treasure, he has yet one jewel left; ye cannot bereave 105 him of his covetousness. Banish all objects of lust, shut up

all youth into the severest discipline that can be exercised
in any hermitage, ye cannot make them chaste that came not
thither so.

8. Suppose we could expel sin by this means; look how
much we thus expel of sin, so much we expel of virtue: for 110
the matter of them both is the same; remove that and ye
remove them both alike. This justifies the high providence
of God, who, though He commands us temperance, justice,
continence, yet pours out before us even to a profuseness
all desirable things and gives us minds that can wander 115
beyond all limit and satiety. Why should we then affect a
rigor contrary to the manner of God and of nature, by
abridging or scanting those means which books, freely
permitted, are both to the trial of virtue and the exercise
of truth?   120

9. Well knows he who uses to consider, that our faith
and knowledge thrive by exercise, as well as our limbs and
complexion. Truth is compared in scripture to a streaming
fountain; if her waters flow not in a perpetual progression,
they sicken into a muddy pool of conformity and tradition. 125
A man may be a heretic in the truth; and if he believe
things only because his pastor says so or the assembly so
determines, without knowing other reason, though his belief be true, yet the very truth he holds becomes his heresy.
There is not any burden that some would gladlier post off 130
to another than the charge and care of their religion.

10. A wealthy man, addicted to his pleasure and to his
profits, finds religion to be a traffic so entangled and of so
many piddling accounts that of all mysteries he cannot skill
to keep a stock going upon that trade. What should he do? 135
Fain he would have the name to be religious; fain he would
bear up with his neighbors in that. What does he therefore
but resolves to give over toiling and to find himself out
some factor, to whose care and credit he may commit the
whole managing of his religious affairs; some divine of 140
note and estimation that must be. To him he adheres, re-
signs the whole warehouse of his religion, with all the
locks and keys, into his custody, and indeed makes the very

person of that man his religion, esteems his associating with
145 him a sufficient evidence and commendatory of his own
piety. He entertains him, gives him gifts, feasts him, lodges
him; his religion comes home at night, prays, is liberally
supped and sumptuously laid to sleep, rises, is saluted, and
after the malmsey, or some well-spiced brewage, and better
150 breakfasted than He whose morning appetite would have
gladly fed on green figs between Bethany and Jerusalem,
his religion walks abroad at eight and leaves his kind
entertainer in the shop trading all day without his religion.

11. Another sort there be, who, when they hear that
155 all things shall be ordered, all things regulated and settled,
nothing written but what passes through the custom-house
of certain publicans that have the tonnaging and pounding
of all free-spoken truth, will straight give themselves into
your hands, make them and cut them out what religion ye
160 please: there be delights, there be recreations and jolly
pastimes that will fetch the day about from sun to sun and
rock the tedious year as in a delightful dream. What need
they torture their heads with that which others have taken
so strictly and so unalterably into their own purveying?
165 These are the fruits which a dull ease and cessation of
knowledge will bring forth among the people. How goodly
and how to be wished were such an obedient unanimity as
this! What a fine conformity would it starch us all into!
Doubtless a staunch and solid piece of framework as any
170 January could freeze together.

12. There be who perpetually complain of schisms and
sects, and make it such a calamity that any man dissents
from their maxims. It is their own pride and ignorance
which causes the disturbing, who neither will hear with
175 meekness nor can convince, yet all must be suppressed
which is not found in their Syntagma. They are the trou-
blers, they are the dividers of unity, who neglect and permit not others to unite those dissevered pieces which are
yet wanting to the body of truth. To be still searching
180 what we know not, by what we know, still closing up truth
to truth as we find it—for all her body is homogeneal and

proportional,—this is the golden rule in theology as well as in arithmetic, and makes up the best harmony in a church: not the forced and outward union of cold and neutral and inwardly divided minds. 185

13. Lords and commons of England! consider what nation it is whereof ye are and whereof ye are the governors: a nation not slow and dull, but of a quick, ingenious, and piercing spirit, acute to invent, subtle and sinewy to discourse, not beneath the reach of any point the highest that 190 human capacity can soar to. What could a man require more from a nation so pliant and so prone to seek after knowledge? What wants there to such a towardly and pregnant soil but wise and faithful laborers, to make a knowing people, a nation of prophets, of sages, and of 195 worthies? We reckon more than five months yet to harvest; there need not be five weeks, had we but eyes to lift up, the fields are white already. Where there is much desire to learn, there of necessity will be much arguing, much writing, many opinions; for opinion in good men is but knowledge 200 in the making. Under these fantastic terrors of sect and schism we wrong the earnest and zealous thirst after knowledge and understanding which God hath stirred up in this city. What some lament of, we rather should rejoice at, should rather praise this pious forwardness among men to 205 reassume the ill-deputed care of their religion into their own hands again. A little generous prudence, a little forbearance of one another, and some grain of charity might win all these diligencies to join and unite into one general and brotherly search after truth; could we but forego this pre- 210 latical tradition of crowding free consciences and Christian liberties into canons and precepts of men.

14. Methinks I see in my mind a noble and puissant nation rousing herself like a strong man after sleep and shaking her invincible locks; methinks I see her as an eagle 215 mewing her mighty youth and kindling her undazzled eyes at the full midday beam, purging and unscaling her long-abused sight at the fountain itself of heavenly radiance, while the whole noise of timorous and flocking birds, with

220 those also that love the twilight, flutter about, amazed at what she means, and in their envious gabble would prognosticate a year of sects and schisms.

15. What should ye do then, should ye suppress all this flowery crop of knowledge and new light sprung up and 225 yet springing daily in this city? Should ye set an oligarchy of twenty engrossers over it, to bring a famine upon our minds again, when we shall know nothing but what is measured to us by their bushel?

※ ※ ※

The Presbyterian Parliament having ruled that no books should be published until approved by a board of licensers, Milton defied the regulation in his *Areopagitica*. The Puritans, whose clamorous theological bickering had at last provoked Archbishop Laud to a feeble and futile attempt to enforce decorum within the Church, did not, having attained power, repeal their censorship. They agreed with the poet Thomas Dudley, of the Bay Colony:

> Let men of God in courts and churches watch
> O'er such as do a Toleration hatch,
> Lest that ill egg bring forth a cockatrice
> To poison all with heresy and vice.

Milton's pamphlet against the censorship has remained the classic statement of the doctrine of free speech. His argument involves a discussion of the broader question of the nature of virtue, and it is the theoretical framework for the modern faith in the value of free discussion—the open market for ideas—a kind of intellectual *laissez faire*. This excerpt, much abridged, contains the gist of Milton's thought.

1. In which two paragraphs do you find the fullest statement of his theory? Study his several arguments in the passage, formulating them in sentences of your own and trying to reduce them to their common principles. Then summarize the essential doctrine in a few sentences.

2. Nicolo Machiavelli had observed that "men are ungrateful, fickle, false, cowardly, and covetous; as long as you succeed they will offer you their blood, property, life, and chil-

dren, but when your need is urgent, they turn against you."
Thus he advised a prince to be loved if possible, but certainly
feared: "for love is preserved by the link of obligation, which,
owing to the baseness of men, is broken at every opportunity
for their advantage; but fear preserves you by a dread of punishment which never fails." And since the vulgar are easily
deceived by appearances and results, a prince should speak
words of fidelity, friendship, humanity, and religion; but he
need not act on such principles. Thus Machiavelli's rules of government rested on the assumption that man is a fickle, simple-
minded creature. What is Milton's estimate of human nature?
(Give line references.)

3. In the older feudal and agrarian scheme of society, the
common people were supposed to be coarse, humble, hard-
working folk; their overlords protected them, and the Church
offered them its ministrations and simple moral instruction
adapted to their understanding and their manner of life. What
do you infer, from indications throughout the passage, to have
been Milton's notion of an ideal commonwealth? Briefly sketch
its chief features. How do you like it?

Milton's prose is Elizabethan, colorful and exuberant. Ideas
are presented not abstractly but pictorially: instead of "the
exercise of discrimination," we have Psyche sorting seeds
(ll. 5-7). Or compare with lines 15-18 such an abstract phrasing
as "The truly virtuous man must be able to recognize the attractiveness of evil without yielding to temptation." Milton,
though a master of prose, does not get all the credit, for this
pictorial quality is inherent in the language of his age: for instance, whereas "apprehend" now signifies merely a mental
operation, in Elizabethan English it retained its suggestion
of physical grasping. Yet Milton was temperamentally fitted to
make the most of this language. He does not merely analyze
a psychological situation; he makes it dramatic. His words
impart vigor and action. The twins are not merely joined; they
cleave. The knowledge of good and evil does not emerge; it
leaps forth. The seeds must be sorted *asunder*. In such words
one may feel the violent energy of the underlying thought.

4. To examine this style, note the metaphors and similes
in which it abounds. The distinction is formal and need not be
taken too seriously: a simile is an explicit comparison or

analogy, like that between moral discrimination and Psyche's task (ll. 2–7); in metaphor, the comparison is implied or assumed, as the Christian in line 18 is made a warrior. Find six more similes and twelve more metaphors. (There are also, as has been indicated, many metaphors inherent in words which still retained their etymological allusions—e.g., *apprehend*—but these can hardly be counted.)

5. The beautiful story of Psyche may be read in *The Golden Ass* of Apuleius (Books IV–VI), in Pater's *Marius* (Chapter V), or in Sylvia Townsend Warner's *The True Heart*. This textbook does not provide a footnote explaining that Psyche was a figure in Greek mythology. Why not?

6. There can be no question woven to catch the Elizabethan music of this prose. Mechanically viewed, it seems to derive from the length and complexity of the sentences. In addition to the marked cadence at the end of each sentence, there are minor cadences and suspensions within the sentence, and these vary in quality. Within the rhythms thus established, the syllables may flow rapidly or in slower measure. But these phrasings are not formal or external; they derive from the sense and the arrangement of the words, as in the subtly magic "from out the rind of one apple tasted." Nor is one precise music prescribed; here is the score for each reader to make of what he will.

Now that you have digested the sense of the essay, read the paragraphs aloud, and decide which you think the most notable in music. Be prepared to defend your choice.

How do you account for the fact that modern prose is so unmusical? Or find a passage in a modern author which refutes this charge.

7. A theory so broad and so basic as is Milton's raises many questions for discussion in your essay. Here are suggestions:

a) The free discussion of Milton's contemporaries dealt largely with matters of religion. The plain man, having learned to read, started on his pathway to heaven by reading the Bible by whatever light was available to him. Read 30 or 40 pages in Richard Baxter's *Autobiography* or George Fox's *Journal* or John Bunyan's *Grace Abounding* (all in the Everyman Library); then, using these data, write an essay describing and commenting on the popular theological activities of the period.

b) Milton thought that the religious sects might cooperatively accumulate the fragments of the Whole Truth; Thomas Browne, in his *Religio Medici,* presented a more orthodox personal attitude. Read sections i-xvi in his book; then write an essay describing his attitude and evaluating it in comparison with Milton's.

c) Read the "Epistle Dedicatory" of Jeremy Taylor's *Liberty of Prophesying;* summarize this churchman's program of tolerance and point out any ways in which his perspective differs from Milton's.

d) The schisms which seemed so hopeful to Milton have resulted in our hundreds of religious denominations and storefront sects. The pew-holder, freed from the intellectual domination of the parish priest, has evolved his own religious notions and sometimes enforces them upon the pulpit. Religious life has become democratic, individualistic, sectarian, evangelistic. Do not suppose Milton peculiarly responsible for these tendencies: he merely provided a theory to justify the process. Take some one phase of current religious activity which you have observed and write an essay describing and evaluating it. (Mrs. Humphry Ward's *Robert Elsmere,* chapters 38, 40, 41, 46, Harold Frederic's *Damnation of Theron Ware,* or Sinclair Lewis's *Elmer Gantry* may stimulate your observation, although you may find none of these pictures accurate.)

e) For modern views, read in William James's *Varieties of Religious Experience* the chapter on "The Divided Self" or several chapters in H. E. Fosdick's *On Being a Real Person.* Use this as material for an essay, noting the difference between the modern and the Miltonic perspective.

f) In an actual society, the theory of free publication may need tacit qualification; Milton conceded that in some matters "the law is to bid restraint and punishment." The unscrupulous may issue literature seditious, obscene, or likely to create social disturbance. Sometimes the mere raising of a question may work the mischief: Is it true that Republicans eat Democratic babies? Does Maine intend to repudiate her state debts when she secedes from the Union? Irresponsible advertisers inculcate depraved ideals. Or it may seem unwise to acquaint the public with some point of military or scientific or historical information. Select some one matter in which the value of free publication or discussion may be questioned, make up your mind about it, and present your opinion in an essay.

THE PSYCHOLOGY OF SOCIAL
INSTITUTIONS[1]

THURMAN ARNOLD

•

1. WHEREVER MEN BECOME ABSORBED IN A MEDIEVAL SEARCH for the magic formula of universal truth the creeds of government grow in importance and the practical activities of government are mismanaged. Holy wars are fought, orators 5 and priests thrive, but technicians perish. Color and romance abound in such an era, as in all times of conflict, but practical distribution of available comfort and efficient organization are impossible.

2. When we attempt to analyze the actual operation of 10 creeds in society, we discover the surprising fact that their content and their logic are the least important things about them. Socialists, thrown into power against a background of confusion, become more conservative than Tories. On the other hand, whoever obtains power in times of na- 15 tional humiliation and defeat is apt to express and intensify the persecution manias which that atmosphere develops in any people. This happened in Russia and Germany. It was not the result of the doctrines of Communism or Fascism. It would have occurred under any doctrine. Only 20 those leaders who can respond to current aspirations and ideals can survive. Therefore, any governmental creed that is professed by actual leaders must change to fit the emotional needs of their people. The theoretical systems of government are only argumentative tools by which priests 25 and scholars condemn heresy or else attack the established Church.

3. The study of the actual operation of the social creeds

[1] Abridged from *The Folklore of Capitalism*, by Thurman Arnold; reprinted by permission of the Yale University Press, Publishers.

which give logical form and unity to our so-called systems
of government is confused by the fact that it is hard for us
not to think of them as guiding principles which we choose 30
or reject. For example, a recent book, *In Defense of Capitalism,* by James H. R. Cromwell and Hugo E. Czerwonky,
carries this statement on the jacket, which not only represents the attitude of the authors but also that of most conservative people today: 35

The insecurity and degradation of the American working
masses is attributable, not to capitalism, but to ignorance concerning its functioning. The fact is that capitalism is an ideal
which never has been achieved. Before discarding capitalism
and economic freedom for a system of regimentation and ration- 40
ing, we contend that the defects of our monetary organization
should first be remedied and capitalism thereby given a fair
chance to show what it can do.

In other words, from this point of view Capitalism is studied
apart from the living organizations which profess it as a 45
creed. If it is found to be good our troubles must come from
a sinful refusal to follow Capitalism logically. If it is found
to be bad our troubles are the result of not voluntarily aban-
doning it.

4. Such a point of view makes it impossible to observe 50
how creeds actually operate in the world of temporal affairs. It leads only to pounding the table and preaching
the evils of sin. This chapter will therefore be based on the
assumption that social creeds, law, economics, and so on
have no meaning whatever apart from the organization to 55
which they are attached. To say that the organizations
voluntarily choose them is as meaningless as to say that
the Catholic Church voluntarily chose the Catholic religion
in preference to Protestantism. To blame organizations for
not living up to them is as meaningless as blaming feudal 60
barons for not living up to the precepts of chivalry. Books
like *In Defense of Capitalism* are an automatic response
to an emotional conflict. They are not an explanation of
the creed; they are part of it. In order to understand this

65 we must discuss the psychology of social institutions which produces similar results regardless of the form into which the statement of the creed is cast.

5. The social organization of a nation is the unifying force which binds a people together. It is a complex thing 70 based on habit and acceptance of certain common values. It creates an atmosphere in which thousands of smaller organizations with opposing interests succeed in getting along together. It does this by the force of public opinion which makes dissent, or even doubt, subject to various 75 kinds of ostracism.

6. The elements which all social organizations share in common may tentatively be described as follows: (1) A creed or a set of commonly accepted rituals, verbal or ceremonial, which has the effect of making each individual 80 feel an integral part of the group and which makes the group appear as a single unit. (2) A set of attitudes which makes the creed effective by giving the individual prestige, or at least security, when he subordinates what are ordinarily called "selfish interests" to those of the group. (3) A 85 set of institutional habits by means of which men are automatically able to work together without any process of conscious choice as to whether they will coöperate or not. (4) The mythological or historical tradition which proves that an institutional creed has been ordained by more than 90 human forces. This mythology may take every conceivable form, depending on the culture. It may emphasize humanitarian values or nonhumanitarian values, warlike or peacetime diversities. However, although the emphasis may differ in different cultures, all the common human values 95 will be found represented in some form or other, whether the organization be a primitive tribe or the New York Stock Exchange. Granted these essentials, we find successful organizations. Without them, organization can be maintained only by force, and force cannot continue long be-100 cause it is too exhausting.

7. Because words and ceremonies are our only methods of communication, everywhere we find that the creed is re-

garded as the cornerstone of social institutions. Therefore, the folklore of every people runs in something like this form. A long time ago, with the aid of some sacred and infallible force, certain exceptionally gifted forebears formulated a lot of principles which contained the fundamentals of social organization. Nations which, like the United States, trace their beginnings to some single event think that their principles were discovered all at one time. This circumstance gives them a *written* constitution. Nations like England, which do not claim any sudden birth, always find their principles in a whole series of historical events, and hence their "constitution" is unwritten.

8. In this country we like to think that we decided to write down all our governmental principles in one document called the Constitution. Actually, the Constitution consists of thousands of documents written at various times. Yet since our origin as an independent nation centered around one historic event, we emphasize what was written at that time and call it a written constitution. This folklore has caused many naïve books to be written on the advantages of a people getting together and deciding to write their constitution. The writer recalls a course in college in which one of the matters discussed was whether England had not made a mistake in not reducing her constitution to definite written form. In a similar way the myths of primitive governments may center either on a single event or on a series of events in which the actors are individuals of more than human capabilities. In an age where Reason is God, constitutions or fundamental creeds are always supposed to be the result of rational thought on the part of our forebears. Thus Rousseau depicted a social contract by which men agreed to stop fighting, because this seemed such an eminently reasonable hypothesis to a peace-loving man. In an age of mysticism the tables are handed down from on high instead of being discovered by reason.

9. Having acquired a constitution through the intervention of exceptionally gifted men, the folklore of every nation then assumes that the people accepted it as truth

and proceeded to live up to it. Dissenters are shown the light by the process of education. Whatever gaps were left by the physical inability of the forefathers to consider everything are filled by the learned men of the time, with ma-
145 terial which they manufacture, not out of whole cloth but out of the principles of the original document. If this process is questioned it is always answered that the forefathers wanted the constitution to be a growing and not a static thing, and invariably some of them are found who said
150 just that. If, however, a gap is left unfilled, it is always pointed out that a constitution cannot be one thing today and another tomorrow, and invariably there are found a number of great men who stated this with some vehemence in the past. Each argument is used alternately by the Su-
155 preme Court of the United States, but it should be kept in mind that we are talking here not about the United States Constitution but about every organizational creed. The language of the Constitution is immaterial since it represents current myths and folklore rather than rules.
160 Out of it are spun the contradictory ideals of governmental morality. It is essential to constitutionalism as a vital creed that it be capable of being used on both sides of any question, because it must be the creed of all groups in order to function as a unifying symbol. Pride in his early struggles
165 and a clinging to traditions which have been handed to him by better men than he are deep seated within the psychology of the individual.

10. It is considered quite a sophisticated observation in these curious times to say that both political parties are
170 exactly alike. Few, however, understand that the reason for this is that where the center of attention is abstractions rather than practical objectives all parties are bound to be alike. The creed of each must represent all the current conflicting ideals and phobias. Only minority parties which
175 do not expect to get into power can write creeds without internal contradictions. Opposing parties which hope to win will necessarily worship the same gods even while they are denouncing each other because they are talking to

actual voters and not to some ideal society of the future. This is not something to complain about. It follows from the fact that every governmental creed must represent all the contradictory ideals of a people if it is to be accepted by them.

11. The logical content of creeds never realistically describes the institutions to which the creeds are attached. Every phrase in the Constitution designed to protect the submerged individual has become an instrument for the protection of large organizations. Due process of law under the Fifth Amendment unquestionably referred to arbitrary criminal prosecution of individuals. Today this amendment is one of the reasons why railroads are protected from a Federal pension system. Public control of business becomes the same as taking away property. Great national organizations become individuals. Only a short time ago nobody saw anything strange or out of the way in the change. Scholars in law schools proved that it was not a change at all and were generally believed.

12. It is therefore not the content of the governmental creed which molds institutions, but the imaginary personalities which make up the national mythology. Every culture has its hierarchy of divinities, like the ancient Greeks. This hierarchy is never recognized as a mythology during the period when it is most potent. The power of any currently accepted mythology lies in the fact that its heroes are thought to have a real existence. There is always a large number of them because each mood and aspiration must be represented. Every institution tries to represent all of these heroes at once. Thus the American industrial organization is a hardboiled trader, a scholar, a patron of modern architecture, a thrifty housewife, a philanthropist, a statesman preaching sound principles of government, a patriot, and a sentimental protector of widows and orphans at the same time. Let me designate the heroes of a nation and I care not who writes its constitution.

13. In the days of chivalry national heroes were princes of the Church or warriors seeking high adventure for a holy

motive. These imaginary personalities gave form and logic to governmental structure. King Richard went to the Crusades in an unconscious response to the demand that the
220 Government of England imitate its myths, just as the ruling class of every time unconsciously imitates the little ideal pictures to which it owes its prestige.

14. In the United States the mythology used to be very simple. The predominant figure was the American Busi-
225 nessman. Warriors were respected, but they had a distinctly minor place. The National Government had to imitate the American Businessman. Whenever it failed, people became alarmed. A businessman balances his budget. Hence the unbalanced budget which was actually pulling us out of
230 the depression was the source of greater alarm than administrative failures which were actually more dangerous. The American Businessman bosses his employees. Hence the encouragement of the C.I.O. was thought to be the forerunner of a revolution, in spite of the fact that never
235 had industrial unrest been followed with less actual disorder. The American Businessman was an individual who was free from the control of any other individual and owed allegiance only to the Constitution. It is this mythology, operating long after the American Businessman has dis-
240 appeared as an independent individual, which gives the great industrial organization an established place in our temporal government. Every demand on these great industrial structures is referred to the conception of the American Businessman as a standard.

245 15. Thus pension systems for great corporations are all right provided businessmen inaugurate them. Economic coercion is permitted provided these heroes accomplish it. Boondoggling of every kind is subject to no criticism if businessmen finance it. Charity and welfare work, provided
250 they are used to portray businessmen in their softer and more sentimental moods, are lovely things. When undertaken by the Government, they are necessary evils because such activity impairs the dignity and prestige of our great

national ideal type. The businessman is the only divinity
supposed to conduct such affairs. Therefore one never hears 255
a community chest spoken of as a necessary evil as the dole
is. Private charity even in times when it is an obvious failure
is supposed to be more efficient than government relief.

16. Coupled with the national heroes in every institutional mythology is the national Devil. Our Devil is gov- 260
ernmental interference. Thus we firmly believe in the
inherent malevolence of government which interferes with
business. Here are people who are not to be trusted—they
are the bureaucrats, the petty tyrants, the destroyers of a
rule of law. Organizations always tend to assume the char- 265
acters given to them by popular mythology. Hence the
government is no career for an up-and-coming young man.
Governmental institutions are not to be trusted to hire
their employees. We must control their inherent malevolence
by Civil Service rules. Civil Service is a great protection for 270
mediocrity and thus tends to make the government fit the
bureaucratic preconceptions. Thus the powerful influence
of the national hierarchy of gods moves institutions into
patterns from which they cannot escape until the attitudes
change.   275

17. Germany is a country which loves to wear uniforms.
It is said that it is difficult to keep even German railway
conductors from wearing out their uniforms at home. The
national hero is a soldier. Therefore, no economic principles ever designed have prevented Germany from assum- 280
ing the atmosphere of at best a military academy with a
scholarly faculty, and at worst an armed camp.

18. How far nations can be induced to revise their
mythologies is a psychological problem not unlike the problem of how to change the admiration and dislikes of the 285
individual. The politician does not attempt to change the
mythology. He works with it unscrupulously to get results.
The trouble with him is not that his technique is bad but
that his ends are not broad or humanitarian. Yet in our
present medieval atmosphere it is his techniques which are 290

condemned. His ends, in so far as they are selfish, are supposed to work for the greatest benefit of all in a free economic system.

19. Probably the only way in which mythologies actually change is through the rise to power of a new class whose traditional heroes are of a different mold. This can be observed in revolutions of all kinds, peaceful as well as violent. A ruling class ceases to perform the functions necessary to distribute goods according to the demands of a people. A new class appears to satisfy those demands. At first it is looked down on. Gradually it accumulates a mythology and a creed. Finally all searchers for universal truth, all scholars, all priests (except, of course, unsound radicals), all educational institutions of standing, are found supporting that class and everyone feels that the search for legal and economic truth has reached a successful termination. We can observe the rise of a race of traders and money lenders against the system of law and economics of chivalry and feudalism which today looks incredibly romantic, but which then looked like the very bedrock of reality. No one would have dreamed in the Middle Ages that the despised creed of the trader and the money lender —a creed of selfishness and worship of the then lowest material values—should rise to be a compendium of everything most respectable in temporal affairs.

20. Today we can observe the rise of a class of engineers, salesmen, minor executives, and social workers—all engaged in actually running the country's temporal affairs. Current mythology puts them in the rôle of servants, not rulers. Social workers are given a subordinate rôle. For purposes of governmental policy their humanitarian ideas are positively dangerous, because they put consideration of actual efficiency in the distribution of goods above reverence for the independence and dignity of the businessman. It is as if a usurer attempted to sit at the table in social equality with the medieval baron to whom he was lending money. Nevertheless, it is this great class of employees, working for salaries, which distributes the goods of the world.

Traders still are possessed of the symbols of power. The new class, however, has already shown signs of developing a creed of its own and a set of heroes. Older universities look at their new economic thinking with suspicion, but its prestige grows with the prestige of the class of business and social technicians which it represents. Its mythology does not include the worship of the American Businessman. So far it is destructive only. However, one should remember that a fully developed creed and mythology are not found until the class which they support is securely in power. Adam Smith did not think up principles by which the merchant and manufacturer gained power. He supplied them with a philosophy after they had taken charge of the temporal government.

21. Curiously enough, in all the holy war against Communism and Fascism to make the world safe for our prevailing divinity, we find very little spiritual conflict about the principles of democracy. Democracy was accepted as a political fact, not as something to be chosen or rejected. The democratic tradition had become recognized as a tradition and had ceased to be regarded as a set of guiding principles. All over the world, except perhaps in the Orient, there was a recognition that popular majorities were necessary for a successful government regardless of what the creed happened to be. A strange thing had happened to democracy as a creed. Few believed any more that it was a peculiarly sacred or divine thing. The "principles" of democracy were not worshiped as they once were, as fundamental truths. Everyone recognized the limitations of the average man—and few thought that these limitations disappeared in a group.

22. Democracy ceased being a creed. It simply became a name for a type of organization controlled by voters. Men discovered that it is immaterial whether democracy is morally beautiful or not. They recognized as a fact that it was more important that an institution keep in touch with the mass of its members than that it follow rational principles. The word "democracy" therefore came to represent

the notion that political techniques which had nothing to do with rational principles were a necessary part of social control. This was first discovered in connection with the distribution of goods by large organizations. Advertising men used slogans rather than descriptions of their products. Politicians soon found the advantages of such techniques over either appeals to pure reason or the grosser forms of vote buying. Polls began to be taken on public questions—experts began to develop in the ascertaining of public attitudes. Principles and political platforms became more and more of a ceremony and less a matter of belief to those who wrote them.

23. This sort of political realism about democracy was brought home to us by the success of the dictatorships in Russia and Germany. In these countries the revolutionary governments undertook deliberately to arouse the intense enthusiasm of their peoples and to keep it at a high pitch. The method used was not rational; it was the rhythm of uniforms, salutes, marching feet, and national games. The strength of Hitler lay in the fact that he put everyone to work and managed to develop national pride. His weakness lay in his persecutions.

24. Such persecutions are not, I believe, *necessary* to the exercise of national power or the development of national morale. The reason why they are apt to occur in times of change is that respectable people in such times are too devoted to principles to solve immediate problems or to build up morale by the objective use of ceremony. They are too obsessed with the principles of government by the people to know how it works.

25. The old creed of democracy as our fathers knew it was a useful slogan to bind together those who rose to fill the gaps left by an incompetent aristocracy. It was a useful slogan to stir national pride in a people who had no ruling class. Like all creeds it was in no way descriptive. It borrowed the old symbols of aristocracy since it had to represent all the current conflicting ideals. Thus the lack of an ecclesiastical hierarchy was filled by the slogan, "The voice

of the people is the voice of God." The gap left by the ab- 405
sence of an aristocracy was bridged by the constant reference to the "nobility" of the common people. The necessity to personify a ruler and invest him with divine
power was filled in the personification of the people. Under
these slogans a small ruling class developed in the United 410
States.

26. The democratic creed of that ruling class, however,
was full of so many hidden conflicts that it developed in
America more *sub rosa* institutions than in any other Western nation. The "people" in this democracy were supposed 415
to choose sound economic principles in preference to unsound ones like a scholargarchy. They were to reject unsound legal principles like a theocracy. Only one thing they
were not permitted to do in public, and that was to think
realistically about their government. Therefore our real gov- 420
ernment was conducted by non-respectable politicians. Exceptions there were, such as Jefferson and Roosevelt, who
combined political technique with aristocratic background.
Such men incurred the bitter enmity of their friends as
traitors to their class. Actual political leaders in the pe- 425
culiar democracy we established were generally the type
who theoretically should have been distrusted by the people,
because they appealed to the emotions instead of reasoning
analytically for the benefit of thinking men. When the
people of New York City or Chicago sought real repre- 430
sentation they were forced to choose organizations like
Tammany Hall or the Thompson machine, since respectable
people could not think politically.

27. The only class which was permitted to think objectively about what it was doing without violating its 435
own creed was big business. In this area both learned and
popular philosophy proved that whatever mistakes business made cancelled each other, that its greed was only
a form of unselfishness, and that its corruption was only
the work of an occasional emissary of Satan sent up from 440
below to plague mankind. Of course, the law and the
economics which permitted this class to act practically al-

lowed its members to be respectable and efficient at the same time. In this favorable atmosphere their natural or-
445 ganizing ability was not hampered by taboos. They developed a productive plant which was the marvel of the modern world. As a creed, democracy never even remotely resembled the actual democracy which existed in this country, but as a political fact it produced a spiritual
450 government in Washington to represent its ideals and a temporal government in our industrial centers which gave scope for the productive energy of its people and which, at the same time, never lost their support, violated their taboos, or contradicted the mythology they had set up for
455 themselves.

28.   In our thinking about democracy we have dropped to a large extent the medieval atmosphere. We have ceased to write books describing how sacred it is. We realize that in its essence it means that an effective leader must main-
460 tain the morale as well as the discipline of his army. Even respectable people today are acquiring skill in the use of political techniques. The effects are noticeable. A better class of political leaders is in charge of our political machines. Grosser and more unpleasant forms of political chicanery
465 are not used to the same extent as in 1900. As men have gradually ceased to believe in the democratic slogans as truths, political techniques have become less the exclusive property of unscrupulous people.

29.   Today, when sophisticated men speak of democracy
470 as the only workable method of government, they mean that a government which does not carry its people along with it emotionally, which depends on force, is insecure. They mean that it is better for a government to do foolish things which can have popular support than wise things
475 which arouse people against it. They mean that if a man is not contented, material comforts will do him no good. They mean that the art of government consists in the technique of achieving willing popular acceptance; that what people *ought* to want is immaterial; that democratic gov-

ernment consists only in giving them what they *do* want; 480
that progress in government can come only by improving
the *wants* of the people through the technique of removing
their prejudices; and, finally, that the removal of prejudice
must come first or material and humanitarian progress,
imposed by force, will fail. When we consider democracy 485
as a political fact, we are no longer concerned with the
question of whether it ought to be admired as a fine thing
or condemned as a stupid thing.

30. Our thinking about symbols of money and credit
seldom takes such a fact-minded point of view. Here we 490
are caught in formulas which pretend to be universal truths.
We believe in the capitalistic system, as we used to believe
in democracy, not as a tool, but as a set of abstract principles to be followed. The systems of government over
which we have our theological disputes are no longer 495
monarchy, aristocracy, and democracy, but Capitalism,
Communism, and Fascism. Capitalism is a good thing in
the abstract. It has its following of learned men and philosophers. It is no more descriptive of social organization
today than the theology of the monarchy was descriptive 500
before the French Revolution. It is instead an arsenal of
weapons to be used against new organizations, rising because of a compelling need, but hampered because they
have as yet found no place in accepted institutional mythology. The terms Communism and Fascism are used to de- 505
nounce these new organizations as breeders of heresy. The
acceptance of the slogans of Capitalism as tools rather than
as truths is still over the horizon.

❦ ❦ ❦

1. Thurman Arnold's *Folklore of Capitalism* is the standard exposition of the sophisticated modern view of social action, political and economic. This specimen is included in the
text in order that you may be indoctrinated with sound ideas
and that false ideas may be exposed. As the essay is highly abstract, expounding a general principle, you may best approach

it by determining what Arnold says or implies about several specific questions. To do this, you may have to gather evidence from several parts of the essay.

a) Would he scrap the United States Constitution? Is this the hidden drift of his argument?

b) Would he dispense with the Supreme Court? Or render its functions merely ceremonial?

c) What is his attitude toward big corporations? What would you expect him to say about trusts?

d) Summarize his views on Fascist Germany, noting any points on which you think him wrong.

2. Mark off the several main divisions of the essay and state the topic of each.

3. Clip an editorial or newspaper column which adduces what Arnold calls the national creed or mythology. Analyze it; what action or program is advocated or denounced? How is the particular issue related to the guiding principle? (Or examine a radio speech in the same way.)

4. In Pars. 12-15 there is described a kind of social *bovarysme,* in which certain idealized types—the hard-boiled trader, the philanthropist, etc.—are made the patterns or standards of institutional behavior. Look through the advertising pages of a popular magazine to see how such heroic figures are utilized in the distribution of goods and services. Explain briefly, with illustrations.

5. Is Arnold of the school of Machiavelli or that of Milton? In what ways?

6. What do you think happens to ethical values and the responsibility of governors in Arnold's picture of social organization?

7. Here are suggestions for themes:

a) Arnold intends his analysis to apply to any social organization, large or small. Analyze the psychology of a lodge or a luncheon club or a labor organization or a college, etc., in these terms.

b) Does his account of the creed or constitution apply to the church? Would a churchman agree?

c) If you find Arnold's perspective congenial, you might try applying it to the left wingers. He argues that liberal critics of political or economic wickedness have "strengthened the creed by showing that in it lay the way of salvation." And the proper Socialist—"never identified with an organization that seemed about to do anything practical"—has been the sort of man "for whom romantic college professors could vote." Discuss the psychological workings of the Communist movement in the United States with regard both to its supporters and to the commonwealth at large.

d) Test the ideas of Par. 19 against the data provided in Chapter I or Chapters I-II of R. H. Tawney's *Religion and the Rise of Capitalism*. Present your conclusions in an essay.

e) If revolutions fascinate you, read the *Communist Manifesto* and the Preface and Chapter XI, on "Dual Power," of Trotzky's *History of the Russian Revolution,* vol. I. Mix the Marxist analysis of history well with Thurman Arnold's psychologizing, and present some conclusion of yours in a temperate essay.

f) If you find Arnold's perspective distasteful, in whole, in part, or in implication, write an essay explaining what you find ugly or implausible in his view of society. You need not attempt to refute the obnoxious attitude as though it were an objective fact; you need only show it incompatible with an effectual scheme of values. But you should represent his view accurately, whatever color you may see it in.

ROCOCO[1]

EGON FRIEDELL

•

1. WATTEAU WAS SO PERFECT A MIRROR OF HIS TIME BE-
cause, in his destiny and his personality, he was its most
speaking symbol. He was a dying man, and his whole life
and creative work the euphoria of the consumptive. And
5 Rococo also was a dying age, and its joy in life nothing
but a sort of tubercular sensuality, a last craving for illusion
to carry one over the gateway of death: the cheerful red
on its cheeks is either rouge or a hectic spot. Rococo is the
agony and euthanasia of the Baroque, its sunset—that hour
10 of the day which Watteau most loved to paint. Loving and
dying: that is the formula for Watteau and the whole of
Rococo.

2. It was, in contrast to the Baroque, a *disintegrating*
style, purely picturesque and decorative, playful and orna-
15 mental, smothering everything in festoons of garlands, shells,
and twining plants—swamp motives, these, that now obtain
the mastery, while the fine earlier forms begin to dissolve in
an aristocratic decay. Over all there is the soft cool breeze
of evening, the fading blue and tender rose which herald
20 the close of the day. A grey autumnal mood is settling
upon humanity and is reflected in the faded tints of its
external covering, which, for choice, was of honey-yellow
and tea-green, dark grey and pale red, violet and brown.
This decadence-style *par excellence* is weary, toned down,
25 anaemic, and, above all, feminine: affectedly infantine and
naïvely obscene, as a woman is; veiled and boudoirish;
perfumed and painted; satiny and sweet-toothed; without

[1] Reprinted from *A Cultural History of the Modern Age*, by Egon
Friedell, by permission of and special arrangement with Alfred A. Knopf,
Inc., authorized publishers.

masculine depth and worthiness, but equally without virile
heaviness and pedantry; lightly poised as if dancing, and
so achieving the miracle of an architecture that almost 30
defies the laws of gravitation; forever ambiguously smiling,
but seldom with a whole-hearted laugh; amusing, piquant,
capricious, epicurean, witty, coquettish; full of anecdote,
short story, and point; chattering and open-minded, scep-
tical and popular, with the atmosphere of comedy, theatrical 35
and yet domestic: even the caryatids of the age, such as
Frederick the Great, Bach, and Voltaire, were in a sense
genre figures of more than life-size.

3. This late Baroque has indeed an intimate character
which the High Baroque never possessed. It is in the best 40
sense a tapestry style, which sets out purely to please, to
decorate and refine, and regards violence of expression as
not only vulgar, but inconvenient. The characteristic building to which invention and care were devoted was no
longer the pompous palace, but the *petite maison*, the small 45
pleasure-house, furnished with all the charms of a luxury
of intimacy rather than display, and, as compared with
the preceding architecture, having something discreet, reserved, and personal about it. Under Louis XIV men lived
only in public: that is, for and by reason of the court; 50
they counted only when they appeared before the King
and as long as they continued so to appear. For that reason
every vital manifestation, from a profound thought to a
graceful bow, was designed for parade and calculated for
the effect it would make at Versailles. Now, however, 55
fifty years of gala performances had left them weary, and
they began to appreciate the joys of retirement, of letting
themselves go, of belonging to themselves. The very names
of these villas—*Érémitage, Monrepos, Solitude, Sans-souci*
—are an index to the change in taste. Gone are Jove-like 60
aloofness and heaviness of line; their aspect is now gracious,
unconstrained, hospitable. In the rooms within there are
no longer the stiff ceremonial chairs with high, hard backs,
or the imposing decorative pieces of heavy material, but
comfortable upholstered chairs, sofas with silken cushions, 65

and small white lacquered tables with fine gold lining. Even such quiet effects as these were further toned down by replacing the gold with silver, or shading it to mat; here as in all else the positive was avoided and preference given
70 to broken, fading, mixed colours and delicate materials such as rosewood, violet-wood, tulip-wood. The items of the inventory begin to wear the subjective stamp of their owners and to serve their personal aims. A host of new articles of furniture, expressive of the new mood, came into
75 fashion about this time. There was the *boîte à surprises*, a *secretaire* with cunningly contrived secret drawers and surprise mechanisms, and the lady's writing-table prettily called *"bonheur du jour."* All the objects in daily use were impregnated with scent, and enamelled perfume-pans filled
80 the apartments with exquisite odours. The leading artists took an interest in every one of these details and were able, by bringing them all into harmony, to create a finely graded atmosphere of artistic satisfaction and comfort. Watteau painted fashion-plates and shop signs, and Boucher designed
85 headings for note-paper, menus, and business papers.

4. A special note of these Rococo interiors was the predominance of pastel and porcelain. Indeed, no kind of painting could have expressed so well the intellectual attitude of this whole period—its delicate, fleeting, pale, ex-
90 piring character, so well attuned to a soft velvet background —as the pastel, even apart from the fact that it is a medium particularly suited to the intimate portrait. European porcelain was first manufactured in 1709 by the Saxon Johann Friedrich Böttcher, whom Augustus the Strong kept in
95 captivity for himself as his alchemist; and, as it turned out, this discovery of his did in fact develop into a sort of gold-making, for the new material made a conquest of the whole continent. The Meissen factory, which was founded shortly after, supplied everyone with cheap, handsome, and
100 practical eating-utensils and drove not only earthenware and pewter, but even silver from the table. The classic maker of German porcelain was, however, Joachim Kändler, whose enamoured shepherds and shepherdesses and life-size birds,

monkeys, and dogs were the delight of the elegant world.
As for Augustus the Strong, he was so obsessed by his [105]
new craze that he sacrificed half his fortune to it and
filled a whole castle with porcelain. In Vienna, too, a fine
porcelain-factory was opened in 1718, but the German
manufactures had a powerful rival later in the Sèvres factory, built on the initiative of the Pompadour. In England [110]
Josiah Wedgwood invented the material named after him,
using it chiefly for masterly reproductions of Classical vases.
Finally all Europe was seized by a veritable mania for china.
Not only candlesticks and lustres, clocks and stones, flower-
pieces and inlays for furniture were made of it, but whole [115]
rooms and coaches and more than life-size monuments were
formed out of it. All this sort of thing was of course merely
the diversion into inappropriate paths of a very subtle art
that, so long as it respected the nature of its material, was
a vital and pregnant expression of the soul of the times; [120]
the reason why it found the eager response that it did in
the Rococo soul was precisely that it was so extraordinarily
and exclusively suited to the polished, coquettish, select,
fragile, and demure art of miniature.

5. In 1765—when a new spirit was already stirring— [125]
Diderot remarked about Boucher that he "went in too
much for petty play of feature." We can well apply this
remark to the whole Rococo. Voltaire, already, had called
his age the *siècle des petitesses*. In every sphere its only
genuine products were charming trifles. Baroque shouted [130]
and placarded, Rococo whispered and hushed. Both were
fond of flourishes, but in Baroque the flourish was a passionate exclamation-mark, which Rococo changed into a
discrete and elegant mark of interrogation.

6. Boredom had to be avoided at all costs. Accordingly [135]
in the eighteenth century French culture received a new
fillip. *Esprit* was born, the spirit of champagne, which is
froth and wine in one. But with this almost morbid straining to be, under all circumstances, stimulating and brilliant,
aromatic and effervescent, the old monumental air, the dig- [140]
nity, seriousness, and depth disappeared. Great tracts of the

soul wholly withered, were contemptuously avoided or flippantly ignored. The glitter which streams from the departing Baroque is the phosphorescence of corruption.

145 7. Men thought no longer in laboriously built-up and compartmented systems or heavy drugging syllogistic chains, but in close piquant polemics, faceted epigrams, time-killing satires, peppered pamphlets, and razor-edged aphorisms or, again, in *poésies fugitives,* lyric-epigrammatic *niai-*
150 *series* that had only a shimmering streak of any train of thought in them. Dialogue, novel, short story, all became vessels for philosophy. Even the conscientious and profound Montesquieu draws the coloured ribbon of a scandalous harem adventure through his *Lettres persanes.* It was essen-
155 tial to be understood by everyone, even the half-educated, the society man, the public, and, above all, the ladies.

8. This speaks out of the portraits too. Scholars are no longer painted with book, pen, and spectacles, but as smiling, nonchalant men of the world. Nothing is allowed
160 to disillusion us by suggesting the technical aids to their work; nor indeed must this work itself smell of oil, ink, and work-room, for it would have you believe that it is nothing more than a light, tasteful, and pleasant article of luxury, one of the many indispensable superfluities of
165 the self-indulgent life of society. The gardens of science, guarded from the eyes of the profane as holy ground in the Middle Ages, hedged in by the barbed wire fence of Latin learning in the Renaissance, were thrown open for general use in the eighteenth century and publicly set out
170 for the entertainment, refreshment, and instruction of all: of nobility and bourgeoisie, of man and wife, of clergy and laity. The People are still not admitted; not because they are despised, but from a still more curious reason—namely, that the fact of their existence has not yet been noticed.

175 9. Seeing that this age knew how to turn even science and philosophy into highly select stimulants, to be swallowed like a gum-tickling *apéritif,* it goes without saying that it was equally well able to deal with all the other aspects of life. There was but one desire, to make life an

uninterrupted round of pleasure. "For safety," as Madame 180
de la Verrue said, "we get in our paradise on earth." Moreover, one insisted on having one's fun without paying for
it: the fruits of riches without the trouble of working, the
glitter of an influential social position without its duties,
the joys of love without its pains. Therefore the grand 185
passion was avoided, and even branded as not *chic,* and
only the sweet frothy cream of love was tasted: one was
always amorous, never seriously in love. "We take each
other," wrote Crébillon *fils,* "without loving; we leave each
other without hating." Love and hate were passions, and 190
passions were uncomfortable things, besides indicating a
lack of *esprit.* Love was to be enjoyed without much fuss,
like a tasty bonbon which soon melts on the tongue and
is only there to be followed by a second of a different
flavour.
195

10. Eroticism became a graceful society game, which
imitated love in an amusing way and was subject to definite
rules. Love was turned into an *amateur stage,* a mapped-out
comedy with everything foreseen and prearranged—the
casting, in which the lady always receives the part of the 200
capricious mistress, the man that of the chivalrous adorer;
the speeches and gestures with which the several stages are
to be marked—wooing, hesitation, granting, happiness,
surfeit, parting. It is a complete scenario, created by long
tradition and art, in which everything has its conventional 205
place and everything is permitted, excepting only "scenes";
for to have seriously upset one's partner would have been
to betray a deplorable lack of tact and good manners. Even
jealousy was only allowed to be of a playful character:
"*la gelosia è passione ordinaria e troppo antica,*" said 210
Goldoni.

11. A requisite article which appears often in the pictures of the time is the swing, which was set up everywhere
and with the utmost nonchalance. Coming into fashion
about this time, it expressed many typical Rococo elements, 215
such as playfulness, the pretence of infantile innocence,
the dawning feeling for fresh air, the gallantry of man

and the coquetry of woman; and the agreeable giddiness
which it produced acted more or less as an aphrodisiac. In
220 Rococo, a woman could not look feminine and childish
enough, and the prevailing ideal was one of fragility, in
conscious imitation of the china doll. Health was considered
uninteresting, strength plebeian. The aristocratic ideal was
now transformed into an ideal of refinement, hypersensi-
225 bility, and elegant languor, an emphasis on unfitness for
life, and morbidity. The beauty-patch—which had already
come up in Louis XIV's time, but only now became the
dominating element in the physiognomy of the woman of
the world and ought really to be called the ugliness patch
230 —was meant to serve as a piquant interruption in the regu-
larity of a face and thereby emphasized the tendency to
asymmetry, innate in Rococo; while at the same time it
suggested a beauty-defect, a wart, thus making of every
woman a *belle-vilaine* and endowing her with a new and
235 perverse charm—it was, in fact, one more trait of morbidity.

12. Powdering, which was indispensable for well-
groomed people, whether they wore real or false hair, was
an extremely laborious performance. Usually the powder
was flung up towards the ceiling and allowed to float down
240 on to the head, the face being protected by a cloth. Prince
Kaunitz used to walk through a double row of lackeys
whose duty it was to powder him as evenly as possible.
Count Brühl owned five hundred wigs, which were all
kept permanently powdered—"a lot for a man without a
245 head," was Frederick the Great's comment. Faces, too, had
to be kept under a heavy layer of powder. The Rococo
powder, like the Baroque *allonge*, was no freak of fashion,
but the most eloquent symbol of the age. In the Rococo a
man past forty had done with life, and a woman far sooner.
250 Marriages were earlier than at the present day. Girls often
married at fourteen or fifteen, youths at twenty. In his
letters Voltaire calls himself an old man from his forty-
fifth year on. As late as the end of the nineteenth century
a woman of thirty acted as chaperon at a ball; now she
255 takes dancing-lessons at fifty. In the French dramas of

morals of the eighties the philosopher who looked on at
life and love with the eyes of a resigned observer was
seldom over forty; the modern films like to make the un-
principled seducer a man of fifty. The Rococo felt itself to
be old, while at the same time it was filled with the des- 260
perate longing of life for the youth that is vanishing, and
that is why it eliminated differences in age by ordering
grey hair for all. Rococo felt sick and anaemic, and therefore powder had to give it, as it were, a uniform of pallor
and anaemia. The young or young-painted face with its 265
white hair is a moving symbol of the Rococo soul, the *tragic
mask* of the time: for every age wears its appointed charac-
ter-mask, in which all its *velléités* are consciously or unconsciously summed.

❊ ❊ ❊

Friedell's *History* is in effect a series of character sketches.
As one may exhibit the personality of an individual in terms
of his mannerisms, his clothes, his house and its furnishings, his
preferences in art, so Friedell has here drawn a psychological
portrait of the rococo period—or of the rococo soul—in terms
of its behavior and tastes.

We are accustomed to speak of the spirit of an age, assuming
that the men and women of any historical period, however
they may differ from one another, have certain common qualities of temperament which distinguish them from the men
and women of another period. But Friedell employs the term
as something more than a metaphor. He constantly implies that
the spirit of an age is an entity, an active force in history,
that it is not merely a reflection or a consequence of the material
environment but actually shapes that environment in its own
image. Which is the prime mover in human affairs, a spirit,
evolving according to its own laws, or material things, tools and
trinkets, developing according to their laws? The question is
metaphysical. Both the idealistic and the materialistic views
open interesting lines of speculation to the historian, and
neither theory, when carried to its logical extreme, is quite
plausible. For there is an ambiguity in the aspect of human
history: spirit and substance have an astonishing way of keeping
pace with one another. Did the invention of oil paints, the print-

ing press, the cannon, and the telescope determine the course
of the human spirit, or did the Renaissance spirit seek and find
among the potentialities of physical nature precisely the utensils
it needed to express itself? In the nineteenth century Mrs.
Grundy used Elias Howe's new sewing machine to make herself a dress hideously furbished with pleats and ruffles and
flounces and ribbons; which was the creator, Howe or Mrs.
Grundy?—the science of machinery or the petty bourgeois
soul? Reality is mysterious, eluding our blunt questions. The
practical charm of Friedell's work is that it suffuses objects
with meaning; the merely quaint stage properties of historical
romance are made eloquently significant of the moods of the
humanity whose drama is enacted. Whatever our metaphysics,
this extension of our sensibilities is a valid enrichment of our
experience.

1. Without rereading the essay, make a list of the objects or
manners which you remember as expressive of the mood of
the period. If you recall fewer than five, read the essay again.

2. A great many phrases throughout the essay attribute
qualities of character to the period; what three or four terms
—your own words, if you like—best summarize the spirit of
the age?

3. Define *euphoria* (l. 4), *hectic* (l. 8), *euthanasia* (l. 9),
anaemic (l. 25), *virile* (l. 28), *caryatid* (l. 36), *syllogism* (l. 146),
polemic (l. 147).

4. How is the essay organized: as a list of things or as a
list of qualities? Is there a logical development of thought, or
do the various parts merely contribute to a unified impression?

5. What, roughly, are the dates of baroque and of rococo?
Name a notable work of architecture in each style. The derivation of the word *rococo* throws light on what feature of the
period? Was Chardin a typical rococo painter? Name several
writers to whose works the comments of Par. 7 apply. What
musicians composed in the spirit of this period?

6. Compare Par. 3 with the Lynds' description of homes in
Middletown. What is the chief rhetorical difference?

7. What a fact means depends upon its interpreter.
a) Rococo had a woman's distrust of the fine arts, and paid
her artists so poorly that they had to earn their living by doing
odd jobs for commercial houses.—Compare this statement with

that in lines 83-85. Which do you think more plausible, more consistent with the rest of the essay?

b) What interpretation by no means harmonious with Friedell's might be put upon the facts mentioned in lines 108-110?

c) Do the porcelain coaches in Par. 4 strengthen or weaken Friedell's argument?

d) How are the "young-painted faces" and powdered hair contradictory, and how has Friedell reconciled them?

8. Friedell has elsewhere listed characteristic utensils of each modern age: the compass in the sixteenth century, the microscope in the seventeenth, the mirror in this middle eighteenth, the newspaper in the nineteenth, the telephone in the twentieth. What is the significance of each of his symbols?

9. Apply Friedell's method to your own environment.

a) What are some of the characteristic buildings (cf. Par. 3) of our age? What do they signify?

b) Cf. Pars. 7-8. What do you make of the fact that we publish so many digests, surveys, outlines of history, medicine, law, philosophy, etc., selling them in drug stores?

c) Cf. lines 157-161. In the advertising pages of our magazines we have a pictorial record of contemporary man, as he is or as he would like to be. Collect at least a dozen such items of evidence and interpret it.

d) A comparison of the daguerreotypes in your family album with the candid products of the modern camera may suggest what change in the quality of human self-consciousness?

e) Cf. lines 226-235. Discuss briefly some recent feminine style—of dress, coiffure, hat, make-up—with reference to the qualities of character implicit in it. Have women any character independent of that imposed upon them by the fashions they follow?

f) What phenomena do you think a future historian of culture might select as peculiarly expressive of the spirit of our age? Explain your answers—and give them some thought: does the radio, for instance, make man powerful by extending his perceptions, or does it isolate and browbeat him? What meanings—if any—have the cigarette, the calculating machine, the paper cup?

10. Explain the derivations of *boudoir, chaperon, demure, index, menu, paradise, passion, scandal.*

THE LAW OF NATIONS[1]

HENRY SUMNER MAINE

•

1. THE ROMANS DESCRIBED THEIR LEGAL SYSTEM AS CON-
sisting of two ingredients. "All nations," says the Institutional Treatise published under the authority of the Emperor Justinian, "who are ruled by laws and customs, are
5 governed partly by their own particular laws, and partly by
those laws which are common to all mankind. The law
which a people enacts is called the Civil Law of that people,
but that which natural reason appoints for all mankind is
called the Law of Nations, because all nations use it." The
10 part of the law "which natural reason appoints for all mankind" was the element which the Edict of the Praetor was
supposed to have worked into Roman jurisprudence. Elsewhere it is styled more simply Jus Naturale, or the Law of
Nature; and its ordinances are said to be dictated by Natural
15 Equity (*naturalis aequitas*) as well as by natural reason.

2. The most superficial student of Roman history must
be struck by the extraordinary degree in which the fortunes
of the republic were affected by the presence of foreigners,
under different names, on her soil. The causes of this immi-
20 gration are discernible enough at a later period, for we can
readily understand why men of all races should flock to the
mistress of the world; but the same phenomenon of a large
population of foreigners and denizens meets us in the very
earliest records of the Roman State. No doubt, the instability
25 of society in ancient Italy, composed as it was in great measure of robber tribes, gave men considerable inducement to
locate themselves in the territory of any community strong
enough to protect itself and them from external attack, even
though protection should be purchased at the cost of heavy

---

[1] From *Ancient Law*, by Henry Sumner Maine.

taxation, political disfranchisement, and much social hu- 30 miliation. It is probable, however, that this explanation is imperfect, and that it could only be completed by taking into account those active commercial relations which, though they are little reflected in the military traditions of the republic, Rome appears certainly to have had with 35 Carthage and with the interior of Italy in pre-historic times. Whatever were the circumstances to which it was attributable, the foreign element in the commonwealth determined the whole course of its history, which, at all its stages, is little more than a narrative of conflicts between 40 a stubborn nationality and an alien population. Nothing like this has been seen in modern times; on the one hand, because modern European communities have seldom or never received any accession of foreign immigrants which was large enough to make itself felt by the bulk of the native 45 citizens, and on the other, because modern states, being held together by allegiance to a king or political superior, absorb considerable bodies of immigrant settlers with a quickness unknown to the ancient world, where the original citizens of a commonwealth always believed themselves to 50 be united by kinship in blood, and resented a claim to equality of privilege as a usurpation of their birthright. In the early Roman republic the principle of the absolute exclusion of foreigners pervaded the Civil Law no less than the constitution. The alien or denizen could have no share in any 55 institution supposed to be coeval with the State. He could not have the benefit of the Quiritarian law. He could not be a party to the *nexum* which was at once the conveyance and the contract of the primitive Romans. Still, neither the interest nor the security of Rome permitted him to be quite 60 outlawed. All ancient communities ran the risk of being overthrown by a very slight disturbance of equilibrium, and the mere instinct of self-preservation would force the Romans to devise some method of adjusting the rights and duties of foreigners, who might otherwise have decided 65 their controversies by armed strife. Moreover, at no period of Roman history was foreign trade entirely neglected. It

was therefore probably half as a measure of police and half
in furtherance of commerce that jurisdiction was first assumed in disputes to which the parties were either foreigners or a native and a foreigner. The assumption of such
jurisdiction brought with it the immediate necessity of dis-
covering some principles on which the questions to be
adjudicated upon could be settled, and the principles applied
to this object were eminently characteristic of the time. They
refused, as I have said before, to decide the new cases by
pure Roman Civil Law. They refused, no doubt because it
seemed to involve some kind of degradation, to apply the
law of the particular State from which the foreign litigant
came. The expedient to which they resorted was that of
selecting the rules of law common to Rome and to the different Italian communities in which the immigrants were
born. In other words, they set themselves to form a system
answering to the primitive and literal meaning of Jus Gentium, that is, Law common to all Nations. Jus Gentium was,
in fact, the sum of the common ingredients in the customs
of the old Italian tribes, for they were *all the nations* whom
the Romans had the means of observing, and who sent successive swarms of immigrants to Roman soil. Whenever a
particular usage was seen to be practised by a large number
of separate races in common, it was set down as part of the
Law common to all Nations, or Jus Gentium. Thus, although the conveyance of property was certainly accompanied by very different forms in the different commonwealths surrounding Rome, the actual transfer, tradition, or
delivery of the article intended to be conveyed was a part of
the ceremonial in all of them. It was, for instance, a part,
though a subordinate part, in the Mancipation or conveyance peculiar to Rome. Tradition, therefore, being in all
probability the only common ingredient in the modes of
conveyance which the jurisconsults had the means of observing, was set down as an institution Juris Gentium, or
rule of the Law common to all Nations. A vast number of
other observances were scrutinised with the same result.
Some common characteristic was discovered in all of them,

which had a common object, and this characteristic was classed in the Jus Gentium. The Jus Gentium was accordingly a collection of rules and principles, determined by observation to be common to the institutions which prevailed among the various Italian tribes.   110

3. The circumstances of the origin of the Jus Gentium are probably a sufficient safeguard against the mistake of supposing that the Roman lawyers had any special respect for it. It was the fruit in part of their disdain for all foreign law, and in part of their disinclination to give the foreigner 115 the advantage of their own indigenous Jus Civile. It is true that we, at the present day, should probably take a very different view of the Jus Gentium, if we were performing the operation which was effected by the Roman jurisconsults. We should attach some vague superiority or preced- 120 ence to the element which we had thus discerned underlying and pervading so great a variety of usage. We should have a sort of respect for rules and principles so universal. Perhaps we should speak of the common ingredient as being of the essence of the transaction into which it entered, and 125 should stigmatise the remaining apparatus of ceremony, as adventitious and accidental. Or it may be, we should infer that the races which we were comparing once obeyed a great system of common institutions of which the Jus Gentium was the reproduction, and that the complicated 130 usages of separate commonwealths were only corruptions and depravations of the simpler ordinances which had once regulated their primitive state. But the results to which modern ideas conduct the observer are, as nearly as possible, the reverse of those which were instinctively brought home 135 to the primitive Roman. What we respect or admire, he disliked or regarded with jealous dread. The parts of jurisprudence which he looked upon with affection were exactly those which a modern theorist leaves out of consideration as accidental and transitory; the solemn gestures of the 140 mancipation; the nicely adjusted questions and answers of the verbal contract; the endless formalities of pleading and procedure. The Jus Gentium was merely a system forced on

his attention by a political necessity. He loved it as little as
145 he loved the foreigners from whose institutions it was derived and for whose benefit it was intended. A complete
revolution in his ideas was required before it could challenge his respect, but so complete was it when it did occur,
that the true reason why our modern estimate of the Jus
150 Gentium differs from that which has just been described, is
that both modern jurisprudence and modern philosophy
have inherited the matured views of the later jurisconsults
on this subject. There did come a time when, from an ig-
noble appendage of the Jus Civile, the Jus Gentium came to
155 be considered a great though as yet imperfectly developed
model to which all law ought as far as possible to conform.
This crisis arrived when the Greek theory of a Law of
Nature was applied to the practical Roman administration
of the Law common to all Nations.

160   4. It becomes necessary to investigate the Greek concep-
tions of Nature and her law. The word φύσις, which was
rendered in the Latin *natura* and our *nature,* denoted originally the material universe, but it was the material universe
contemplated under an aspect which it is not very easy to
165 delineate in modern language. Nature signified the physical
world regarded as the result of some primordial element or
law. The oldest Greek philosophers had been accustomed
to explain the fabric of creation as the manifestation of
some single principle which they variously asserted to be
170 movement, fire, moisture, or generation. In its simplest and
most ancient sense, Nature is precisely the physical universe
looked upon in this way as the manifestation of a principle.
Afterwards, the later Greek sects added the *moral* to the
physical world in the conception of Nature. They extended
175 the term till it embraced not merely the visible creation, but
the thoughts, observances, and aspirations of mankind. Still,
as before, it was not solely the moral phenomena of human
society which they understood by *Nature,* but these phenomena considered as resolvable into some general and
180 simple laws.

  5. Now, just as the oldest Greek theorists supposed that

the sports of chance had changed the material universe from its simple primitive form into its present heterogeneous condition, so their intellectual descendants imagined that but for untoward accident the human race would have conformed itself to simpler rules of conduct and a less tempestuous life. To live according to *nature* came to be considered as the end for which man was created, and which the best men were bound to compass. To live according to *nature* was to rise above the disorderly habits and gross indulgences of the vulgar to higher laws of action which nothing but self-denial and self-command would enable the aspirant to observe. It is notorious that this proposition—live according to nature—was the sum of the tenets of the famous Stoic philosophy. Now on the subjugation of Greece that philosophy made instantaneous progress in Roman society. It possessed natural fascinations for the powerful class who, in theory at least, adhered to the simple habits of the ancient Italian race, and disdained to surrender themselves to the innovations of foreign fashions. Such persons began immediately to affect the Stoic precepts of life according to nature—an affectation all the more grateful and all the more noble from its contrast with the unbounded profligacy which was being diffused through the imperial city by the pillage of the world and by the example of its most luxurious races. In the front of the disciples of the new Greek school, we might be sure, even if we did not know it historically, that the Roman lawyers figured.

6. The alliance of the lawyers with the Stoic philosophy lasted through many centuries. Some of the earliest names in the series of renowned jurisconsults are associated with Stoicism, and ultimately we have the golden age of Roman jurisprudence fixed by general consent at the era of the Antonine Caesars, the most famous disciples to whom that philosophy has given a rule of life. The long diffusion of these doctrines among the members of a particular profession was sure to affect the art which they practised and influenced. But it is a serious, though a very common, error to measure the influence of Stoicism on Roman law by

220 counting up the number of legal rules which can be confidently affiliated on Stoical dogmas. It has often been observed that the strength of Stoicism resided not in its canons
of conduct, which were often repulsive or ridiculous, but in
the great though vague principle which it inculcated of
225 resistance to passion. Just in the same way the influence on
jurisprudence of the Greek theories, which had their most
distinct expression in Stoicism, consisted not in the number
of specific positions which they contributed to Roman law,
but in the single fundamental assumption which they lent
230 to it. After Nature had become a household word in the
mouths of the Romans, the belief gradually prevailed among
the Roman lawyers that the old Jus Gentium was in fact
the lost code of Nature, and that the Praetor in framing
an Edictal jurisprudence on the principles of the Jus Gen-
235 tium was gradually restoring a type from which law had
only departed to deteriorate. The inference from this belief
was immediate that it was the Praetor's duty to supersede
the Civil Law as much as possible by the Edict, to revive as
far as might be the institutions by which Nature had gov-
240 erned man in the primitive state. Of course there were
many impediments to the amelioration of law by this
agency. There may have been prejudices to overcome even
in the legal profession itself, and Roman habits were far
too tenacious to give way at once to mere philosophical
245 theory. But on the whole, the progress of the Romans
in legal improvement was astonishingly rapid as soon as
stimulus was applied to it by the theory of Natural Law.
The ideas of simplification and generalization had always
been associated with the conception of Nature; simplicity,
250 symmetry, and intelligibility came therefore to be regarded
as the characteristics of a good legal system, and the taste
for involved language, multiplied ceremonials, and useless difficulties disappeared altogether. The strong will and
unusual opportunities of Justinian were needed to bring
255 the Roman law into its existing shape, but the ground plan

of the system had been sketched long before the imperial reforms were effected.

❊ ❊ ❊

1. Find approximate dates for Justinian, the Roman republic, the oldest Greek philosophers (l. 167), the Stoics (l. 195), the subjugation of Greece, the age of the Antonines. Enter these dates in the margin of the text, so as to indicate the chronology of the several stages of the process here explained. Also make a separate list of these items in their proper order.

2. Consult the Britannica and write brief accounts of Justinian's Institutes, the Edict of the Praetor, and the Mancipation. Include such details as help you to understand Maine's discussion.

3. Notice the phrasing "are said to be dictated" (l. 14) instead of "are dictated." Which phrases in Par. 2 similarly distinguish between supposition and actuality? The history of an institution includes not only an account of the forms or mechanisms of society, but also. . . . What else?

4. In this history of an institution, the Jus Gentium, what is it that remains constant, and what changes? Define the change: from what to what? What, in a few words, was the cause of that change?

5. Does Par. 2 present a number of causes leading to a common effect, or a number of effects springing from a common cause? What is the common cause or effect? Make an analytic outline of the *logic* of the paragraph. (Each proposition will be a cause—or each an effect—of the heading under which it is placed.)

6. Consider the plan of the whole essay.

a) Divide it into several sections and state the topic of each.

b) You have seen in answering Question 1 that there are several departures from chronological order. Why should Justinian rather than the Antonines or the legal procedures of the early republic have been used as the starting point of the essay?

c) Why should the origins of the Jus Gentium have been described before the ideas of the oldest Greek philosophers?

d) Why does Maine offer his conjectures (Par. 3) as to what *we* might think of the Jus Gentium?

e) Why should he do so at this point, rather than before Par. 2 or later in the essay?

7. The division between Pars. 4 and 5 might have been made, with possible advantage, where instead of at line 180?

8. Where is the point of Par. 2 stated? (Cf. Question 5.) Write a sentence which might be placed at the head of the paragraph to serve as a signpost.

9. Do you think that people in modern times regard moral relationships as resolvable into some general, simple, primeval laws? Explain.

10. Did the Stoic concept of a natural morality enable the moralists to determine the "higher laws of action," or did it simply lend dignity to moral traits independently arrived at? (ll. 181-195.)

11. We are told (ll. 224-225) that Stoicism inculcated the principle of resistance to passion. Did the Stoics, then, regard passions as natural or unnatural? What was the attitude of Christianity on these questions? What early attitude toward passion may be inferred from the derivation of the word? What do you take to be the modern or the correct attitude?

12. If you expect to study law, read and summarize the title essay in Chief Justice Holmes's *The Common Law,* a classic and epoch-making analysis of the way in which a fixed form may be given a new meaning.

13. Find cognates of *alien, community, franchise, police.*

14. Explain the derivations of *canon, denizen, foreign, Stoic, subjugation.*

THE CHAMPION[1]

HENRY C. LEA

●

1. The employment of champions was sufficiently extended to deserve some special notice. It has been seen that those unable to wield the sword or club were not therefore exempted from the duel, and even the scantiest measure of justice would require that they should have 5 the right to delegate their vindication to some more potential vehicle of the Divine decision. This would seem originally to have been the office of some member of the family, as in the cognate procedure of sacramental purgation. Among the Alamanni, for instance, a woman when accused 10 could be defended by a kinsman "cum tracta spata"; the same rule is prescribed by the Lombard law, and by that of the Angli and Werini; while the far-pervading principle of family unity renders the presumption fair that it prevailed throughout the other races in whose codes it is not 15 specifically indicated. Restricted to cases of disability, the use of champions was a necessity to the battle ordeal, but at a very early period the practice received a remarkable extension, which was directly in conflict with the original principles of the judicial duel, in permitting able-bodied 20 antagonists to put forward substitutes who fought the battle for their principals. With regard to this there appears to have been a considerable diversity of practice among the races of primitive barbarians. The laws of the Franks, of the Alamanni, and of the Saxons make no allusion to such 25 a privilege, and apparently expect the principal to defend his rights himself; and yet an instance occurs in 590, where, in a duel fought by order of Gontran, the defendant was allowed to intrust his cause to his nephew, though, as he

---

[1] From *Superstition and Force*, by Henry C. Lea.

30 was accused of killing a stag in the king's forest, physical infirmity could hardly have been pleaded. With the Lombards the judicial combat and the champion seem to have been convertible terms. In a charter of the latter half of the tenth century in France, recording a judicial duel to decide

35 a contest concerning property, the judge, in ordering the combat, calls upon the antagonists to produce skilled champions to defend their claims at the time and place indicated, which would show that the principals were not expected to appear personally. There is in this something

40 so repugnant to the fierce and self-relying spirit in which the wager of battle found its origin, and the use of a professional gladiator is so inconsistent with the pious reference to the judgment of God, which formed the only excuse for the whole system, that some external reason is re-

45 quired to account for its introduction. This reason is doubtless to be found in the liberty allowed of challenging witnesses. The prevalence of this throughout Western Europe readily enabled parties, unwilling themselves to encounter the risks of a mortal struggle, to put forward some trucu-

50 lent bravo who swore unscrupulously, and whose evidence would require him to be forced out of court at the sword's point. That this, indeed, was frequently done is proved by a remark of Bracton, who states that a witness suspected of being a hired gladiator was not allowed to proceed to

55 the combat, but was tried for the attempt by a jury, and if convicted was punished by the loss of a foot and hand.

2. Although the custom of hiring champions existed from a very early period, since the Frisian laws give the fullest license for employing and paying them, still, their

60 identity with witnesses cannot be readily proved from the simple records of those primitive times. It becomes very evident, however, in the more detailed regulations of the twelfth and thirteenth centuries. In England, for instance, until the first statute of Westminster, issued by Edward I.,

65 in 1275, the hired champion of the defendant, in a suit concerning real estate, was obliged to assume the position of a witness, by swearing that he had been personally pres-

ent and had seen seizin given of the land, or that his father
when dying had enjoined him by his filial duty to maintain the defendant's title as though he had been present. 70
This curious legal fiction was common also to the Norman
jurisprudence of the period, where in such cases the champion of the plaintiff was obliged to swear that he had heard
and seen the matters alleged in support of the claim, while
the opposing champion swore that they were false. A more 75
distant indication of the same origin is observable in the
regulation of the Assises de Jerusalem and of the Sicilian
constitutions, which directed that the champion should swear
on the field of battle as to his belief in the justice of the
quarrel which he was about to defend. 80

3. Looking on the profession of a champion in this
light, as that of a false witness, we can understand the
heavy penalties to which he was subjected in case of defeat,
a severity which would otherwise appear to be a purpose-
less expression of the savage barbarity of the times. Thus, 85
in the Norman coutumier above referred to, in civil suits
as to disputed landed possessions, the champion swearing
to the truth of his principal's claim was, if defeated, visited
with a heavy fine and was declared infamous, being thence-
forth incapable of appearing in court either as plaintiff 90
or as witness, while the penalty of the principal was merely
the loss of the property in dispute. In criminal cases, from
a very early period, while the principal perhaps escaped
with fine or imprisonment, the hired ruffian was hanged,
or at best lost a hand or foot, the immemorial punishment 95
for perjury; while the laws of the Crusaders prescribe that
in combats between champions, the defeated one shall be
promptly hanged, whether dead or alive. In later times,
when the origin of the champion's office had been lost sight
of, and he was everywhere recognized as simply a bravo 100
who sold his skill and courage to the highest bidder, a
more practical reason was found for maintaining this
severity—the more necessary, because the principal was
bound by law to pay his champion, even when defeated,
the full sum agreed upon as the price of his services in both 105

swearing and fighting. Beaumanoir thus defends it on the ground of the liability of champions to be bought over by the adverse party, and he therefore commends the gentle stimulus of prospective mutilation as necessary to prevent them from betraying their employers. In the same spirit, the Emperor Frederic II. prohibited champions from bargaining with each other not to use teeth and hands. He commanded them to inflict all the injury possible on their adversaries, and decreed that they should, in case of defeat, share the punishment incurred by the principal, if the judge of the combat should consider that through cowardice or treachery they had not conducted the duel with proper energy and perseverance.

4. With such risks to be encountered, it is no wonder that the trade of the champion offered few attractions to honest men, who could keep body and soul together in any other way. In primitive times, the solidarity of the family no doubt caused the champion in most cases to be drawn from among the kindred; at a later period he might generally be procured from among the freedmen or clients of the principal. In the palmy days of chivalry, it was perhaps not uncommon for the generous knight to throw himself boldly into the lists in defense of persecuted and friendless innocence, as he was bound to do by the tenor of his oath of knighthood. Even as late as the fifteenth century, indeed, in a collection of Welsh laws, among the modes by which a stranger acquired the rights of kindred is enumerated the act of voluntarily undergoing the duel in the place of a principal unable or unwilling to appear for himself. A vast proportion of pleaders, however, would necessarily be destitute of these chances to avoid the personal appearance in the arena for which they might be unfitted or disinclined, and thus there gradually arose the regular profession of the paid gladiator. Reckless desperadoes, skilled at quarter-staff, or those whose familiarity with sword and dagger, gained by a life spent in ceaseless brawls, gave them confidence in their own ability, might undertake it as an occupation which exposed them to little

risk beyond what they habitually incurred, and of such
was the profession generally composed. This evil must have 145
made itself apparent early, for we find Charlemagne endeavoring to oppose it by decreeing that no robber should
be allowed to appear in the lists as a champion; and the
order needed to be frequently repeated.

5. When the Roman law commenced to exercise its pow- 150
erful influence in moulding the feudal customs into a
regular body of procedure, and admiring jurists lost no
opportunity of making use of the newly-discovered treasures of legal lore, whether applicable or not, it is easy to
understand that the contempt and the civil disabilities 155
lavished by the Imperial jurisprudence on the gladiator of
antiquity came to be transferred to the medieval champion;
although the latter, by the theory of the law, stood forth
to defend the innocent, while the former ignobly exposed
his life for the gratification of an imbruted populace. This 160
curious legacy of shame is clearly traceable in Pierre de
Fontaines. To be a gladiator or an actor was, by the Roman
law, a competent cause for disinheritance. One of the texts
prescribing it is translated bodily by de Fontaines, the
"arenarius" of the Roman becoming the "champions" of 165
the Frenchman; and in another similar transcription from
the Digest, the "athleta" of the original is transformed
into a "champion." By the thirteenth century, the occupation of champion had thus become infamous. Its professors
were classed with the vilest criminals, and with the un- 170
happy females who exposed their charms for sale, as the
champion did his skill and courage. They were held incapable of appearing as witnesses, and the extraordinary
anomaly was exhibited of seeking to learn the truth in
affairs of the highest moment by a solemn appeal to God, 175
through the instrumentality of those who were already
considered as convicts of the worst kind, or who, by the
very act, were branded with infamy if successful in justify-
ing innocence, and if defeated were mutilated or hanged.
By the codes in force throughout Germany in the thirteenth 180
and fourteenth centuries, they were not only deprived of

all legal privileges, such as succeeding to property, bearing
witness, etc., but even their children were visited with the
same disabilities. The utter contempt in which they were
185 held was moreover quaintly symbolized in the same code
by the provisions of a tariff of damages to be assessed for
blows and other personal injuries. A graduated list of fines
is given for such insults offered to nobles, merchants,
peasants, etc., in compensation of their wounded honor;
190 below the serf come the mountebank and juggler, who
could only cuff the assailant's shadow projected on a wall;
and last of all are rated the champion and his children,
whose only redress was a glance of sunshine cast upon them
by the offender from a polished shield. Deemed by law
195 incapable of receiving an insult, the satisfaction awarded
was as illusory as the honor to be repaired. That this
poetical justice was long in vogue is proved by the commentary upon it in the Richstich Landrecht, of which the
date is shown to be not earlier than the close of the four-
200 teenth century by an allusion in the same chapter to accidental deaths arising from the use of firearms.

6. The Italians, however, took a more sensible and practical view of the matter. Accepting as a necessity the existence of champions as a class, they were disposed rather
205 to elevate than to degrade the profession. In the Veronese
code of 1228, they appear as an established institution, consisting of individuals selected and appointed by the magistrates, who did not allow them to receive more than one
hundred sous for the performance of their office.

210 7. It is evident that the evils attendant upon the employment of champions were generally recognized, and it is
not singular that efforts were occasionally made to abrogate
or limit the practice. Otho II., whose laws did so much to
give respectability to the duel, decreed that champions
215 should be permitted only to counts, ecclesiastics, women,
boys, old men, and cripples. That this rule was strictly
enforced in some places we may infer from the pleadings
of a case occurring in 1010 before the Bishop of Aretino,
concerning a disputed property, wherein a crippled right

hand is alleged as the reason for allowing a champion to 220
one of the parties. In other parts of Italy, however, the
regulation must have been speedily disregarded, for about
the same time Henry II. found it necessary to promulgate
a law forbidding the employment of substitutes to able-
bodied defendants in cases of parricide or of aggravated 225
murder. The English law manifests considerable variation
at different periods with respect to this point. In 1150, Henry
II. strictly prohibited the wager of battle with hired champions in his Norman territories, and we learn from Glan-
ville that a champion suspected of serving for money might 230
be objected to by the opposite party, whence arose a secondary combat to determine his fitness for the primary one.
It is evident from this that mercenary champions were not
recognized as legal in England. This, however, was probably little regarded in practice. There exists a charter of 235
Bracton's date, by which John, "quondam porcarius de
Coldingham," grants to the Priory of Coldingham a tract
of land which he had received from Adam de Riston in
payment for victoriously fighting a duel for him. When
John thus proclaimed himself to be a hired champion there 240
could have been little danger that legal disabilities would
be visited either on him or his principal. The custom gradually became general, for eventually, in civil cases, both
parties were compelled by law to employ champions, which
presupposes, as a matter of course, that in a great majority 245
of instances, the substitutes must have been hired. In criminal cases, however, the rule was generally reversed; in
felonies, the defendant was obliged to appear personally,
while in cases of less moment he was at liberty to put forward a witness as champion; and when the appellant, 250
from sex or other disability, or the defendant from age,
was unable to undergo the combat personally, it was forbidden, and the case was decided by a jury. By the Scottish
law of the twelfth century, it is evident that champions
were not allowed in any case, since those disabled by age 255
or wounds were forced to undergo the ordeal in order to
escape the duel. This strictness became relaxed in time,

though the practice seems never to have received much encouragement. By a law of David II., about the year 1350, 260 it appears that a noble had the privilege of putting forward a substitute; but if a peasant challenged a noble, he was obliged to appear personally, unless his lord undertook the quarrel for him and presented the champion as from himself.

� 襲 襲

1. Distinguish between the *evidence* and the *discourse* which interprets it. (Do not regard the second, third, and eighth sentences (ll. 2-7, 31-33) as evidence.) Enclose *each item* of evidence—e.g., "Among the Alamanni '. . . spata!' "—in brackets. Then, in what remains, indicate by marginal lines those sentences which contain the leading ideas of each paragraph and which, read consecutively, present the argument of the whole passage.

2. Lea has discussed the principle of family unity (l. 14) earlier in his book. But it can be understood by reference to the present context. State briefly what the principle was.

3. Explain why the "extension . . . was directly in conflict with the original principles of the judicial duel." (ll. 19-20.) Where else in Par. 1 is this contradiction between theory and practice remarked?

4. Why is the phrase, "immemorial punishment for perjury" (ll. 95-96), essential to Lea's argument?

5. "A more practical reason was found. . . ." (l. 102.) What was the old reason? Why was it no longer sufficient?

6. Why should Lea have written "even as late as . . ." in line 130? Would not "as early as . . ." or "no later than . . ." have been better?

7. Study the inference from the evidence in lines 53-56. The principle may be broadly stated: The existence of a law against a practice indicates that the practice itself existed.

a) Which two items of evidence in Par. 3 are used according to this principle?

b) Find two passages in Pars. 4-7 in which Lea infers the existence of a practice from its prohibition.

8. What about the evidence presented in lines 227-229? What might be inferred from it in accordance with the principle just stated? Lea, however, has used it as proof of what proposition?

9. Formulate general principles—such as that stated in Question 7—which will show how Lea has reasoned from each of the following items of evidence:
   a) "Since the Frisian laws . . . paying them." (ll. 58-59.)
   b) "In criminal cases . . . perjury." (ll. 92-96.)
   c) "One of the texts . . . champion." (ll. 163-168.)
   d) "There exists a charter . . . for him." (ll. 235-239.)

10. What two principles are involved in the inference of lines 198-201?

11. Write a 150- to 200-word summary of the whole selection. Here, of course, you can present only the argument, not the evidence; allow one or two sentences to the thought of each paragraph. Be sure that your summary in itself constitutes a logically coherent statement.

12. Suppose that our account of the duel fought in 590 (ll. 27-31) did not mention the crime of which the defendant was accused. What should we then be able to infer from it? At what point in the essay might the episode then have been introduced as evidence?

13. At what point in the essay might each of the following facts be introduced as evidence?
   a) A law of Louis I, son of Charlemagne, decrees that "the right hand of the defeated champion shall be amputated, because of the perjury committed prior to the combat."
   b) In the ninth century, Agobard, Archbishop of Lyons, wrote against the trial by combat; one of his objections was its unfairness to the defendant who happened to be old or crippled.
   c) Henry de Bracton, d. 1268, wrote, in his *De Legibus et Consuetudinibus Angliae:* "Thus anyone who wished was able in such an event to name a stranger as a hired champion, the which privilege is no longer sustained."
   d) A Norman code of the twelfth or thirteenth century prescribes that champions shall be taken to see the lands and buildings in dispute, in the same manner as a jury of view.

14. Some light may be thrown upon the historical significance of the combat by a sentence of Henri Pirenne, in his discussion of urban institutions: "Traditional law, with its narrow formal procedure, its ordeals, its judicial duels, its judges
recruited from among the rural population, and knowing no
other custom than that which had been gradually elaborated
to regulate the relations of men living by the cultivation or
the ownership of the land, was inadequate for a population
whose existence was based on commerce and industry." (*Economic and Social History of Medieval Europe,* New York,
1937, p. 52. Cf. also William Robertson, "A View of the Progress of Society in Europe," Section I.) Which of the following
do you think the most progressive?

    a) The regulations of Frederic II (ll. 111-118.)
    b) The German codes (l. 180 f.)
    c) The Veronese code (ll. 205-209.)
    d) The decree of Otho II (ll. 214-216.)
    e) The Scottish law (ll. 253-257.)
    f) The law of David II (ll. 260-264.)

Write an essay explaining your choice and commenting on the
others.

15. Explain the derivations of *challenge, champion, cowardice, cripple, gladiator, juggler, mountebank, ordeal, spade*
(of playing cards), *treachery.*

THE ICONOCLASTS OF ANTWERP[1]

JOHN LOTHROP MOTLEY

•

1. THE CHURCH, PLACED IN THE CENTRE OF THE CITY, WITH the noisy streets of the busiest metropolis in Europe eddying around its walls, was a sacred island in the tumultuous main. Through the perpetual twilight, tall columnar trunks in thick profusion grew from a floor chequered with pris- 5 matic lights and sepulchral shadows. Each shaft of the petrified forest rose to a preternatural height, their many branches intermingling in the space above, to form an impenetrable canopy. Foliage, flowers and fruit of colossal luxuriance, strange birds, beasts, griffins and chimeras in 10 endless multitudes, the rank vegetation and the fantastic zoology of a fresher or fabulous world, seemed to decorate and to animate the serried trunks and pendant branches, while the shattering symphonies or dying murmurs of the organ suggested the rushing of the wind through the forest, 15 —now the full diapason of the storm and now the gentle cadence of the evening breeze.

2. Internally, the whole church was rich beyond expression. All that opulent devotion and inventive ingenuity could devise, in wood, bronze, marble, silver, gold, precious 20 jewelry, or blazing sacramental furniture, had been profusely lavished. The penitential tears of centuries had incrusted the whole interior with their glittering stalactites. Divided into five naves, with external rows of chapels, but separated by no screens or partitions, the great temple 25 forming an imposing whole, the effect was the more impressive, the vistas almost infinite in appearance. The wealthy citizens, the twenty-seven guilds, the six military associations, the rhythmical colleges, besides many other

[1] From *The Rise of the Dutch Republic*, by John Lothrop Motley.

30 secular or religious sodalities, had each their own chapels
and altars. Tombs adorned with the effigies of mailed crusaders and pious dames covered the floor, tattered banners
hung in the air, the escutcheons of the Golden Fleece, an
order typical of Flemish industry, but of which Emperors
35 and Kings were proud to be the chevaliers, decorated the
columns. The vast and beautifully-painted windows glowed
with scriptural scenes, antique portraits, homely allegories,
painted in those brilliant and forgotten colors which Art
has not ceased to deplore. The daylight melting into gloom
40 or colored with fantastic brilliancy, priests in effulgent robes
chanting in unknown language, the sublime breathing of
choral music, the suffocating odors of myrrh and spikenard,
suggestive of the oriental scenery and imagery of Holy
Writ, all combined to bewilder and exalt the senses. The
45 highest and humblest seemed to find themselves upon the
same level within those sacred precincts, where even the
bloodstained criminal was secure, and the arm of secular
justice was paralyzed.

3. But the work of degeneration had commenced. The
50 atmosphere of the cathedral was no longer holy in the eyes
of increasing multitudes. Better the sanguinary rites of
Belgic Druids, better the yell of slaughtered victims from
the "wild wood without mercy" of the pagan forefathers
of the nation, than this fantastic intermingling of divine
55 music, glowing colors, gorgeous ceremonies, with all the
burning, beheading and strangling work which had characterized the system of human sacrifice for the past half-
century.

4. Such was the church of Notre Dame at Antwerp.
60 Thus indifferent or hostile towards the architectural treasure were the inhabitants of a city, where in a previous age
the whole population would have risked their lives to defend what they esteemed the pride and garland of their
metropolis.

65 5. Upon the 18th August, the great and time-honored
ceremony of the Ommegang occurred. Accordingly, the
great procession, the principal object of which was to con-

duct around the city a colossal image of the Virgin, issued
as usual from the door of the cathedral. The image, be-
dizened and effulgent, was borne aloft upon the shoulders 70
of her adorers, followed by the guilds, the military associations, the rhetoricians, the religious sodalities, all in glittering
costume, bearing blazoned banners, and marching tri-
umphantly through the streets with sound of trumpet and
beat of drum. The pageant, solemn but noisy, was exactly 75
such a show as was most fitted at that moment to irritate
Protestant minds and to lead to mischief. No violent explo-
sion of ill-feeling, however, took place. The procession was
followed by a rabble rout of scoffers, but they confined
themselves to words and insulting gestures. The image was 80
incessantly saluted, as she was borne along the streets, with
sneers, imprecations, and the rudest ribaldry. "Mayken!
Mayken!" (little Mary) "your hour is come. 'Tis your last
promenade. The city is tired of you." Such were the greet-
ings which the representative of the Holy Virgin received 85
from men grown weary of antiquated mummery. A few
missiles were thrown occasionally at the procession as it
passed through the city, but no damage was inflicted. When
the image was at last restored to its place, and the pageant
brought to a somewhat hurried conclusion, there seemed 90
cause for congratulation that no tumult had occurred.

6. On the following morning there was a large crowd
collected in front of the cathedral. The image, instead of
standing in the centre of the church, where, upon all former
occasions, it had been accustomed during the week suc- 95
ceeding the ceremony to receive congratulatory visits, was
now ignominiously placed behind an iron railing within
the choir. It had been deemed imprudent to leave it exposed to sacrilegious hands. The precaution excited derision.
Many vagabonds of dangerous appearance, many idle ap- 100
prentices and ragged urchins were hanging for a long time
about the imprisoned image, peeping through the railings,
and indulging in many a brutal jest. "Mayken! Mayken!"
they cried, "art thou terrified so soon? Hast flown to thy
nest so early? Dost think thyself beyond the reach of 105

mischief? Beware, Mayken! thine hour is fast approaching!"
Others thronged around the balustrade, shouting *"Vivent
les gueux!"* and hoarsely commanding the image to join in
the beggars' cry. Then, leaving the spot, the mob roamed
110 idly about the magnificent church, sneering at the idols,
execrating the gorgeous ornaments, scoffing at crucifix and
altar.

7. Presently one of the rabble, a ragged fellow of me-
chanical aspect, in a tattered black doublet and an old
115 straw hat, ascended the pulpit. Opening a sacred volume
which he found there, he began to deliver an extemporane-
ous and coarse caricature of a monkish sermon. Some of the
bystanders applauded, some cried shame, some shouted
"long live the beggars!" some threw sticks and rubbish at
120 the mountebank, some caught him by the legs and strove
to pull him from the place. He, on the other hand, manfully maintained his ground, hurling back every missile,
struggling with his assailants, and continuing the while to
pour forth a malignant and obscene discourse. At last a
125 young sailor, warm in the Catholic Faith, and impulsive
as mariners are prone to be, ascended the pulpit from behind, sprang upon the mechanic, and flung him headlong
down the steps. The preacher grappled with his enemy as
he fell, and both came rolling to the ground. Neither was
130 much injured, but a tumult ensued. A pistol-shot was
fired, and the sailor wounded in the arm. Daggers were
drawn, cudgels brandished, the bystanders taking part generally against the sailor, while those who protected him
were somewhat bruised and belabored before they could
135 convey him out of the church. Nothing more, however,
transpired that day, and the keepers of the cathedral were
enabled to expel the crowd and to close the doors for the
night.

8. Information of this tumult was brought to the senate,
140 then assembled in the Hotel de Ville. That body was
thrown into a state of great perturbation. In losing the
Prince of Orange, they seemed to have lost their own
brains, and the first measure which they took was to

despatch a messenger to implore his return. In the mean-
time, it was necessary that they should do something for 145
themselves. It was evident that a storm was brewing. The
pest which was sweeping so rapidly through the provinces
would soon be among them. Symptoms of the dreaded visitation were already but too manifest. What precaution should
they take? Should they issue a proclamation? Such docu- 150
ments had been too common of late, and had lost their
virtue. It was the time not to assert but to exercise authority.
Should they summon the ward-masters, and order the instant arming and mustering of their respective companies?
Should they assemble the captains of the military associa- 155
tions? Nothing better could have been desired than such
measures in cases of invasion or of ordinary tumult, but
who should say how deeply the poison had sunk into the
body politic; who should say with how much or how little
alacrity the burgher militia would obey the mandates of 160
the magistracy? It would be better to issue no proclamation
unless they could enforce its provisions; it would be better
not to call out the citizen soldiery unless they were likely to
prove obedient. Should mercenary troops at this late hour
be sent for? Would not their appearance at this crisis rather 165
inflame the rage than intimidate the insolence of the sec-
taries? Never were magistrates in greater perplexity. They
knew not what course was likely to prove the safest, and
in their anxiety to do nothing wrong, the senators did
nothing at all. After a long and anxious consultation, the 170
honest burgomaster and his associates all went home to
their beds, hoping that the threatening flame of civil tumult
would die out of itself, or perhaps that their dreams would
supply them with that wisdom which seemed denied to
their waking hours.   175

9. In the morning, as it was known that no precaution
had been taken, the audacity of the Reformers was naturally
increased. Within the cathedral a great crowd was at an
early hour collected, whose savage looks and ragged appearance denoted that the day and night were not likely to pass 180
away so peacefully as the last. The same taunts and impre-

cations were hurled at the image of the Virgin; the same howling of the beggars' cry resounded through the lofty arches. For a few hours, no act of violence was committed,
185 but the crowd increased. A few trifles, drifting, as usual, before the event, seemed to indicate the approaching convulsion. A very paltry old woman excited the image-breaking of Antwerp. She had for years been accustomed to sit before the door of the cathedral with wax-tapers and wafers,
190 earning a scanty subsistence from the profits of her meagre trade, and by the small coins which she sometimes received in charity. Some of the rabble began to chaffer with this ancient hucksteress. They scoffed at her consecrated wares; they bandied with her ribald jests, of which her public
195 position had furnished her with a supply; they assured her that the hour had come when her idolatrous traffic was to be forever terminated, when she and her patroness, Mary, were to be given over to destruction together. The old woman, enraged, answered threat with threat, and gibe with
200 gibe. Passing from words to deeds, she began to catch from the ground every offensive missile or weapon which she could find, and to lay about her in all directions. Her tormentors defended themselves as they could. Having destroyed her whole stock-in-trade, they provoked others to
205 appear in her defence. The passers-by thronged to the scene; the cathedral was soon filled to overflowing; a furious tumult was already in progress.

10.   Many persons fled in alarm to the town-house, carrying information of this outbreak to the magistrates. John
210 Van Immerzeel, Margrave of Antwerp, was then holding communication with the senate, and awaiting the arrival of the ward-masters, whom it had at last been thought expedient to summon. Upon intelligence of this riot, which the militia, if previously mustered, might have prevented,
215 the senate determined to proceed to the cathedral in a body, with the hope of quelling the mob by the dignity of their presence. The margrave, who was the high executive officer of the little commonwealth, marched down to the cathedral accordingly, attended by the two burgomasters

and all the senators. At first their authority, solicitations, 220
and personal influence, produced a good effect. Some of
those outside consented to retire, and the tumult partially
subsided within. As night, however, was fast approaching,
many of the mob insisted upon remaining for evening mass.
They were informed that there would be none that night, 225
and that for once the people could certainly dispense with
their vespers.

11.   Several persons now manifesting an intention of leaving the cathedral, it was suggested to the senators that if
they should lead the way, the populace would follow in 230
their train, and so disperse to their homes. The excellent
magistrates took the advice, not caring, perhaps, to fulfil
any longer the dangerous but not dignified functions of
police officers. Before departing, they adopted the precaution of closing all the doors of the church, leaving a single 235
one open, that the rabble still remaining might have an
opportunity to depart. It seemed not to occur to the senators
that the same gate would as conveniently afford an entrance
for those without as an egress for those within. That un-
looked-for event happened, however. No sooner had the 240
magistrates retired than the rabble burst through the single
door which had been left open, overpowered the margrave,
who, with a few attendants, had remained behind, vainly
endeavoring by threats and exhortations to appease the
tumult, drove him ignominiously from the church, and 245
threw all the other portals wide open. Then the populace
flowed in like an angry sea. The whole of the cathedral
was at the mercy of the rioters, who were evidently bent
on mischief. The wardens and treasurers of the church,
after a vain attempt to secure a few of its most precious 250
possessions, retired. They carried the news to the senators,
who, accompanied by a few halberdmen, again ventured
to approach the spot. It was but for a moment, however,
for, appalled by the furious sounds which came from
within the church, as if subterranean and invisible forces 255
were preparing a catastrophe which no human power could
withstand, the magistrates fled precipitately from the scene.

Fearing that the next attack would be upon the town-house,
they hastened to concentrate at that point their available
260 forces, and left the stately cathedral to its fate.

12. And now, as the shadows of night were deepening
the perpetual twilight of the church, the work of destruction commenced. Instead of evening mass rose the fierce
music of a psalm, yelled by a thousand angry voices. It
265 seemed the preconcerted signal for a general attack. A band
of marauders flew upon the image of the Virgin, dragged
it forth from its receptacle, plunged daggers into its inani-
mate body, tore off its jewelled and embroidered garments,
broke the whole figure into a thousand pieces, and scat-
270 tered the fragments along the floor. A wild shout succeeded, and then the work, which seemed delegated to a
comparatively small number of the assembled crowd, went
on with incredible celerity. Some were armed with axes,
some with bludgeons, some with sledge-hammers; others
275 brought ladders, pulleys, ropes, and levers. Every statue was
hurled from its niche, every picture torn from the wall,
every wonderfully painted window shivered to atoms,
every ancient monument shattered, every sculptured decora-
tion, however inaccessible in appearance, hurled to the
280 ground. Indefatigably, audaciously, endowed, as it seemed,
with preternatural strength and nimbleness, these iconoclasts clambered up the dizzy heights, shrieking and chattering like malignant apes, as they tore off in triumph the
slowly-matured fruit of centuries. In a space of time won-
285 derfully brief, they had accomplished their task.

13. A colossal and magnificent group of the Saviour
crucified between two thieves adorned the principal altar.
The statue of Christ was wrenched from its place with
ropes and pulleys, while the malefactors, with bitter and
290 blasphemous irony, were left on high, the only representatives of the marble crowd which had been destroyed. A
very beautiful piece of architecture decorated the choir,—
the "repository," as it was called, in which the body of
Christ was figuratively enshrined. This much-admired work
295 rested upon a single column, but rose, arch upon arch,

pillar upon pillar, to the height of three hundred feet, till quite lost in the vault above. "It was now shattered into a million pieces." The statues, images, pictures, ornaments, as they lay upon the ground, were broken with sledge-hammers, hewn with axes, trampled, torn, and beaten into shreds. A troop of harlots, snatching waxen tapers from the altars, stood around the destroyers and lighted them at their work. Nothing escaped their omnivorous rage. They desecrated seventy chapels, forced open all the chests of treasure, covered their own squalid attire with the gorgeous robes of the ecclesiastics, broke the sacred bread, poured out the sacramental wine into golden chalices, quaffing huge draughts to the beggars' health, burned all the splendid missals and manuscripts, and smeared their shoes with the sacred oil, with which kings and prelates had been anointed. It seemed that each of these malicious creatures must have been endowed with the strength of a hundred giants. How else, in the few brief hours of a midsummer night, could such a monstrous desecration have been accomplished by a troop which, according to all accounts, was not more than one hundred in number. There was a multitude of spectators, as upon all such occasions, but the actual spoilers were very few.

14. The noblest and richest temple of the Netherlands was a wreck, but the fury of the spoilers was excited, not appeased. Each seizing a burning torch, the whole herd rushed from the cathedral, and swept howling through the streets. "Long live the beggars!" resounded through the sultry midnight air, as the ravenous pack flew to and fro, smiting every image of the Virgin, every crucifix, every sculptured saint, every Catholic symbol which they met with upon their path. All night long, they roamed from one sacred edifice to another, thoroughly destroying as they went. Before morning they had sacked thirty churches within the city walls. They entered the monasteries, burned their invaluable libraries, destroyed their altars, statues, pictures, and descending into the cellars, broached every cask which they found there, pouring out in one great flood all

the ancient wine and ale with which these holy men had
335 been wont to solace their retirement from generation to
generation. They invaded the nunneries, whence the occupants, panic-stricken, fled for refuge to the houses of their
friends and kindred. The streets were filled with monks and
nuns, running this way and that, shrieking and fluttering,
340 to escape the claws of these fiendish Calvinists. The terror
was imaginary, for not the least remarkable feature in these
transactions was, that neither insult nor injury was offered
to man or woman, and that not a farthing's value of the
immense amount of property destroyed, was appropriated.
345 It was a war not against the living, but against graven
images; nor was the sentiment which prompted the on-
slaught in the least commingled with a desire of plunder.
The principal citizens of Antwerp, expecting every instant
that the storm would be diverted from the ecclesiastical
350 edifices to private dwellings, and that robbery, rape, and
murder would follow sacrilege, remained all night expecting the attack, and prepared to defend their hearths, even
if the altars were profaned. The precaution was needless.
It was asserted by the Catholics that the confederates and
355 other opulent Protestants had organized this company of
profligates for the meagre pittance of ten stivers a day. On
the other hand, it was believed by many that the Catholics
had themselves plotted the whole outrage in order to bring
odium upon the Reformers. Both statements were equally
360 unfounded. The task was most thoroughly performed, but
it was prompted by a furious fanaticism, not by baser
motives.

15. Two days and nights longer the havoc raged un-
checked through all the churches of Antwerp and the
365 neighboring villages. Hardly a statue or picture escaped
destruction. Fortunately, the illustrious artist, whose labors
were destined in the next generation to enrich and ennoble
the city, Rubens, most profound of colorists, most dramatic
of artists, whose profuse tropical genius seemed to flower
370 the more luxuriantly, as if the destruction wrought by
brutal hands were to be compensated by the creative energy

THE ICONOCLASTS OF ANTWERP 333

of one divine spirit, had not yet been born. Of the treasures
which existed the destruction was complete. Yet the rage
was directed exclusively against stocks and stones. Not a
man was wounded nor a woman outraged. Prisoners, in- 375
deed, who had been languishing hopelessly in dungeons
were liberated. A monk, who had been in the prison of the
Barefoot Monastery, for twelve years, recovered his freedom. Art was trampled in the dust, but humanity deplored
no victims.

❋ ❋ ❋

Motley's prose is magnificent in an old-fashioned way. It is
too late in the years to imitate his style—or to condemn it. We
may profitably define its quality and examine its mechanics. It
is leisurely and expansive, suffused with a few not very complicated emotions and ideas. Motley's intent was to produce an
historical painting, rich in detail and highly colored, much in
the grandiloquent vein of Raphael or Rubens or Delacroix.

1. Analyze the design of the whole passage.

a) Where does the narrative begin? List the topics of the
narrative paragraphs. (You may regard Pars. 12-13 as a unit.)
Indicate the chronology.

b) Explain the relation between the descriptive and the
narrative sections. How does the subject of Par. 2 differ from
that of Par. 1?

c) What portion of the action is the climax of the whole
passage? What lesser moments of climax precede it?

d) An element of opposition to the iconoclasts, giving the
narrative a dramatic quality, appears at what points? And with
what effect?

2. Observe the construction of Par. 13. A single ornament is
described in the first sentence, destroyed in the second, where
it remains in the nominative, taking passive verbs. This pattern
is repeated in the next three sentences. (ll. 291-298.) In the sixth
sentence, which concludes the section, the ornaments are presented in general terms, but the syntactical structure is the same.
In the second section, the destroyers appear in the nominative,
taking a series of active verbs, which, with their objects, develop
the theme of desecration. (ll. 303-310.) After each section there

are indications of lighting effects: the tapers lifted by the
harlots and the midsummer night enfolding the whole scene.
The "brief hours" is a subdued echo of the time suggestion
closing the preceding paragraph. The design of Par. 13 is
definite enough to be felt and to seem intentional. This calculated design gives Motley's narrative a static, picturesque quality,
very different from the rush of Froude's narrative or the serene
flow of Parkman's.

Make a similar analysis of the construction of Par. 12.

3. The static, sustained quality of Motley's prose is also a
matter of diction. Lines 200-202 deal with vigorous action:
"Passing from words to deeds, she began to catch from the
ground every offensive missile or weapon which she could find,
and to lay about her in all directions." The idea *offensive* recurs
in *missile,* which in turn is contained in *weapon. Passing from
words to deeds* is repeated in *lay about her,* and *about her* is
reiterated: *in all directions. Which she could find* is gratuitous.
These groups of words overlap, with only slight variations of
meaning. Such a technic sustains thought and mood. At the
same time, the narrative has no impetus; it seems hardly to move.

a) Note, in Par. 5, every reiteration of the idea of *procession.*
What other reiterations do you find here?

b) Analyze lines 113-129 in the same way.

4. The events of the successive days constitute a series of
climaxes. In Motley's stately and proportioned narrative, the
crescendos are gradual; at first the rabble is held in check, and
there are moments of interruption or of falling action. In Par. 5,
for instance, the Protestants appear in prepositional phrases,
syntactically minor parts of the sentences. As nominatives, in
line 79, they *confine themselves.* The action is subdued with
passives and with negatives.

a) Trace the rising and falling action in Pars. 6 and 7,
commenting on the closing sentences of each, on the series:
vagabonds—apprentices—urchins (ll. 100-101), and on the
passives in lines 130-134.

b) Outline the rise or fall of the action through the whole
narrative, commenting on the tendencies of the paragraph conclusions and on any notable instances of restraint or suspense
or intensification.

c) Comment on the action and mood of Pars. 14-15.

THE STRENGTH OF PRIMITIVE CHRISTIANITY[1]

EDWARD GIBBON

•

1. WE HAVE ALREADY DESCRIBED THE RELIGIOUS HARMONY of the ancient world, and the facility with which the most different and even hostile nations embraced, or at least respected, each other's superstitions. A single people refused to join in the common intercourse of mankind. The Jews, who, under the Assyrian and Persian monarchies, had languished for many ages the most despised portion of their slaves, emerged from obscurity under the successors of Alexander; and, as they multiplied to a surprising degree in the East, and afterwards in the West, they soon excited the curiosity and wonder of other nations. The sullen obstinacy with which they maintained their peculiar rites and unsocial manners seemed to mark them out a distinct species of men, who boldly professed, or who faintly disguised, their implacable hatred to the rest of human kind. Neither the violence of Antiochus, nor the arts of Herod, nor the example of the circumjacent nations, could ever persuade the Jews to associate with the institutions of Moses the elegant mythology of the Greeks.[2] According to the maxims of universal toleration, the Romans protected a superstition which they despised. The polite Augustus condescended to give orders that sacrifices should be offered for his prosperity in the temple of Jerusalem; while the

---

[1] From *The Decline and Fall of the Roman Empire,* by Edward Gibbon.

[2] A Jewish sect, which indulged themselves in a sort of occasional conformity, derived from Herod, by whose example and authority they had been seduced, the name of Herodians. But their numbers were so inconsiderable, and their duration so short, that Josephus has not thought them worthy of his notice. [Gibbon's note.]

meanest of the posterity of Abraham, who should have
25 paid the same homage to the Jupiter of the Capitol, would
have been an object of abhorrence to himself and to his
brethren. But the moderation of the conquerors was insufficient to appease the jealous prejudices of their subjects,
who were alarmed and scandalized at the ensigns of pagan-
30 ism, which necessarily introduced themselves into a Roman
province. The mad attempt of Caligula to place his own
statue in the temple of Jerusalem was defeated by the
unanimous resolution of a people who dreaded death much
less than such an idolatrous profanation. Their attachment
35 to the law of Moses was equal to their detestation of foreign
religions. The current of zeal and devotion, as it was contracted into a narrow channel, ran with the strength, and
sometimes with the fury, of a torrent.

2.   This inflexible perseverance, which appeared so odious,
40 or so ridiculous, to the ancient world, assumes a more awful
character, since Providence has deigned to reveal to us the
mysterious history of the chosen people. But the devout,
and even scrupulous, attachment to the Mosaic religion, so
conspicuous among the Jews who lived under the second
45 temple, becomes still more surprising, if it is compared with
the stubborn incredulity of their forefathers. When the law
was given in thunder from Mount Sinai; when the tides
of the ocean and the course of the planets were suspended
for the convenience of the Israelites; and when temporal
50 rewards and punishments were the immediate consequences
of their piety or disobedience; they perpetually relapsed
into rebellion against the visible majesty of their Divine
King, placed the idols of the nations in the sanctuary of
Jehovah, and imitated every fantastic ceremony that was
55 practised in the tents of the Arabs or in the cities of
Phoenicia. As the protection of Heaven was deservedly with-
drawn from the ungrateful race, their faith acquired a pro-
portionable degree of vigour and purity. The contemporaries
of Moses and Joshua had beheld, with careless indifference,
60 the most amazing miracles. Under the pressure of every
calamity, the belief of those miracles has preserved the Jews

of a later period from the universal contagion of idolatry; and, in contradiction to every known principle of the human mind, that singular people seems to have yielded a stronger and more ready assent to the traditions of their remote ancestors than to the evidence of their own senses.

3. The Jewish religion was admirably suited for defence, but it was never designed for conquest; and it seems probable that the number of proselytes was never much superior to that of apostates. The divine promises were originally made, and the distinguishing rite of circumcision was enjoined, to a single family. When the posterity of Abraham had multiplied like the sands of the sea, the Deity, from whose mouth they received a system of laws and ceremonies, declared himself the proper and, as it were, the national God of Israel; and, with the most jealous care, separated his favourite people from the rest of mankind. The conquest of the land of Canaan was accompanied with so many wonderful and with so many bloody circumstances that the victorious Jews were left in a state of irreconcilable hostility with all their neighbours. They had been commanded to extirpate some of the most idolatrous tribes; and the execution of the Divine will had seldom been retarded by the weakness of humanity. With the other nations they were forbidden to contract any marriages or alliances. The obligation of preaching to the Gentiles the faith of Moses had never been inculcated as a precept of the law, nor were the Jews inclined to impose it on themselves as a voluntary duty. The descendants of Abraham were flattered by the opinion that they alone were the heirs of the covenant; and they were apprehensive of diminishing the value of their inheritance, by sharing it too easily with the strangers of the earth. A larger acquaintance with mankind extended their knowledge without correcting their prejudices; and, whenever the God of Israel acquired any new votaries, he was much more indebted to the inconstant humour of polytheism than to the active zeal of his own missionaries.

4. Under these circumstances, Christianity offered itself to the world, armed with the strength of the Mosaic law,

100 and delivered from the weight of its fetters. An exclusive zeal for the truth of religion and the unity of God was as carefully inculcated in the new as in the ancient system; and whatever was now revealed to mankind, concerning the nature and designs of the Supreme Being, was fitted to
105 increase their reverence for that mysterious doctrine. The divine authority of Moses and the prophets was admitted, and even established, as the firmest basis of Christianity. From the beginning of the world, an uninterrupted series of predictions had announced and prepared the long ex-
110 pected coming of the Messiah, who, in compliance with the gross apprehensions of the Jews, had been more frequently represented under the character of a King and Conqueror, than under that of a Prophet, a Martyr, and the Son of God. By his expiatory sacrifice, the imperfect sacrifices of
115 the temple were at once consummated and abolished. The ceremonial law, which consisted only of types and figures, was succeeded by a pure and spiritual worship, equally adapted to all climates, as well as to every condition of mankind; and to the initiation of blood was substituted
120 a more harmless initiation of water. The promise of divine favour, instead of being partially confined to the posterity of Abraham, was universally proposed to the freeman and the slave, to the Greek and to the barbarian, to the Jew and to the Gentile. Every privilege that could raise the proselyte
125 from earth to Heaven, that could exalt his devotion, secure his happiness, or even gratify that secret pride which, under the semblance of devotion, insinuates itself into the human heart, was still reserved for the members of the Christian church; but at the same time all mankind was permitted,
130 and even solicited, to accept the glorious distinction, which was not only proffered as a favour, but imposed as an obligation. It became the most sacred duty of a new convert to diffuse among his friends and relations the inestimable blessing which he had received, and to warn them against
135 a refusal that would be severely punished as a criminal disobedience to the will of a benevolent but all-powerful deity.

5. The enfranchisement of the church from the bonds of the synagogue was a work however of some time and of some difficulty. . . . [Here follows an account of the several sects of Christians.]

6. But, whatever difference of opinion might subsist between the Orthodox, the Ebionites, and the Gnostics, concerning the divinity or the obligation of the Mosaic law, they were all equally animated by the same exclusive zeal and by the same abhorrence for idolatry which had distinguished the Jews from the other nations of the ancient world. The philosopher, who considered the system of polytheism as a composition of human fraud and error, could disguise a smile of contempt under the mask of devotion, without apprehending that either the mockery or the compliance would expose him to the resentment of any invisible, or, as he conceived them, imaginary powers. But the established religions of Paganism were seen by the primitive Christians in a much more odious and formidable light. It was the universal sentiment both of the church and of heretics that the daemons were the authors, the patrons, and the objects of idolatry. Those rebellious spirits who had been degraded from the rank of angels, and cast down into the infernal pit, were still permitted to roam upon earth, to torment the bodies, and to seduce the minds, of sinful men. The daemons soon discovered and abused the natural propensity of the human heart towards devotion, and, artfully withdrawing the adoration of mankind from their Creator, they usurped the place and honours of the Supreme Deity. By the success of their malicious contrivances, they at once gratified their own vanity and revenge, and obtained the only comfort of which they were yet susceptible, the hope of involving the human species in the participation of their guilt and misery. It was confessed, or at least it was imagined, that they had distributed among themselves the most important characters of polytheism, one daemon assuming the name and attributes of Jupiter, another of Aesculapius, a third of Venus, and a fourth per-

175 haps of Apollo;[3] and that, by the advantage of their long
experience and aerial nature, they were enabled to execute,
with sufficient skill and dignity, the parts which they had
undertaken. They lurked in the temples, instituted festivals
and sacrifices, invented fables, pronounced oracles, and
180 were frequently allowed to perform miracles. The Christians, who, by the interposition of evil spirits, could so
readily explain every praeternatural appearance, were disposed and even desirous to admit the most extravagant
fictions of the Pagan mythology. But the belief of the
185 Christian was accompanied with horror. The most trifling
mark of respect to the national worship he considered as a
direct homage yielded to the daemon, and as an act of
rebellion against the majesty of God.

7. In consequence of this opinion, it was the first but
190 arduous duty of a Christian to preserve himself pure and
undefiled by the practise of idolatry. The religion of the
nations was not merely a speculative doctrine professed in
the schools or preached in the temples. The innumerable
deities and rites of polytheism were closely interwoven with
195 every circumstance of business or pleasure, of public or of
private life; and it seemed impossible to escape the observance of them, without, at the same time, renouncing the
commerce of mankind and all the offices and amusements
of society. The important transactions of peace and war
200 were prepared or concluded by solemn sacrifices, in which
the magistrate, the senator, and the soldier were obliged
to preside or to participate. The public spectacles were an
essential part of the cheerful devotion of the Pagans, and
the gods were supposed to accept, as the most grateful offer-
205 ing, the games that the prince and people celebrated in
honour of their peculiar festivals. The Christian, who with
pious horror avoided the abomination of the circus or the
theatre, found himself encompassed with infernal snares

[3] Tertullian (Apolog. c. 23) alleges the confession of the Daemons
themselves as often as they were tormented by the Christian exorcists
[Gibbon's note.]

in every convivial entertainment, as often as his friends, invoking the hospitable deities, poured out libations to each 210 other's happiness. When the bride, struggling with well-affected reluctance, was forced in hymenaeal pomp over the threshold of her new habitation, or when the sad procession of the dead slowly moved towards the funeral pile; the Christian, on these interesting occasions, was compelled 215 to desert the persons who were the dearest to him, rather than contract the guilt inherent to those impious ceremonies. Every art and every trade that was in the least concerned in the framing or adorning of idols was polluted by the stain of idolatry; a severe sentence, since it devoted 220 to eternal misery the far greater part of the community, which is employed in the exercise of liberal or mechanic professions. If we cast our eyes over the numerous remains of antiquity, we shall perceive that, besides the immediate representations of the Gods and the holy instruments of 225 their worship, the elegant forms and agreeable fictions, consecrated by the imagination of the Greeks, were introduced as the richest ornaments of the houses, the dress, and the furniture, of the Pagans. Even the arts of music and painting, of eloquence and poetry, flowed from the same impure 230 origin. In the style of the fathers, Apollo and the Muses were the organs of the infernal spirit, Homer and Virgil were the most eminent of his servants, and the beautiful mythology which pervades and animates the compositions of their genius is destined to celebrate the glory of the 235 daemons. Even the common language of Greece and Rome abounded with familiar but impious expressions, which the imprudent Christian might too carelessly utter, or too patiently hear.

8. The dangerous temptations which on every side 240 lurked in ambush to surprise the unguarded believer assailed him with redoubled violence on the days of solemn festivals. So artfully were they framed and disposed throughout the year that superstition always wore the appearance of pleasure, and often of virtue. Some of the most sacred 245

festivals in the Roman ritual were destined to salute the new
calends of January with vows of public and private felicity,
to indulge the pious remembrance of the dead and living,
to ascertain the inviolable bounds of property, to hail, on
250 the return of spring, the genial powers of fecundity, to per-
petuate the two memorable aeras of Rome, the foundation
of the city and that of the republic, and to restore, during
the humane license of the Saturnalia, the primitive equality
of mankind. Some idea may be conceived of the abhorrence
255 of the Christians for such impious ceremonies, by the
scrupulous delicacy which they displayed on a much less
alarming occasion. On days of general festivity, it was the
custom of the ancients to adorn their doors with lamps
and with branches of laurel, and to crown their heads with
260 a garland of flowers. This innocent and elegant practise
might, perhaps, have been tolerated as a mere civil institution. But it most unluckily happened that the doors were
under the protection of the household gods, that the laurel
was sacred to the lover of Daphne, and that garlands of
265 flowers, though frequently worn as a symbol either of joy
or mourning, had been dedicated in their first origin to
the service of superstition. The trembling Christians, who
were persuaded in this instance to comply with the fashion
of their country and the commands of the magistrate,
270 laboured under the most gloomy apprehensions, from the
reproaches of their own conscience, the censures of the
church, and the denunciations of divine vengeance.

9. Such was the anxious diligence which was required
to guard the chastity of the gospel from the infectious breath
275 of idolatry. The superstitious observances of public or private
rites were carelessly practised, from education and habit, by
the followers of the established religion. But, as often as
they occurred, they afforded the Christians an opportunity
of declaring and confirming their zealous opposition. By
280 these frequent protestations, their attachment to the faith
was continually fortified, and, in proportion to the increase
of zeal, they combated with the more ardour and success

in the holy war which they had undertaken against the empire of the daemons.

❊ ❊ ❊

1.   Determine the meaning of the following words or phrases in their present context: superstition (l. 21), condescended (ll. 21-22), meanest (l. 24), awful (l. 40), proper (l. 75), humanity (l. 84), apprehensions (l. 111), partially (l. 121), patrons (l. 158), the style of the fathers (l. 231), destined (l. 246), denunciations (l. 272).

2.   State the argument of the whole passage in one sentence.

3.   Which paragraph (apart from the truncated Par. 5) might have been omitted without impairing the cogency of the argument? Why did Gibbon include it?

4.   Gibbon's wordings are meticulous.

a) How would the thought of each sentence differ if he had written *despicable* for *despised* (l. 7)—*allay* for *appease* (l. 28)—*scrupulous* for *even scrupulous* (l. 43)—*advantage* for *convenience* (l. 49)—*righteousness* for *purity* (l. 58)?

b) Do the following terms (ll. 11-15) indicate the pagan view or Gibbon's objective characterization of the Jews: sullen obstinacy—peculiar—unsocial—implacable hatred?

c) "Their detestation of foreign religions was equal to their attachment to the law of Moses." How does this differ in import from the present version? (ll. 34-36.)

d) Why did not Gibbon write "Apollo" in line 264?

5.   Gibbon endured the reproach that his treatment of Christianity was irreligious and unkind. Suppose yourself a censor, set to guard the public faith. Precisely which sentences might be advanced as evidence that Gibbon has denied the authority of the Christian religion? Consider especially lines 56-57 and 126-127. Does he not, in attributing to the Christians a convenient facility in demonology (ll. 180-184), discredit the faith? May his phrase "beautiful mythology" be regarded, in its context, as an aspersion upon true religion? Write a decision upon these passages, and look for other evidence of Gibbon's apostasy.

6.   Now suppose yourself Gibbon's advocate, intent on demonstrating that he has explicitly and unequivocally ac-

knowledged the Christian faith. Consider lines 103-105, 108-110, 133-134, or such other evidence as you can find.

[The paradoxes of Pars. 2-3 have been dissolved, since Gibbon's time, by a more scientific study of the Old Testament documents which has thrown the religious evolution of Israel into intelligible perspective. In sum, it is now understood that instead of the Whole Law having been revealed at the outset, beliefs and practices were achieved gradually, in response to changing circumstances, and largely through the insight of the prophets. For details, see the Britannica article on "Hebrew Religion," or Julius Bewer, *Literature of the Old Testament*. For the relations of the early Christians with their neighbors, discussed in Pars. 6-8, see James Moffatt's commentary on *The First Epistle of Paul to the Corinthians*, pp. 60-65, 101-114, 134-145.]

7. Motley chose his words to expand and intensify his statements, and for him the question must usually have been, "Does this word mean enough?" For Gibbon, the function of the word was to mark the limits of his statement: "Does not this word mean too much?" And whereas Motley's phrasings rise toward a baroque crescendo, the sentences of Gibbon subside in elegant diminuendos. Consider the modulations of the first sentence: religious harmony—facility with which nations embraced—or at least respected—superstitions. Observe how "facility," a term merely accurate, implies at first a certain cordiality of toleration and later a moral flaccidity or apathy. Truly this music has a dying fall. Find instances of a similar cadence throughout the essay.

Anticlimax may be ingeniously employed upon enthusiasms for which one has little sympathy, and if Gibbon had adjusted his artful decrescendos only to the zeal of the Christians, he might be defined as a wit. But there is line 215. The style of Gibbon traces, with an exquisite accuracy, that discrete mark of interrogation which Egon Friedell took for a symbol of the rococo soul. And after that melancholy backward glance at garlands of laurel over antique porticoes, which represents Gibbon's nearest approach to enthusiasm, the deliberate equanimity of the final paragraph (cf. l. 276) becomes in itself an emotion.

COLUMBUS[1]

LORD ACTON

•

1. WHILE THE ASIATIC EMPIRE [OF PORTUGAL] WAS BUILT up by the sustained and patient effort of a nation, during seventy years, the discovery of the West was due to one eager and original intellect, propelled by medieval dreams. Columbus had sailed both North and South; but the idea 5 which changed the axis of the globe came to him from books. He failed to draw an inference favourable to his design from the driftwood which a tropical current carries to Iceland, and proceeded on the assurance of Pierre d'Ailly and of Toscanelli, that Asia reaches so far east as 10 to leave but a moderate interval between Portugal and Japan. Although he rested his case on arguments from the classics and the prophets, his main authority was Toscanelli; but it is uncertain whether, as he affirmed, they had been in direct correspondence, or whether Columbus obtained 15 the letter and the Chart of 1474 by means which were the cause of his disgrace.

2. Rejected by Portugal, he made his way into Spain. He was found, starving, at the gate of a Franciscan convent; and the place where he sank down is marked by a 20 monument, because it is there that our modern world began. The friar who took him in and listened to his story soon perceived that this ragged mendicant was the most extraordinary person he had known, and he found him patrons at the court of Castile. The argument which Colum- 25 bus now laid before the learned men of Spain was this: The eastern route, even if the Portuguese succeed in finding it, would be of no use to them, as the voyage to Cipango,

[1] From *Lectures on Modern History*, by Lord Acton. By permission of The Macmillan Company, publishers.

to Cathay, even to the spice islands, would be too long for
30 profit. It was better to sail out into the West, for that route
would be scarcely 3000 miles to the extremity of Asia; the
other would be 15,000, apart from the tremendous circuit
of Africa, the extent of which was ascertained by Diaz
while Columbus was pursuing his uphill struggle. The
35 basis of the entire calculation was that the circumference
of the earth is 18,000 miles at the equator, and that Asia
begins, as is shown in Toscanelli's chart, somewhere about
California. Misled by his belief in cosmographers, he
blotted out the Pacific, and estimated the extent of water
40 to be traversed at one-third of the reality. The Spaniards
who were consulted pointed out the flaw, for the true
dimensions were known; but they were unable to demonstrate the truth against the great authorities cited on the
other side. The sophisms of Columbus were worth more
45 than all the science of Salamanca. The objectors who called
him a visionary were in the right, and he was obstinately
wrong. To his auspicious persistency in error Americans
owe, among other things, their existence.

3. A majority reported favourably—a majority com-
50 posed, it would appear, of ignorant men. Years were spent
in these preliminaries, and then the war with Granada absorbed the resources and the energies of the Crown. Columbus was present when the last Moorish king kissed the hand
of Isabella, and he saw the cross raised over the Alhambra.
55 This victory of Christendom was immediately followed by
the expulsion of the Jews, and then the Catholic queen
gave audience to the Genoese projector. His scheme belonged to the same order of ideas, and he was eloquent
on its religious aspect. He would make so many slaves as
60 to cover all expenses, and would have them baptized. He
would bring home gold enough in three years to reconquer
Palestine. He had one impressive argument which was
not suggested by the situation at Court. Toscanelli had
been at Rome when envoys came from the Grand Khan,
65 petitioning for missionaries to instruct his people in the
doctrines of Christianity. Two such embassies were sent,

but their prayer was not attended to. Here were suppliants calling out of the darkness: Come over and help us. It was suitable that the nation which conquered the Moslem and banished the Jews should go on to convert the heathen. 70 The Spaniards would appear in the East, knowing that their presence was desired. In reality they would come in answer to an invitation, and might look for a welcome. Making up by their zeal for the deficient enterprise of Rome, they might rescue the teeming millions of Farthest 75 Asia, and thus fulfil prophecy, as there were only a hundred and fifty-five years to the end of the world. The conversion of Tartary would be the crowning glory of Catholic Spain.

4. All this was somewhat hypothetical and vague; but nothing could be more definite than the reward which he 80 demanded. For it appeared that what this forlorn adventurer required for himself was to be admiral of the Atlantic, ranking with the constable of Castile, Viceroy, with power of life and death, in regions to be occupied, and a large proportion of the intended spoil. And he would accept no 85 less. None divined what he himself knew not, that the thing he offered in return was dominion over half the world. Therefore, when he found that this would not do, Columbus saddled his mule and took the road to France. In that superb moment he showed what man he was, and 90 the action was more convincing than his words had been. An Aragonese official, Santangel, found the money, the £1500 required for the expedition, and the traveller was overtaken by an alguazil a couple of leagues away, and recalled to Granada. Santangel was, by descent, a Jew. 95 Several of his kindred suffered under the Inquisition, before and after, and he fortified himself against the peril of the hour when he financed the first voyage of Columbus. Granada fell on the 2nd of January 1492. The Jews were expelled on the 20th of March. On the 17th of April the 100 contract with Columbus was signed at Santa Fe. The same crusading spirit, the same motive of militant propagandism, appears in each of the three transactions. And the explorer, at this early stage, was generally backed by the clergy.

105 Juan Perez, the hospitable Franciscan, was his friend; and Mendoza, the great cardinal of Toledo, and Deza, afterwards Archbishop of Seville. Talavera, the Archbishop of Granada, found him too fanciful to be trusted.

5. Sailing due west from the Canaries he crossed the 110 Atlantic in its widest part. The navigation was prosperous and uneventful until, changing their course to follow the flight of birds, they missed the continent and came upon the islands. It was the longest voyage that had ever been attempted in the open sea; but the passage itself and the 115 shoals and currents of the West Indies were mastered with the aid of nautical instruments from Nuremberg, and of the *Ephemerides* of Regiomontanus. These were recent achievements of the Renaissance, and without them the undertaking was impossible. Even with the new appli-120 ances, Columbus was habitually wrong in his measurements. He put Cuba 18° too far to the west; he thought San Domingo as large as Spain; and he saw mountains 50,000 feet high in Yucatan. Indeed, he protested that his success was not due to science, but to the study of the prophet Isaiah. 125 Above all things, he insisted that Cuba was part of the Asiatic continent, and obliged his companions to testify to the same belief, although there is evidence that he did not share it.

6. He had promised Cathay. If he produced an un-130 known continent instead, a continent many thousands of miles long, prohibiting approach to Cathay, he would undo his own work; the peasants who had exposed his fallacies would triumph in his failure, and the competing Portuguese would appropriate all that he had undertaken to add to the 135 crown of Castile. Without civilisation and gold his discoveries would be valueless; and there was so little gold at first that he at once proposed to make up for it in slaves. His constant endeavour was not to be mistaken for the man who discovered the new world. Somewhere in the near 140 background he still beheld the city with the hundred bridges, the crowded bazaar, the long train of caparisoned elephants, the palace with the pavement of solid gold. Naked

savages skulking in the forest, marked down by voracious cannibals along the causeway of the Lesser Antilles, were no distraction from the quest of the Grand Khan. The 145 facts before him were uninteresting and provisional, and were overshadowed by the phantoms that crowded his mind. The contrast between the gorgeous and entrancing vision and the dismal and desperate reality made the position a false one. He went on seeking gold when it was 150 needful to govern, and proved an incapable administrator. Long before his final voyage he had fallen into discredit, and he died in obscurity.

※ ※ ※

1. Outline the passage as a narrative, listing the paragraph topics.

2. What theses are developed as comments upon the events of each paragraph? Where possible, find the phrase which states the idea most fully and succinctly.

3. The texture of this prose is logical rather than pictorial; the pageantry has been handled elsewhere, and the writer would get on with the story. Yet he has the knack of deftly visualizing a significant scene: thus in lines 18-25, after the broad narrative statement, the focus is suddenly narrowed to the moment at the convent gate; then the narrative broadens again. What other instances of this use of imagery do you find?

4. Lord Acton's prose is not stylized, not mannered, hence not easily characterized. He is at ease in the language and takes its varied resources for granted. He manages to say much in surprisingly few words. Read several paragraphs aloud. The rhythms are short, crisp; the sentences end sooner than one expects. One quality of this style, then, is its terseness. Taking the shortest way to its mark, the prose is energetic; but the implicit logical connection between successive statements makes it sinewy too. There is no attempt at formal syntactical balance, but rather a defiance of symmetry. The language is aristocratically colloquial in tone—"too long for profit" (ll. 29-30)—for the blunt phrase is brief. The sentences are sometimes aphoristic —"The sophisms of Columbus were worth more than all the science of Salamanca"—but they keep this side of epigram. The terseness may enforce an irony, as in lines 59-60. Pick out half

a dozen other striking sentences, and comment on several of them.

5. The evaluation of a prose style must be largely a matter of personal taste. But it is good to decide on one's preferences, making taste conscious and so sharpening it. Of the styles of the following writers—Macaulay, Froude, Parkman, Parrington, Motley, Gibbon—which do you prefer to Lord Acton's?

Try to rule out the interest of the subject matter. Explain your preferences the best you can. You may not be able to rationalize them or define your criteria. Here are questions that may help you in your appraisals. Is the style showy or unobtrusive? Is it artificial, unlike good colloquial forms of speech? (This need not be a defect.) Can it be read aloud with pleasure—or without undue pain? Are its rhythms varied, or monotonous, or awkward? Have the statements been shaped by the pressure of rhetorical forms, or have the rhetorical forms been evolved to express the thought? Does the style express a temperament? Is it witty, whimsical, stodgy, colorful, abstract? Would it wear well? (Or would one tire of the style before having read one's fill of the subject matter?) Does it make the language exciting? (Good art affords a delight in the medium.)

Now sort out your preferences among the styles of the following writers: Chase, Pater, Beer, Tinker, Raleigh, Mather, Mumford, Adams, Lea. Are the best of these superior to any of the former group? How do you rate Addison, Thoreau, Holmes, Milton?

Which of the passages in this text do you think least distinguished in style?

Of the several authors you have read during the year, which have you imitated, consciously or not, in your own prose? From which have you learned the most useful tricks? Which do you think exerted the best influence? Draw up a short list of authors whose style a writer might most profitably study.

[The prose in this book, though often drawn from historians of one kind or another, has been analyzed as exposition, and there has been no systematic consideration of historiographical methods and perspectives. The student intending to major in history, who will want to explore such matters, may read J. B. Black, *The Art of History,* Allan Nevins, *The Gateway to History,* Sidney Hook, *The Hero in History,* and Lord Acton's "Inaugural Lecture" in his *Lectures on Modern History.*]

DERIVATIONS

•

In many of the exercises you are asked to explain the
derivations of words. Your merciless instructor, not content
that you should know what the group of letters stands
for in the text and in current usage, wants you to consider
what other meanings it has had.

If language were a fixed system of symbols, each word
representing one certain object or action or quality, it would
often come in handy. Such words arranged in sentences
would make diagrams of portions of the world, flat and
unequivocal as a blueprint. Laborious men have so devised
universal languages, intended to nip international mis-
understandings in the bud and to expedite tourists. You
too may construct one: first list or classify the elements of
the real world; then assign a pronounceable group of
vowels and consonants, i.e., a word, to each element; there
should be no irregular verbs and no metaphors. But you
foresee the futility of any such attempt to make language
orderly, uniform, and stable. New inventions would require names. New scientific and social concepts would
render the established terms obsolete. Slang and other
kinds of poetry would creep into this logician's paradise,
generating dialects peculiar to cultural groups. Local pro-
nunciations would dissolve the universal dictionary into
disparate languages. For human beings have little talent
for precise discourse; they will fill their tongues with poetic
confusions of thought and feeling.

You may hear this delightful music of growing language
all about you if you only listen. Even simple descriptive
names are pleasant conceits: *alarm clock, fountain pen,
elevator, funny bone, snapshot, brunch*. Some common
nouns began as trade names: *victrola, nabisco*; others com-
memorate persons: *volt* and *ampere, chesterfield, sandwich,*

a *Brody*, a *Micky Finn*. Some words remind us of older fashions: the *comics*, now stories told in crude pictures, were once supposed to be funny, and *paper*, now made of wood pulp, was once made of papyrus. Our everyday speech is full of witty allusion: the thwarted man *cannot get to first base*; he is *stymied, behind the eight ball*; he may as well *throw up the sponge*. The candid man is *aboveboard*; he *puts his cards on the table*; he is not a *four-flusher*, not *underhanded*; he has nothing *up his sleeve*.

One must feel a little sorry for the person so deaf or indifferent to allusion that he misses the point of these phrases. Other phrases have been so thoroughly worked into the common speech that unless we are attentive we may not appreciate their flavor: *horse sense, sob sister, every whipstitch, to talk a blue streak, to get a word in edgewise*—words being long and narrow! Others elude us: what *music* does one *face*? See how many of these vivid expressions you can notice in the next day or so; you will soon get the habit.

This kind of attention to words is more than an aesthetic amusement. The more you sense the overtones of words, the more deftly you will handle them. Language is a subtle instrument of expression just because the meanings of words have not been assigned by a dictionary maker but have rather been gradually evolved from the way in which thoughtful, emotional people applied the words to their human experience throughout changing centuries. Your first step toward an appreciation of the richness of language is to recognize the wit and poetry of contemporary word play. But a similar evolution has always been at work. To call an erratic fellow *off his trolley* is no more ingenious than to call him, in an agricultural community, *out of his furrow* or, as the Romans pronounced it, *delirious*. Again, we get our opponent *on the ropes*, in a boxing phrase; but *to pounce* on him is also an allusion to a sport, the feudal pastime of hawking, for it was originally the hawk that *pounced* on its quarry, swooped and struck with its talons or *pounces*. Not all derivations are so picturesque as these, but nearly every word has something curious in its history.

The current meanings and implications of our words have been shaped by the people who used them and handed them down to us. The fruitful study of a derivation is not simply to memorize the successive meanings of the word as listed in the dictionary; rather we would see the human spirit at work in the shaping of its meaning. In order thus sympathetically to understand a derivation, we must consider more precisely just what happens as a word evolves. Plainly the significant phases in the life of a word are the transitions from one meaning to another. But to describe this process as "a change of meaning" is inept and confusing. A more accurate account of the usual process, from the point of view of the shapers of language, is a little more complicated. In general terms, it may be put as follows: a familiar noise, already meaningful, is applied in a new way or in a new situation. Let us examine this formulation of the process in detail. Some of the details may seem obvious; nevertheless they are worth noting.

A word comprises a sound and a meaning. At the moment in which a new meaning is developed, the sound of the word does not change. Of course, pronunciation varies from one locality to another, from one person to another. Moreover, it may vary extremely from one age to another, and this development is called *phonetic* change, in distinction to *semantic* change, with which we are concerned. The phonetic evolution of words is largely a physiological process, an affair of the speech muscles in throat and mouth, and it is unconscious. All the syllables of a certain sound type vary in their pronunciation over a given period in the same way: Anglo-Saxon *cu* has become modern English *cow,* and AS. *nu* has become *now*; AS. *disc* and *fisc* have become *dish* and *fish*. In the days before printing, spellings were based on pronunciation and thus preserved for us the older sounds of the words. But as the changes in sound were unnoticed by the speakers who made them, they had nothing to do with the shifts in the application of the word. For instance, AS. *ceorfan* and *steorfan* have become *carve* and *starve*; one of these words has also undergone a change of meaning, for *steorfan* meant simply "to die," not necessarily of hunger. But this change of meaning was neither cause nor effect of the change in sound. Thus in your study of semantic changes, you may disregard the phonetic changes; you need not hope to remember the curiously spelled older forms of the word which you find in the dictionary or be perplexed by them. A change of pronunciation may also occur when a word is taken from a foreign country or language, as by merchants, who import cargoes, or by the learned, who import books and ideas. Such a borrowed word is promptly naturalized: its inflectional ending may be dropped, and it is sounded in an English way. The *bovis* of the Romans was pronounced *bœuf* by the French, which in turn was pronounced *beef* in England; the application of the word was narrowed in English, but you need not trace the phonetic change in order to understand the semantic change. Sound changes are of interest to the philologist and indispensable clues to the history of a word; but since you wish simply to understand the results of professional investigation, you may, like the speakers of the language, disregard the variations of pronunciation. At the moment of semantic development, the noise of the word was familiar and constant.

Moreover, the noise was already meaningful. It is unprofitable to speculate about how sounds and meanings came to be associated in the first place—i.e., the origin of language. There are, no doubt, a few words which are sheer invention from meaningless raw materials. *Kodak* is such a word, but most trade names are made from existing words; thus *bovril* alludes to beef and virility. *Honk* and *burp* may imitate the sounds of nature; *ouch* may have been an unmeditated response. But normally the noise has an established meaning when, by being newly applied, it comes under our observation.

In order to understand the human significance of the word's evolution, you must imagine yourself in the position of the individual who applied his familiar word in a novel way. Thus you must know what the familiar meaning was and what was the new application. At this point it is easy to go astray. For instance, an *arachnid* is a spider, and *Arachne* is the girl in the fable who challenged Athena to a weaving match and was turned into a spider; did the fablist name his heroine from the creature into which she was metamorphosed, or did a scientist name his class of animals from the girl in the old story? Again, did the citizens of *Corinth* name their town from the currants which grew there, or did *currant* merchants name the little raisins after the place they came from? Again, *pink* means, among other things, a flower and a color, and one meaning was derived from the other; was the flower named from the color or the color from the flower?

Obviously, then, to understand a naming you must know which of the two meanings was, at the moment of semantic development, the familiar one, the one in the mind of the speaker, and which represents the new application. This is simply to distinguish the older from the newer meaning. Thus we find that both *Arachne* and *arachnid* are derived from the Greek word ἀράχνη; these letters were presumably the Greek way of indicating the appropriate noise which meant "spider." Hence the first hypothesis was correct, and the fablist named his heroine from the animal.

Often a word has passed through a series of such developments, so that the several meanings must be arranged in pairs, one leading into the next. Thus of *canaries*: the islands were named from the dogs (Latin *canis*) found there; the wine and the birds were named from the islands; and the color was named from the birds. *Pink* is more complicated; how would you group the meanings contained in *the garden pink, the parlor pink, the pink of condition, the pink ribbon, pinking shears,* and *to pink an adversary?*

To distinguish the older from the more recent meaning, one must know the history of the noise or consult someone who does. As words are spoken as well as written, their tracks fade in air, and no complete history of a word is possible. The *Oxford English Dictionary,* in thirteen huge volumes, lists under each entry all the senses in which the word was known to have been written, with a series of dated examples of each usage; the *Dictionary of American English,* in four volumes, is likewise made on historical principles. You should know these works, but the O.E.D. provides rather too much information for the novice to handle. The *Shorter Oxford Dictionary,* an abridgement of the O.E.D., outlines the semantic evolution of words more compactly and dates the emergence of each meaning— an important feature. Ernest Weekley's *Concise Etymological Dictionary of Modern English* is authoritative and inexpensive; buy it if you can. The etymologies in the good college dictionaries are often too sketchy to be complete and clear; they do, however, afford a necessary practice, and you should learn to read them.

musket . . . [F. *mousquet,* fr. It. *moschetto,* formerly, a kind of hawk, fr. L. *musca* a fly.] (*Webster's Collegiate*)

apricot . . . [< Sp. *albaricoque* < Arab. *al,* the + *burquq* < Gk. *praikokion* < Lat. *praecoquum,* early ripe; ending influenced by Fr. *abricot*] (*Winston Simplified*)

stirrup . . . [< AS. *stīrap, stīgrap* < *stīgan,* to climb + *rāp,* rope] (*Winston Simplified*)

The symbol < or "fr." means "from." The word is traced back through several languages, indicated by the abbreviations; thus *apricot* began as a Latin word and migrated through Greece, westward along Arabic North Africa into Spain, and thence to England. The italicized forms represent the spellings of the word in the various languages and thus, read from right to left, suggest the stages of a gradually changing pronunciation. To you these forms are of secondary importance, for they occurred either unconsciously as part of the general phonetic evolution of the language or as the adaptation of a foreign word to the established speech. It is interesting to note that the first syllable of *apricot* is a vestige of the Arabic definite article (as in *alcohol, almanac*), but this is not part of the semantic development.

The words in roman type, again read from right to left, represent the successive meanings of the noise. It is these meanings that you must consider. Thus of *apricot*: the Romans called the fruit the "early ripe," a simple descriptive term. *Musket* evolves in two stages: the Italians called one of their hawks "the little fly" (It. *moschetto* being a diminutive); then they called their gun "the hawk," presumably in affectionate suggestion of ferocity.

In summarizing such namings, it is well to employ a set form in order to avoid possible confusions. For instance, should one say that the stirrup was called a mounting-rope or that the mounting-rope was called a stirrup? *Silly* is derived from AS. *gesaelig,* happy; should one infer that happy people were regarded as foolish? And what is one to make of the explanation that a nickel is called nickel because it is made of nickel? As you have seen, three things are involved in these situations: (1) the sound, which was constant; (2) the new application, the thing named, indicated by the later meaning; and (3) the designation or thought contained in the sound, indicated by the earlier meaning. An intelligible explanation must distinguish these three elements and relate them properly. The following form is convenient:

Of *nickel*: the coin was named from "the metal it was made of." Here we use the word itself, italicized, to denote the constant sound. Then, rather than repeat this ambiguous term, we find paraphrases for the two meanings, enclosing the earlier meaning in quotation marks to suggest that it existed as the thought in the speaker's mind. And to show the psychology of the process accurately, we must get the terms in the proper order:

Of *silly*: a weak-witted person was described as "happy."

Of *stirrup*: the loop in which a horseman placed his foot was called a "mounting-rope."

Now take your dictionary and work through the following examples of how you will be expected to interpret the data given there:

Of *halibut*: the fish was called a "holy flounder," perhaps because it was eaten on holy days.

Of *forceps*: the blacksmith's tool was called a "taker of hot things."

Of *arena*: the fighting place was referred to as "the sand."

Of *capuchin*: monks of a certain order were named from the long "hoods" they wore.

Of *cravat*: the neck-scarf was named from the "Croatian" soldiers who wore it.

Of *poplin*: a cloth was named from the "papal" city, Avignon, where it was woven.

Of *melancholy*: a gloomy person was described as having an excess of "black bile."

Of *flirt*: an insincere coquette was described as "moving nimbly about." (Here, since the semantic development occurred in modern English, the successive meanings are found not in the derivation but in the definition.)

Of *disease*: a serious malady was euphemistically minimized as a mere "discomfort." (Again the two senses appear in the definition.)

Of *pagan*: the Roman soldier called the civilian a "hick" or "countryman"; then the Christian, regarding himself as a soldier of Christ, called the unbeliever a "civilian."

Of *dragoon*: a soldier was named from "the gun he carried." And the gun had been called "a fire-breathing monster."

Such a formulation usually makes the psychology of the situation plain enough. One must, of course, exercise a certain ingenuity in the choice of synonyms. It would not, for instance, make sense to say, of *dragon,* that part of a soldier's equipment was called "a non-existent animal."

So far we have analyzed semantic development as a conscious naming procedure. But a further stage of the process promptly follows: the lapse of reference. The first persons who use the word in the new way are aware of the metaphor; but as the new name is generally accepted, its allusion to the older meaning of the sound is soon forgot. Obviously the reference is lost when the word passes into another language: in English, *arena* carries no allusion to sand; *apricot* meant "early ripe" to the Romans who named the fruit, but to the Greeks and Arabs and Spaniards who transmitted the word it signified merely the fruit itself. Or this may happen as a result of cultural change: we no longer think of *travel* as "work" or of *silly* people as "happy." It happens anyway: boarding a street car we do not think of a *nickel* as "made of a certain metal," nor, in the chemistry laboratory, does *nickel* suggest "money"; the two meanings have become independent. Thus our account of the psychology of semantic development is accurate for only the brief, colorful ambiguous moments in the life of the word. The duration of such moments varies: although one may speak of the *mother* of vinegar without thinking of "parent," it is unlikely that the seventeenth-century roisterers who dubbed the proprietress of a bawdy-house *mother* ever used the term without committing a filial sacrilege. In general, however, the allusion soon fades.

This loss of reference is governed by an obvious law: words take their meanings from the things they are applied to. For language is learned empirically: by *duck,* baby may mean "the wooden toy to be pulled about on a string"; the child who called the spider web a *parlor* had learned the word from the nursery rime. With further experience, the individual conforms his noise meanings to the common sense, which is likewise empirical. We know that a *mediocre* performance is not "of medium quality" but "inferior." We regard the *intoxicated* man not as "poisoned" but as "having drunk too much"; the metaphor has lost its threat.

This general law, that words take their meanings from their applications, underlies a second and psychologically distinct process of semantic development. The naming process which we have analyzed so far is the work of more or less conscious manipulators of language. But meanings may also be unconsciously modified as the speakers, applying the word to its conventional object, modify their conception of that object; they think the word differently. For instance, the Greek *daimon* was a guardian spirit, but the early Christians looked on pagan spirits as potential enemies or devils; thus a *demon* is an agent of hell. A *prudefemme* or *prude* was originally a fine, modest woman, but gay young fellows regarded such women as affected, and overattentive to the proprieties, as no doubt they were; now *prude* is understood from its derogatory application. The *cavaliers* were gallant servants of King Charles, but partly because their manners declined with their fortunes, partly because the middle-class users of the phrase resented them, *cavalier treatment* came to mean irresponsible and arrogant behavior. In developments of this type, the meaning may truly be said to change. The process involves no conscious metaphorical naming; rather the nature of the object or the speakers' view of it produces a gradual, unconscious shift in the meaning inferred from the word's application. Sometimes, as in *demon* and *cavalier,* the revision is of historical interest; sometimes it amounts merely to a change of focus. Thus of *comrade*: a roommate (the original sense of the word) was regarded as a "loyal associate" (its present meaning); here the sense has widened. Likewise *paper* (made of papyrus) must have been understood in the more general sense of "writing material," so that later the term was applied without incongruity to sheets made of linen or wood pulp. Conversely *meat,* originally applied to any food (as in *nut meats, sweetmeats*), was later regarded as "the flesh of animals," perhaps because such flesh constituted the interesting bulk of the gentry's diet. The passage of the word into another language, entailing loss of reference, may facilitate such widening or narrowing of sense.

A set form will prove helpful in recognizing and explaining semantic developments of this second main type. Thus: of *bourgeoisie*: town-dwellers were regarded as "the commercial class," for so, in contrast to the feudal classes, they were. Here again the italicized word itself denotes the constant sound. The first paraphrase is the earlier denotation; the second is enclosed in quotation marks to suggest that it developed as the thought in the speaker's mind.

Of *slave*: the conquered Slavs, reduced to servitude, were regarded not as of a particular race but, more generally, as "human property."

Of *smug*: the dapper, fastidiously groomed person was thought to be "self-satisfied and conceited."

Of *cheat*: the man who, under feudal law, took possession of an estate as forfeit or fine was regarded as a "trickster and thief."

Whereas the naming process involves an intentional descriptive allusion, conscious for a period and later lost, the second kind of semantic development is unconscious: the speakers intend the words in a strictly conventional sense but gradually understand them in a new way. The two processes differ psychologically, as the two formulations suggest. Compare them.

I.   Naming (intentional allusion): 2 was called "1."

II.   Change of concept (unintended): 1 was regarded as "2."

The numbers 1 and 2 stand for the earlier and later meanings. In each case, the first term is the object referred to; the second term, in quotation marks, is the idea in the speaker's mind.

But how are you to tell which explanation accounts for the development of the given word? The second type is rare. The great majority of meanings are developed through the naming process and so may be accounted for by an explanation of Type I. If, however, this proves psychologically implausible or unconvincing, try Type II. The two formulas do not unlock word histories automatically, without the exercise of intelligence on your part; they are handy testing devices to help you avoid confusion as you decide which of the two semantic processes was probably at work.

For instance, to say of *companion* that a close associate (2) was called a "bread-sharer" (1) is not quite satisfactory; the metaphor seems far-fetched. But one's messmates (1) might naturally have been regarded simply as "close associates" (2).

Of *knave*: should one say that a miscreant (2) was harshly addressed as "boy" (1)? Actually the development seems to have occurred in two steps: a menial servant (2) was literally described as the "boy" (1); then such servants (1) were regarded as "good-for-nothing rascals" (2).

Of *poison*: a deadly draught was called "a drink." Or: a drink was regarded, in some Renaissance circles, as likely to be "fatal." Weekley comments that the semantic change seems "to date from treacherous times." Very likely. Yet of the two explanations the first is the more plausible and exhibits the naming as a grimly ironic euphemism.

Sometimes there is little to choose between the two explanations, as in *urbane,* where the two processes may both have been at work. Similarly of *immorality* in its middle-class sense: sexual misbehavior is sometimes described simply as "wrongdoing" in order to avoid harsher words; at the same time, smug souls regard wickedness as consisting chiefly of "sexual misbehavior," thus disregarding other sins in order to concentrate their reproach on the fault which they are not themselves inclined to.

Now consider *starve,* which originally meant simply "to die." Both forms of explanation suggest a period in which there was an awful equivalence of "to die" and "to die of hunger." But neither is quite convincing. The data available in the O.E.D. show that the word was used until quite recently in such phrases as *to starve of cold* and *to starve of hunger,* where, since it must be qualified, it evidently retains its broader meaning. Presumably, then, the latter phrase was contracted to plain *starve.* This contraction was facilitated by the fact that a familiar word, *to die,* already covered the general idea, whereas no other word existed for the special sense, "to perish of hunger." We may also infer that fewer people died from cold than from lack of food.

In such contractions or ellipses, the surviving word absorbs the sense of the rest of the phrase. Thus Weekley surmises that the surviving noun in such phrases as *im-*

pudent hussy or *idle hussy* may have absorbed the sense of the adjectives; in effect, a housewife (1) was commonly regarded as "an impudent, idle woman." The strangely varying meanings of adjectives (e.g., *arrant, buxom, dainty, nice*) may similarly have been drawn from the nouns with which they were habitually used, so that etymologically the noun modified the adjective. Thus of *buxom*: the good-natured (woman) or obedient (wife) was thought of as "hearty, comely, plump."

As a beginner, you were assured that the sound of a word need not be considered in connection with its meaning. In general, phonetic and semantic evolution are independent. Sometimes, however, the sound of a word does affect its meaning. Thus the *sea rover*, literally "sea robber" or "pirate," is naturally understood as a "wanderer," a sense drawn from the unrelated word *to rove*. *Sorry*, originally "painfully" and later understood from such phrases as *sore afraid* to mean "extremely," has also absorbed some of the meaning of the unrelated word *sorrow*. *Fulsome*, literally "full," may have drawn from ME. *ful*, foul, its present sense of "offensive," as in *fulsome flattery*. *Pester* has been colored by *pest*, a plague. Again, of *tornado* [from Sp. *tronada*, from Sp. *tronar*, to thunder]: in Spanish, the storm was described as a "thunderer"; but the English, confusing Sp. *tronar* and Sp. *tornar*, to turn, identified the storm as our "twister." In this instance the pronunciation was revised in accordance with the misunderstood allusion.

As you become adept in the study of derivations, you will learn also to consider the languages through which the word has passed, for the social history of a word may be intrinsically interesting or even color its meaning. Though *fatherly* and *paternal* stem from the same Indo-European source word, they have not quite the same tone; *father* was spoken by a Teutonic people, the Anglo-Saxons, and is thus native English; *pater*, the Latin form of the Indo-European word, was later adopted into English, but its forms have never acquired quite the homely sense of *father*; we decry benevolent legislation as *paternalistic*, not as *fatherly*. *Carpenter,* originally "chariot-maker," was a Celtic word picked up by the Roman invaders of Gaul and later, in its more general sense of "woodworker," transmitted by way of Norman French into English, where it forestalled a corresponding generalization of the specific Anglo-Saxon *wainwright*. Portuguese explorers carried *deòs*, god, to Java and China, where it became *joss;* they carried *curral,* corral, to South African Kaffirs and Dutch, who gave it to English as *kraal*. The British in India acquired *chiz*, thing, whence *it's the cheese*. We need not in this essay review the dispersion of Indo-European into its several language groups or the circumstances in which English, basically Anglo-Saxon, has from time to time drawn words from this language or that.

Word studies call for some knowledge of our cultural tradition and in turn enliven history. The arrogant austerity of Calvinism is contained in the Puritan epithet *carnal,* applied to men who respected cakes and ale. The dapper rationalism of the eighteenth century is summarized in the sneer with which Lord Chesterfield's contemporaries pronounced *enthusiasm*. The current *underprivileged* represents the new sociological salesmanship among a people unmoved by the unadorned *poor*. And what rumors of urban degradation are implicit in the fact that in the Bronx, a section of New York City, green vegetation is referred to with horror as *ivry perzin!*

It has become apparent that a word does not evolve as an isolated psychological unit; rather it develops in a context of language and in the special circumstances of human history. Its whole story may involve the phrases in which it was commonly used, the availability of other words for the expression of a similar idea, the semantic influence of other words of similar sound. The changing social environment—tools and occupations, architecture and warfare, perils and amusements, religious and political practices—is reflected in the language. As value judgments are revised, meanings are modified. Thus the succinct derivation provided in your dictionary only hints at the actual history of the living word. When you have learned to make the most of these hints, you may attempt a more precise understanding of the word's evolution, using the data of the *Oxford English Dictionary* and the *Dictionary of American English*. Among the many interesting books on the subject, Ernest Weekley's *Romance of Words, Adjectives and Other Words,* and *Words Ancient and Modern* are full of historical elucidations.

While you are beginning your career as an amateur etymologist, you may consider a derivation acceptably explained by a statement of one of the types formulated above, together with whatever brief comment you may deem relevant. Even when your investigations acquire more historical precision, these formulations will prove helpful devices for grasping the psychology of semantic change. Word studies are not guaranteed to enlarge your vocabulary in ten days; if you want merely a bigger word, copy it from a thesaurus. But as you savor the implicit humanity of words, it is to be presumed that your own language will become richer and more subtly expressive.